Mathematics for Elementary Teachers

An Activity Approach

Eighth Edition

Mathematics for Elementary Teachers

An Activity Approach

Albert B. Bennett, Jr.
University of New Hampshire

Laurie J. Burton
Western Oregon University

L. Ted Nelson
Portland State University

 Higher Education

Boston   Burr Ridge, IL   Dubuque, IA   New York   San Francisco   St. Louis
Bangkok   Bogotá   Caracas   Kuala Lumpur   Lisbon   London   Madrid   Mexico City
Milan   Montreal   New Delhi   Santiago   Seoul   Singapore   Sydney   Taipei   Toronto

Higher Education

MATHEMATICS FOR ELEMENTARY TEACHERS: AN ACTIVITY APPROACH, EIGHTH EDITION

Published by McGraw-Hill, a business unit of The McGraw-Hill Companies, Inc., 1221 Avenue of the Americas, New York, NY 10020. Copyright © 2010 by The McGraw-Hill Companies, Inc. All rights reserved. Previous editions © 2007, 2004, and 2001. No part of this publication may be reproduced or distributed in any form or by any means, or stored in a database or retrieval system, without the prior written consent of The McGraw-Hill Companies, Inc., including, but not limited to, in any network or other electronic storage or transmission, or broadcast for distance learning.

Some ancillaries, including electronic and print components, may not be available to customers outside the United States.

This book is printed on recycled, acid-free paper containing 10% postconsumer waste.

1 2 3 4 5 6 7 8 9 0 QPD/QPD 0 9

ISBN 978—0—07—723750—9
MHID 0—07—723750—1

Editorial Director: *Stewart K. Mattson*
Sponsoring Editor: *Dawn R. Bercier*
Director of Development: *Kristine Tibbetts*
Developmental Editor: *Michelle Driscoll*
Developmental Editor: *Christina A. Lane*
Marketing Manager: *John Osgood*
Senior Project Manager: *Vicki Krug*
Senior Production Supervisor: *Sherry L. Kane*
Lead Media Project Manager: *Judi David*
Senior Designer: *David W. Hash*
Interior Designer: *Ellen Pettergell*
Cover/Designer Illustration: *Precision Graphics*
Lead Photo Research Coordinator: *Carrie K. Burger*
Photo Research: *Connie Mueller*
Supplement Producer: *Mary Jane Lampe*
Compositor: *Macmillan Publishing Solutions*
Typeface: *10/12 Times Roman*
Printer: *Quebecor World Dubuque, IA*

The credits section for this book begins on page C-1 and is considered an extension of the copyright page.

Standards 2000 quotations reprinted with permission from Principles and Standards for School Mathematics, copyright 2000, by the National Council of Teachers of Mathematics. All rights reserved.

To Future Teachers

This book was written to help you teach elementary- and middle-school mathematics. You will experience firsthand how the use of models and manipulatives contribute to the understanding of mathematics concepts.

You will find that the models and manipulatives used in the activities in this book are commonly used for teaching elementary- and middle-school mathematics. Many of these activities can be easily adapted for use in school classrooms, and we encourage you to do this. To assist you, there is an *Elementary School Activity* at the end of each chapter to illustrate how ideas from the chapter can be adapted for use in the elementary classroom. If you have the opportunity, we encourage you to try these adapted activities with children.

In this course, you are the student. Each activity in this book asks you to look for patterns and relationships and to explain in your own words how they make sense.[1] This is the same process you will someday be using with your students.

This is an important time for you to begin thinking like the teacher you are becoming and about the process of teaching and learning mathematics. You can do this by

- Monitoring your own thoughts and feelings about math as you learn to explore and investigate

- Thinking about how you can use, change, or adapt the activities in this book for use in an elementary- or middle-school classroom

- Observing your classmates and asking them questions to try to understand how they are thinking about mathematics

This book offers a variety of resources to help you achieve these goals.

The **Manipulative Kit** bundled with this book contains 10 colorful manipulatives commonly used in elementary schools. The Activity Sets in this book require the use of manipulatives from this kit as well as additional materials found on **Material Cards** at the back of the book.

You can enter the Student Center Companion Website for this book (without a password) and access:

- **Virtual Manipulatives,** electronic versions of the items in the **Manipulative Kit**

- Eleven interactive applets ("Filling 3D Shapes" is shown here)

- Downloadable color copies of the materials in the Manipulative Kit

- A variety of grids for homework assignments, as well as bibliographies and Internet links for each section

- Thirty-four open-ended mathematics and laboratory investigations for active exploration of key concepts, including Geometer's Sketchpad® student modules for exploring geometry topics.

---

[1]Answers to selected questions in the Activity Sets (marked *) are available in the back of the book.

Just for Fun Activities and Elementary School Activities

Contents

Activity Sets

Material Cards

1. Algebra Pieces (1.3)
2. Algebraic Expression Cards (1.3)
3. Attribute Label Cards (2.1)
4. Attribute-Game Grid (2.1)
5. Two-Circle Venn Diagram (2.1)
6. Three-Circle Venn Diagram (2.1, 9.1)
7. Follow-Up Activities and Questions No. 3 (2.1)
8. Rectangular Geoboard Template (2.2, 6.4, 9.1, 10.2)
9. Coordinate Guessing and Hide-a-Region Grids (2.2)
10. Logic Problem Clue Cards and People Pieces (Problem 1) (2.3)
11. Logic Problem Clue Cards and People Pieces (Problem 2) (2.3)
12. Logic Problem Clue Cards, Prize and People Pieces (Problem 3) (2.3)
13. Logic Problem Clue Cards, Career, Singer, People, and Location Pieces (Problem 4) (2.3)
14. Logic Problem Clue Cards (Problem 5) (2.3)
15. Logic Problem Object Pieces (Problem 5) (2.3)
16. Pica-Centro Recording Sheet (2.3)
17. Mind-Reading Cards (3.1)
18. Interest Gameboard (6.3)
19. Metric Ruler, Protractor, and Compass (7.1, 9.1, 10.1, 10.3, 11.1, 11.2, 11.3)
20. Table of Random Digits (7.2, 7.3, 8.1)
21. Two-Penny Grid (8.1)
22. Three-Penny Grid (8.1)
23. Simulation Spinners (8.2)
24. Trick Dice (8.2)
25. Geoboard Recording Paper (9.1)
26. Circular Geoboard Template (9.1)
27. Grids for Game of Hex (9.2)
28. Regular Polyhedra (9.3)
29. Regular Polyhedra (9.3)
30. Two-Centimeter Grid Paper (9.3)
31. Cube Patterns for Instant Insanity (9.3)
32. Perpendicular Lines for Symmetry (9.4)
33. Metric Measuring Tape (10.1)
34. Centimeter Racing Mat (10.1)
35. Pentominoes (10.2)
36. Pentomino Game Grid (10.2)
37. Prism, Pyramid, and Cylinder (10.3)
38. Hypsometer-Clinometer (11.3)

Preface

The primary purpose of *Mathematics for Elementary Teachers: An Activity Approach* is to engage prospective elementary- and middle-school teachers in mathematical activities that will enhance their conceptual knowledge, introduce them to important manipulatives, and model the kind of mathematical learning experiences they will be expected to provide for their students.

The National Council of Teachers of Mathematics' *Principles and Standards for School Mathematics* ("Standards 2000") and its predecessor, *Curriculum and Evaluation Standards for School Mathematics* ("Standards 1989"), strongly assert that students learn mathematics well when they construct their own mathematical thinking. Information can be transmitted from one person to another, but mathematical understanding and knowledge come from within the learner as that individual explores, discovers, and makes connections.

The National Council of Teachers of Mathematics' *Professional Standards for Teaching Mathematics* presents a vision of mathematics teaching that "redirects mathematics instruction from a focus on presenting content through lecture and demonstration to a focus on active participation and involvement." In this vision, "mathematics instructors do not simply deliver content; rather, they facilitate learners' construction of their own knowledge of mathematics."

This book contains activities and materials to actively engage students in mathematical explorations. It provides prospective elementary- and middle-school teachers the opportunity to examine and learn mathematics in a meaningful way. It also provides instructors with a variety of resources for making an interactive approach to mathematics the focus of their teaching.

OUR PHILOSOPHY

Mathematics for Elementary Teachers: An Activity Approach is a collection of activities for prospective teachers that involves and develops inductive and deductive reasoning. The activities enable students to think deeply about how manipulatives and visual models contribute to understanding mathematical concepts. Students experience mathematics directly by using models that embody concepts and promote mathematical thinking. This book reflects the beliefs that:

- Prospective teachers who learn mathematics through appropriate use of manipulatives, models, and diagrams are more likely to develop a solid conceptual basis and a deeper understanding of the mathematics they will teach.
- Prospective teachers who learn mathematics by being actively involved in doing mathematics will be more likely to teach in the same manner.
- Prospective teachers who use manipulatives effectively in their learning will experience how manipulatives assist understanding and will be more likely to use them effectively in their teaching.
- Becoming familiar with manipulatives and models in structured activities will give prospective teachers confidence to develop lessons that use manipulatives and models.
- A concrete approach diminishes the mathematical anxiety that often accompanies a more abstract approach.
- Tactile and visual approaches provide mental images that, for some students, can be easily retained to provide understanding for symbolic representations.

COOPERATIVE LEARNING AND USING MANIPULATIVES

Each Activity Set can be done individually or in small groups. Small group instruction provides opportunities for discussion and for listening to others explain their reasoning. Guidelines for cooperative learning in small groups are outlined in Activity Set 2.3.

It is well known that effective teachers have a good understanding of the mathematics they teach and are skillful in choosing and using a variety of appropriate instructional techniques. The importance of using manipulatives in mathematics teaching and learning is well documented and amply illustrated in the pages of NCTM's *Standards and Expectations 2000*. Research has shown that the appropriate use of manipulative materials has a significant positive effect on students' attitudes to learning and potential for achievement in mathematics.

Interviews with teachers successfully using manipulatives in classrooms revealed the following commonalities: the teachers had all received training for using manipulatives; they designed their own lessons and worked through them using manipulatives themselves; and they prepared for classroom use of the manipulatives by anticipating how the class would react to each activity.

FEATURES OF THE EIGHTH EDITION

Mathematics for Elementary Teachers: An Activity Approach consists of 34 Activity Sets and accompanying materials, which, collectively, constitute a self-contained mathematics laboratory. It contains many special features designed to enhance learning.

Discovery Based Activity Sets   Each Activity Set uses materials and/or visual models to provide a context for understanding. The questions and activities in each Activity Set are sequentially developed to encourage discovery and to provide an in-depth exploration of a topic. Students are asked to describe patterns, form conjectures, look for relationships, and discuss their thinking.

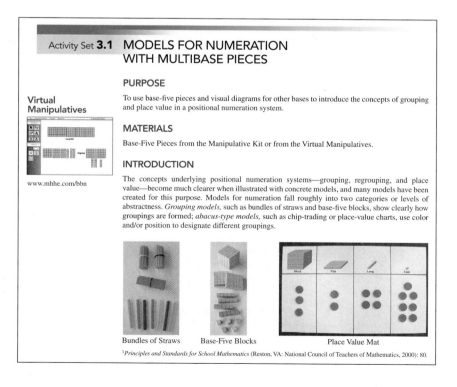

New Full-Color Diagrams   Using color diagrams that match the actual manipulatives strengthens pedagogy and conceptual learning

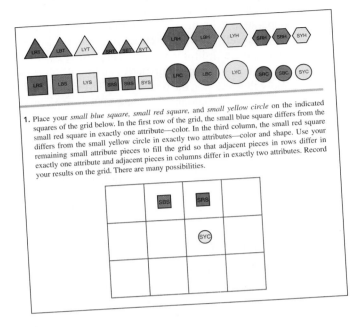

1. Place your *small blue square*, *small red square*, and *small yellow circle* on the indicated squares of the grid below. In the first row of the grid, the small blue square differs from the small red square in exactly one attribute—color. In the third column, the small red square differs from the small yellow circle in exactly two attributes—color and shape. Use your remaining small attribute pieces to fill the grid so that adjacent pieces in rows differ in exactly one attribute and adjacent pieces in columns differ in exactly two attributes. Record your results on the grid. There are many possibilities.

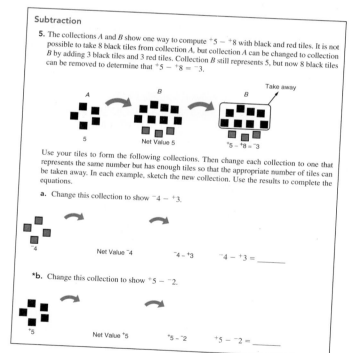

Subtraction

5. The collections A and B show one way to compute $^+5 - {}^+8$ with black and red tiles. It is not possible to take 8 black tiles from collection A, but collection A can be changed to collection B by adding 3 black tiles and 3 red tiles. Collection B still represents 5, but now 8 black tiles can be removed to determine that $^+5 - {}^+8 = {}^-3$.

Use your tiles to form the following collections. Then change each collection to one that represents the same number but has enough tiles so that the appropriate number of tiles can be taken away. In each example, sketch the new collection. Use the results to complete the equations.

a. Change this collection to show $^-4 - {}^+3$.

Net Value $^-4$ $^-4 - {}^+3$ $^-4 - {}^+3 =$ _____

*b. Change this collection to show $^+5 - {}^-2$.

Net Value $^+5$ $^+5 - {}^-2$ $^+5 - {}^-2 =$ _____

New Full Color Elementary School Text Pages   Pages taken from current grade school textbooks show future teachers how key concepts from the activity set are presented to K–8 students and new *Follow-Up Questions and Activities* allow your students to explore these ideas.

Colored Cardstock Manipulatives   Manipulatives designed for use with each Activity Set (and selected *Follow-Up Questions and Activities*) are packaged with each text. A Manipulative Kit holds resealable, labeled bags for each type of manipulative.

Virtual Manipulatives   There are corresponding Virtual Manipulatives and work areas on the companion website (www.mhhe.com/bbn).

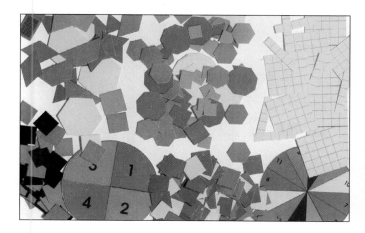

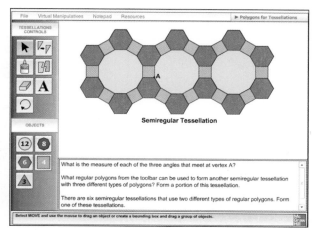

(Updated) Material Cards   In addition to the Manipulative Kit, the *Activity Approach* text also offers 38 Material Cards (some of which are colored) with additional manipulatives, models, grids, templates, and game mats.

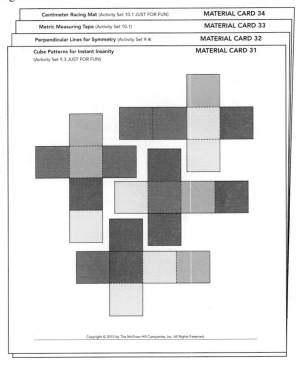

(Updated) Elementary School Activity   At the end of each chapter, there is field-use-ready Elementary School Activity that illustrates how ideas and manipulatives from the chapter can be adapted for use in the elementary classroom. Activities are now illustrated with engaging photographs of elementary school students using manipulatives.

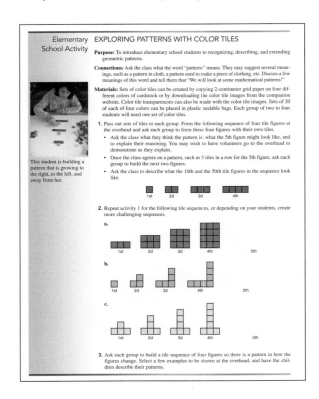

(Updated) Follow-Up Questions and Activities   *Follow-Up Questions and Activities* at the end of each Activity Set ask students to relate the activity set to three important areas: connections to the elementary classroom, related mathematics concepts, and the NCTM *Standards and Expectations* from the *Principle and Standards for School Mathematics*.

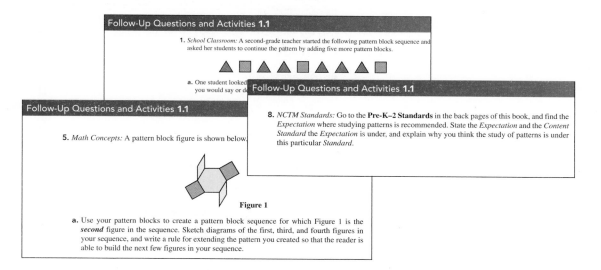

NCTM Standards and Expectations   A durable, removable cardstock table of the **NCTM Standards and Expectations for Grades Pre-K–2, 3–5, and 6–8** is provided in the back of the book so students can answer end of section *Follow-Up Questions and Activities* and see what mathematics is recommended at various grade levels.

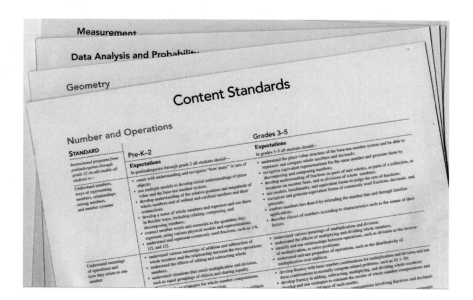

Technology Connection through Applets

Each chapter directs students to an appropriate interactive applet from the companion website (www.mhhe.com/bbn). The applets pose questions for student explorations.

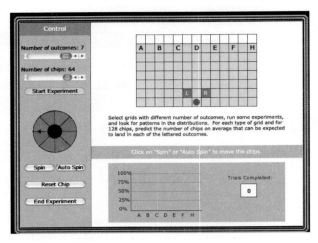

Distributions Applet, Chapter 7
www.mhhe.com/bbn

(Updated) Just for Fun

Each Activity Set is followed by a "Just for Fun" activity. These are related to the topics of the Activity Sets and often relate to recreational activities or have an artistic aspect.

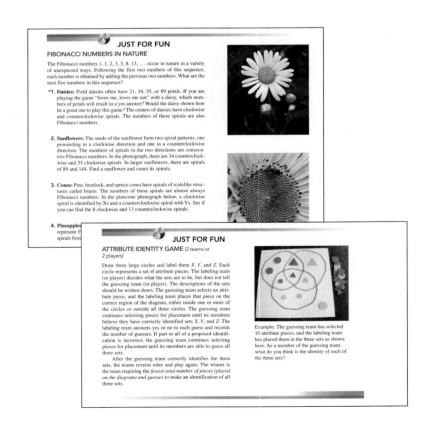

Answer Section   Answers to selected questions (marked with an asterisk) in the Activity Sets appear in the back of the book.

ADDITIONAL RESOURCES

Mathematics for Elementary Teachers: A Conceptual Approach, **eighth edition (ISBN-13: 978-0-07-351945-6; ISBN-10: 0-07-351945-6)**
This is an optional companion volume to the *Activity Approach*. Each of the 34 sections in it corresponds to one of the Activity Sets. The text also contains a one-page Math Activity at the beginning of each section that utilizes the same Manipulative Kit materials as the *Activity Approach*. As with previous editions, the *Activity Approach* and the *Conceptual Approach* are both available packaged together and with the Manipulative Kit ISBN-13: 978-0-07-729794-7, ISBN-10: 0-07-729794-6

Instructor's Resource Manual   The *Instructor's Resource Manual* to accompany *Mathematics for Elementary Teachers: An Activity Approach*, eighth edition, contains an updated set of section-by-section Planning Guides with detailed suggestions for teaching a course using the *Activity Approach*. The *Instructor's Manual* includes answers for all of the Activity Set questions and the Just for Fun activities, as well as selected answers for the updated end-of-section *Follow-Up Questions and Activities*. The *Instructor's Manual* also provides a set of sample test questions, with answers, for each chapter of the *Activity Approach*. The *Instructor's Resource Manual* can be found at the companion website for *Mathematics for Elementary Teachers: An Activity Approach*, accessible at www.mhhe.com/bbn

Companion Website (www.mhhe.com/bbn)   The website for the *Activity Approach* offers a variety of resources for both instructors and students. The companion website enables you to:

- Use Virtual Manipulatives to carry out various activities online using printable virtual colored manipulative pieces
- Access Interactive Mathematics Applets, one for each chapter, for exploring key mathematical concepts
- Explore 34 open-ended Math Investigations, one per Activity Set, including 14 investigations that use Mathematics Investigator software to generate data and eight investigations with corresponding, student friendly, Geometer's Sketchpad® modules
- Download color masters for transparencies of the manipulatives in the Manipulative Kit and black-and-white masters for a variety of grid and dot papers
- Access extended bibliographies and Internet links for further research
- Download instructions and exercises for Network Graphs and Logo

COURSE FORMATS

Many of the Activity Sets in *Mathematics for Elementary Teachers: An Activity Approach* are independent of each other and can be covered out of sequence (see the *Instructor's Resource Manual* for information on the Activity Set dependencies). The flexible coverage of the *Activity Approach* makes it possible for the book to be used effectively in a variety of course formats:

- A lab course based on the Activity Sets and supplemented with outside readings from a reference text or journals, with the *Follow-Up Questions and Activities* used for assignments
- A combination lab and recitation course in which the Activity Sets are integrated with discussions or lectures extending the ideas raised in the Activity Sets and developed further in *Mathematics for Elementary Teachers: A Conceptual Approach*
- A traditional lecture/recitation course in which the Activity Sets and *Follow-Up Questions and Activities* in the *Activity Approach* are used to supplement *Mathematics for Elementary Teachers: A Conceptual Approach*.

ACKNOWLEDGMENTS

The authors would like to thank the students and instructors who have used the previous editions of this book, along with the instructors who reviewed this book and *Mathematics for Elementary Teachers: A Conceptual Approach.* The following reviewers contributed excellent advice and suggestions for the eighth edition of *Mathematics for Elementary Teachers: An Activity Approach*:

Paul Ache, *Kutztown University*
Margo Alexander, *Georgia State University*
Babette Benken, *California State University, Long Beach*
Dr. Joy W. Black, *University of West Georgia*
Patty Bonesteel, *Wayne State University*
Kristin Chatas, *Washtenaw Community College*
Eddie Cheng, *Oakland University*
Joy Darley, *Georgia Southern University*
Linda Dequire, *California State University, Long Beach*
Ana Dias, *Central Michigan University*
Mary C. Enderson, *Middle Tennessee State University*
Larry Feldman, *Indiana University of Pennsylvania*
Maria Fung, *Western Oregon University*
Dr. Marilyn Hasty, *Southern Illinois University, Edwardsville*
Karen Heinz, *Rowan University*
Kathy Johnson, *Volunteer State Community College*
Joan Jones, *Eastern Michigan University*
Greg Klein, *Texas A&M University, College Station*
Robert Koff, *Georgia Perimeter*
Peggy Lakey, *University of Nevada, Reno*
Pamela Lasher, *Edinboro University of Pennsylvania*
Judy McBride, *Indiana University–Purdue University Indianapolis*
J. Lyn Miller, *Slippery Rock University*
Sue Purkayastha, *University of Illinois–Champaign*
Laurie Riggs, *California State Polytechnic University–Pomona*
Kathleen Rohrig, *Boise State University*
Lisa Rombes, *Washtenaw Community College*
Pavel Sikorskii, *Michigan State University*
Agnes Tuska, *California State University, Fresno*
Laura Villarreal, *University of Texas at Brownsville*
Dr. Andrew M. White, *Eastern Illinois University*

In particular, Laurie Burton would like to especially thank all of the Western Oregon University students who have willingly class-tested new materials and provided many helpful suggestions and corrections. The authors are sincerely grateful for all of this continued support as we seek to update and improve our materials. Finally, we would like to thank the people at McGraw-Hill who have dedicated their time and creativity to enhance and improve this edition of *Mathematics for Elementary Teachers: An Activity Approach.*

1

Problem Solving

In grades 3–5, students should investigate numerical and geometric patterns and express them mathematically in words or symbols. They should analyze the structure of the pattern and how it grows or changes, organize this information systemically, and use their analysis to develop generalizations about the mathematical relationships in the pattern.[1]

Activity Set 1.1 ## SEEING AND EXTENDING PATTERNS WITH PATTERN BLOCKS

PURPOSE

To recognize, describe, construct, and extend geometric patterns.

Virtual Manipulatives

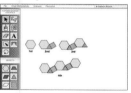

www.mhhe.com/bbn

MATERIALS

Pattern Blocks and Color Tiles from the Manipulative Kit or from the Virtual Manipulatives.

INTRODUCTION

In this first activity set, colored geometric shapes called pattern blocks will be used to recognize, study, and extend geometric patterns. The set of pattern blocks consists of six different polygons: a green triangle, an orange square, a red trapezoid, a blue rhombus, a tan rhombus, and a yellow hexagon.

Human beings are pattern-seeking creatures. Babies begin life's journey listening for verbal patterns and looking for visual patterns. Scientists in search of extraterrestrial intelligence send patterned signals into the universe and listen for incoming patterns on radio telescopes. Mathematics is also concerned with patterns. Many mathematicians and educators involved in reforming mathematics teaching and learning at the elementary and middle school levels are suggesting that the notion of mathematics as the study of number and shape needs to be expanded. Some suggest that "mathematics is an exploratory science that seeks to understand every kind of pattern."[2]

In this set we will look at a variety of sequences. A *sequence* is an ordered set of mathematical objects. There are many possibilities for sequences. A few examples of sequences are a sequence of pattern block figures, a sequence of tile figures, a sequence of letter groupings, a sequence of whole numbers, and a sequence of fractions.

---

[1]*Principles and Standards for School Mathematics* (Reston, VA: National Council of Teachers of Mathematics, 2000): 159.

[2]Lynn A. Steen, *On the Shoulders of Giants: New Approaches to Numeracy* (Washington, DC: National Academy Press, 1990): 1–8.

HANDS ON Activity

Shape Patterns

Name_____

Learn You can make a pattern of shapes. Use pattern blocks. Then use letters to show the pattern another way.

Math Word

unit

unit

A B   A   B   A   B   A   B

To find a pattern, look for the shapes that repeat. The shapes that repeat make a unit.

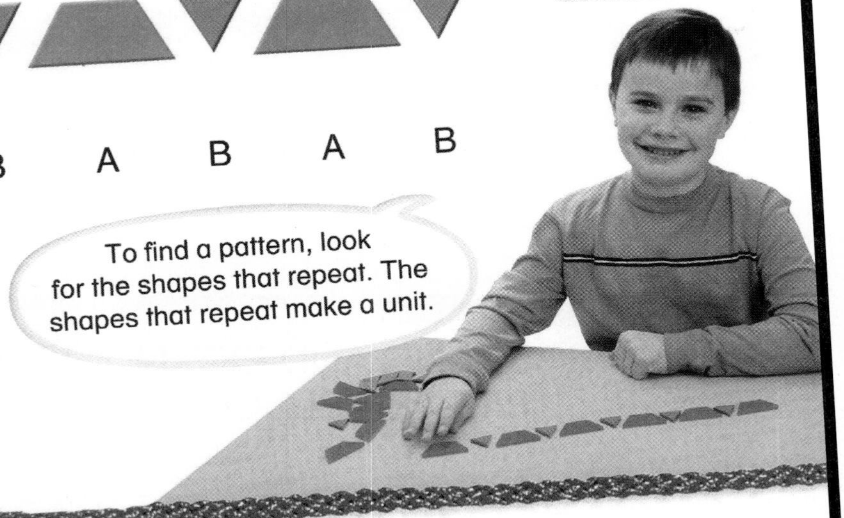

Your Turn Use pattern blocks to show the pattern. Then circle the pattern unit.

1

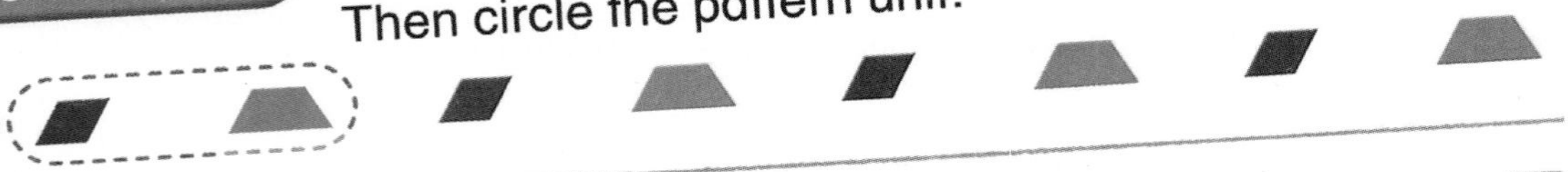

2

3

4

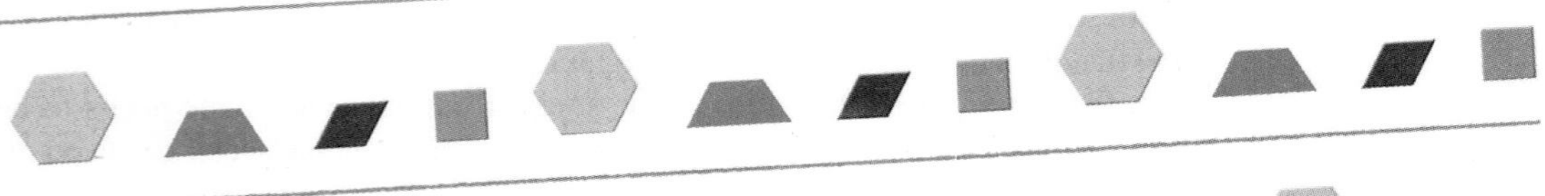

5

6 **Write About It!** How can you tell which shapes come next?

1. The pattern block figures shown here form the first five figures of a sequence. Use your green triangles to construct the sixth and seventh figures that you think extend the given pattern, and sketch these figures.

1st   2d   3d   4th   5th   6th   7th

*a. Describe in writing at least three ways that the seventh figure in your sequence differs from the sixth figure.

*b. Describe in writing what the 15th figure in this sequence would look like so that someone reading your description, who had not seen this sequence, could build the same figure.

2. Use your pattern blocks to construct the sixth figure of the sequence below, and sketch that figure.

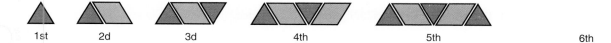

1st   2d   3d   4th   5th   6th

a. Describe in writing how new figures are created as this sequence is extended.

b. Will the 10th figure in an extended sequence have a green triangle or a blue rhombus on the right end? Explain your reasoning.

c. How many triangles and how many rhombuses are in the 25th figure of the extended sequence? Explain how you arrived at your answer.

d. Complete the following statement that will enable readers to determine the number of triangles and rhombuses in any figure they choose.

In the nth figure, where n is an even number, there will be $n \div 2$ triangles and $n \div 2$ rhombuses. If n is an odd number, the nth figure will contain _____ triangles and _____ rhombuses.

3. The pattern block sequence started below uses three different types of pattern blocks. Use your pattern blocks to build and sketch the next figure in the extended sequence.

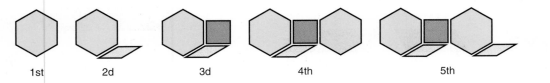

1st   2d   3d   4th   5th   6th

*a. Describe in writing how new figures are created as this sequence is extended.

*b. What pattern block will be attached to the right end of the 16th figure to obtain the 17th figure in this sequence?

*c. Determine the number of hexagons, squares, and rhombuses in the 20th figure of the sequence. Explain how you thought about it.

*d. Repeat part c for the 57th figure in the sequence.

4. Use your pattern blocks to build and sketch the sixth figure of the sequence here.

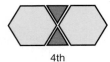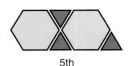

1st   2d   3d   4th   5th   6th

a. Determine the number of triangles and hexagons in the 10th figure of the extended sequence. Do the same for the 15th figure.

b. Any figure number that is a multiple of 3 has 1/3 that number of hexagons and 2/3 that number of triangles. Explain how you can determine the number of hexagons and triangles if the figure number is 1 more than a multiple of 3. One less than a multiple of 3.

5. The third and fourth figures of a pattern block sequence are given below. Use your pattern blocks to construct and sketch the first, second, and fifth figures in this sequence.

1st   2d   3d

4th   5th

a. Describe how the odd-numbered figures differ from the even-numbered figures.

b. Sketch the missing figures for the next sequence. Explain how you can determine the number of hexagons in any even-numbered figure of the sequence, then explain it for any odd-numbered figure.

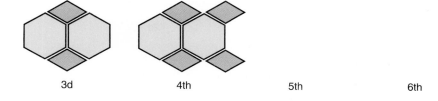

1st   2d   3d   4th   5th   6th

Explanation:

*6. The third term of a color tile sequence is shown below. Use your color tiles to create more than one sequence for which the given figure is the third figure. Sketch diagrams of the first, second, and fourth figures. Write a rule for extending each pattern you create so that the reader is able to build the next few figures in the sequence.

Sequence I

1st   2d   3d   4th

Rule:

Sequence II

1st   2d   3d   4th

Rule:

Sequence III

1st   2d   3d   4th

Rule:

7. Pattern block sequences I and II begin repeating in the fifth figure and pattern block sequence III begins repeating in the sixth figure. Build and sketch the next figure in each sequence with your pattern blocks. For the 38th figure in each sequence, determine which pattern block is at its right end and how many of each type of pattern block the 38th figure contains. Describe how you reached your conclusion in each case.

Sequence I

  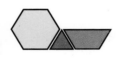 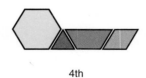 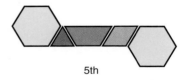

1st   2d   3d   4th   5th

Explanation

6th

*Sequence II

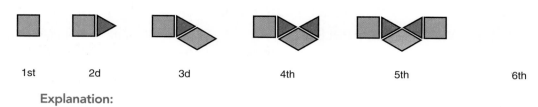

1st   2d   3d   4th   5th   6th

Explanation:

Sequence III

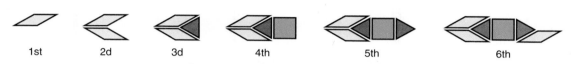

1st   2d   3d   4th   5th   6th

Explanation:

7th

8. Devise your own sequence of figures with pattern blocks. Pose at least three questions about your sequence. Ask another person to build your sequence and answer your questions. Sketch at least the first four figures from your sequence and record your questions.

JUST FOR FUN

TOWER PUZZLE APPLET

This ancient puzzle is sometimes referred to as the "Tower of Brahma." The story says that at creation, the priests were given three golden spindles. One golden spindle has 64 golden disks with the largest disk at the bottom of the spindle and each successive disk getting smaller up to the top smallest disk. Day and night the priests were to transfer disks from one spindle to another, moving the disks one at a time but never placing a larger disk on a smaller one until all the disks are transferred to another spindle—in the original order. When the priests finished transferring the spindle of 64 disks, the world was to come to an end.

Use a model, or the interactive applet from the companion website, and the problem-solving strategies of simplifying, making a table, and looking for a pattern as you try to form a conjecture about the minimum number of moves to transfer all 64 disks from one spindle to another spindle. By experimenting with special cases, such as 2 disks, 3 disks, etc., data can be gathered that lead to conjectures for predicting the number of moves for transferring 64 disks.

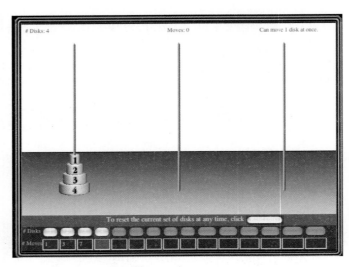

Tower Puzzle Applet, Chapter 1
www.mhhe.com/bbn

Follow-Up Questions and Activities 1.1

1. *School Classroom:* A second-grade teacher started the following pattern block sequence and asked her students to continue the pattern by adding five more pattern blocks.

   a. One student looked at the sequence and said he did not know what to do. Describe what you would say or do as the teacher.

   b. Another student continued the pattern block sequence as follows. Describe what you believe this student was thinking. What questions can you ask to encourage the student to reveal how she perceived and extended the pattern?

2. *School Classroom:* Design a pattern block sequence that you believe is appropriate for an elementary school student and write a few questions that you can ask about your sequence. Try this activity on an elementary school age child of your choice. Record your sequence, your questions, and the student's responses.

3. *School Classroom:* On page 2, the example from the **Elementary School Text** shows a student using pattern blocks to extend and show patterns: Question 6 says "Write About It! How can you tell which shapes come next?" Describe what you would say or do as the teacher to help a student who is struggling with writing about the patterns, without just telling the student what to write.

4. *Math Concepts:* Make up two secret pattern block or color tile sequences that have the same first four figures but different figures after that. Show the first four figures to a partner and challenge them to find both of your secret sequences. Illustrate your sequences and explain the results of your challenge.

5. *Math Concepts:* A pattern block figure is shown below.

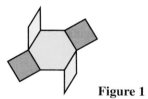

Figure 1

   a. Use your pattern blocks to create a pattern block sequence for which Figure 1 is the *second* figure in the sequence. Sketch diagrams of the first, third, and fourth figures in your sequence, and write a rule for extending the pattern you created so that the reader is able to build the next few figures in your sequence.

   b. Use your pattern blocks to create a second pattern block sequence for which Figure 1 is the *fourth* figure in the sequence. Sketch diagrams of the first, second, third, and fifth figures in your sequence, and write a rule for extending the pattern you created so that the reader is able to build the next few figures in your second sequence.

*c. Write a sentence or two describing what the 50th figure would look like and how many tiles it would contain.

*d. Write a statement that will enable readers to determine the number of tiles for any figure number, *n*.

2. The first three terms of the number sequence represented by the tile figures here are 7, 12, and 17. Build and sketch the fourth figure, and record the number of tiles needed to build it.

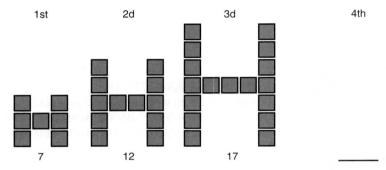

a. Write directions for constructing the eighth figure so that someone who has not seen any of the figures could build the figure by following your directions.

b. How many tiles are in the eighth figure?

c. Determine the number of tiles in the 15th figure. (Imagine how you would construct that figure.)

d. Describe in words what the 50th figure would look like and how many tiles it would contain.

e. Write a procedure using words or an algebraic expression to determine the number of tiles for any figure, *n*.

3. Here are three sets of tile figures and the number sequences they represent. Build the fourth figure and record the fourth number in each number sequence. Determine the 10th number in each number sequence by imagining how you would construct the 10th figure in each tile sequence. Write a procedure using words or an algebraic expression that would enable the reader to determine the number of tiles in any figure, given the figure number, *n*.

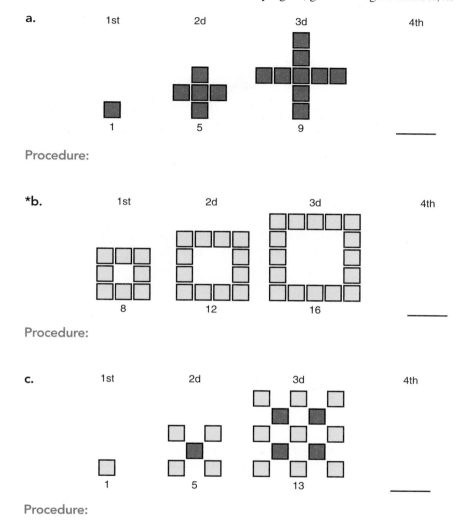

a.

Procedure:

***b.**

Procedure:

c.

Procedure:

4. Using red and blue tiles, construct and then sketch the fourth and fifth figures in this sequence of rectangles and determine the fourth and fifth terms of the corresponding number sequence.

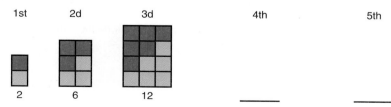

a. Describe the 10th rectangle in the sequence, including height, width, total number of tiles, number of red tiles, and number of blue tiles.

b. Explain how you can determine the number of red tiles and the number of blue tiles in the 50th rectangle.

5. The following figures resemble a stairstep pattern. Use your tiles to construct and then sketch the fifth figure (fifth stairstep).

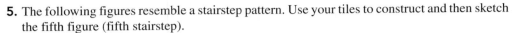

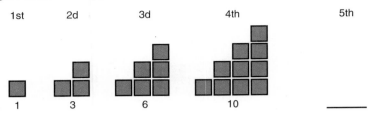

*a. What number does the fifth stairstep represent? The 10th stairstep?

*b. Explain how the results from activity 4b above can help to determine the number of tiles in the 50th stairstep.

*c. Which stairstep corresponds to Gauss's sum $1 + 2 + 3 + 4 + \cdots + 99 + 100$?

*d. Explain how stairsteps and activity 4 can be used to determine Gauss's sum in part c.

*e. Write a paragraph explaining how the sum of consecutive whole numbers from 1 to any given number, n, can be obtained by using stairsteps.

6. Suppose young Gauss had been asked to compute the sum

$$2 + 4 + 6 + 8 + 10 + 12 + 14 + \cdots + 78 + 80$$

How might he have computed this sum quickly? Devise a method of your own to compute the sum. (*Hint:* One way is to build a stairstep sequence similar to that in activity 5, except for the height of the steps.) Record your method and any diagrams or sketches you use.

JUST FOR FUN

FIBONACCI NUMBERS IN NATURE

The Fibonacci numbers 1, 1, 2, 3, 5, 8, 13, . . . occur in nature in a variety of unexpected ways. Following the first two numbers of this sequence, each number is obtained by adding the previous two numbers. What are the next five numbers in this sequence?

*1. **Daisies:** Field daisies often have 21, 34, 55, or 89 petals. If you are playing the game "loves me, loves me not" with a daisy, which numbers of petals will result in a yes answer? Would the daisy shown here be a good one to play this game? The centers of daisies have clockwise and counterclockwise spirals. The numbers of these spirals are also Fibonacci numbers.

2. **Sunflowers:** The seeds of the sunflower form two spiral patterns, one proceeding in a clockwise direction and one in a counterclockwise direction. The numbers of spirals in the two directions are consecutive Fibonacci numbers. In the photograph, there are 34 counterclockwise and 55 clockwise spirals. In larger sunflowers, there are spirals of 89 and 144. Find a sunflower and count its spirals.

3. **Cones:** Pine, hemlock, and spruce cones have spirals of scalelike structures called bracts. The numbers of these spirals are almost always Fibonacci numbers. In the pinecone photograph below, a clockwise spiral is identified by Xs and a counterclockwise spiral with Ys. See if you can find the 8 clockwise and 13 counterclockwise spirals.

4. **Pineapples:** The sections of a pineapple are also arranged in spirals that represent Fibonacci number patterns. Find a pineapple, and count its spirals from upper left to lower right and from lower left to upper right.

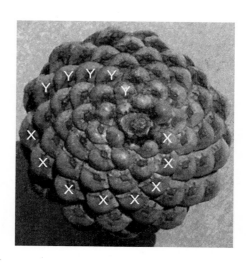

Follow-Up Questions and Activities **1.2**

1. *School Classroom:* Suppose you were teaching a middle school class and helping students understand how to use tile patterns to quickly compute sums such as $2 + 4 + 6 + \cdots + 20$. If one of your students simply chose to count the individual color tiles, explain how you would help him understand how to use this pattern to find the sum of the first 10 consecutive even numbers without just counting the individual tiles or without just adding $2 + 4 + 6 + \cdots + 20$.

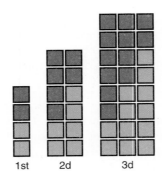

1st   2d   3d   . . .

2. *School Classroom:* One *Expectation* in the **Pre-K–2 Algebra Standard** in the back pages of this book says that students should be able to transfer from one representation of a pattern to another.

   a. Create a pattern with color tiles that you believe children at the Pre-K–2 level can "transfer" from a tile pattern to a number pattern. Record your tile pattern and the corresponding number pattern.

   b. Create a number pattern that you believe children at the Pre-K–2 level can transfer from a number pattern to a color tile pattern. Record your number pattern and the corresponding tile pattern.

   c. If you were to try the patterns you created with children at the Pre-K–2 level, what difficulties might you expect them to encounter, and how would you prepare them to overcome those difficulties?

3. *Math Concepts:*

   a. Use color tiles to build and then sketch the next two figures of this tile sequence. Record the number of tiles in each tile figure and the sum each figure represents to continue the number sequence.

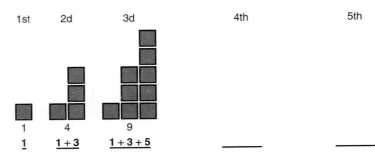

1st   2d   3d   4th   5th

1   4   9

<u>1</u>   **1 + 3**   **1 + 3 + 5**   _____   _____

b. By duplicating each of the figures in part a and inverting the duplicate copy, rectangles are formed. Build and sketch the 4th figure in the sequence of rectangles. Explain how you can use the 4th rectangular array in the tile sequence to find the sum of the odd numbers $1 + 3 + 5 + 7$ without just adding.

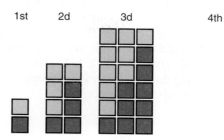

1st   2d   3d   4th

c. Explain how you can use rectangular arrays to obtain the sum of the odd numbers from 1 to 191 without just adding $1 + 3 + 5 + 7 + 9 + \cdots + 191$.

4. *Math Concepts:* Design and sketch the first three figures of a color tile sequence that grows in an interesting pattern such as the tile sequences in activities 2 and 3.

    a. Write a procedure in words that enables you to determine the number of tiles in the 10th figure of your tile sequence without actually constructing the 10th figure. How many tiles are in the 10th figure of your tile sequence?

    b. Write a procedure using words or an algebraic expression to determine the number of tiles for any figure, *n*, in your tile sequence. Explain your thinking.

5. *Math Concepts:* Open the **Math Investigation 1.2: Read Me—Triangular Numbers Instructions** from the companion website, and investigate the units digit patterns as described in questions 1 and 2 of the *Starting Points for Investigations 1.2.* State a few of your patterns or conclusions and explain your thinking.

6. *Math Concepts:* Here are the first three figures in a color tile sequence.

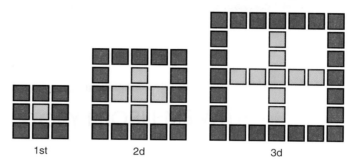

1st   2d   3d

    a. Write directions for constructing the eighth figure of this color tile sequence so that someone who has not seen any of the figures could build the figure by following your directions.

    b. What are the first eight terms in the number sequence represented by the total number of tiles in each of the first eight figures in the above color tile sequence?

    c. Determine the total number of tiles in the 15th figure. How many are red? How many are blue?

Two numbers   Sum of two numbers   Product of two numbers

    In this activity set, we will represent and solve algebra story problems using a geometric model similar to that of the Greeks. Our model will consist of two types of pieces: a variable piece and a unit piece. The variable piece will be used to represent an arbitrary line segment or an arbitrary number. Each unit piece will represent a length of 1 unit.

Unit   Variable piece

    The algebra pieces can be placed together to form different expressions.

An arbitrary number

Twice a number

3 more than a number

2 more than 3 times a number

---

1. If a variable piece represents a whole number, then two consecutive whole numbers are represented by the algebra pieces in figure a. Figure b illustrates the sum of the two consecutive whole numbers.

Two consecutive whole numbers (a)

The sum of two consecutive whole numbers (b)

d. Write a procedure using words or an algebraic expression to determine the number of red tiles for any figure, n. Write a procedure using words or an algebraic expression to determine the number of blue tiles for any figure, n.

e. Write a procedure using words or an algebraic expression to determine the total number of tiles for any figure, n.

7. *NCTM Standards:* Go to the **Algebra Standards** in the back pages of this book, and for each grade level, Pre-K–2, 3–5, and 6–8 find: "Understand patterns, relations and functions." Using the tile sequence in question 3a, describe how a child at each level is expected to work with this tile sequence.

 ## BENNETT-BURTON-NELSON WEBSITE

www.mhhe.com/bbn

Virtual Manipulatives   Grid and Dot Paper   Links and Readings
Interactive Chapter Applets   Color Transparencies   Geometer Sketchpad Modules
Puzzlers   Extended Bibliography

JUST FOR FUN

ALGEBRAIC EXPRESSIONS GAME[3]
(2 TEAMS)

In this game, players match algebraic expressions to word descriptions. Copies of algebraic expression cards appear on Material Card 2. There are two decks of 12 cards, one for each team of 12 students. Each student has an expression card similar to the samples shown here.

Play: Team A plays through its 12 cards and the amount of time required is recorded. Then team B plays through its 12 cards and records its time. On team A, the player who has the $n + 1$ card begins by saying, "I have $n + 1$. Who has two less than a number?" Then the player on team A, who has the card with $n - 2$, says, "I have $n - 2$. Who has one more than two times a number?" The game continues in this manner.

On team B, the first player is the player with the $n + 2$ card, and the next player is the player with an algebraic expression matching the word description on the first player's card.

Each deck of 12 cards is circular. That is, the last card in the deck calls the first card. Therefore, all the cards in the deck should be used. If there are fewer than 12 students on a team, some students can use more than one card. If there are more than 12 students on a team, two students can share a card, or more cards can be made.

Objective: The two teams compete against each other to complete the cycle of cards in the shortest amount of time.

Variation: The game can be changed so that word descriptions are matched to algebraic expressions. Two sample cards are shown here. In this case, player 1 says, "I have two more than three times a number. Who has $4x - 1$?" Player 2 says, "I have one less than four times a number. Who has $3x + 5$?" Make a deck of these cards and play this version of the game.

First Player

> **I have**
>
> $n + 1$
>
> **Who has**
>
> two less than
> a number

Next Player

> **I have**
>
> $n - 2$
>
> **Who has**
>
> one more than
> two times a number

First Player

> **I have**
>
> two more than three
> times a number
>
> **Who has**
> $4x - 1$

Next Player

> **I have**
>
> one less than four
> times a number
> **Who has**
>
> $3x + 5$

[3]T. Giambrone, "I HAVE . . . WHO HAS . . .?" *The Mathematics Teacher* 73 (October 1980): 504–506.

Follow-Up Questions and Activities **1.3**

1. *School Classroom:* Suppose you were working with a student who was struggling with the idea of using a variable and could not understand that the variable was not a fixed value. Explain how you could use algebra pieces to help the student understand how the variable is just a placeholder. Give an example question that you would use to help the student.

2. *School Classroom:* Devise a problem that you believe is appropriate for an upper elementary school student to solve using algebra pieces and mental arithmetic. Write out the problem and notes on "getting started" questions you may wish to ask your student. Try this activity on an upper elementary school age child of your choice. Record your problem, questions or hints you posed, and the student's responses.

3. *Math Concepts:* Use algebra pieces and mental arithmetic to determine four consecutive odd numbers whose sum is 64. Sketch and label your algebra piece model, and explain how you solved the problem.

4. *Math Concepts:* Use your algebra pieces to construct a rectangle whose length is twice its width. Draw a sketch of this rectangle. Using algebra pieces and mental arithmetic, explain how you can determine the length and width of this rectangle if you know the perimeter of the rectangle is 54 units.

5. *Math Concepts:* Five-eighths of the pieces of candy in a bowl of candy are chocolate, one-fourth of the pieces are strawberry, and the remaining pieces are sour apple. If the number of strawberry pieces is tripled, there will be 108 pieces of candy all together. Use algebra pieces and mental arithmetic to determine how many pieces of chocolate candy are in the bowl. Sketch and label your algebra piece model, and explain how you solved the problem.

6. *Math Concepts:* A box contains a total of $11.40 in nickels, dimes, and quarters. There are twice as many nickels as dimes and three times as many quarters as dimes. Use algebra pieces and mental arithmetic to determine how many of each coin are in the box. Sketch and label your algebra piece model, and explain how you solved the problem.

7. *NCTM Standards:* Go to http://illuminations.nctm.org/ and under "Lessons" select grade levels K–2, 3–5, and 6–8 and all of the **Content Standards.** Search for the keyword "pattern." Choose a lesson that involves extending and analyzing patterns.

    a. State the title of the lesson and briefly summarize the lesson.

    b. Referring to the **Standards Summary** in the back pages of this book as necessary, list the *Problem-Solving Standard Expectations* that the lesson addresses, and explain how the lesson addresses these *Expectations*.

8. *NCTM Standards:* One of the **Grades 3–5 Algebra Expectations** in the back of this book states "Model problem situations with objects and use representations such as graphs, tables and equations to draw conclusions." Explain why you think using algebra pieces and mental arithmetic as a problem-solving tool addresses this *Expectation*.

BENNETT-BURTON-NELSON WEBSITE

www.mhhe.com/bbn

Virtual Manipulatives	Grid and Dot Paper	Links and Readings
Interactive Chapter Applets	Color Transparencies	Geometer Sketchpad Modules
Puzzlers	Extended Bibliography	

Elementary School Activity

EXPLORING PATTERNS WITH COLOR TILES

Purpose: To introduce elementary school students to recognizing, describing, and extending geometric patterns.

Connections: Ask the class what the word "patterns" means. They may suggest several meanings, such as a pattern in cloth, a pattern used to make a piece of clothing, etc. Discuss a few meanings of this word and tell them that "We will look at some mathematical patterns!"

Materials: Sets of color tiles can be created by copying 2-centimeter grid paper on four different colors of cardstock or by downloading the color tile images from the companion website. Color tile transparencies can also be made with the color tile images. Sets of 20 of each of four colors can be placed in plastic sealable bags. Each group of two to four students will need one set of color tiles.

This student is building a pattern that is growing to the right, to the left, and away from her.

1. Pass out sets of tiles to each group. Form the following sequence of four tile figures at the overhead and ask each group to form these four figures with their own tiles.
   - Ask the class what they think the pattern is, what the 5th figure might look like, and to explain their reasoning. You may wish to have volunteers go to the overhead to demonstrate as they explain.
   - Once the class agrees on a pattern, such as 5 tiles in a row for the 5th figure, ask each group to build the next two figures.
   - Ask the class to describe what the 10th and the 50th tile figures in the sequence look like.

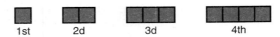

2. Repeat activity 1 for the following tile sequences, or depending on your students, create more challenging sequences.

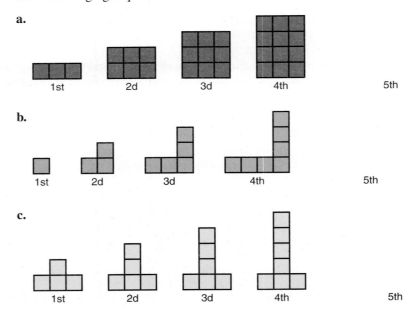

3. Ask each group to build a tile sequence of four figures so there is a pattern in how the figures change. Select a few examples to be shown at the overhead, and have the children describe their patterns.

2 Sets, Functions, and Reasoning

Being able to reason is essential to understanding mathematics. By developing ideas, exploring phenomena, justifying results, and using mathematical conjectures in all content areas and—with different expectations of sophistication—at all grade levels, students should see and expect that mathematics makes sense. Building on the considerable reasoning skills that children bring to school, teachers can help students learn what mathematical reasoning entails.[1]

Activity Set 2.1 SORTING AND CLASSIFYING WITH ATTRIBUTE PIECES

PURPOSE

To use attribute pieces in games and activities for sorting and classifying, reasoning logically, formulating and verifying hypotheses, and introducing set terminology and operations.

Virtual Manipulatives

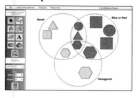

www.mhhe.com/bbn

MATERIALS

Attribute Pieces from the Manipulative Kit or from the Virtual Manipulatives, Attribute Label Cards from Material Card 3, and scissors to cut them out, Attribute Game Grids from Material Card 4 and the Two-Circle and Three Circle Venn Diagrams on Material Cards 5 and 6, respectively.

INTRODUCTION

"Mathematics is reasoning. One cannot do mathematics without reasoning. The standard does not suggest, however, that formal reasoning strategies be taught in grades K–4. At this level, the mathematical reasoning should involve the kind of informal thinking, conjecturing, and validating that helps children to see that mathematics makes sense.

"Manipulatives and other physical models help children relate processes to their conceptual underpinnings and give them concrete objects to talk about in explaining and justifying their thinking. Observing children interact with objects in this way allows teachers to reinforce thinking processes and evaluate any possible misunderstandings."[2]

---

[1]*Principles and Standards for School Mathematics* (Reston, VA: National Council of Teachers of Mathematics, 2000): 56.

[2]*Curriculum and Evaluation Standards for School Mathematics* (Reston, VA: National Council of Teachers of Mathematics, 1989): 29.

Unit 3
Enrichment

Venn Diagrams

You can use data from a diagram
to draw conclusions.

Look! Ken attends
all 3 clubs.

School Clubs

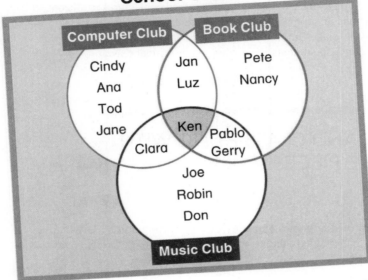

Computer Club

Cindy
Ana
Tod
Jane

Jan
Luz

Book Club

Pete
Nancy

Ken
Clara

Pablo
Gerry

Joe
Robin
Don

Music Club

Solve.

1. Who attends only the Book Club?

_____

2. How many children attend the

   Computer Club? _____ children

3. How many children attend

   more than 1 club? _____

Show your work.

In the late 1960s, sets of geometric figures called attribute pieces became a popular physical model for activities that promote logical thinking. These attribute pieces are also well suited for introducing ideas and terminology related to sets. The 24 attribute pieces used in this activity set vary in shape, color, and size. There are four shapes (triangle, square, hexagon, and circle), three colors (red, blue, and yellow), and two sizes (large and small). Each attribute piece differs from every other piece in at least one of the attributes of shape, color, or size. The letters on each piece refer to its three attributes. (For example, LRT means large, red, triangle.) Most of the games and activities in this activity set can be adapted for use with children.

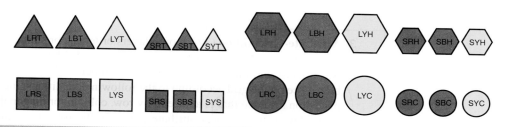

1. Place your *small blue square, small red square,* and *small yellow circle* on the indicated squares of the grid below. In the first row of the grid, the small blue square differs from the small red square in exactly one attribute—color. In the third column, the small red square differs from the small yellow circle in exactly two attributes—color and shape. Use your remaining small attribute pieces to fill the grid so that adjacent pieces in rows differ in exactly one attribute and adjacent pieces in columns differ in exactly two attributes. Record your results on the grid. There are many possibilities.

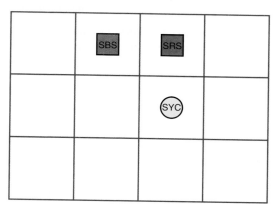

2. **Attribute Guessing Game** (2 players): To play this game, display all 24 attribute pieces on a flat surface. One player thinks of a specific attribute piece. The other player tries to determine that piece by asking questions that can be answered yes or no. Pieces that are ruled out by questions may be physically separated from the rest. The score is the number of questions needed to identify the piece. Players alternate roles. Low score wins.

   *a. If the player trying to guess the piece restricts all questions to the attributes of color, size, and shape, what is the minimum number of guesses necessary to ensure the identification of a randomly chosen piece? List the questions you would ask in order to identify a piece in the minimum number of guesses.

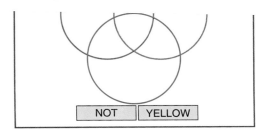

   b. Record the set of attribute pieces in the *union* of the following two sets.

     Circular *or* Not Blue: _____

     _____

   c. Using only word combinations found on the attribute label cards of Material Card 3, describe the pieces that are outside both circles in the Venn diagram on the previous

Follow-Up Questions and Activities 2.2

1. *School Classroom:* A fourth-grade student was confused about how a negative slope could be referred to as rise over run; they argued that you "rise up" and that you "run over (to the right)." Explain how you would help this student make sense of using the idea of rise over run for negative slope and slopes of 0. Illustrate your explanation.

2. *School Classroom:* Suppose that after you introduced your students to slopes, a student asks you if it is possible to have a line with slope $2\frac{1}{3}$. Explain how you would help the student understand that this is possible. Write a series of questions you could ask the student to bring about his understanding and ability to draw lines given similar mixed number slopes.

3. *Math Concepts:* With a classmate, play the Hide-a-Region game described in the **Just for Fun Activity** in this section. List several strategies that helped you determine the hidden target and explain how they helped you.

4. *Math Concepts:*
   a. Of all possible lines, how many lines have a *y*-intercept of 3? Explain your thinking and write equations in slope-intercept form to illustrate your answer.
   b. Of all possible lines, how many lines have a slope of 3? Explain your thinking and write equations in slope-intercept form to illustrate your answer.
   c. Of all possible lines, how many lines have a slope of 3 and a *y*-intercept of 3? Explain your thinking and write equations in slope-intercept form to illustrate your answer.

5. *Math Concepts:* Consider the following lines:

$y = \frac{1}{3}x + 3$	$y = \frac{1}{3}x - 3$	$y = -\frac{1}{3}x + 3$	$y = -\frac{1}{3}x - 3$
$y = 3x + \frac{1}{3}$	$y = 3x - \frac{1}{3}$	$y = -3x + \frac{1}{3}$	$y = -3x - \frac{1}{3}$

Determine three different ways to categorize this set of lines into groups. Illustrate your categories and explain your thinking.

6. *Math Concepts:* Twelve different line segments, each with different nonnegative slopes, can be formed on the 5 × 5 geoboard. *Note:* Vertical line segments have undefined slopes.

   a. Sketch and count the number of line segments with different nonnegative slopes that can be formed on 2 × 2, 3 × 3, and 4 × 4 geoboards. Copy Rectangular Geoboards from the website or use printable Virtual Manipulatives.

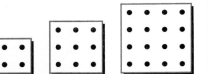

   b. Predict the number of line segments with different nonnegative slopes that can be formed on a 6 × 6 geoboard and give your prediction. Then sketch the geoboard line segments to check your prediction. You may find it helpful to sketch the line segments on more than one geoboard. Copy Rectangular Geoboards from the website or use printable Virtual Manipulatives.

7. *NCTM Standards:*

a. In order to determine the slopes of lines, students need an understanding of the Cartesian coordinate system and how to plot points given their coordinates. Look through the **Standards** summary in the back pages of this book to determine specifically where such experience is recommended. Record the *Expectation(s),* the grade level(s), and the *Content Standard(s)* the recommendations are under.

b. Return to the **Standards** summary in the back pages of this book and find an *Expectation* that specifically mentions slope. State the *Expectation* and the *Content Standard* the *Expectation* is under, and explain why you think slope is under this particular *Standard* and grade level.

BENNETT-BURTON-NELSON WEBSITE

www.mhhe.com/bbn

Virtual Manipulatives
Interactive Chapter Applets
Puzzlers

Grid and Dot Paper
Color Transparencies
Extended Bibliography

Links and Readings
Geometer Sketchpad Modules

Elementary School Activity

REASONING WITH ATTRIBUTE PIECES

Purpose: To introduce elementary school students to testing conjectures and reasoning logically by comparing and contrasting attribute pieces.

Connections: "How many of you have a dog or a cat?" "What other animals do you have?" "Have you ever looked at two animals to compare them to see how they are alike or how they are different?" Today we will use colored pieces called attribute pieces, and you will compare them to see how they are alike and how they are different.

Materials: Masters for classroom sets of attribute pieces can be downloaded from the companion website and printed on cardstock. The masters can also be used to create colored overhead transparencies. Sets of 24 attribute pieces can be placed in plastic sealable bags. Each group of two to four students will need one set of attribute pieces.

1. Pass out a set of attribute pieces to each group and allow them some time to look at them. Often students will sort the pieces by color, shape, or size. Select a few groups to describe what they noticed or what they did with the pieces. Discuss the three major ways the pieces differ: color, shape, and size.

2. Place these four pieces in a row on the overhead and ask how each piece differs from the previous piece. This row of pieces is called a one-difference train because each piece differs from the previous piece by one attribute.

Ask students to determine some of the different pieces for the fifth piece in this train, and to use their pieces to continue building this one-difference train as long as is possible.

3. Form the following two-difference train on the overhead and repeat activity 2 by asking students to compare each piece to the next piece. Ask them what kind of a train this is. (two-difference train) Ask them to form and to continue building this train. *Note:* this activity can be played like a game, with each student in turn trying to place a new piece on the train, until no further moves are possible.

4. Place the following three pieces on the overhead and ask what kind of a train this forms. (three-difference train) Ask for suggestions for a few more pieces for this train.

5. Draw a circle on the overhead, and tell the students you are thinking about a set of attribute pieces for the circle, such as all the yellow pieces, or all triangular pieces, and that they can guess what type of pieces are in the circle by selecting an attribute piece, one at a time, and you will either place it in the circle or on the outside of the circle. Repeat this activity using a variety of "Secret Attribute" sets such as all yellow pieces, all square pieces, all large pieces, all large square pieces, etc.

6. (Optional) Repeat activity 5 for a two-circle Venn diagram. You may want to first show an example and note how each piece inside the overlapping part of the circles has the attributes of both circles. You may use this to lead a conversation about the intersection of sets.

This second grader is building a one-difference train.

3 Whole Numbers

Concrete models can help students represent numbers and develop number sense; they can also help to bring meaning to students' use of written symbols and can be useful in building place-value concepts. But using materials, especially in a rote manner, does not ensure understanding. Teachers should try to uncover students' thinking as they work with concrete materials by asking questions that elicit students' thinking and reasoning.[1]

Activity Set 3.1 MODELS FOR NUMERATION WITH MULTIBASE PIECES

Virtual Manipulatives

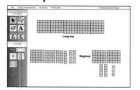

www.mhhe.com/bbn

PURPOSE

To use base-five pieces and visual diagrams for other bases to introduce the concepts of grouping and place value in a positional numeration system.

MATERIALS

Base-Five Pieces from the Manipulative Kit or from the Virtual Manipulatives.

INTRODUCTION

The concepts underlying positional numeration systems—grouping, regrouping, and place value—become much clearer when illustrated with concrete models, and many models have been created for this purpose. Models for numeration fall roughly into two categories or levels of abstractness. *Grouping models,* such as bundles of straws and base-five blocks, show clearly how groupings are formed; *abacus-type models,* such as chip-trading or place-value charts, use color and/or position to designate different groupings.

Bundles of Straws

Base-Five Blocks

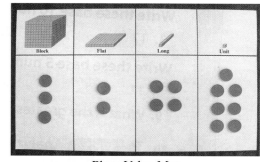
Place Value Mat

[1]*Principles and Standards for School Mathematics* (Reston, VA: National Council of Teachers of Mathematics, 2000): 80.

d. Explain why you never have to write a numeral greater than 4 in the table for a minimal collection of base-five pieces.

2. Using the base-five pieces, you can represent a collection of 28 units by a minimal collection of 1 flat, 0 longs, and 3 units. This is recorded in the table below. Using base-five pieces to aid visualization, supply the missing numbers in the following table for minimal collections.

	No. of Unit Squares	Long-Flats	Flats	Longs	Units
a.	28	0	1	0	3
b.	31				
*c.	126				
d.	200				
e.		0	1	2	3
*f.		3	3	0	3
g.		4	4	4	4

3. Minimal collections of base-five pieces can be recorded without using tables. For example, the first entry in the table above can be written as 103_{five}. In doing this, we must agree that the positions of the digits from right to left represent the numbers of units, longs, flats, and long-flats. This method of writing numbers is called *positional numeration,* and 103_{five} is called a *base-five numeral.* Write the base-five numerals for each of the other entries in the table in activity 2.

a. 103_{five} **b.**   ***c.**   **d.**

e.   ***f.**   **g.**

4. The base-five pieces that represent the numeral 2034_{five} are shown here. There is a total of 269 unit squares in these pieces.

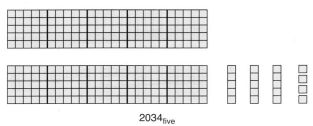

2034_{five}

Represent the following numbers with your base-five pieces, and determine the total number of unit squares in each.

	Base-Five Numeral	Total Number of Unit Squares
a.	2304_{five}	
*b.	1032_{five}	
c.	2004_{five}	

5. Here are the first three pieces for base seven. Draw the first three pieces for base three and base ten in the space provided below.

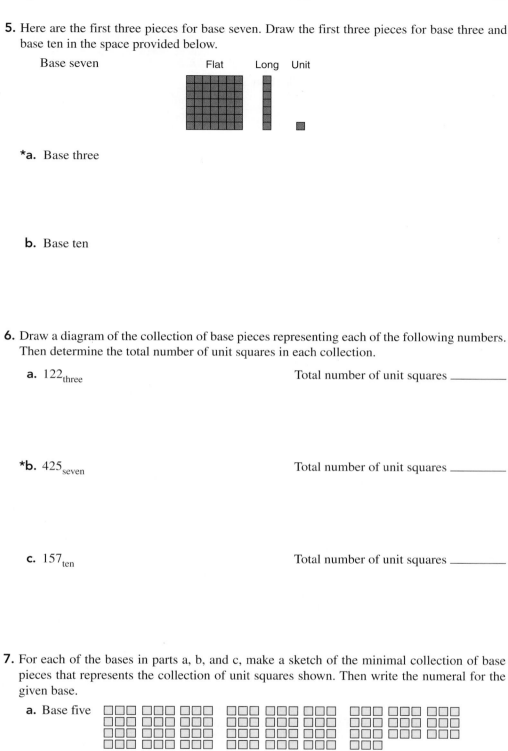

Base seven

Flat   Long   Unit

*a. Base three

b. Base ten

6. Draw a diagram of the collection of base pieces representing each of the following numbers. Then determine the total number of unit squares in each collection.

a. 122_{three} Total number of unit squares _____

*b. 425_{seven} Total number of unit squares _____

c. 157_{ten} Total number of unit squares _____

7. For each of the bases in parts a, b, and c, make a sketch of the minimal collection of base pieces that represents the collection of unit squares shown. Then write the numeral for the given base.

a. Base five

Minimal Collection Sketch:

Base-five numeral _____

*b. Base nine

Minimal Collection Sketch:

Base-nine numeral _____

c. Base ten

Minimal Collection Sketch:

Base-ten numeral _____

JUST FOR FUN

The numbers 1, 2, 4, 8, 16, 32, and so on are called *binary numbers*. Following 1, each number is obtained by doubling the previous number. There are a variety of applications of binary numbers. Many of these applications provide solutions to games and puzzles, such as the intriguing mind-reading cards (shown on the next page) and the ancient game of Nim (shown on the next page).

MIND-READING CARDS

With the five cards in Figure 1 on page 61, you can determine the age of any person who is not over 31. Which of these cards is your age on? If you selected card 4 and card 16, then you are 20 years old. If you selected cards 1, 2, and 16, then you are 19 years old.

1. The number in the upper left-hand corner of each of these cards is a binary number. Write your age as the sum of the fewest possible binary numbers. On which cards do the binary numbers that sum to your age appear? On which cards does your age appear?

*2. Write the number 27 as the sum of the fewest number of binary numbers. On which cards do these binary numbers occur? On which cards does 27 occur?

3. If someone chooses a number that is only on cards 1, 2, and 8, what is this number?

*4. Explain how the mind-reading cards work.

*5. The mind-reading cards can be extended to include greater numbers by using more cards. The next card is card 32 (see Figure 2). To extend this system to six cards, more numbers must be placed on all six cards. For example, $33 = 32 + 1$, so 33 must be put on card 1 as well as on card 32. On which cards should 44 be placed?

6. Write the additional numbers that must be put on cards 1, 2, 4, 8, 16, and 32 in Figure 2 to extend this system to six cards. What is the greatest age on this new six-card system?

7. Cut out the mind-reading cards from Material Card 17 and use them to intrigue your friends or students. Ask someone to select the cards containing his or her age, or to pick a number less than 64 and tell you which cards it is on. Then, amaze them by revealing that number.

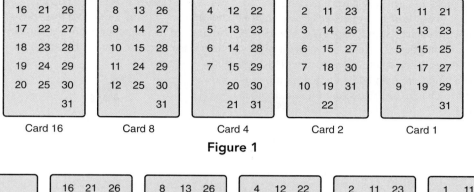

Figure 1

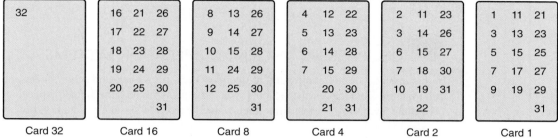

Figure 2

GAME OF NIM (2 players)

The game of Nim is said to be of ancient Chinese origin. In its simplest form, it is played with three rows of toothpicks or markers. On a turn, a player may take any number of toothpicks from any one row. The winner of the game is the player who takes the last toothpick or group of toothpicks. Try a few rounds of this game with a classmate.

With a little practice, it is easy to discover some situations in which you can win. For example, if it is your opponent's turn to play and there is a 1-2-3 arrangement, as shown below, you will be able to win. Sketch three more situations in which you will win if it is your opponent's turn to play.

Winning Strategy: A winning strategy for the game of Nim involves binary numbers.

1. On your turn, group the remaining toothpicks in each row by binary numbers, using the largest binary numbers possible in each row, as shown in the following example.

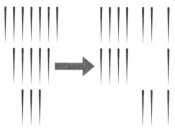

2. Then remove toothpicks so that there is an *even number* of each type of pile left. In the example above, you will see an even number of 4s, an even number of 2s, and an odd number of 1s. So 1 toothpick must be taken from one of the rows. Show that the 1-2-3 arrangement shown in the column at the left has an even number of binary groups.

*3. Assume it is your turn and you have the arrangement shown below. Cross out toothpick(s) so that your opponent will be left with an even number of binary groups.

*4. After the toothpicks in each row have been grouped by binary numbers, there will be either an *even situation* (an even number of each type of binary group) or an *odd situation* (an odd number of at least one type of binary group). Experiment to see whether one turn will always change an even situation to an odd situation. Is it possible in one turn to change an even situation into another even situation?

Generalized Nim: Play the game of Nim with any number of rows and any number of toothpicks in each row. Try the strategy of leaving your opponent with an even situation each time it is his or her turn. Is this still a winning strategy?

 ## DECIPHERING ANCIENT NUMERATION SYSTEMS APPLET

In this applet, you are challenged to decipher the Attic-Greek and other ancient numeration systems. To decipher the systems, you drag the symbols onto the workspace and click "Translate Symbols" to determine their value. There are six ancient numeration systems for you to decipher.

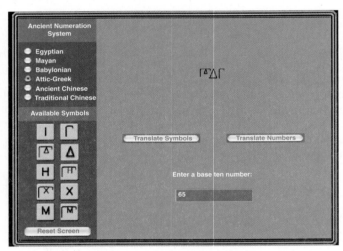

Deciphering Ancient Numeration Systems Applet, Chapter 3
www.mhhe.com/bbn

Follow-Up Questions and Activities 3.1

1. *School Classroom:* Suppose you have asked your students to imagine there is another culture that uses base five to count and they need to devise a way to communicate numbers with this culture. Explain how you would help your students solve this problem.

2. *School Classroom:* Devise an activity you think will help elementary school students understand how the digits in a base-ten number relate to the value of the number. In your activity; use base-ten pieces and use the 1-6 spinner from your Manipulative Kit to pick digits. Write a few questions you can ask your students about your activity.

3. *School Classroom:* Read the **Elementary School Text** page at the beginning of this section. Describe a way to use both of your hands to count in base four. Then create a chart for base four similar to the chart for base five on that page.

4. *Math Concepts:* Explain why the digits in a place value system with base, b, are 0, 1, ..., $b - 1$ and why no digits for numbers greater than $b - 1$ are needed.

5. *Math Concepts:* For any base, b, the base piece after a long-flat is called a flat-flat.
   a. Sketch what you think a flat-flat should look like and explain why it is a logical choice for the next base piece regardless of the base.
   b. Determine the minimal collection of base-seven pieces and the corresponding base-seven numeral for 30,000 unit squares. Draw a generic sketch of the base-seven pieces and explain how you arrived at your answer.

6. *Math Concepts:* The place value chart model for numeration (see the Introduction to this Activity Set) consists of a chart with columns on which markers are placed. This model can represent any base, with the columns, starting on the right, representing units, longs, flats, and blocks, respectively, in the given base. Using base five, for example, each group of five markers is replaced by one marker in the next column to the left. In this diagram, 13 markers in the units column, grouped by fives, result in two markers in the longs column and three markers in the units column, or 23_{five}.

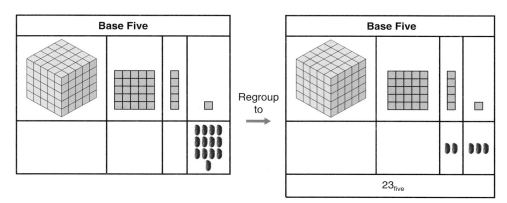

When grouped by fours (base four), regrouping the same starting set of 13 markers, as shown on page 64, results in three markers in the longs column and one marker in the units column, or 31_{four}.

Activity Set **3.2**   ADDING AND SUBTRACTING WITH MULTIBASE PIECES

PURPOSE

Virtual Manipulatives

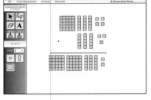

www.mhhe.com/bbn

To use multibase pieces to visually illustrate addition and subtraction.

MATERIALS

A pair of dice and Base-Five Pieces from the Manipulative Kit or from the Virtual Manipulatives.

INTRODUCTION

The operations of addition and subtraction are inverses of each other. *Addition* is explained by putting together sets of objects, and *subtraction* can be explained by taking away a subset of objects from a given set. This dual relationship between subtraction and addition can be seen in the trading-up game, which introduces addition, and the trading-down game, which introduces subtraction.

Algorithms for addition and subtraction are step-by-step procedures for adding and subtracting numbers. One of the best ways to gain insight into the addition and subtraction algorithms is by thinking the process through using manipulatives that represent other number bases. The base-five pieces will be used in the following activities.

Addition

1. **Trading-Up Game** (2 to 5 players): Use your base-five pieces to play. On a player's turn, two dice are rolled. The total number of dots facing up on the dice is the number of base-five units the player wins. At the end of a player's turn, the player's pieces should be traded (regrouped), if necessary, so that the total winnings are represented by the fewest number of base-five pieces (minimal collection). The base-five numeral for the minimal collection should be recorded. The first player to get one long-flat wins the game.

   Example: On the player's first turn, shown below, the eight units won were traded for a minimal collection and the corresponding base-five numeral was recorded.

   On the player's second turn, the eight additional pieces won were added to the player's collection. After trading to get a minimal collection, the player recorded the base-five numeral for the total collection.

	Dice	Collection	Minimal collection	Numeral
1st turn	⚁ ⚅	▢▢▢▢ ▢▢▢▢	▢▢ ▢ ▢	13_{five}
2d turn	⚄ ⚂	▢▢▢▢ ▢▢▢▢ ▢▢▢▢	▢▢▢ ▢	31_{five}

2. Answer the following questions for the trading-up game described in activity 1.

 a. What is the minimal collection for the greatest number of units you can win in one roll of the two dice?

 *b. By comparing the maximum collection for one turn (part a) to the long-flat, determine the minimum possible number of rolls in which a game can be won. Explain your reasoning.

 c. Determine the maximum number of turns it can take to obtain a long-flat. Explain how you arrived at your conclusion. (*Hint:* Compare the least possible winnings from one roll of the dice to the long-flat.)

 *d. If your total is 421_{five} after several turns, will it be possible for you to win on your next roll? Explain why or why not.

 e. Suppose your total score is 333_{five}. What is the fewest number of turns in which you can reach a long-flat, 1000_{five}? Explain how you reached your conclusion. (*Hint:* Use your base-five pieces to represent 333_{five}.)

3. Numbers written as base-five numerals can be added using base-five pieces. For example, $324_{\text{five}} + 243_{\text{five}}$ can be added by representing each number with base-five pieces, combining the collections, and trading (regrouping) to find the minimal collection, as shown below.

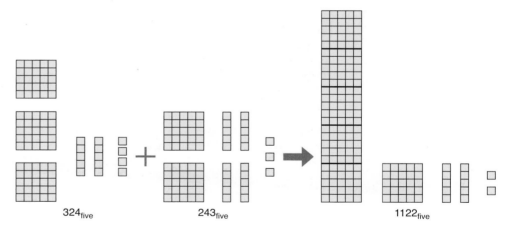

324_{five} 243_{five} 1122_{five}

Use base-five pieces to represent each of the following sums. Then regroup to obtain the minimal collection, and record the base-five numeral for this collection.

*a. $43_{\text{five}} + 24_{\text{five}} =$ **b.** $313_{\text{five}} + 233_{\text{five}} =$

*c. $304_{\text{five}} + 20_{\text{five}} + 120_{\text{five}} + 22_{\text{five}} =$ **d.** $1000_{\text{five}} + 100_{\text{five}} + 10_{\text{five}} =$

Subtract 2-Digit Numbers

Name_____

Learn   Subtract 53 − 17.

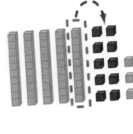

Step 1

Show 53.
Are there enough ones to subtract
7 ones?

tens	ones
□	□
5	3
− 1	7

Step 2

There are not enough ones to subtract.
Regroup 1 ten as 10 ones.
Now there are 13 ones.

tens	ones
4	13
5̶	3̶
− 1	7

Step 3

Subtract the ones.

tens	ones
4	13
5̶	3̶
− 1	7
	6

Step 4

Subtract the tens.

tens	ones
4	13
5̶	3̶
− 1	7
3	6

$$53 - 17 = \underline{36}$$

Try It   Subtract. You can use 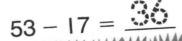 and ▪ to help.

1.

tens	ones
2	15
3̶	5̶
− 1	8
1	7

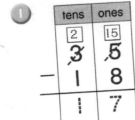

2.

tens	ones
□	□
4	7
− 2	4

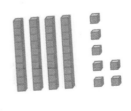

3. **Write About It!** How is subtracting 42 − 26 different
from subtracting 42 − 6?

From *McGraw-Hill National Mathematics*, Grade 2, by Macmillan/McGraw-Hill. Copyright © 2007 by The McGraw-Hill Companies, Inc.
Reprinted by permission of The McGraw-Hill Companies, Inc.

4. Numbers in other bases can be added mentally by visualizing or by making sketches of the appropriate base pieces. For example, in order to add $1221_{three} + 122_{three}$, the following diagrams show what regrouping must be done to obtain a minimal collection of 2 long-flats, 1 flat, and 2 longs.

$$\begin{array}{r} 1221_{three} \\ + \ 122_{three} \\ \hline 2120_{three} \end{array}$$

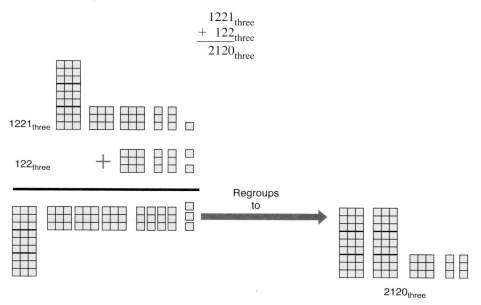

Make sketches of base pieces representing the following sums and their regroupings (as above). Record the numeral for each sum.

*a. $\begin{array}{r} 201_{three} \\ + \ 102_{three} \\ \hline \end{array}$

b. $\begin{array}{r} 2312_{four} \\ + \ 203_{four} \\ \hline \end{array}$

*c. $\begin{array}{r} 255_{six} \\ + \ 134_{six} \\ \hline \end{array}$

Subtraction

5. **Trading-Down Game** (2 to 5 players): Use your base-five pieces to play. Each player begins the game with 1 long-flat. On a player's turn, two dice are rolled. The total number of dots facing up on the dice is the number of units the player discards. The object of the game is to get rid of all base-five pieces. The first player to do so wins the game. On some turns the player will have to trade (regroup) in order to discard the exact number of pieces. At the end of each player's turn, the player's remaining pieces should be a minimal collection, and the base-five numeral should be recorded. See the next page for an example of this game.

Follow-Up Questions and Activities 3.2

1. *School Classroom:* Write three different short story problems appropriate for elementary school students that illustrate the three subtraction methods. Explain your thinking.

2. *School Classroom:* A student in your class repeatedly makes the same type of addition error; for example, when they add 23 + 18, they write 311 and when they add 34 + 18, they write 412. What error is the student making? Explain how you would use base-ten pieces to help this student understand how to resolve this issue.

3. *School Classroom:* The **Elementary School Text** page at the beginning of this section illustrates how the standard subtraction algorithm corresponds to subtracting with base-ten pieces. Illustrate with similar diagrams what the steps would look like if the students decided to subtract the tens before subtracting the units in 53 − 17. Explain why you believe one method is better than the other.

4. *Math Concepts:* For each of the following, sketch a base piece model to compute the sum or difference and explain how the base pieces can be used to model the standard paper-and-pencil algorithm.

   a. $431_{\text{five}} + 233_{\text{five}}$ **b.** 1982 + 2189

   c. $431_{\text{five}} - 233_{\text{five}}$ **d.** 2912 − 1189

5. *Math Concepts:* Using sticks bundled for base-five (see Introduction to Activity Set 3.1), sketch a simple stick bundle model to compute each of the following sums or differences and explain how the stick bundles can be used to model the standard paper-and-pencil algorithm.

   a. $432_{\text{five}} + 144_{\text{five}}$ **b.** $411_{\text{five}} - 333_{\text{five}}$

6. *Math Concepts:* With beans as single units (1), gluing 10 beans on a popsicle stick for a bean stick (10) and gluing 10 bean sticks together for a bean raft (100) is another easy and inexpensive manipulative to use in the elementary school classroom. For each of the following, sketch a bean stick model to compute the sum or difference and explain how the beans and bean sticks can be used to model the standard paper-and-pencil algorithm (use very simple outline sketches to save time). *Hint:* You can trade 1 bean stick for 10 beans, etc.

   a. 335 + 134   **b.** 3000 − 1982

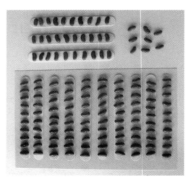

7. *Math Concepts:* Do an Internet search and find a website that features a game or math applet focused on whole number addition or subtraction. Describe the game or applet and critique its quality and usefulness. Give the URL of the game or math applet you found.

8. *NCTM Standards:* Read the *Expectation* in the **Pre-K–2 Number and Operations Standards** in the back pages of this book under the *Standard* "Understand meanings of operations . . ." that involves "understand the effects of adding . . ." Give examples of how the activities in this activity set address this expectation.

9. *NCTM Standards:* Go to http://illuminations.nctm.org/ and under "Lessons" select grade levels Pre-K–2 and the **Number and Operation Standard.** Choose a lesson that involves adding or subtracting whole numbers.

    a. State the title of the lesson and briefly summarize the lesson.

    b. Referring to the **Standards Summary** in the back pages of this book as necessary, list the *Number and Operation Standard Expectations* that the lesson addresses and explain how the lesson addresses these *Expectations*.

 # BENNETT-BURTON-NELSON WEBSITE

www.mhhe.com/bbn

Virtual Manipulatives
Interactive Chapter Applets
Puzzlers

Grid and Dot Paper
Color Transparencies
Extended Bibliography

Links and Readings
Geometer Sketchpad Modules

I will multiply 2-digit numbers by 2-digit numbers.

11.4 Multiply by 2-Digit Numbers

VOCABULARY

Distributive Property
of Multiplication

Learn

It's fun to take a boat tour on Lake Michigan. Each month the boat makes 32 tours. How many miles does the boat travel in one month?

The **Distributive Property of Multiplication** says that you can multiply the addends of a sum by a number, and then add the products.

Use the Distributive Property of Multiplication to break apart factors to find a product.

Let's connect models to paper and pencil.

Take a 14-Mile Tour on Lake Michigan

Wisconsin   Lake Michigan   Michigan

Illinois   Indiana   Ohio

Make Connections

Use Models

Draw a rectangle on graph paper, using the factors as the dimensions. Separate tens and ones with a heavy line.

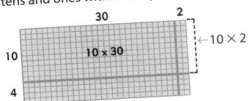

$$(10 + 4) \times 32$$

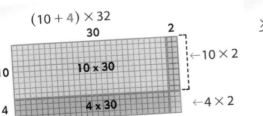

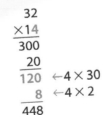

$$300 + 120 + 20 + 8 = 448$$

Use Paper and Pencil

```
   32
  ×14
  300  ←10 × 30
   20  ←10 × 2
```

```
   32
  ×14
  300
   20
  120  ←4 × 30
    8  ←4 × 2
  448
```

Use a Calculator

Press:

Display:

32×14=448

*4. Explain how it is possible, using base-ten pieces, to multiply a two-digit number by a two-digit number without using any multiplication facts. Draw a diagram to illustrate your explanation for 21 × 23.

5. The rectangular model for multiplication corresponds very closely to the traditional paper-and-pencil algorithm for multiplication. Use your base-ten pieces to form the rectangle representing 23 × 24.

  *a. Here is a paper-and-pencil procedure that uses four partial products for multiplication. Make a diagram of the base-ten piece rectangle representing 23 × 24. Clearly match each partial product with the corresponding region of your diagram.

$$
\begin{array}{r}
24 \\
\times\ 23 \\
\hline
12 \quad (3 \times 4) \\
60 \quad (3 \times 20) \\
80 \quad (20 \times 4) \\
400 \quad (20 \times 20) \\
\hline
552
\end{array}
\quad
\begin{array}{l}
\text{Partial} \\
\text{products}
\end{array}
$$

  b. The following procedure uses two partial products for multiplication. Make another sketch of your base-ten piece rectangle, and match the parts of the rectangle with the corresponding partial products.

$$
\begin{array}{r}
24 \\
\times\ 23 \\
\hline
72 \quad (3 \times 24) \\
480 \quad (20 \times 24) \\
\hline
552
\end{array}
\quad
\begin{array}{l}
\text{Partial} \\
\text{products}
\end{array}
$$

6. Once you become familiar with the base-ten piece model, it is easy to sketch diagrams of rectangles in order to compute products. For example, to compute 33 × 41, you would outline the rectangle as in the first sketch below and fill it with flats, longs, and units as in the second sketch. The product is obtained by counting the base-ten pieces, 12 hundreds, 15 tens, and 3 units, and regrouping to obtain 1 thousand, 3 hundreds, 5 tens, and 3 units (1353).

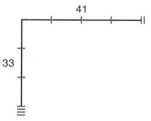
Figure 1

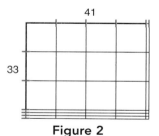
Figure 2

For each of the products on the following page,

(1) Draw a base-ten piece sketch, similar to Figure 2, in the first column.

(2) Determine the product from the sketch and record it below the sketch.

(3) In column 2, compute the product using the paper-and-pencil algorithm with *four* partial products and match the partial products to the corresponding parts of your sketch by marking the partial products on the sketch.

(4) In column 3 compute the product using the paper-and-pencil algorithm with *two* partial products and match the partial products to the corresponding parts of your sketch by marking the partial products on the sketch.

Follow-Up Questions and Activities **3.3**

1. *School Classroom:* How would you answer the following elementary school student's question: "I know that to multiply a number by 10 you just put a zero at the end, but why? Write your reply and include any necessary diagrams or sketches.

2. *School Classroom:* Design an activity that you believe is appropriate for helping an elementary school student understand what partial products are and how they work while multiplying one two-digit number by another two-digit number. Write a few questions to go with your activity. Explain how your activity will help a typical child learning about multiplication.

3. *School Classroom:* Explain how the distributive property of multiplication over addition is illustrated visually in the model for 14×32 in the **Elementary School Text** page at the beginning of this section.

4. *Math Concepts:* Use base-five pieces to model $13_{\text{five}} \times 4_{\text{five}}$, regroup the base pieces to form the minimal collection, and give the solution to $13_{\text{five}} \times 4_{\text{five}}$ in base five. Illustrate your model and explain your thinking.

5. *Math Concepts:* Using your base-five pieces only (no pencil and paper), build a rectangle similar to the base-ten rectangle in activity 3 to determine the product $12_{\text{five}} \times 13_{\text{five}}$. Draw a sketch of your rectangle, label the dimensions, and record the product in base five. Explain how you used the base-five pieces to determine the product.

6. *Math Concepts:* Use a place value chart (see Follow-Up Questions and Activities 3.1) and answer the following questions:

   a. Sketch a base-five place value chart with 4 markers in the units column, 1 marker in the long column, and 3 markers in the flat column to represent 314_{five}. Explain, using place value chart diagrams, how you can multiply $3 \times 314_{\text{five}}$ using just the markers and the chart.

   b. Explain, using place value chart diagrams, how you can multiply $10_{\text{five}} \times 314_{\text{five}}$ using just the markers and the chart.

7. *NCTM Standards:* Read the **Grades 3–5 Number and Operations Standards** in the back pages of this book. Pick two *Expectations* that the activities in this section address. State the *Expectations* and the *Standards* they are under. Explain which activities address these *Expectations* and how they do so.

 BENNETT-BURTON-NELSON WEBSITE

www.mhhe.com/bbn

Virtual Manipulatives	Grid and Dot Paper	Links and Readings
Interactive Chapter Applets	Color Transparencies	Geometer Sketchpad Modules
Puzzlers	Extended Bibliography	

Activity Set **3.4**   DIVIDING WITH BASE-TEN PIECES

Virtual Manipulatives

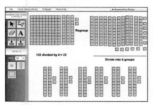

www.mhhe.com/bbn

PURPOSE

To use base-ten pieces to illustrate two physical interpretations of division and the long-division algorithm.

MATERIALS

Base-Ten Pieces from the Manipulative Kit or from the Virtual Manipulatives.

INTRODUCTION

In this activity set we will begin by using base-ten pieces to look at two different ways to approach division. The *measurement* or *subtractive* approach to division is illustrated by answering the question "How many piles of 3 cards can you make from a total of 39 cards?"

The *sharing* or *partitive* approach to division is illustrated by answering the question "If 39 cards are separated into 3 piles, how many are in each pile?"

Each question can be answered by computing 39 ÷ 3. The answer to both questions is 13. With physical objects, however, the first question would be modeled by repeatedly subtracting groups of 3 objects and counting the number of groups, and the second by dividing the objects into 3 groups and counting the number of objects in each group.

Base-ten pieces also will be used to illustrate the inverse relationship between multiplication and division and to provide a concrete interpretation of the long-division algorithm.

---

1. Using base-ten pieces, we can determine the quotient 36 ÷ 3 by simple counting procedures.

With the ***sharing*** method (Figure 1), 36 is shared equally among 3 groups. Each group has 1 long and 2 units.

The ***measurement*** approach (Figure 2) to division asks how many groups of 3 can be formed from 36. In this case, all the longs must be traded for units so that groups of 3 can be formed.

36 ÷ 3 = 12 (12 in each of 3 equal groups)
Sharing
Figure 1

36 ÷ 3 = 12 (12 groups of 3)
Measurement
Figure 2

I will explore dividing.

5.3 Explore Dividing by 1-Digit Divisors

Hands On Activity

Ms. Meir works for the Miami Metrozoo. She has equally divided 148 maps among 4 zoo guides. How many maps did she give to each guide?

You Will Need
- place-value models

You can use place-value models to divide 148 by 4.

Use Models

STEP 1

Model 148. Draw rectangles to show 4 equal groups.

STEP 2

Regroup to show 1 hundred as 10 tens.
Place an equal number of tens in each group.

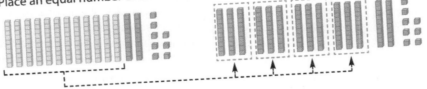

STEP 3

Regroup to show the extra tens as ones.
Place an equal number of ones in each group.

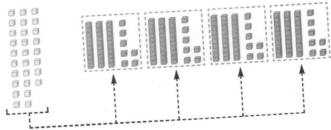

a. Represent 24 as a minimal collection of base-ten pieces. Then, regrouping when necessary, determine 24 ÷ 6 using the measurement interpretation of division. Record your results with sketches of base-ten pieces.

*b. Represent 132 as a minimal collection of base-ten pieces. Determine 132 ÷ 12 using the sharing interpretation of division. Record your results with sketches of base-ten pieces.

2. Many times division with whole numbers does not come out evenly, so there is a remainder. When we divide 20 by 3 using the measurement approach, there are 6 groups of 3 units and 2 remaining units. Dividing 20 by 3 using the sharing method, we have 3 groups of 6 with 2 remaining.

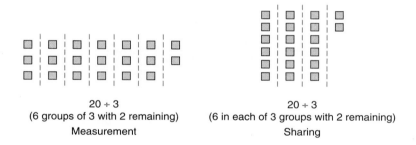

20 ÷ 3	20 ÷ 3
(6 groups of 3 with 2 remaining)	(6 in each of 3 groups with 2 remaining)
Measurement	Sharing

Use base-ten pieces to determine each of the following quotients and record your results in a diagram.

a. 57 ÷ 4 (sharing approach)

*b. 114 ÷ 12 (measurement approach)

3. When 36 was divided by 3 in activity 1, the answer 12 was obtained in two different ways. Notice that with either approach the base-ten pieces can be pushed together to form a rectangular array of 36 squares with one dimension of 3. So *division can be thought of as finding the missing dimension of a rectangle when the total number of unit squares and one dimension are known.*

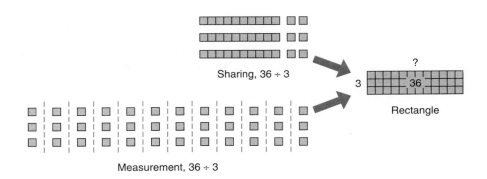

Sharing, 36 ÷ 3

Measurement, 36 ÷ 3

Rectangle

In each of the following activities, use the specified base-ten pieces to construct a rectangle with the given dimension. You may have to trade pieces for other pieces of equal value. Sketch a diagram of your result, and record the missing dimension of the rectangle.

a. Start with 9 longs and 6 units, and build a rectangle that has one dimension of 4 units.

*b. Start with 2 flats, 7 longs, and 3 units, and build a rectangle that has one dimension of 13 units.

c. Start with 4 flats, 6 longs, and 2 units, and build a rectangle that has one dimension of 21 units.

4. To divide 143 by 11 using the base-ten pieces, form the minimal collection of base-ten pieces for 143. Then draw a line segment of length 11 units to represent one dimension of the rectangle. Finally, distribute the base pieces representing 143 (regrouping as necessary) until a rectangle has been formed. In this example we can see that the other dimension is 13, so $143 \div 11 = 13$.

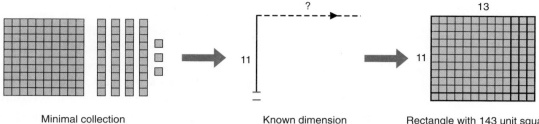

| Minimal collection for 143 | Known dimension of the rectangle | Rectangle with 143 unit squares and dimensions 11 by 13 |

In a similar manner, use your base-ten pieces to determine each of the following quotients. Sometimes you may need to trade pieces. Draw a sketch of your results. (*Note:* If there is a remainder, you will get a rectangle with pieces left over.)

a. $221 \div 17$

*b. $529 \div 23$

c. $397 \div 34$

5. The paper-and-pencil algorithm for long division can be visualized using base-ten pieces and the rectangular model. Suppose the goal is to compute $477 \div 14$. Notice that the usual symbol for division, $14\overline{)477}$, suggests two sides of a rectangle, where the length of one side is 14, the total number of units is 477, and the length of the other side (the quotient) is unknown. The following steps and full-page diagram on the following page show how the rectangular model for division is related to the long-division algorithm.

Step 1: First select the base-ten pieces to represent 477.

Step 2: Draw a line segment of 14 units to represent one dimension of the rectangle. Begin distributing the base-ten pieces representing 477 to form a rectangle of width 14.

Step 3: Three sections each of width 10 can be incorporated into the rectangle. This requires 4 flats and 2 longs and leaves 5 longs and 7 units, which is not enough to complete another section of 10 (1 flat had to be traded for 10 longs to build this much).

Step 4: Four sections of width 1 can be added onto the rectangle (1 long was traded for 10 units). This uses 5 longs and 6 units and leaves 1 unit remaining—not enough to make the rectangle any wider unless the remaining unit is cut into pieces.

Step 5: The desired dimension of the rectangle (the quotient) is 34, and there is a remainder of 1.

Use your base-ten pieces to compute $255 \div 11$. Make a sketch below of your base-ten piece rectangle and describe how it relates to the long-division algorithm.

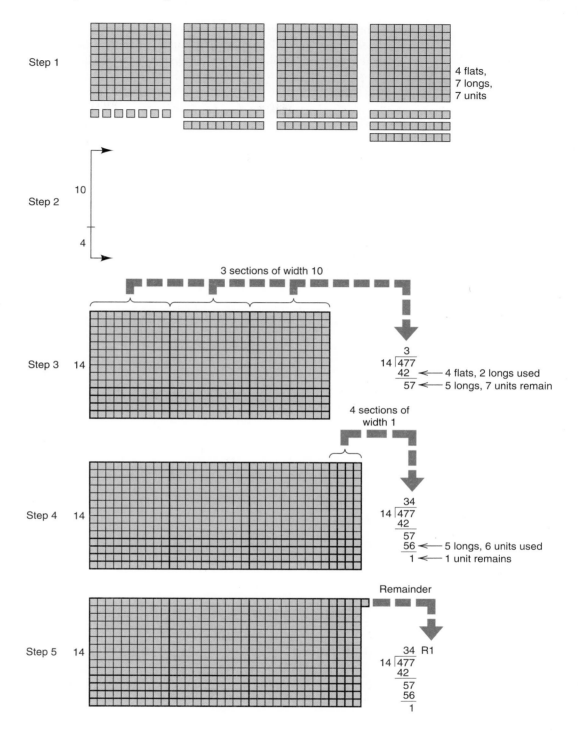

Step 1

4 flats,
7 longs,
7 units

Step 2

10

4

3 sections of width 10

Step 3   14

$$
\begin{array}{r}
3 \\
14\overline{\smash{)}477} \\
42 \\
\hline
57
\end{array}
$$

← 4 flats, 2 longs used
← 5 longs, 7 units remain

4 sections of
width 1

Step 4   14

$$
\begin{array}{r}
34 \\
14\overline{\smash{)}477} \\
42 \\
\hline
57 \\
56 \\
\hline
1
\end{array}
$$

← 5 longs, 6 units used
← 1 unit remains

Remainder

Step 5   14

$$
\begin{array}{r}
34 \;\; R1 \\
14\overline{\smash{)}477} \\
42 \\
\hline
57 \\
56 \\
\hline
1
\end{array}
$$

6. Compute the following quotients using your base-ten pieces and the rectangular model illustrated in activity 5. Record your results by making a sketch of each final base-ten piece rectangle and showing how each digit in the quotient relates to the long-division algorithm.

a. $144 \div 6$

$$6\overline{)144}$$

b. $134 \div 3$

$$3\overline{)134}$$

*c. $587 \div 23$

$$23\overline{)587}$$

JUST FOR FUN

Here are several games and number tricks to try using a calculator.

ARABIAN NIGHTS MYSTERY

Select any three-digit number, such as 837, and enter it on your calculator twice to form a six-digit number (in this case, 837837). Then carry out the following steps: divide this number by 11, then divide the result by 7, and finally divide the result by 13. You may be surprised by the outcome. This trick has been called the Arabian Nights Mystery because it can be explained by using the number 1001, in reference to the book *Tales from the Thousand and One Nights*. Try this trick for some other three-digit numbers. Explain why it works.

KEYBOARD GAME (2 players)

The first player begins the game by entering a whole number on a calculator. The players then take turns subtracting single-digit numbers, with the following restriction: each player must subtract a nonzero digit, using a digit button adjacent to the one used by the preceding player. For example, if a player subtracts 6, the next player must subtract 9, 8, 5, 2, or 3. When a player's turn results in a number less than 0, that player loses the game.

MAGIC FORMULAS

Usually if someone asks you to select a number on which to perform some operations, you will choose an easy one. With the aid of a calculator, however, you do not have to be so careful about the number you select. For example, try a three- or four-digit number in the following formula.

• Select any number (remember this number, as it will be needed later), add 221, multiply by 2652, subtract 1326, divide by 663, subtract 870, divide by 4, and subtract the number you started with. Your result will be 3.

Follow-Up Questions and Activities 3.4

1. *School Classroom:*
   a. Describe two real-world examples, appropriate for elementary school students, of using the sharing division concept.
   b. Describe two real-world examples, appropriate for elementary school students, of using the measurement division concept.

2. *School Classroom:* How would you help this student? Carlie was watching Adam divide 12 by 3 using the measurement method and then declared the answer to 12 ÷ 3 to be 3. Carlie explained her method as: If you put 12 chips in 3 piles and then count the number of piles, you get 3.

3. *School Classroom:* The division example on the **Elementary School Text** page at the beginning of this section uses the partitive or sharing method to determine 148 ÷ 4. Draw a sketch to show how you would do this same division using the rectangular model as illustrated in activity 5 of this section.

4. *Math Concepts:* Using your base-five pieces only (no pencil and paper), build a rectangle similar to the base-ten rectangle in activity 4 to determine the quotient $1402_{five} \div 22_{five}$. Draw a sketch of your rectangle, label the dimensions, and record the quotient in base five. Explain how you used the base-five pieces to determine the solution.

5. *Math Concepts:* Read the Arabian Nights Mystery described in the **Just for Fun Activity** for this activity set. Explain why the mystery always works.

6. *Math Concepts:* Open the **Math Calculator Investigation 3.4: Read Me—Sums and Differences of Squares Instructions** from the companion website and investigate the divisibility of the sums and differences of the squares as described in questions 1, 2, 3, and 4 of the *Starting Points for Investigations 3.4.* Give a few of your examples and explain your thinking.

7. *NCTM Standards:* Read the *Expectation* in the **Grades 3–5 Number and Operations Standards** in the back pages of this book under the *Standard* "Understand meanings of operations . . ." that involves "division as the inverse of multiplication." Explain how the base-ten piece models can be used to see this relationship.

 BENNETT-BURTON-NELSON WEBSITE

www.mhhe.com/bbn

Virtual Manipulatives	Grid and Dot Paper	Links and Readings
Interactive Chapter Applets	Color Transparencies	Geometer Sketchpad Modules
Puzzlers	Extended Bibliography	

Elementary School Activity

INTRODUCING PLACE VALUE WITH BASE-TEN PIECES

Purpose: To provide elementary school students with an understanding of base-ten positional numeration.

Connections: "Thousands of years ago before we had cities, automobiles, planes, and computers, we lived in caves and did not have numbers like we have today. One early number system used marks like / / / / to write the number four. How do you think the number for nine was written? We will use base-ten pieces to help you learn about the types of numbers that are used today."

Materials: Sets of base-ten pieces may be created by copying base-ten grid paper from the companion website onto cardstock and cutting out units, longs, and flats. Base-ten piece transparencies can also be made with the base-ten pieces image. Sets of base-ten pieces can be placed in plastic sealable bags. Each group of two to four students will need one set of base-ten pieces.

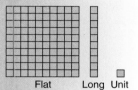

Flat   Long Unit

1. Pass out sets of base-ten pieces to pairs of students and ask them what they notice about the pieces. Discuss the relationship of the pieces to each other and the value of each piece, if the smallest piece has value 1. (*Note:* Depending on the level of the students, you may want to use only units and longs and adjust the numbers in the following activities as needed.)

2. Write numbers such as 36 and 253 on the board and ask students to represent the number with their base-ten pieces. Have the students discuss other collections of base-ten pieces that also represent these numbers. Discuss finding or using the fewest number of pieces (minimal collection) for these numbers and make sure the children are comfortable with trading (such as 10 units for 1 long or 1 long for 10 units). Ask the students how the early cave people might have written the number for 36 and discuss the convenience of today's numbers. (*Note:* The purpose of this portion of the activity is to encourage students to think in terms of units, tens, and hundreds.)

This student is modeling 2237 with 3-dimensional base-ten blocks that are commonly found in schools.

3. Ask students to use their base-ten pieces to compute the results of the following expressions. You may adjust the numbers and operations to match the level of the students you are working with. Have the students discuss their methods and reasoning with the class.

    a. $68 + 57$ **b.** $274 + 63$ **c.** $321 - 74$ **d.** 4×13 **e.** $141 \div 3$

4. Using the preceding expressions, ask students to make up a story problem involving the given numbers and operation. (*Note:* Depending on the level of the students, examples or explanations may be needed, such as, thinking of division by 3 as sharing among 3 people.)

5. (Optional) Chips numbered from 0 to 9 in a bag are needed for each pair of students. Have each student sketch a place-value table as shown here. Taking turns, each student selects one chip from the bag and writes this number in one of the columns of their table. Each player takes three turns and the object is to form the greatest three-digit number.

Hundreds	Tens	Ones

4 Number Theory

Number theory offers many rich opportunities for explorations that are interesting, enjoyable, and useful.

. . . Challenging but accessible problems from number theory can be easily formulated and explored by students. For example, building rectangular arrays with a set of tile can stimulate questions about divisibility and prime, composite, square, even, and odd numbers . . . .[1]

MODELS FOR EVEN NUMBERS, ODD NUMBERS, FACTORS, AND PRIMES

Virtual Manipulatives

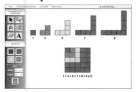

www.mhhe.com/bbn

PURPOSE

To use models to provide visual images of basic concepts of number theory.

MATERIALS

Color Tiles from the Manipulative Kit or from the Virtual Manipulatives.

INTRODUCTION

Some problems in number theory are simple enough for children to understand yet are unsolvable by mathematicians. Maybe that is why this branch of mathematics has intrigued so many people, novices and professionals alike, for over 2000 years. For example, is it true that every *even number* greater than 2 can be expressed as the sum of two *prime numbers?* It is true for the first few even numbers:

$$4 = 2 + 2 \qquad 6 = 3 + 3 \qquad 8 = 3 + 5 \qquad 10 = 5 + 5 \qquad 12 = 5 + 7 \qquad 14 = 7 + 7$$

However, mathematicians have not been able to prove it is true for all even numbers greater than 2.

The ideas of odd, even, factors, and primes are basic concepts of number theory. In this activity set, these ideas will be given geometric form to show that visual images can be associated with them.

---

[1]*Curriculum and Evaluation Standards for School Mathematics* (Reston, VA: National Council of Teachers of Mathematics, 1989): 91–93.

Prime Factors

 **Mini Lab**

Materials
• square tiles

What You'll LEARN

Find the prime factorization of a composite number

NEW Vocabulary

factor
prime number
composite number
prime factorization

Work with a partner.

Any given number of squares can be arranged into one or more different rectangles. The table shows the different rectangles that can be made using 2, 3, or 4 squares. A 1 × 3 rectangle is the same as a 3 × 1 rectangle.

STEP 1 Copy the table.

Number of Squares	Sketch of Rectangle Formed	Dimensions of Each Rectangle
2		1 × 2
3		1 × 3
4		1 × 4, 2 × 2
5		1 × 5
6		1 × 6, 2 × 3
⋮ 20		

STEP 2 Use square tiles to help you complete the table.

1. For what numbers can more than one rectangle be formed?
2. For what numbers can only one rectangle be formed?
3. For the numbers in which only one rectangle is formed, what do you notice about the dimensions of the rectangle?

When two or more numbers are multiplied, each number is called a **factor** of the product.

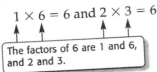

$$1 \times 7 = 7$$

The factors of 7 are 1 and 7.

$$1 \times 6 = 6 \text{ and } 2 \times 3 = 6$$

The factors of 6 are 1 and 6, and 2 and 3.

READING
in the Content Area

For strategies in reading this lesson, visit **msmath1.net/reading**.

A whole number that has exactly two unique factors, 1 and the number itself, is a **prime number**. A number greater than 1 with more than two factors is a **composite number**.

Even and Odd Numbers

1. The nonzero whole numbers (counting numbers) can be represented geometrically in many different ways. Here the first five consecutive numbers are represented as a sequence of tile figures. Extend the sequence by drawing the figures for the numbers 6, 7, and 8.

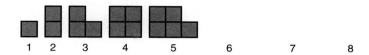

Describe, in your own words, how the figures for the even counting numbers differ from those for the odd counting numbers in the sequence above.

2. Here is a tile sequence for the first four *even numbers*.

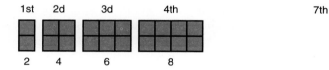

   a. Draw the figure for the seventh even number above. What is the seventh even number?

   Seventh even number _____

   *b. Describe in words what the figure for the 125th even number would look like. What is the 125th even number?

   125th even number _____

   c. Describe in words what the figure for the *n*th even number would look like. Write a mathematical expression for the *n*th even number.

   *n*th even number _____

3. This tile sequence represents the first four *odd numbers*.

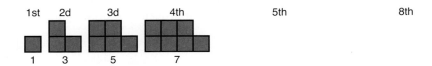

a. Draw the figures for the fifth and eighth odd numbers. What is the fifth odd number? What is the eighth odd number?

5th odd number _____   8th odd number _____

*b. Describe in words how to draw the figure representing the 15th odd number. What is the 15th odd number?

15th odd number _____

c. Determine the 50th, 100th, and *n*th odd numbers by imagining what their figures would look like, based on the model shown above.

50th odd number _____   100th odd number _____   *n*th odd number _____

*d. When the odd numbers, beginning with 1, are arranged in consecutive order, 7 is in the fourth position and 11 is in the sixth position. In what position is 79? 117? (*Hint:* Think about the tile figures for these numbers. You may wish to draw a rough sketch of the figures.)

79 is in the _____ position.   117 is in the _____ position.

4. The following diagram illustrates that when an even number is added to an odd number, the sum is an odd number. Determine the oddness or evenness of each of the sums and differences below by drawing similar diagrams.

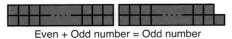

Even number   Odd number   Even + Odd number = Odd number

a. The sum of any two even numbers

*b. The sum of any two odd numbers

c. The sum of any two consecutive counting numbers

d. The sum of any three consecutive counting numbers

*e. The difference of any two odd numbers

f. The sum of any three odd numbers and two even numbers

5. The tiles for the figures in the tile sequence for consecutive odd numbers can be rearranged as follows:

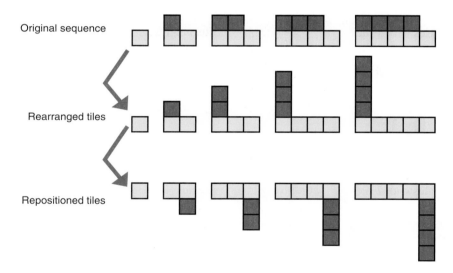

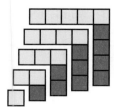

a. The L-shaped figures for the first five consecutive odd numbers can be pushed together to form a square. What does this tell you about the sum of the first five consecutive odd numbers?

*b. Visualize the L-shaped figures for the first 10 consecutive odd numbers. What size square can be formed from these figures? What is the sum of the first 10 consecutive odd numbers?

c. Consider the sum of all odd numbers from 1 to 79.

$$1 + 3 + 5 + 7 + \cdots + 77 + 79$$

How many numbers are in this sum? Determine the sum of the consecutive odd numbers from 1 to 79 by visualizing L-shaped figures forming a square.

Factors and Primes

6. All possible rectangular arrays that can be constructed with exactly 4 tiles, exactly 7 tiles, and exactly 12 tiles are diagrammed below. Use the tiles from your Manipulative Kit or from the Virtual Manipulatives to form all possible rectangular arrays that can be constructed for the remaining numbers from 1 to 12 (remember a square is a rectangle). Sketch these arrays in the spaces provided below.

Rectangles with 1 tile   Rectangles with 2 tiles   Rectangles with 3 tiles

Rectangles with 4 tiles   Rectangles with 5 tiles   Rectangles with 6 tiles

Rectangles with 7 tiles   Rectangles with 8 tiles   Rectangles with 9 tiles

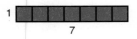

Rectangles with 10 tiles   Rectangles with 11 tiles   Rectangles with 12 tiles

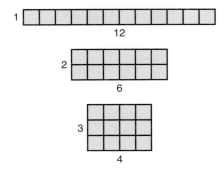

7. The dimensions of a rectangular array are factors of the number the array represents. For example, the number 12 has a 1×12 array, 2×6 array, and 3×4 array, and the factors of 12 are 1, 2, 3, 4, 6, and 12. Use your results from activity 6 to complete the following table by listing all the factors of each number and the total number of factors. Then extend the table to numbers through 20.

Number	Factors	Number of Factors
1	_____	_____
2	_____	_____
3	_____	_____
4	1, 2, 4	3
5	_____	_____
6	_____	_____
7	1, 7	2
8	_____	_____
9	_____	_____
10	_____	_____
11	_____	_____
12	1, 2, 3, 4, 6, 12	6
13	_____	_____
14	_____	_____
15	_____	_____
16	_____	_____
17	_____	_____
18	_____	_____
19	_____	_____
20	_____	_____

8. Numbers with more than one rectangle, such as 12 and 4, are called *composite numbers.* Except for the number 1, all numbers that have exactly one rectangle are called *prime numbers.*

a. Write a sentence or two to explain how you can describe prime and composite numbers in terms of *numbers of factors.*

*b. How does the number 1 differ from the prime and composite numbers?

    c. Is there another counting number, like 1, that is neither prime nor composite? Explain why or why not in terms of rectangles.

    d. Some numbers are called *square numbers* or *perfect squares.* Look at the sketches in activity 6. Which numbers from 1 to 12 do you think could be called square numbers? State your reason.

    *e. Examine the rectangles representing numbers that have an odd number of factors. What conclusions can you draw about numbers that have an odd number of factors?

9. The numbers listed in your chart have either 1, 2, 3, 4, 5, or 6 factors.

    a. Identify another number that has exactly 5 factors. Are there other numbers with exactly 5 factors? Explain.

    b. Find two numbers greater than 20 that have more rectangles than the number 12. What are the factors of each of these numbers?

10. The numbers 6, 10, 14, and 15 each have exactly 4 factors. Looking at the factors for these numbers, determine what special characteristics the numbers with exactly 4 factors possess. List a few more numbers with exactly 4 factors, and explain how you could generate more of the numbers.

JUST FOR FUN

NUMBER CHART PRIMES AND MULTIPLES

A seventh-grade student, Keith, chose to do a math project based on identifying prime numbers with the sieve of Eratosthenes.[2] Keith's innovation to the sieve added extra information. He used a number chart like the one here and put a triangle around 1 because it is neither prime nor composite. Then he circled 2 because it was prime and put a black dot above each multiple of 2. Next he moved from 2 to the next undotted number, 3, circled 3 and put a blue dot to the right of each multiple of 3.

The chart below has been started using Keith's method. The multiples of 2 have a black dot above them. Circle 3 and put a blue dot to the right of each multiple of 3. Circle 5 and put a green dot beneath all multiples of 5. Circle 7 and put a red dot to the left of all multiples of 7. Finally, circle all the remaining numbers which have no colored dots in their squares.

1. How can we be sure that all the circled numbers are prime?
2. How can you use the chart to find all numbers which are multiples of 3 and 5?
3. Keith's chart actually included all numbers up to 1000. How many different colors did he use?

1	2	3	•4	5	•6	7	•8	9	•10
11	•12	13	•14	15	•16	17	•18	19	•20
21	•22	23	•24	25	•26	27	•28	29	•30
31	•32	33	•34	35	•36	37	•38	39	•40
41	•42	43	•44	45	•46	47	•48	49	•50
51	•52	53	•54	55	•56	57	•58	59	•60
61	•62	63	•64	65	•66	67	•68	69	•70
71	•72	73	•74	75	•76	77	•78	79	•80
81	•82	83	•84	85	•86	87	•88	89	•90
91	•92	93	•94	95	•96	97	•98	99	•100
101	•102	103	•104	105	•106	107	•108	109	•110
111	•112	113	•114	115	•116	117	•118	119	•120

neither prime
nor composite

prime numbers

black dot   multiple of 2
blue dot   multiple of 3
green dot   multiple of 5
red dot   multiple of 7

[2]C. L. Bradford, "Keith's Secret Discovery of the Sieve of Eratosthenes," *Arithmetic Teacher* 21 (March 1974): 239–241.

Follow-Up Questions and Activities **4.1**

1. *School Classroom:* How would you help a student in your class who, after building rectangular arrays to find factors, insisted that the factors of 16 are 1, 2, 4, 4, 8, and 16 because "every side of the array has to have a number that goes with it"?

2. *School Classroom:* One of the students in your class said that it was easy to find the sum of the first n odd numbers because it is just n^2. However, when asked to find the sum of consecutive odd numbers from 1 to 219 she couldn't do it because she didn't know how many odd numbers there were from 1 to 219. Explain how you would help her understand how to find the number of consecutive odd numbers from 1 to any other odd number.

3. *School Classroom:* Suppose that your students finished the table shown on the **Elementary School Text** page at the beginning of this section by sketching all rectangles for the numbers 7 through 20 and recording their dimensions. After finishing, one group of students insisted that 1 was a prime number because it has only one rectangle like 2, 3, 5, and the other primes. Explain how you would resolve this issue without simply telling them a rule to remember.

4. *Math Concepts:* The tile sequence below represents the first four consecutive odd numbers. Sketch a tile figure that represents the nth odd number. Write an algebraic expression for this nth odd number and describe how your algebraic expression can be seen in the shape of the tile figure you have sketched.

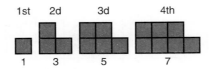

```
1st     2d      3d       4th
 1       3       5        7
```

5. *Math Concepts:* How many numbers less than 100 have an odd number of factors? Explain your answer in terms of rectangular arrays.

6. *Math Concepts:* For the following questions, use specific prime number examples to help draw conclusions about the general statements.
   a. If p is a prime number, how many factors does p^2 have? Explain whether or not the number of factors of p^2 varies with different primes.
   b. If p is a prime number and n is a counting number, how many factors does p^n have?
   c. Explain how you can use the results in part b to find a number with exactly 6 factors? Exactly 8 factors?

7. *Math Concepts:* If p, q, and r, are three different prime numbers, determine the number of factors for each of the following numbers. Use specific prime number examples to help draw conclusions about the general statements.
   a. $p \times q$
   b. $p^2 \times q$
   c. $p^2 \times q^2$
   d. $p \times q \times r$

8. *NCTM Standards:*

    a. In the **Grades 3–5 Number and Operations Standards** in the back pages of this book, one *Expectation* says, "Describe classes of numbers according to characteristics such as the nature of their factors." As a grades 3–5 teacher, explain what this statement would mean to you.

    b. Determine if there are any other *Expectations* at the grades 3–5 level or higher that specifically refer to the number theory topics explored in the activities in this section, and, if so, record what they suggest.

9. *NCTM Standards:* Go to http://illuminations.nctm.org/ and under "Lessons" select grade levels 3–5 and the **Number and Operation Standard.** Choose a lesson that involves even and odd numbers or factors of whole numbers; search for the keyword "factor."

    a. State the title of the lesson and briefly summarize the lesson.

    b. Referring to the **Standards Summary** in the back pages of this book as necessary, list the *Number and Operation Standard Expectations* that the lesson addresses and explain how the lesson addresses these *Expectations.*

 # BENNETT-BURTON-NELSON WEBSITE

www.mhhe.com/bbn

Virtual Manipulatives	Grid and Dot Paper	Links and Readings
Interactive Chapter Applets	Color Transparencies	Geometer Sketchpad Modules
Puzzlers	Extended Bibliography	

Activity Set **4.2** MODELS FOR GREATEST COMMON FACTOR AND LEAST COMMON MULTIPLE

PURPOSE

To use a linear model to illustrate the concepts of greatest common factor and least common multiple and show how they are related.

MATERIALS

No supplementary materials are needed.

INTRODUCTION

Greatest common factor (GCF) and least common multiple (LCM) are important concepts that occur frequently in mathematics. The GCF of two numbers is usually introduced by listing all the factors of two numbers, identifying the *common factors,* and then choosing the *greatest* of the common factors.

Factors of 12: 1, 2, 3, 4, ⑥, 12

Factors of 18: 1, 2, 3, ⑥, 9, 18

The LCM of two numbers is often introduced by listing multiples of each number, identifying *common multiples,* and choosing the *least* of the common multiples.

Multiples of 12: 12, 24, ㊱, 48, 60, 72, 84, 96, 108, 120, 132, 144, . . .

Multiples of 18: 18, ㊱, 54, 72, 90, 108, 126, 144, 162, 180, 198, . . .

In this activity set, the concepts of GCF and LCM will be visually represented by rods. The GCF will be viewed as the greatest common length into which two (or more) rods can be cut.

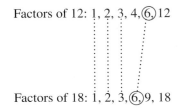

The LCM will be viewed as the shortest common length into which two (or more) rods will fit. This will be determined by placing copies of each rod end to end.

Greatest Common Factor

1. Here are rods of length 36 units and 54 units. Both rods can be cut evenly into pieces with a common length of 6 units, since 6 is a factor of 36 and 6 is a factor of 54.

54

36

a. There are five other ways to cut both rods evenly into pieces of common length. Mark those on the following five pairs of rods.

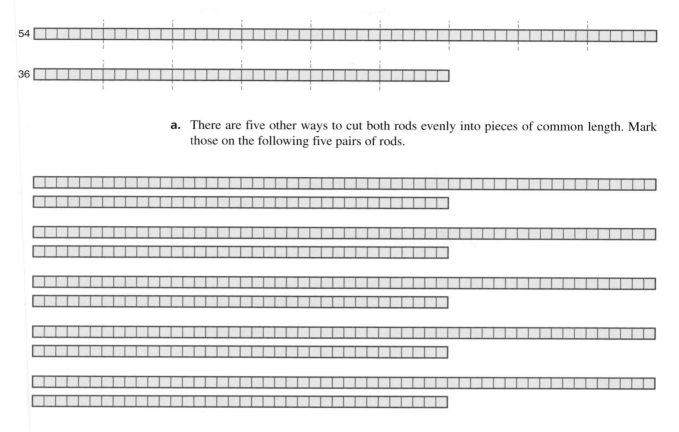

*b. Because rods of length 36 and 54 can both be cut evenly into pieces of length 6, 6 is called a *common factor* of 36 and 54. List the other common factors of 36 and 54.

Common factors of 36 and 54: 6, _____, _____, _____, _____, _____

c. Circle the *greatest common factor*[3] of 36 and 54. The greatest common factor of 36 and 54 is abbreviated as GCF(36, 54).

2. Determine the greatest common factor of each pair of numbers below by indicating how you would cut the rods into common pieces of greatest length. Record your answer next to the diagram.

a. 36

24

GCF (36, 24) =

*b. 18

25

GCF (18, 25) =

c. 42

28

GCF (42, 28) =

[3]Also commonly called the *greatest common divisor* or GCD.

3. a. Determine the greatest common factor of the numbers 20 and 12 by indicating how you would cut the two rods below into pieces of greatest common length.

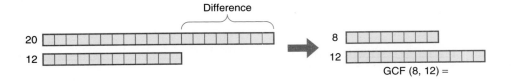

GCF (20, 12) =

b. The amount by which one rod exceeds the other is represented by the *difference rod*. Determine the GCF of the difference rod and the shorter rod using the diagram below.

GCF (8, 12) =

4. For each pair of rods shown below, determine the GCF of the shorter rod and the difference rod. Indicate how you would cut the difference rod and the smaller rod on the diagrams.

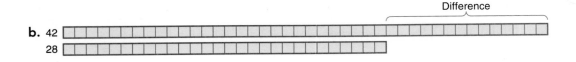

*a. 40
     24

b. 42
    28

c. 21
     12

*5. You may have noticed in activities 1–4 that the longer rod is always cut at a point coinciding with the end of the shorter rod. So, the GCF of two numbers can be determined by comparing the difference rod and the smaller rod. Use your results from activity 4 to determine the following.

GCF(40, 24) =   GCF(42, 28) =   GCF(21, 12) =

6. The preceding activity suggests that the GCF of two numbers can be determined by computing the difference of the two numbers and then finding the GCF of the difference and the smaller of the two numbers. If the GCF of the smaller numbers is not apparent, this method of taking differences can be continued. For example,

$$GCF(198, 126) = GCF(72, 126) = GCF(72, 54) = GCF(18, 54)$$
$$= GCF(18, 36) = GCF(18, 18) = 18$$

Use this difference method to find the GCF of the following pairs of numbers. Show each step.

a. GCF(144, 27) =

*b. GCF(280, 168) =

c. GCF(714, 420) =

*d. GCF(306, 187) =

Least Common Multiple

7. In the following diagram, the numbers 3 and 5 are represented by rods. When the rods of length 3 are arranged end to end alongside a similar arrangement of rods of length 5, the distances at which the ends evenly match are *common multiples* of 3 and 5 (15, 30, 45, etc.). The least distance at which they match, 15, is the *least common multiple* of 3 and 5. This least common multiple is written LCM(3, 5) = 15.

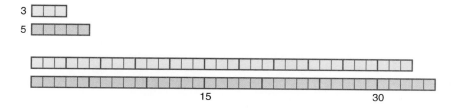

Find the LCM of each of the following pairs of numbers by drawing the minimum number of end-to-end rods of each length needed to make both rows the same length.

a. 8
   12

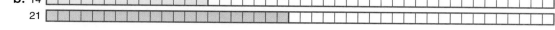

LCM (8, 12) = _____

*b. 14
    21

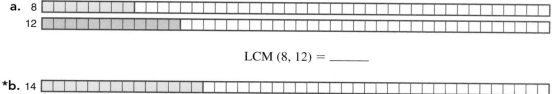

LCM (14, 21) = _____

c. 5
    7

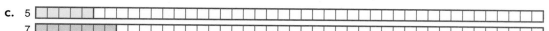

LCM (5, 7) = _____

*d. 8
    10

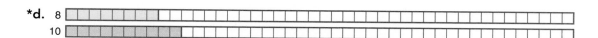

LCM (8, 10) = _____

8. There is a relationship between the GCF and the LCM of two numbers. The first figure below shows the numbers 6 and 15; GCF(6, 15) = 3 is indicated by marks on the rods. The second figure shows that LCM(6, 15) = 30.

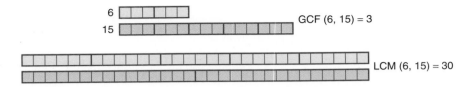

a. GCF(6, 15) = 3 and 3 divides the 6-unit rod into 2 parts and the 15-unit rod into 5 parts. Notice that 2 rods of length 15 or 5 rods of length 6 equal 30, the LCM(6, 15). Use the rod diagrams in activity 7 to complete the following table. Look for a relationship involving the GCF, LCM, and the product of the two numbers.

	A	B	GCF (A, B)	LCM (A, B)	A × B
(1)	6	15	3	30	90
(2)	8	12	___	___	___
*(3)	14	21	___	___	___
(4)	5	7	___	___	___
*(5)	8	10	___	___	___

b. Based on your observations from the table in part a, write a brief set of directions for finding the LCM of two numbers once you have determined the GCF.

9. For each of the following pairs of numbers, first compute the GCF of the pair and then use the relationship from activity 8b to compute the LCM.

*a. GCF(9, 15) =

LCM(9, 15) =

b. GCF(8, 18) =

LCM(8, 18) =

*c. GCF(140, 350) =

LCM(140, 350) =

d. GCF(135, 42) =

LCM(135, 42) =

JUST FOR FUN

STAR POLYGONS

Star polygons are often constructed to provide decorative and artistic patterns. The star polygon pictured here was formed from colored yarn around a circle of 16 equally spaced tacks on a piece of plywood. Starting at the red tack in the lower left and moving in a clockwise direction, the yarn goes a step of 5 to the next red tack and then another step of 5 to a third red tack. This procedure continues until the yarn gets back to its starting point. In the following activities, star polygons are analyzed by using the concepts of factor, multiple, greatest common factor, and least common multiple.[4]

Star polygons can be constructed by taking steps of a given size around a circle of points. The following star (14, 3) was constructed by beginning at point p and taking a step of 3 spaces to point q. Three spaces from q is point r. Through this process we eventually come back to point p, after having hit all 14 points. The resulting figure is a star polygon.

In general, for whole numbers n and s, where $n \geq 3$ and $s < n$, star (n, s) denotes a star polygon with n points and steps of s.

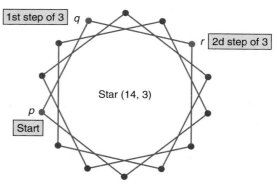

Star (14, 3)

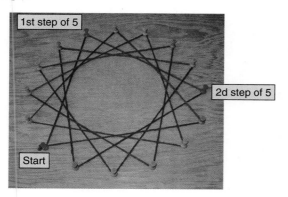

[4]A. B. Bennett, Jr., "Star Patterns," *Arithmetic Teacher* 25 (January 1978): 12–14.

*1. Sketch the star polygons, given below, by beginning at point *x* and taking steps of *s* in a clockwise direction.

Will the same star polygons be obtained if the steps are taken in a counterclockwise direction?

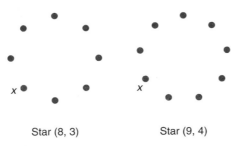
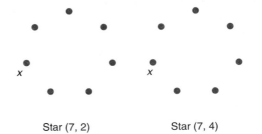

Star (8, 3)   Star (9, 4)   Star (7, 2)   Star (7, 4)

*2. Sketch the following pairs of star polygons. Make a conjecture about star (*n*, *s*) and star (*n*, *r*), where *r* + *s* = *n*.

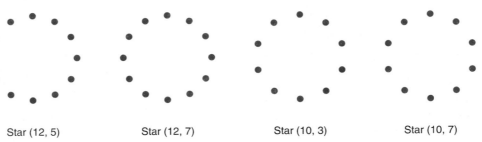

Star (12, 5)   Star (12, 7)   Star (10, 3)   Star (10, 7)

Conjecture:

*3. The star polygons in activities 1 and 2 can each be completed by beginning at any point and drawing one continuous path. In each of those examples, the path returns to the starting point after hitting all points. For star (15, 3), however, the path closes after hitting only 5 points. To complete this star, 3 different paths are needed. Determine the number of different paths to complete each of the following star polygons.

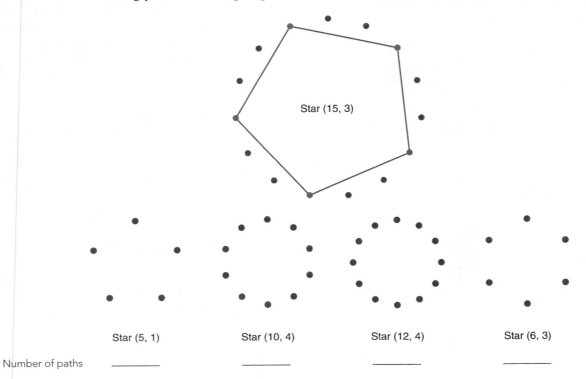

Star (15, 3)

Star (5, 1)   Star (10, 4)   Star (12, 4)   Star (6, 3)

Number of paths   _____   _____   _____   _____

*4. What conditions must n and s satisfy in order for star (n, s) to be formed with 1 continuous path? Use your conjecture to sketch 15-point star polygons that can be formed by 1 continuous path. There are 4 of these star polygons. Star $(15, 1)$, which is congruent to star $(15, 14)$, is one of them. Determine and sketch the remaining three star polygons, and write the size of the steps for each.

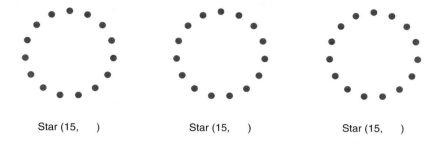

Star (15,   )   Star (15,   )   Star (15,   )

Size of step   _____   _____   _____

*5. Star $(14, 3)$ (shown at the right) was constructed by beginning at point p and taking steps of 3 to points q, r, s, t, and so forth. After point t, the next step of 3 passes the starting point, p, completes the first *orbit* (once around the circle, shown as red edges) and starts us on the second orbit (shown as blue edges). When the last step in the second orbit passes p, the third and final orbit (shown as green edges) begins. For star $(14, 3)$ it takes three orbits before the path returns to the starting point, p. The individual orbits are shown below.

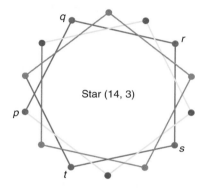

Star (14, 3)

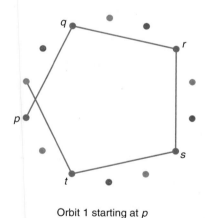

Orbit 1 starting at *p*

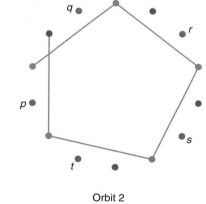

Orbit 2

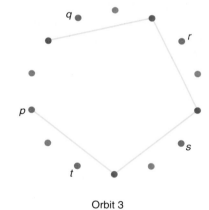

Orbit 3

For the star polygons given below, how many orbits are needed before a given path will return to its starting point? For each star polygon, you may pick any point as the starting point.

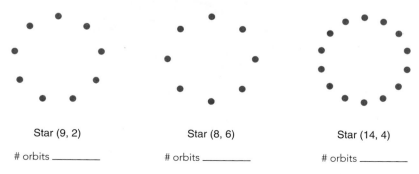

Star (9, 2)   Star (8, 6)   Star (14, 4)

orbits _____   # orbits _____   # orbits _____

6. Star (7, 3) was drawn by starting at point 1 and connecting the points in the following order: 1, 4, 7, 3, 6, 2, 5, and 1. Three orbits are needed to complete this star. The number of orbits is just the number of times we need to go around the 7 points of the circle before the steps of 3 bring us back to the beginning point. That is, after taking steps of 3 for 21 spaces, we arrive back at the beginning point. The 21 spaces represent the least common multiple of 7 and 3.

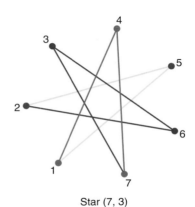

Star (7, 3)

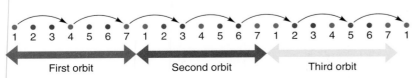

a. Explain how the concept of least common multiple can be used to determine the number of orbits for 1 path of star (15, 6). Check your answer.

*b. Make a conjecture about the number of orbits needed to complete 1 path for star (n, s).

7. Create a star polygon. Any number of points can be used and any shape can be used; the points do not have to lie on a circle. Star polygons can be made by drawing with colored pencils (different colors for steps of different sizes) or by using colored thread or yarn. With a needle and thread, they can be stitched on posterboard. Several star polygons can be formed on the same set of points. Three star polygons have been stitched from 36 holes on the posterboard pictured here. One star polygon is made from green thread

with steps of 6, another from red thread with steps of 11, and a third from blue thread with steps of 15.

a. The star polygon with steps of 11 is the only one of the three star polygons in this photograph that can be constructed by 1 continuous path. Why?

*b. How many orbits are needed to complete star (36, 11)?

ANALYZING STAR POLYGONS APPLET

In this applet, you will draw star polygons by choosing the number of points and size of the steps. Star (9, 2) was drawn by beginning at one of 9 points and taking steps of size 2 around the circle of points until returning to the original point. What is the relationship between the numbers of points and sizes of steps? This applet enables you to form more than one star polygon on a given set of points to create colorful designs.

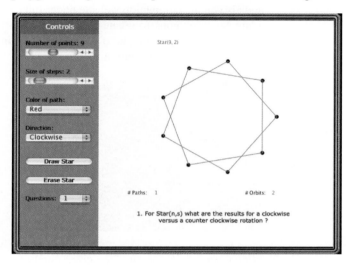

Analyzing Star Polygons Applet, Chapter 4
www.mhhe.com/bbn

Follow-Up Questions and Activities **4.2**

1. *School Classroom:* Devon's teacher has told his class that *Relatively Prime* numbers are numbers whose greatest common factor is 1. Devon would like to know how 4 and 9 can be relatively prime since neither 4 nor 9 are prime numbers. How can you help Devon's teacher explain this idea?

2. *School Classroom:* Star Polygons are described in the **Just for Fun** activity in this section and also on the companion website under Interactive Math Applets. Describe how you could adapt Star Polygons to create a math-art project for children using, for example, colored pencils or yarn as in the photo at the left. Explain how the project you design contributes to the math curriculum for children.

Yarn and tack star polygon created by a student at Western Oregon University.

3. *Math Concepts:* For each of the given number pairs (*A*, *B*), determine the GCF(*A*, *B*) and the LCM(*A*, *B*). Then record the prime factorizations of *A*, *B*, GCF(*A*, *B*), and LCM(*A*, *B*) as demonstrated here:

			Prime Factorizations			
(*A*, *B*)	GCF(*A*, *B*)	LCM(*A*, *B*)	*A*	*B*	GCF(*A*, *B*)	LCM(*A*, *B*)
(8, 12)	4	24	$2 \times 2 \times 2$	$2 \times 2 \times 3$	2×2	$2 \times 2 \times 2 \times 3$
(20, 24)						
(12, 25)						
(15, 60)						

   a. Find the relationship between the prime factors of each of the two numbers and the prime factors of the GCF of the two numbers. Explain how you can determine the GCF of two numbers by using the prime factorizations of both numbers.

   b. Find a relationship between the prime factors of each of the two numbers and the prime factors of the LCM of the two numbers. Explain how you can determine the LCM of two numbers by using the prime factorizations of both numbers.

4. *Math Concepts:*

   a. Let Set A be all multiples of 8 and let Set B be all multiples of 12. How can you use these two sets and a two-circle Venn diagram to find the LCM(8, 12)? Explain your solution path and illustrate it with a two-circle Venn diagram.

   b. Let Set C be all factors of 8 and let Set D be all factors of 12. How can you use these two sets and a two-circle Venn diagram to find the GCF(8, 12)? Explain your solution path and illustrate it with a two-circle Venn diagram.

5. *Math Concepts:* Color rods such as Cuisenaire Rods[5] shown here are often found in elementary schools.

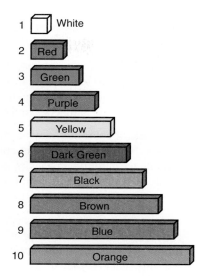

1   White
2   Red
3   Green
4   Purple
5   Yellow
6   Dark Green
7   Black
8   Brown
9   Blue
10 Orange

   a. Putting several same-color rods end to end forms a train. Using the rods, is it possible to make a purple train and a black train that are the same length? Explain your answer.

   b. Can any two different nonwhite trains always be made the same length? Are different lengths possible? What do these lengths represent? Explain your reasoning.

   c. How would you explain the concept of *least common multiple* in terms of same-color trains? Demonstrate your explanation by showing how to use rods to find LCM(12, 15).

6. *Math Concepts:* Any whole number can be represented by joining various rods. For example, 18 can be represented by putting an orange and brown rod end to end and 12 can be formed with an orange and a red rod. Explain how you can illustrate the concepts of *common factors* and *greatest common factor* using Cuisenaire rods. You'll need trains of rods for your original numbers and comparison trains of other (shorter) rods. Demonstrate your explanation by showing how to use rods to find the common factors of 12 and 16 and then the GCF(12, 16).

7. *Math Concepts:* In this activity set we explored the relationship between the greatest common factor and the least common multiple of two numbers. Does this relationship hold if you are considering the greatest common factor or the least common multiple of three numbers? Experiment with several sets of three numbers. Explain your thinking.

8. *NCTM Standards:* Explain where you believe the concepts of GCF and LCM are used in elementary and middle school mathematics, then look through the **Number and Operations Standards** in the back pages of this book to determine whether or not GCF and LCM are referenced. If the GCF and LCM are not mentioned specifically, what *Expectations* address these topics? Explain your thinking.

BENNETT-BURTON-NELSON WEBSITE

www.mhhe.com/bbn

Virtual Manipulatives	Grid and Dot Paper	Links and Readings
Interactive Chapter Applets	Color Transparencies	Geometer Sketchpad Modules
Puzzlers	Extended Bibliography	

[5]Cuisenaire Rods is a registered trademark of the Cuisenaire Company of America, Inc.

Elementary School Activity

EXPLORING FACTORS AND PRIMES WITH COLOR TILES

Purpose: To introduce elementary school students to a visual model for prime and composite numbers.

Connection: Prime numbers are usually defined as numbers with exactly two factors. By representing numbers as rectangular arrays and looking at factors of numbers as the dimensions of rectangles, students have a visual model for partitioning the counting numbers into three distinct groups; prime numbers, composite numbers, and 1.

Materials: Sets of color tiles may be created by copying 2-centimeter grid paper from the companion website on four different colors of cardstock. Color tile transparencies may also be made with the color tile images. Sets of 20 of each of four colors can be placed in plastic sealable bags. Each group of two to four students will need one set of color tiles. Students will also need centimeter grid paper for recording rectangles.

This sixth grader has formed all the possible rectangles with 12 or fewer tiles.

1. Form the three figures shown here on the overhead. Point out that rectangular arrays must be solid (no holes) and that two arrays are the same if one can fit exactly on top of the other. Ask the students to build other rectangular arrays with 12 color tiles. To summarize and make sure that everyone understands, display the three different arrays of 12 tiles with their dimensions written beneath each. (The one other 12-tile array is the 2 by 6 array.)

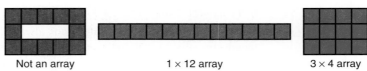

Not an array   1 × 12 array   3 × 4 array

2. Point out that the numbers in the dimensions of the rectangles, 1, 12, 3, 4, 2 and 6, are all factors of 12. Ask them if they can find any other factors of 12 and have them make a chart with headings like the one here. Show them how to record the data for the number 12.

Number	Number of Rectangles	Dimensions	Factors of the Number
12	3	1 × 12, 2 × 6, 3 × 4	1, 2, 3, 4, 6, 12

3. Ask each pair of students to form all possible rectangles with fewer than 12 tiles and record their results in descending order in the chart.

Number	Number of Rectangles	Dimensions	Factors of the Number
11			
10			
⋮			

4. Tell the students numbers like 7, with exactly one possible rectangle with exactly two different dimensions, are called prime numbers. Numbers with more than one possible rectangle are called composite numbers. The number 1 is different than the others because it has only one possible rectangle and the dimensions are both the same. The number 1 is neither prime nor composite. Ask the students to list the prime numbers from their chart and then use their tiles to find and record all the prime numbers less than 20.

5. (Optional) Ask the students which numbers less than 12 have arrays that are squares (Answer: 1, 4, 9). Tell them that these are called square numbers. Ask them to find two more square numbers.

CHAPTER

5 Integers and Fractions

By using an area model in which part of a region is shaded, students can see how fractions are related to a unit whole, compare fractional parts of a whole, and find equivalent fractions. . . . Students who have a solid conceptual foundation in fractions should be less prone to committing computational errors than students who do not have such a foundation.[1]

Activity Set 5.1 BLACK AND RED TILE MODEL FOR INTEGERS

PURPOSE

To use black and red tiles to provide a model for adding, subtracting, multiplying, and dividing integers.

Virtual Manipulatives

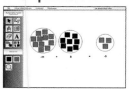

www.mhhe.com/bbn

MATERIALS

Black and Red Tiles from the Manipulative Kit or from the Virtual Manipulatives.

INTRODUCTION

The *integers* (sometimes called *positive and negative numbers* or *signed numbers*) are the numbers . . . $^-6$, $^-5$, $^-4$, $^-3$, $^-2$, $^-1$, 0, $^+1$, $^+2$, $^+3$, $^+4$, $^+5$, $^+6$. . . . Two thousand years ago, the Chinese dealt with positive and negative numbers by using black and red rods. We will use a similar model, black and red tiles, to illustrate addition, subtraction, multiplication, and division of integers. Black tiles will represent positive numbers and red tiles will represent negative numbers.

In this model every collection of red and black tiles has a *net value*. The *net value* of a collection is the value of the number of red or black tiles remaining after all possible red and black tiles have been matched. As the figures below show, an excess of red tiles will be designated by a negative integer and an excess of black tiles by a positive integer. The + and − signs are usually written as superscripts so as not to be confused with the operations of addition and subtraction.

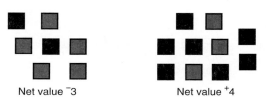

Net value $^-3$ Net value $^+4$

[1]*Principles and Standards for School Mathematics* (Reston, VA: National Council of Teachers of Mathematics, 2000): 150, 218.

I will use models to explore subtracting integers.

17.4 Explore Subtracting Integers

Hands On Activity

You can use two-color counters to subtract integers.

Use two-color counters to find 3 − ⁻2.

You Will Need
- two-color counters

Use Models

STEP 1

Represent the integer 3.

STEP 2

You can't take away 2 red counters from 3 yellow counters, but you can add 2 red counters and 2 yellow counters and still have a model of the integer 3.

Think:
Adding 2 zero pairs is like adding 0.

STEP 3

Subtract the integer ⁻2 by taking away the 2 red counters that represent negative integers.

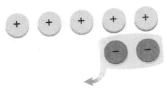

So 3 − ⁻2 = 5.

STEP 4

Use two-color counters to find each difference. Record your work.
Add as many zero pairs as you need in order to subtract.

positive − positive	8 − 6	7 − 8	4 − 7
positive − negative	5 − ⁻3	6 − ⁻8	9 − ⁻9
negative − positive	⁻2 − 7	⁻6 − 3	⁻4 − 4
negative − negative	⁻3 − ⁻5	⁻5 − ⁻4	⁻7 − ⁻10

Using this model every integer can be represented in many ways. For example, the following three collections of tiles each have a net value of ⁻2 because when pairs of red and black are matched there is an excess of 2 red tiles in each collection.

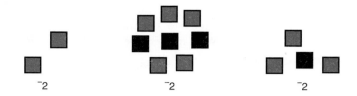

⁻2   ⁻2   ⁻2

If there are the same number of black tiles as there are red tiles in a collection, the collection has *net value 0*. In this case, the positive integer for the black tiles and the negative integer for the red tiles are called *opposites* of each other.

1. Take a small handful of red and black tiles from the Manipulative Kit (or using the random tile feature in the Virtual Manipulatives) and drop them on a flat surface. Record the information about your collection in part a of the following table. Repeat the above directions three times and record the information in parts b, c, and d.

	Total Number of Tiles	Number of Red Tiles	Number of Black Tiles	Net Value
a.	_____	_____	_____	_____
b.	_____	_____	_____	_____
c.	_____	_____	_____	_____
d.	_____	_____	_____	_____

2. The following table contains partial results from collections of red and black tiles that have been dropped. Use your red and black tiles to determine the missing table entries.

	Total Number of Tiles	Number of Red Tiles	Number of Black Tiles	Net Value
*a.	_____	8	29	_____
b.	42	26	_____	_____
*c.	_____	_____	14	⁺8
d.	17	_____	_____	⁺5
e.	20	_____	_____	⁻4
*f.	_____	_____	11	⁻2

Addition

3. These two collections represent the integers $^-3$ and $^+2$, respectively. Form each collection with your tiles. Combine the two collections to determine the sum, $^-3 + {}^+2$. What integer represents the sum of the two collections?

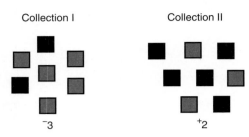

Collection I

$^-3$

Collection II

$^+2$

a. Represent $^-3$ with the fewest number of tiles. Do the same for $^+2$. Sketch these collections and show that, when combined, they represent the same sum as the preceding collections.

b. Use your red and black tiles to determine these sums. Draw a sketch to indicate how you got your answer.

$^+7 + {}^-3 =$

$^-4 + {}^-3 =$

$^-8 + {}^+2 =$

*c. Try to visualize black and red tiles as you determine these sums.

$^+50 + {}^-37 =$ $\qquad$ $^-34 + {}^-25 =$ $\qquad$ $^-132 + {}^+70 =$

4. Write directions that will enable the reader to do the following. Use the black and red tile terminology in your directions.

   a. Add any two negative integers.

   *b. Add a positive integer and a negative integer.

Subtraction

5. The collections A and B show one way to compute $^+5 - ^+8$ with black and red tiles. It is not possible to take 8 black tiles from collection A, but collection A can be changed to collection B by adding 3 black tiles and 3 red tiles. Collection B still represents 5, but now 8 black tiles can be removed to determine that $^+5 - ^+8 = ^-3$.

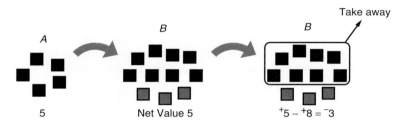

Use your tiles to form the following collections. Then change each collection to one that represents the same number but has enough tiles so that the appropriate number of tiles can be taken away. In each example, sketch the new collection. Use the results to complete the equations.

   a. Change this collection to show $^-4 - ^+3$.

   *b. Change this collection to show $^+5 - ^-2$.

   c. Change this collection to show $^-3 - ^-5$.

*6. Explain how parts a, b, and c of activity 5 can be used to show that subtraction can be performed by adding opposites. That is, taking away a given number of one color is the same as adding the same number of the opposite color. Symbolically this is written $a - b = a + {}^-b$. (*Hint:* Reconstruct the sets in parts a, b, and c with your black and red tiles and watch what happens when you bring in extra tiles and then subtract.)

Multiplication[2]

7. The red and black tiles can be used to illustrate a model for multiplication if we agree that in the product $n \times s$, n tells the number of times we *put in* (+) or *take out* (−) s red or black tiles. For example, ${}^-2 \times {}^+3$ means that 2 times we take out 3 black tiles. This changes set *A*, which represents 0, to set *B*, which represents ${}^-6$. This shows that ${}^-2 \times {}^+3 = {}^-6$.

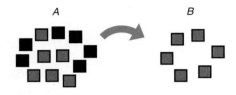

For each of the following activities, start with a collection of 8 red and 8 black tiles, that is, a set that has value zero. Make the described changes to the collection. Sketch the resulting collection and record its value. Then write the complete number equation that has been illustrated.

a. Three times, put in 2 red tiles.

*b. Two times, take out 4 red tiles.

c. Three times, take out 2 black tiles.

8. Use your tiles to show how you would illustrate ${}^-3 \times {}^-4$ with red and black tiles. Illustrate your results by drawing a sketch. Explain how you determined the number of red and black tiles you used in the initial collection.

---

[2]This model for multiplication can be described as the mail-delivery model. Bringing mail to you is a positive action and taking mail from you is a negative action. The mail contains bills for $1 each (debts) or checks for $1 each (assets). The mail carrier can bring (positive) or take away (negative), bills (negative) or checks (positive). Then, for example, ${}^-2 \times {}^+4$ signifies that 2 times the mail carrier takes away four $1 checks, and your net worth has decreased by $8.

Division

9. Review the measurement and sharing approaches to whole number division discussed in Activity Set 3.4.

   a. Form a collection of 12 red tiles and use the sharing approach to determine the quotient $^-12 \div {}^+3$. Draw a sketch of your tiles to indicate how you obtained your answer.

   b. Form a collection of 12 red tiles and use the measurement approach to determine the quotient $^-12 \div {}^-3$. Draw a sketch of your tiles to indicate how you obtained your result.

   *c. Explain why neither the sharing nor measurement approach can be used to illustrate $^+12 \div {}^-3$.

10. In whole number arithmetic we know that $6 \div 2 = 3$ because $2 \times 3 = 6$; that is, division can be defined in terms of multiplication. This same approach can be used for integer multiplication.

   a. Show that this approach gives the same answers as the methods in 9a and 9b above.

   b. What answer does it give for 9c?

   c. Determine each of the following. Use black and red tiles if possible. Explain your thinking.

   *i. $^+15 \div {}^+3$ ii. $^+15 \div {}^-3$ *iii. $^-15 \div {}^+3$ iv. $^-15 \div {}^-3$

JUST FOR FUN

The following four games for negative numbers require two dice, one white and one red. The white die represents positive numbers, and the red die represents negative numbers.

separately for each die—to the right for the white die and to the left for the red die—it will quickly lead to the rule for adding positive and negative numbers.

GAME 1 (Addition—2 to 4 players)

Each player begins the game with a marker on the zero point of the number line. On a turn, the player rolls the dice and adds the positive number represented by the white die to the negative number represented by the red die. This sum determines the amount of movement on the number line. If it is positive, the marker moves to the right, and if it is negative, the marker moves to the left. If the sum is zero, the player rolls again. The first player to reach either ⁻10 or 10 wins the game. If this game is played at first by moving the marker

GAME 2 (Addition and Subtraction—2 to 6 players)

Each player selects one of the cards shown below. On a player's turn, the dice are rolled and the two numbers are either added or subtracted. Suppose, for example, that you rolled ⁺4 and ⁻6; you could add ⁺4 + ⁻6 = ⁻2, subtract ⁺4 − ⁻6 = 10, or subtract ⁻6 − ⁺4 = ⁻10. The answer is then marked on the player's card. The first player to complete a row, column, or diagonal wins the game.

GAME 1

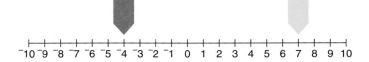

GAME 2

Card 1

⁻9	⁻11	⁻1	8	10
12	3	⁻10	⁻2	⁻6
8	⁻12	⁻7	⁻4	⁻5
2	6	11	7	1
⁻3	0	5	9	4

Card 2

5	12	10	⁻1	⁻9
⁻10	⁻3	7	11	⁻8
⁻4	2	4	⁻6	⁻2
9	⁻7	⁻5	⁻11	1
8	6	3	0	⁻12

Card 3

⁻1	⁻7	9	4	⁻6
8	⁻5	11	⁻12	6
⁻11	1	⁻2	7	⁻9
⁻3	10	12	⁻4	3
2	⁻8	5	0	⁻10

Card 4

⁻8	⁻10	10	5	9
11	7	⁻11	⁻9	3
6	⁻7	4	0	⁻1
⁻4	12	2	⁻12	8
1	⁻5	⁻3	⁻2	⁻6

Card 5

6	⁻2	⁻12	⁻11	⁻10
⁻5	12	1	⁻9	8
4	11	10	2	0
⁻7	5	9	⁻3	3
⁻4	⁻8	⁻6	7	⁻1

Card 6

⁻5	⁻3	2	⁻2	11
4	5	⁻6	⁻1	⁻9
⁻12	⁻11	7	8	⁻8
12	7	6	⁻4	3
1	0	⁻10	5	10

GAME 3 (Multiplication and Inequality—2 to 4 players)

On a turn, the player rolls the dice and multiplies the positive number from the white die by the negative number from the red die. This operation is repeated a second time, and the player then selects the greater of the two products. In the example shown at the right, each player has had four turns. The greater product in each case has been circled. Player B is ahead at this point with the greater score: a total of $^-12$. After 5 rounds, the player with the greater total wins the game.

Chance Option: If a player obtains two undesirable numbers, such as $^-25$ and $^-15$, he or she may use the *chance option*, which involves rolling the dice a third time. If the third product is greater than the other two—say, $^-12$—the player may select this number. If the third product is less than or equal to either of the other two—say, $^-18$—then the smallest of the three numbers ($^-25$ in this example) must be kept as the player's score.

	Player A		Player B	
GAME 3	④	$^-6$	①	$^-3$
	②	$^-18$	$^-6$	②
	⑥	$^-30$	⑤	$^-16$
	$^-15$	⑥	$^-24$	④
	Total	$^-18$	Total	$^-12$

GAME 4 (All four basic operations—1 to 4 players)

Roll the dice four times, and record the four negative numbers from the red die and the four positive numbers from the white die. Using each number no more than once, write as many as possible in the eight blanks of the equations under Round 1 to complete the equations. Repeat this activity for Round 2 and Round 3. You receive 1 point for each equation. If you complete all four equations for a given round, you receive 4 points plus 2 bonus points. The total number of points for the three rounds is your score.

	Round 1	Round 2	Round 3
GAME 4	_____ $+$ $^-1$ $=$ _____	$^+3 +$ _____ $=$ _____	_____ $+$ _____ $=$ $^-6$
	_____ $-$ $^-4$ $=$ _____	$^-1 -$ _____ $=$ _____	_____ $-$ $^-5$ $=$ _____
	$^-2 \times$ _____ $=$ _____	$^-1 \times$ _____ $=$ _____	$^+3 \times$ _____ $=$ _____
	_____ $\div$ $^+3$ $=$ _____	_____ $\div$ _____ $=$ $^+2$	_____ $\div$ $^-1$ $=$ _____

Follow-Up Questions and Activities 5.1

1. *School Classroom:* Write a short word problem appropriate for an elementary school student for each of the following integer addition and subtraction sentences.

   a. $^+7 + {}^-3 = ?$
   b. $^-4 + {}^-3 = ?$
   c. $^-4 - {}^+3 = ?$
   d. $^+5 - {}^-2 = ?$
   e. $^-3 - {}^-7 = ?$

2. *School Classroom:* A seventh-grade student said his father told him to subtract a negative number you just "change the sign and add." So, for example, $^+5 - {}^-7 = {}^+5 + {}^+7 = {}^+12$. How can you use the red and black tile model to help the student see why this rule works?

3. *School Classroom:* Read the integer subtraction activity described in the **Elementary School Text** page at the beginning of this section. Describe what prerequisite knowledge about the red and yellow counter model students need before they can complete this activity.

4. *School Classroom:* Design an activity that you believe is appropriate for helping an elementary school student understand adding and subtracting integers using a temperature model. Write a few questions that you can ask about your activity. Try this activity on an upper elementary or middle school age child of your choice. Record your questions and record the student's responses.

5. *Math Concepts:* For each of the following; sketch a black and red tile model to show computing the sum or difference. In each case, explain your thinking.

   a. $7 + {}^-3 = ?$
   b. $^-4 + {}^-3 = ?$
   c. $^-4 - {}^+3 = ?$
   d. $^+5 - {}^-2 = ?$
   e. $^-3 - {}^-7 = ?$

6. *Math Concepts:* For each of the following, sketch a black and red tile model to show computing the product or quotient. In each case, explain your thinking.

   a. $^+6 \times {}^-2 = ?$
   b. $^-6 \times {}^+2 = ?$
   c. $^-6 \times {}^-2 = ?$
   d. $^-6 \div {}^+2 = ?$
   e. $^-6 \div {}^-2 = ?$

7. *NCTM Standards:* Go to the **Number and Operations Standards** in the back pages of this book and find the *Expectation* that specifically mentions integer operations. State the *Expectation* and the *Standard* it is under. Explain how the activities in this section will help students achieve this *Expectation*.

 BENNETT-BURTON-NELSON WEBSITE

www.mhhe.com/bbn

Virtual Manipulatives	Grid and Dot Paper	Links and Readings
Interactive Chapter Applets	Color Transparencies	Geometer Sketchpad Modules
Puzzlers	Extended Bibliography	

Activity Set **5.2**   FRACTION BAR MODEL FOR EQUALITY AND INEQUALITY

Virtual Manipulatives

www.mhhe.com/bbn

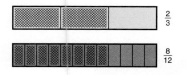
$\frac{5}{6}$

PURPOSE

To use Fraction Bars to provide a visual model for the *part-to-whole* and *division* concepts of fractions, fraction equality and inequality, and fraction rounding and estimation.[3]

MATERIALS

Fraction Bars from the Manipulative Kit or from the Virtual Manipulatives.

INTRODUCTION

The set of Fraction Bars consists of 32 bars divided into 2, 3, 4, 6, or 12 equal parts. The bars are colored (halves—green, thirds—yellow, fourths—blue, sixths—red, and twelfths—orange) so that the user can easily distinguish bars with different numbers of parts. Various fractions are named by shading parts of the bars. For example, the bar to the left represents $\frac{5}{6}$ (five-sixths). The top number in the fraction, the *numerator*, tells the number of shaded parts, and the bottom number, the *denominator*, tells the number of equal parts into which the bar is divided. This model illustrates the *part-to-whole* concept of fractions. It emphasizes the unit and models fractions in relation to this unit. The *division* concept of fractions is introduced in activity 10.

A Fraction Bar with all of its parts shaded is called a whole bar and its fraction equals 1. A bar with no parts shaded is called a zero bar and its fraction equals zero.

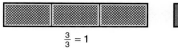   

$\frac{3}{3} = 1$ $\frac{0}{4} = 0$

$\frac{2}{3}$

$\frac{8}{12}$

1. The fractions for the bars in the figure to the left are equal because both bars have the same amount of shading. In the set of 32 Fraction Bars, there are three bars whose fractions equal $\frac{2}{3}$. Sort your set of bars into piles so that the bars with the same shaded amount are in the same pile.

   *a. There are five bars whose fractions are equal to $\frac{0}{4}$. How many bars represent the other fractions listed here?

Fraction	Number of Bars with Equal Fractions
$\frac{0}{4}$	5
$\frac{1}{2}$	_____
$\frac{2}{3}$	_____
$\frac{6}{6}$	_____
$\frac{1}{4}$	_____

[3]Fraction Bars is a registered trademark of Scott Resources, Inc.

b. Complete this table by writing in the sixths, fourths, thirds, and halves that are equal to the twelfths. (*Note:* Many of the squares will be blank.)

Twelfths	$\frac{0}{12}$	$\frac{1}{12}$	$\frac{2}{12}$	$\frac{3}{12}$	$\frac{4}{12}$	$\frac{5}{12}$	$\frac{6}{12}$	$\frac{7}{12}$	$\frac{8}{12}$	$\frac{9}{12}$	$\frac{10}{12}$	$\frac{11}{12}$	$\frac{12}{12}$
Sixths													
Fourths													
Thirds													
Halves													

2. The $\frac{1}{3}$ bar has more shading than the $\frac{1}{4}$ bar, so $\frac{1}{3}$ is greater than $\frac{1}{4}$. This is written $\frac{1}{3} > \frac{1}{4}$ (or $\frac{1}{4} < \frac{1}{3}$).

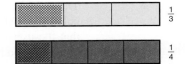

*a. Select the following Fraction Bars from your set of bars:

$$\frac{5}{6}, \frac{1}{4}, \frac{11}{12}, \frac{2}{3}, \frac{1}{6}, \frac{5}{12}, \frac{3}{4}, \frac{1}{3}, \frac{7}{12}, \frac{1}{2}, \text{ and } \frac{1}{12}$$

Place these bars in increasing order from the smallest shaded amount to the largest shaded amount and complete the following inequalities.

$$\underline{\quad} < \frac{1}{6} < \underline{\quad} < \underline{\quad} < \underline{\quad} < \frac{1}{2} < \underline{\quad} < \underline{\quad} < \underline{\quad} < \underline{\quad} < \frac{11}{12}$$

b. Each of the fractions in part a has a common denominator of 12. Rewrite these inequalities using only fractions with a denominator of 12.

$$\underline{\quad} < \frac{2}{12} < \underline{\quad} < \underline{\quad} < \underline{\quad} < \underline{\quad} < \underline{\quad} < \underline{\quad} < \underline{\quad} < \underline{\quad} < \frac{11}{12}$$

3. By placing the five different types of Fraction Bars in a column, we can visualize many equalities and inequalities. For example, by comparing the vertical lines of these bars, we can see that

$$\frac{1}{2} = \frac{6}{12} \qquad \frac{2}{3} < \frac{3}{4} \qquad \frac{5}{6} = \frac{10}{12}$$

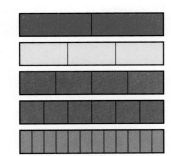

a. List 10 different equalities of pairs of fractions that can be illustrated by comparing the vertical lines of these bars.

*b. List 10 different inequalities of pairs of fractions that can be illustrated by these bars.

4. Many inequalities for fractions can be determined mentally by visualizing the bars representing the fractions. For example, we can determine that $\frac{1}{5}$ is less than $\frac{1}{4}$, because each part of a bar with 5 equal parts is smaller than each part of a bar with 4 equal parts.

Mentally determine the correct inequality sign to put between each pair of fractions. Explain your reasoning in terms of Fraction Bars.

    a. $\frac{1}{3}$ $\frac{1}{10}$

    *b. $\frac{2}{3}$ $\frac{3}{4}$

    c. $\frac{5}{12}$ $\frac{2}{3}$

    *d. $\frac{7}{7}$ $\frac{5}{5}$

5. Rounding fractions to the nearest whole number can be facilitated by sketching or visualizing Fraction Bars. For example, on the bars representing $1\frac{2}{7}$, the shaded amount is closer to 1 whole bar than to 2 whole bars. So to the nearest whole number, $1\frac{2}{7}$ rounds to 1.

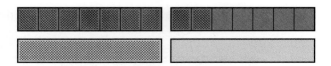

On the other hand, on the bars representing $1\frac{4}{7}$, the shaded amount is closer to 2 whole bars than to 1 whole bar. So to the nearest whole number, $1\frac{4}{7}$ rounds to 2.

Round the following fractions to the nearest whole number. Draw a Fraction Bar sketch to justify your answer.

Fraction	Diagram	Nearest Whole Number
*a. $4\frac{2}{3}$		_____
b. $\frac{1}{8}$		_____
*c. $\frac{10}{12}$		_____
d. $2\frac{5}{7}$		_____

6. Each part of this $\frac{3}{4}$ bar has been split into 2 equal parts. There are now 8 parts, and 6 of these are shaded. Because this splitting has neither increased nor decreased the total shaded amount of the bar, both $\frac{3}{4}$ and $\frac{6}{8}$ are fractions for the same amount.

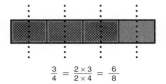

$$\frac{3}{4} = \frac{2 \times 3}{2 \times 4} = \frac{6}{8}$$

   a. Split each part of these bars into 2 equal parts, and complete the equations.

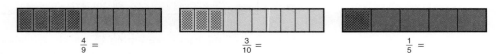

$$\frac{4}{9} = \qquad\qquad \frac{3}{10} = \qquad\qquad \frac{1}{5} =$$

   *b. Split each part of these bars into 3 equal parts, and complete the equations.

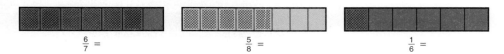

$$\frac{6}{7} = \qquad\qquad \frac{5}{8} = \qquad\qquad \frac{1}{6} =$$

   c. Split each part of these bars into 4 equal parts, and complete the equations.

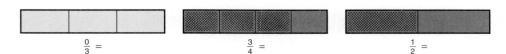

$$\frac{0}{3} = \qquad\qquad \frac{3}{4} = \qquad\qquad \frac{1}{2} =$$

   d. Suppose that each part of the Fraction Bar for $\frac{a}{b}$ is split into 3 equal parts. How many of the parts will be shaded? _____ How many parts will there be in all? _____ Write the fraction for this bar. _____

7. There are an infinite number of fractions that are equal to $\frac{2}{3}$. These fractions can be generated by equally splitting the parts of a $\frac{2}{3}$ bar.

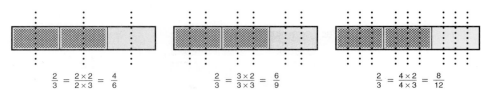

$$\frac{2}{3} = \frac{2 \times 2}{2 \times 3} = \frac{4}{6} \qquad\qquad \frac{2}{3} = \frac{3 \times 2}{3 \times 3} = \frac{6}{9} \qquad\qquad \frac{2}{3} = \frac{4 \times 2}{4 \times 3} = \frac{8}{12}$$

a. If each part of a $\frac{2}{3}$ bar is split into 5 equal parts, what equality of fractions does the bar represent?

*b. If each part of a $\frac{2}{3}$ bar is split into 17 equal parts, what equality of fractions does the bar represent?

c. What effect does splitting each part of any Fraction Bar into 17 equal parts have on the numerator and denominator of the fraction for the bar?

*d. Split each of the following bars to illustrate the given equality.

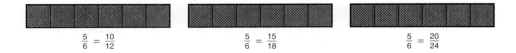

$$\frac{5}{6} = \frac{10}{12} \qquad\qquad\qquad \frac{5}{6} = \frac{15}{18} \qquad\qquad\qquad \frac{5}{6} = \frac{20}{24}$$

8. Each part of a $\frac{2}{3}$ bar is bigger than each part of a $\frac{3}{4}$ bar. If each part of the $\frac{2}{3}$ bar is split into 4 equal parts and each part of the $\frac{3}{4}$ bar is split into 3 equal parts, both bars will then have 12 parts of equal size. The new fractions for these bars will have a common denominator of 12.

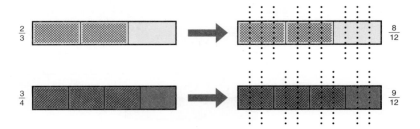

For each of the following pairs of bars, use the fewest number of splits so that all the new parts for both bars are the same size. The corresponding fractions will have the same denominator. Complete the equations.

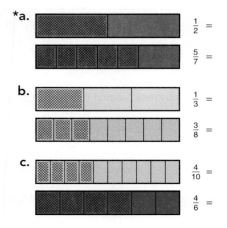

*a. $\frac{1}{2} =$

$\frac{5}{7} =$

b. $\frac{1}{3} =$

$\frac{3}{8} =$

c. $\frac{4}{10} =$

$\frac{4}{6} =$

9. Sketch bars, at the left, for $\frac{3}{5}$ and $\frac{5}{7}$. Sometimes it is difficult to tell from a sketch which fraction is greater.

   a. When both bars are split so that all parts have the same size, the two fractions for these bars will have the same denominator. Complete these equations so that both fractions have the same denominator.

$$\frac{3}{5} = \qquad\qquad \frac{5}{7} =$$

   b. Which is greater, $\frac{3}{5}$ or $\frac{5}{7}$?

   Replace the fractions in each of the following pairs with fractions having the same denominator. Circle the greater fraction in each pair (or state that they are equal).

   c. $\frac{1}{3} =$ *d. $\frac{7}{9} =$ e. $\frac{4}{6} =$ *f. $\frac{11}{15} =$

       $\frac{2}{7} =$ $\frac{8}{10} =$ $\frac{6}{9} =$ $\frac{8}{11} =$

10. The *division* concept of fractions relates quotients of whole numbers to fractions. For example, 3 whole bars are placed end to end to represent the number 3. If this 3-bar is divided into 4 equal parts, each part will be $\frac{3}{4}$ of a whole bar. This shows that $3 \div 4 = \frac{3}{4}$.

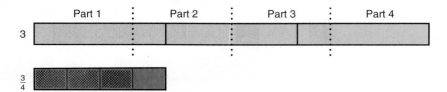

Part 1 : Part 2 : Part 3 : Part 4

3

$\frac{3}{4}$

Illustrate each quotient of whole numbers by dividing the given big bar into equal parts. Then complete the equation by writing a fraction or mixed number.[4]

a. $3 \div 2 =$

*b. $2 \div 3 =$

c. $4 \div 3 =$

JUST FOR FUN

These two fraction games provide extra practice in comparing fractions. In FRIO[5] you compare unequal fractions, and in Fraction Bingo you search for equal fractions.

FRIO (2 to 4 players)

Each player is dealt five bars in a row face up. These bars should be left in the order in which they are dealt. The remaining bars are spread face down. Each player, in turn, takes a bar that is face down and uses it to replace any one of the five bars. The object of the game is to get five bars in order from the *smallest* shaded amount to the *largest* or from the

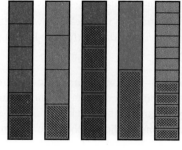

largest to the *smallest*. In this example the five bars will be in order if the $\frac{2}{6}$ bar is replaced by a whole bar and the $\frac{1}{4}$ bar is replaced by an $\frac{11}{12}$ bar. The first player to get five Fraction Bars in decreasing or increasing order wins the game.

FRACTION BINGO (2 to 4 players)

Each player selects a fraction bingo mat from those shown below. The deck of 32 bars is spread face down. Each player, in turn, takes a bar and circles the fraction or fractions on his or her mat that equal the fraction from the bar. The first player to circle four fractions in any row, column, or diagonal is the winner.

Strategy: If the bars are colored green, yellow, blue, red, and orange for halves, thirds, fourths, sixths, and twelfths, respectively, you can increase your chances of winning by selecting bars of the appropriate color.

$\frac{4}{6}$	$\frac{1}{6}$	$\frac{0}{4}$	$\frac{11}{12}$
$\frac{5}{12}$	$\frac{1}{4}$	$\frac{5}{6}$	$\frac{3}{6}$
$\frac{3}{4}$	$\frac{1}{12}$	$\frac{1}{3}$	$\frac{11}{12}$
$\frac{6}{12}$	$\frac{4}{4}$	$\frac{9}{12}$	$\frac{10}{12}$

Mat 1

$\frac{1}{3}$	$\frac{1}{4}$	$\frac{1}{6}$	$\frac{0}{3}$
$\frac{7}{12}$	$\frac{0}{6}$	$\frac{1}{12}$	$\frac{4}{6}$
$\frac{2}{3}$	$\frac{3}{4}$	$\frac{5}{6}$	$\frac{5}{12}$
$\frac{11}{12}$	$\frac{2}{2}$	$\frac{3}{12}$	$\frac{1}{2}$

Mat 2

$\frac{2}{3}$	$\frac{1}{4}$	$\frac{2}{6}$	$\frac{6}{12}$
$\frac{5}{6}$	$\frac{0}{3}$	$\frac{5}{12}$	$\frac{1}{6}$
$\frac{7}{12}$	$\frac{4}{4}$	$\frac{1}{2}$	$\frac{11}{12}$
$\frac{3}{4}$	$\frac{8}{12}$	$\frac{1}{12}$	$\frac{1}{3}$

Mat 3

$\frac{1}{4}$	$\frac{1}{6}$	$\frac{7}{12}$	$\frac{1}{2}$
$\frac{0}{3}$	$\frac{5}{12}$	$\frac{2}{3}$	$\frac{4}{4}$
$\frac{1}{12}$	$\frac{5}{6}$	$\frac{11}{12}$	$\frac{2}{12}$
$\frac{6}{6}$	$\frac{3}{4}$	$\frac{0}{12}$	$\frac{1}{3}$

Mat 4

---

[4]If long strips of paper are available, the big bars such as the 2-bar (the length of 2 whole bars) and the 3-bar (the length of 3 whole bars) can be cut to actual length. A strip can then be folded and the folded amount compared to the fraction bars.

[5]R. Drizigacker, "FRIO, or Fractions In Order," *Arithmetic Teacher* 13 (December 1966): 684–685.

Follow-Up Questions and Activities 5.2

1. *School Classroom:* Jeremy believes that $\frac{1}{6}$ is greater than $\frac{1}{4}$ because 6 is greater than 4. Explain how you would use Fraction Bars to help him determine the correct inequality.

2. *School Classroom:* One of your students says that you can't always say that $\frac{2}{3}$ is greater than $\frac{1}{2}$ because $\frac{1}{2}$ of a large pizza is more than $\frac{2}{3}$ of a small pizza. Describe how you could help the student come to an understanding about fraction inequality by starting with his pizza example.

3. *Math Concepts:* How can you use the Fraction Bars to find fractions between $\frac{1}{4}$ and $\frac{1}{3}$? Explain your thinking.

4. *Math Concepts:* Illustrate and explain two different ways to show the equality relationship between $\frac{1}{6}$ and $\frac{2}{12}$ with Fraction Bars.

5. *Math Concepts:* Illustrate and explain two different ways to show the inequality relationship between $\frac{1}{3}$ and $\frac{1}{4}$ with Fraction Bars.

6. *Math Concepts:* Illustrate and explain how to use Fraction Bars to show $5 \div 4 = ?$, then complete the equation by writing the correct mixed number quotient.

7. *NCTM Standards:* Go to http://illuminations.nctm.org/ and under "Lessons" select grade levels 3–5 and the **Number and Operations Standard.** Choose a lesson about fun with fractions.

   a. State the title of the lesson and briefly summarize the lesson.

   b. Referring to the **Standards Summary** in the back pages of this book as necessary, list the *Number and Operation Standard Expectations* that the lesson addresses and explain how the lesson addresses these *Expectations*.

8. *NCTM Standards:* In the **Grades 3–5 Number and Operations Standards** in the back pages of this book, it is suggested that students need to understand fractions as locations on the number line. Describe how you can use the Fraction Bar model to help students make the transition to the placement of fractions on the number line with understanding.

 # BENNETT-BURTON-NELSON WEBSITE

www.mhhe.com/bbn

Virtual Manipulatives	Grid and Dot Paper	Links and Readings
Interactive Chapter Applets	Color Transparencies	Geometer Sketchpad Modules
Puzzlers	Extended Bibliography	

Activity Set 5.3   COMPUTING WITH FRACTION BARS

PURPOSE

To use Fraction Bars to perform the basic operations of addition, subtraction, multiplication, and division in a visual and intuitive manner.

Virtual Manipulatives

www.mhhe.com/bbn

MATERIALS

Fraction Bars from the Manipulative Kit or from the Virtual Manipulatives.

INTRODUCTION

Piaget has charted the cognitive development of preadolescents, and his research indicates that even at the age of 12, most children deal only with symbols that are closely tied to their perceptions. For example, the symbolic representation $\frac{1}{6} + \frac{2}{3} = \frac{5}{6}$ has meaning for most elementary school children only if they can relate it directly to concrete or pictorial representations.[6]

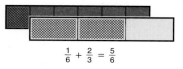

$$\frac{1}{6} + \frac{2}{3} = \frac{5}{6}$$

The following table documents the lack of conceptual understanding of fractions and fraction addition exhibited by 13-year-olds when they were asked to estimate the answer to $\frac{12}{13} + \frac{7}{8}$.[7] Over 50 percent of the students responded with the incorrect answers 19 and 21. What is a reasonable explanation of how students may have arrived at the incorrect answers 19 and 21?

Responses	Percent Responding, Age 13
○ 1	7
● 2	24
○ 19	28
○ 21	27
○ I don't know	14

Students may learn fraction skills at a rote manipulation level, but when their memory fails or they encounter a nonstandard application, they have no conceptual basis to fall back on.

In this activity set, Fraction Bars will be used to develop visual images of fraction operations. These images will provide a conceptual basis for computations, estimations, and problem solving.

Addition and Subtraction

1. **Addition and Subtraction:** Determine the missing fractions and the sum or difference of the fractions for each pair of bars on the page 139. Use Fraction Bars to determine the sums by comparing the addend bars to a sum bar. Use Fraction Bars to determine the differences by drawing two vertical lines on the bars to indicate the difference on the difference bar as illustrated in the examples on page 139.

---

[6]M. J. Driscoll, "The Role of Manipulatives in Elementary School Mathematics," *Research within Reach: Elementary School Mathematics* (St. Louis, MO: Cemrel Inc., 1983): 1.

[7]T. P. Carpenter, H. Kepner, M. K. Corbitt, M. M. Lindquist, and R. E. Reys, "Results and Implications of the Second NAEP Mathematics Assessment: Elementary School," *Arithmetic Teacher* 27 (April 1980): 10–12, 44–47.

I will explore how to multiply a fraction by a fraction.

Explore Multiplication of a Fraction by a Fraction

Hands On Activity

You can draw a diagram to model how to multiply a fraction by a fraction.

You Will Need
- paper
- crayons

Find: $\frac{1}{2}$ of $\frac{3}{4}$

Use Models

STEP 1

Fold the paper in four equal sections. Shade 3 of the sections blue.

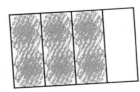

STEP 2

Fold the paper in two equal sections the other way.

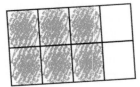

STEP 3

Shade one of the rows red.

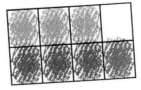

STEP 4

Count the total number of sections. Count the number of sections shaded with both colors. Write the product.

$\frac{3}{8}$ $\leftarrow$ number of sections with both colors
$\phantom{\frac{3}{8}}$ $\leftarrow$ total number of sections

Sum Example:

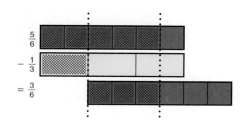

$$\frac{3}{12} + \frac{1}{3} = \frac{7}{12}$$

Difference Example:

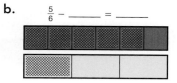

$$\frac{5}{6} - \frac{1}{3} = \frac{3}{6}$$

*a. $\frac{1}{3} + \rule{1cm}{0.4pt} = \rule{1cm}{0.4pt}$

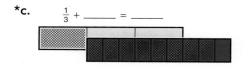

b. $\frac{5}{6} - \rule{1cm}{0.4pt} = \rule{1cm}{0.4pt}$

*c. $\frac{1}{3} + \rule{1cm}{0.4pt} = \rule{1cm}{0.4pt}$

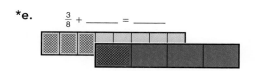

d. $\frac{3}{4} - \rule{1cm}{0.4pt} = \rule{1cm}{0.4pt}$

*e. $\frac{3}{8} + \rule{1cm}{0.4pt} = \rule{1cm}{0.4pt}$

f. $\frac{4}{5} - \rule{1cm}{0.4pt} = \rule{1cm}{0.4pt}$

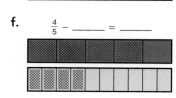

2. Select three pairs of Fraction Bars at random. Complete the following equations for the sum and difference of each pair of fractions. (Subtract the smaller from the larger if the fractions are unequal.)

$\rule{2cm}{0.4pt} + \rule{2cm}{0.4pt} = \rule{2cm}{0.4pt}$ $\rule{2cm}{0.4pt} - \rule{2cm}{0.4pt} = \rule{2cm}{0.4pt}$

$\rule{2cm}{0.4pt} + \rule{2cm}{0.4pt} = \rule{2cm}{0.4pt}$ $\rule{2cm}{0.4pt} - \rule{2cm}{0.4pt} = \rule{2cm}{0.4pt}$

$\rule{2cm}{0.4pt} + \rule{2cm}{0.4pt} = \rule{2cm}{0.4pt}$ $\rule{2cm}{0.4pt} - \rule{2cm}{0.4pt} = \rule{2cm}{0.4pt}$

3. **Obtaining Common Denominators:** If each part of the $\frac{2}{3}$ bar is split into 4 equal parts and each part of the $\frac{1}{4}$ bar is split into 3 equal parts, both bars will have 12 parts of the same size. These new bars show that $\frac{2}{3} + \frac{1}{4} = \frac{11}{12}$ and $\frac{2}{3} - \frac{1}{4} = \frac{5}{12}$.

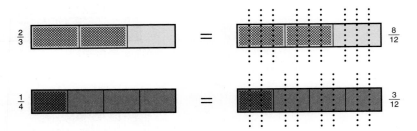

Use the fewest number of splits for the following pairs of Fraction Bars so that each pair of bars has the same number of parts of the same size. Then write two fraction equalities under each pair. For example, in part a, $\frac{5}{6} = \frac{10}{12}$ and $\frac{1}{4} = \frac{3}{12}$.

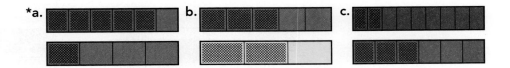

Use the bars from parts a, b, and c above to compute the following sums and differences.

*d. $\frac{5}{6} + \frac{1}{4} =$ **e.** $\frac{3}{5} + \frac{2}{3} =$ **f.** $\frac{2}{9} + \frac{3}{6} =$

*g. $\frac{5}{6} - \frac{1}{4} =$ **h.** $\frac{2}{3} - \frac{3}{5} =$ **i.** $\frac{3}{6} - \frac{2}{9} =$

4. Sketch Fraction Bars for each pair of fractions, and then split the parts of the bars to carry out the operation. Use your diagrams to explain how you reached your conclusions.

*a. $\frac{1}{2} + \frac{5}{6}$ **b.** $\frac{1}{3} + \frac{3}{4}$

c. $\frac{3}{4} - \frac{3}{6}$ **d.** $\frac{1}{2} - \frac{2}{7}$

Multiplication

5. You can determine $\frac{1}{3} \times \frac{1}{6}$ by splitting the shaded part of a $\frac{1}{6}$ bar into 3 equal parts. One of these smaller parts is $\frac{1}{18}$ of a bar, because there are 18 of these parts in a whole bar. (You can think of this as having $\frac{1}{6}$ of an amount and taking $\frac{1}{3}$ of it.)

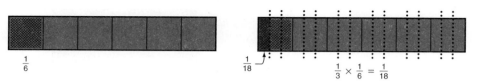

To determine $\frac{1}{3} \times \frac{4}{5}$, split each shaded part of the $\frac{4}{5}$ bar into 3 equal parts. One of these split parts is $\frac{1}{15}$ of the whole bar, and 4 of these split parts is $\frac{4}{15}$ of the whole bar. (You can think of this as having $\frac{4}{5}$ of an amount and taking $\frac{1}{3}$ of each fifth.)

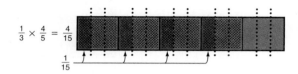

a. Split each part of each bar into 2 equal parts. Use this result to complete the given equations.

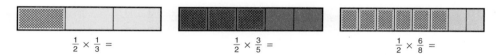

$$\frac{1}{2} \times \frac{1}{3} = \qquad \frac{1}{2} \times \frac{3}{5} = \qquad \frac{1}{2} \times \frac{6}{8} =$$

*b. Split each shaded part of each bar into 3 equal parts, and complete the equations.

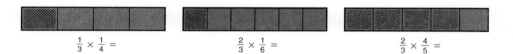

$$\frac{1}{3} \times \frac{1}{4} = \qquad \frac{2}{3} \times \frac{1}{6} = \qquad \frac{2}{3} \times \frac{4}{5} =$$

c. Split each shaded part of each bar into 4 equal parts, and complete the equations.

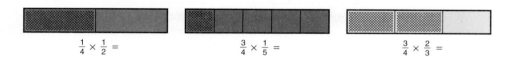

$$\frac{1}{4} \times \frac{1}{2} = \qquad \frac{3}{4} \times \frac{1}{5} = \qquad \frac{3}{4} \times \frac{2}{3} =$$

6. Sketch a Fraction Bar for $\frac{3}{4}$ and visually determine the product $\frac{2}{3} \times \frac{3}{4}$. Write a description of the procedure you used.

Division

7. Using the *measurement* approach to division (see Activity Set 3.4), we can write $\frac{1}{2} \div \frac{1}{6} = 3$, because the shaded portion of the $\frac{1}{6}$ bar can be measured off (or fits into) exactly 3 times on the shaded part of the $\frac{1}{2}$ bar.

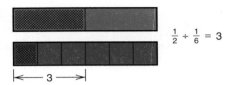

$$\frac{1}{2} \div \frac{1}{6} = 3$$

Similarly, $\frac{5}{6} \div \frac{1}{3} = 2\frac{1}{2}$, because the shaded portion of the $\frac{1}{3}$ bar can be measured off (or fits into) $2\frac{1}{2}$ times on the shaded part of the $\frac{5}{6}$ bar.

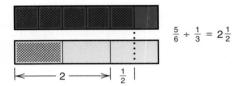

$$\frac{5}{6} \div \frac{1}{3} = 2\frac{1}{2}$$

Sketch Fraction Bars to determine the following quotients. Use your sketch to explain your reasoning.

a. $\frac{3}{4} \div \frac{1}{2} =$

*b. $\frac{10}{12} \div \frac{1}{6} =$

c. $\frac{7}{12} \div \frac{1}{6} =$

*d. $1 \div \frac{2}{3} =$

e. $\frac{3}{2} \div \frac{3}{4} =$

*f. $\frac{7}{8} \div \frac{1}{4} =$

Estimation

8. It is often helpful to draw a sketch or visualize a fraction model when you are trying to estimate with fractions. For example, to estimate the quotient $1\frac{5}{7} \div \frac{1}{8}$, you can compare Fraction Bars representing $1\frac{5}{7}$ to bars representing eighths. There are 8 eighths in 1 whole bar and about 6 eighths in the $\frac{5}{7}$ bar. So, $\frac{1}{8}$ can be measured off about 14 times, and $1\frac{5}{7} \div \frac{1}{8} \approx 14$.

$$1\frac{5}{7} \div \frac{1}{8} \approx 14$$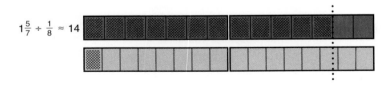

Use a visual approach to estimate the following fraction operations. Draw Fraction Bar sketches and explain how you arrived at your estimation.

a. $1\frac{3}{4} \div \frac{1}{3}$

*b. $\frac{5}{8} - \frac{1}{6}$

c. $\frac{4}{5} + \frac{1}{2}$

*d. $\frac{2}{3} \times \frac{5}{6}$

All Four Operations

9. *a. The following 10 fractions are from the set of Fraction Bars:

$$\frac{1}{6}, \frac{2}{4}, \frac{5}{12}, \frac{2}{6}, \frac{0}{3}, \frac{3}{4}, \frac{3}{12}, \frac{2}{3}, \frac{1}{2}, \frac{1}{4}$$

Using each fraction only once, place these fractions in the 10 blanks to form four equations.

_____ + _____ = _____   3 × _____ = _____

_____ − _____ = _____   _____ ÷ _____ = 2

b. Spread your bars face down and select any 10. Using the fraction from each bar only once, complete as many of these four equations as possible.

Fractions selected: _____, _____, _____, _____, _____,

_____, _____, _____, _____,

_____ + _____ = _____   3 × _____ = _____

_____ − _____ = _____   _____ ÷ _____ = 2

c. Solitaire: The activity in part b can be played like a solitaire game. See how many turns it takes you to complete the four equations by selecting only 10 bars on each turn.

JUST FOR FUN

These three games provide opportunities to perform operations on fractions.

FRACTION BAR BLACKJACK (Addition—2 to 4 players)

Spread the bars face down. The object is to select one or more bars so that the fraction or the sum of fractions is as close to 1 as possible, but not greater than 1. Each player selects bars one at a time, trying to get close to 1 without going over. (A player may wish to take only 1 bar.) Each player finishes his or her turn by saying "I'm holding." After every player in turn has finished, the players show their bars. The player who is closest to a sum of 1, but not over, wins the round.

Examples: Player 1 has a sum greater than 1 and is over. Player 2 has a greater sum than player 3 and wins the round.

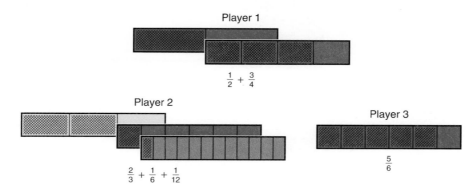

SOLITAIRE (Subtraction)

Spread the Fraction Bars face down. Turn over two bars and compare their shaded amounts. If the difference between the two fractions is less than $\frac{1}{2}$, you win the two bars. If not, you lose the bars. See how many bars you can win by playing through the deck. Will you win the top pair of bars shown here? the bottom pair?

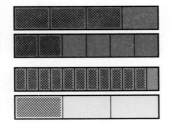

GREATEST QUOTIENT (Division—2 to 4 players)

Remove the zero bars from your set of 32 bars and spread the remaining bars face down. Each player takes two bars. The object of the game is to get the greatest possible quotient by dividing one of the fractions by the other. The greatest *whole* number of times that one fraction divides into the other is the player's score. Each player has the option of taking another bar to improve his or her score or passing. If the player wishes to select another bar, he or she must first discard one bar. The first player to score 21 points wins the game.

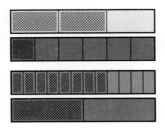

Examples: The whole number part of the quotient can be determined by comparing the shaded amounts of the bars. The score for the top two bars is 4, because the shaded amount of the $\frac{2}{3}$ bar is 4 times greater than the shaded amount of the $\frac{1}{6}$ bar. The score for the bottom two bars is 1, because the shaded amount of the $\frac{1}{2}$ bar fits into the shaded amount of the $\frac{8}{12}$ bar once but not twice.

 TAKE A CHANCE APPLET

In this applet you can play a game with a deck of fractions between 0 and 1 having denominators of 2 through 10. As cards are turned up, you make decisions involving inequalities of two fractions, or four fractions if you decide to take a chance. The sample screen below shows four fractions and asks, "Are two of the fractions less than $\frac{1}{2}$ and the other two greater than or equal to $\frac{1}{2}$?" How would you answer this question to win four cards? If you end up winning 35 cards you beat the deck.

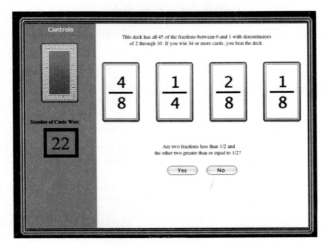

Take a Chance Applet, Chapter 5
www.mhhe.com/bbn

Follow-Up Questions and Activities **5.3**

1. *School Classroom:* One of your students multiplies fractions by getting a common denominator and multiplying the numerators (for example, $\frac{2}{3} \times \frac{3}{4} = \frac{8}{12} \times \frac{9}{12} = \frac{72}{12}$). The student says she does this because you add fractions by getting a common denominator and then adding the numerators. How can you help this student understand why her answer is unreasonable?

2. *School Classroom:* The **Elementary School Text** page at the beginning of this section describes a paper folding method for finding $\frac{1}{2}$ of $\frac{3}{4}$. Draw a series of diagrams to show how you can use this method to find $\frac{2}{3}$ of $\frac{3}{4}$. Sketch shaded diagrams to illustrate each step and describe what is being done for each step.

3. *School Classroom:* Illustrate and explain how you would introduce division of fractions by modeling $\frac{3}{4} \div \frac{1}{6}$ with Fraction Bars.

4. *Math Concepts:* Illustrate and explain each of the steps you would use to model each of the following with Fraction Bars.

   a. $\frac{2}{3} + \frac{3}{4}$

   b. $\frac{5}{6} - \frac{3}{4}$

5. *Math Concepts:* Illustrate and explain each of the steps you would use to model $\frac{1}{6} \times \frac{3}{4}$ with Fraction Bars.

6. *Math Concepts:* Open the **Math Laboratory Investigation 5.3: Read Me—Fraction Patterns Instructions** from the companion website and investigate the fraction patterns described in questions 2 and 3 of the *Starting Points for Investigations 5.3*. State a few of your patterns or conclusions and explain your thinking.

7. *NCTM Standards:* Go to the **Grade 6–8 Number and Operations Standards** in the back pages of this book and find the "Compute Fluently" *Standard*. How will the use of Fraction Bar models for fraction operations help students achieve the first *Expectation* in this *Standard* as it relates to fractions?

 ## BENNETT-BURTON-NELSON WEBSITE

www.mhhe.com/bbn

Virtual Manipulatives	Grid and Dot Paper	Links and Readings
Interactive Chapter Applets	Color Transparencies	Geometer Sketchpad Modules
Puzzlers	Extended Bibliography	

Elementary School Activity

INTRODUCING FRACTIONS WITH FRACTION BARS

Purpose: To introduce elementary school students to fraction notation, equality, and inequality using Fraction Bars.

Connections: Ask the students if they know the meaning of the word "fracture." Discuss some meanings of the word including, "to break into pieces." Tell them that fraction is related to the word fracture and that a fraction is used to talk about a part of something.

Materials: Sets of Fraction Bars can be printed by copying the Fraction Bar images from the companion website. Fraction Bar transparencies can also be made with the Fraction Bar images. Sets of Fraction Bars can be placed in plastic sealable bags. Each pair of students will need one set of Fraction Bars.

Students turn over bars, and the greater shaded amount wins the two bars.

1. Ask each group of students to examine their set of bars to see what they notice. Discuss their observations. (Examples: All red bars have 6 parts; all blue bars have 4 parts; some bars have shaded parts and unshaded parts; etc.)

2. Show them a red bar with 5 parts shaded and ask if anyone knows its fraction. Write $\frac{5}{6}$ and ask them where the "5" comes from and where the "6" comes from. Have them each select a bar and write its fraction. Ask a few volunteers to describe their bar and its fraction.

3. Show them two bars with the same amount of shading and write the equation showing the equality of their fractions. Ask each student to select two new bars with the same amount of shading and to write the equality. Discuss a few examples of fraction equality.

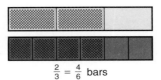

$$\frac{2}{3} = \frac{4}{6} \text{ bars}$$

4. Show them two bars with different amounts of shading and write the inequality for their fractions. Ask each student to select two bars with different shaded amounts and write the inequality for their fractions. Ask volunteers for descriptions of the bars and the inequalities.

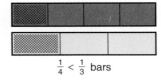

$$\frac{1}{4} < \frac{1}{3} \text{ bars}$$

5. Show two bars whose total shaded amount is one whole bar. Point out that the shaded amount of one bar can be used to "fill in" the other bar to make one whole shaded bar and show the sum is equal to 1 (see the example). Ask them to find two bars that make a whole bar and to write the equation for its sum.

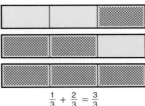

$$\frac{1}{3} + \frac{2}{3} = \frac{3}{3}$$

6. Have each pair turn all of their bars face down and then ask each student to select any two bars and determine if the total shaded amount is less than, equal to, or greater than one whole bar. To make sure that everyone understands, ask for volunteers to describe their amounts. This can be made into a game where the student with the greater total shaded amount wins.

6 Decimals: Rational and Irrational

The approach to decimals should be similar to work with fractions, namely placing strong and continued emphasis on models and oral language and then connecting this work with symbols. . . . Exploring ideas of tenths and hundredths with models can include preliminary work with equivalent decimals.[1]

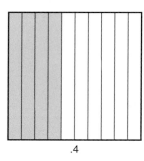 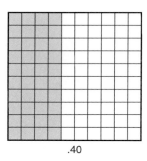

.4   .40

Activity Set 6.1 DECIMAL SQUARES MODEL

PURPOSE

To use Decimal Squares[2] as a visual model for the part-to-whole concept of decimals and for illustrating decimal equality, inequality, place value, and estimation.

Virtual Manipulatives

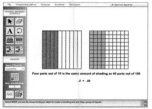

www.mhhe.com/bbn

MATERIALS

Decimal Squares from the Manipulative Kit or from the Virtual Manipulatives.

INTRODUCTION

The results of the second mathematics assessment of the National Assessment of Educational Progress (NAEP) have implications for the use of models in the teaching of decimal concepts.

> In analyzing the computational errors made on the decimal exercises it is evident that much of the difficulty lies in a lack of conceptual understanding. . . . It is important that decimals be thought of as numbers and the ability to relate them to models should assist in understanding.[3]

[1]*Curriculum and Evaluation Standards for School Mathematics* (Reston, VA: National Council of Teachers of Mathematics, 1989): 59.

[2]Decimal Squares is a registered trademark of Scott Resources, Inc.

[3]T. P. Carpenter, M. K. Corbitt, H. S. Kepner, M. M. Lindquist, and R. E. Reys, "Decimals: Results and Implications from National Assessment," *Arithmetic Teacher* 28 (April 1981): 34–37.

I will learn to compare and order decimals.

27.4   Compare and Order Decimals

Earned Run Average (2002 Season)

Player	ERA
Randy Johnson	2.32
Pedro Martinez	2.26

Learn

An ERA, or earned run average, is a decimal that tells how many earned runs a pitcher allows his opponent to score in 9 innings. Which pitcher has the lower ERA?

There's More Than One Way!

Use Models

2.32 > 2.26

Use a Place-Value Chart

Compare each place.

Ones		Tenths	Hundredths
2	.	3	2
2	.	2	6

↑   ↑
2 = 2   3 > 2

2.32 > 2.26

Use Place Value

Line up the decimal points. Compare each place, starting at the greatest place.

```
2  .  3  2
2  .  2  6
↑     ↑
2 = 2   3 > 2     2.32 > 2.26
```

Pedro Martinez has a lower ERA than Randy Johnson.

The Decimal Squares model for decimals is an extension of the number piece model that was used for whole numbers in Chapter 3. The base-ten piece model started with a unit and the pieces increased in size by a factor of 10 (10 units equal 1 long, 10 longs equal 1 flat, etc.). The Decimal Squares model starts with the unit, but the number pieces decrease in size by a factor of 10, as shown here. The number pieces representing 1, $\frac{1}{10}$, $\frac{1}{100}$, and $\frac{1}{1000}$ are indicated by shading one part of each unit number piece.

Unit

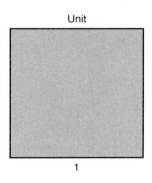

1

1 tenth (red)

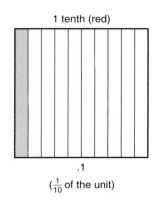

.1

($\frac{1}{10}$ of the unit)

1 hundredth (green)

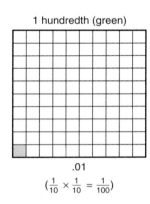

.01

($\frac{1}{10} \times \frac{1}{10} = \frac{1}{100}$)

1 thousandth (yellow)

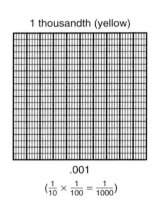

.001

($\frac{1}{10} \times \frac{1}{100} = \frac{1}{1000}$)

The decimals 3 tenths, 37 hundredths, and 379 thousandths are illustrated by the following Decimal Squares.

3 tenths

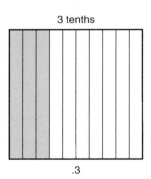

.3

37 hundredths

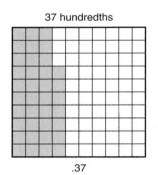

.37

379 thousandths

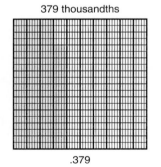

.379

Part to Whole

1. Find the Decimal Squares that represent each of the following decimals. For each decimal, shade the blank Decimal Square to show the decimal and write the name of the decimal below the given decimal.

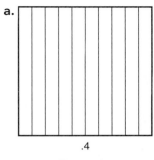

a.

.4

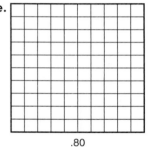

b.

.05

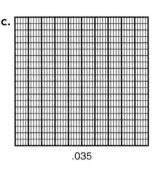

c.

.035

Decimal Name: _____Four tenths_____   _____   _____

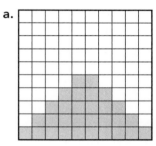

*d.

.7

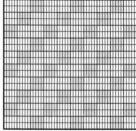

e.

.80

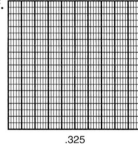

*f.

.325

Decimal Name: _____   _____   _____

2. Below each square write the decimal and the name of the decimal that represents the shaded amount.

a.   ***b.**   **c.**

Decimal: _____   _____   _____

Name: _____   _____   _____

Write the decimal and the name of the decimal that represents each of the following Decimal Squares:

d. 9 shaded parts out of 10   _____

e. 13 shaded parts out of 100   _____

*f. 9 shaded parts out of 100   _____

g. 8 shaded parts out of 1000 _____

*h. 90 shaded parts out of 1000 _____

Equality

The decimals for the following Decimal Squares are equivalent because each Decimal Square is the same size and has the same amount of shading. That is, 4 parts out of 10 is equal to 40 parts out of 100, and 40 parts out of 100 is equal to 400 parts out of 1000.

.4	=	.40	=	.400
Four tenths	=	Forty hundredths	=	Four hundred thousandths

3. a. Sort your Decimal Square card set into sets of equivalent decimals. How many sets are there?

_____ sets of 3 cards   _____ sets of 2 cards   _____ sets of 1 card

b. Pick two of the sets of 3 equivalent decimals and sketch them in the provided blank Decimal Squares here. For each card write the corresponding decimal and the decimal name below the card.

Decimal: _____   _____   _____

Name: _____   _____   _____

Decimal: _____   _____   _____

Name: _____   _____   _____

Fill in the boxes below each Decimal Square to complete the statement and the equation.

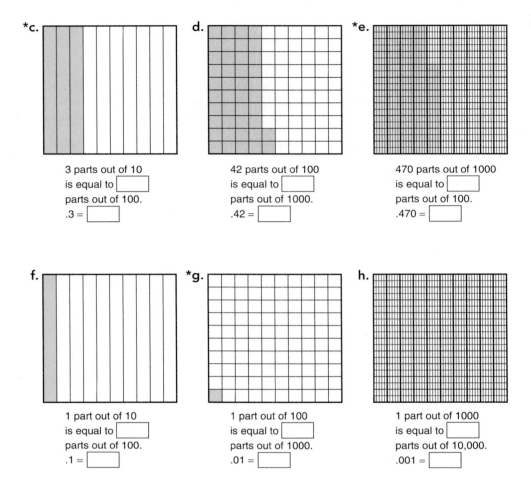

*c.

3 parts out of 10
is equal to ☐
parts out of 100.
.3 = ☐

d.

42 parts out of 100
is equal to ☐
parts out of 1000.
.42 = ☐

*e.

470 parts out of 1000
is equal to ☐
parts out of 100.
.470 = ☐

f.

1 part out of 10
is equal to ☐
parts out of 100.
.1 = ☐

*g.

1 part out of 100
is equal to ☐
parts out of 1000.
.01 = ☐

h.

1 part out of 1000
is equal to ☐
parts out of 10,000.
.001 = ☐

Place Value

The decimal .435 is represented by the shaded parts in both Decimal Squares below. Figure a represents .435 and the way we say its decimal name is "four hundred thirty-five thousandths," because 435 parts out of 1000 are shaded. In Figure b, the encircled parts of the square show that .435 can also be thought of as 4 tenths, 3 hundredths, and 5 thousandths and that each digit has *place value* as recorded in the table.

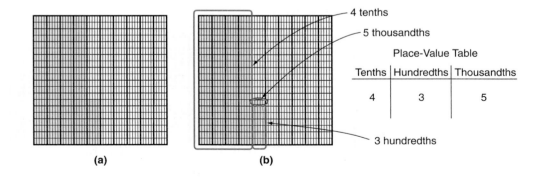

4 tenths

5 thousandths

Place-Value Table

Tenths	Hundredths	Thousandths
4	3	5

3 hundredths

(a)   **(b)**

4. For each of the Decimal Squares, circle the parts that show the decimal in place-value form. Write the digits for each decimal in the place-value table below the square.

a.

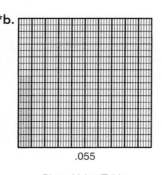

.832

Place-Value Table

Tenths	Hundredths	Thousandths

*b.

.055

Place-Value Table

Tenths	Hundredths	Thousandths

c.

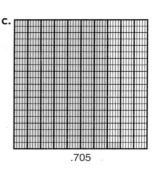

.705

Place-Value Table

Tenths	Hundredths	Thousandths

*d. Explain why it is never necessary to use a digit greater than 9 in any column of a place-value table representing a decimal number.

5. When each part of a Decimal Square for hundredths is partitioned into 10 equal parts, there are 1000 parts. One of these parts is 1 thousandth of the whole square and represents the decimal .001.

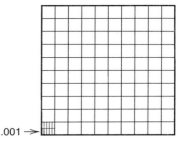

a. Suppose each part of a Decimal Square for thousandths is partitioned into 10 equal parts. What fraction of the whole square is 1 of these parts? What is the decimal for 1 of these small parts, and what is the name of the decimal?

.001 →

*b. Suppose each part of a Decimal Square for thousandths is partitioned into 100 equal parts. What fraction of the whole square is 1 of these parts? What is the decimal for 1 of these small parts, and what is the name of the decimal?

Inequality

The Decimal Squares for .62 and .610 show that .62 is greater than .610, because its square has the greater shaded amount. We can also determine that .62 > .610 by thinking in terms of place value. The digit 6 in .62 and .610 tells us that 6 tenths of both squares are shaded. That is, 6 full columns of both squares are shaded. Looking at the next column, we see that the square for .62 has 2 hundredths (or 20 thousandths) shaded, whereas the square for .610 has 1 hundredth (or 10 thousandths) shaded. So .62 > .610.

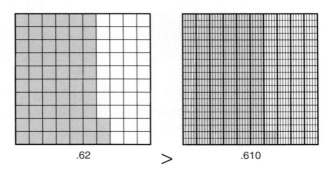

.62   >   .610

6. Determine an inequality for each pair of decimals, and explain the reason for the inequality by describing their Decimal Squares. For example, .4 > .27 because the Decimal Square for .4 has 4 full columns shaded and the square for .27 has less than 3 full columns shaded.

   a. .7   .43

   *b. .042   .04

   c. .3   .285

   Place all of your Decimal Squares face down. For each of parts d–f pick three Decimal Squares at random, place the cards in order, and then write the corresponding decimal equalities or inequalities. For example, draw .2, .15, and .175, rewrite and reorder as .150 < .175 < .200.

   d. _____   _____   _____

   e. _____   _____   _____

   f. _____   _____   _____

7. The following question is from a mathematics assessment test that was given to students entering universities.

Question: Which of the following numbers is the smallest?

   a. .07   **b.** 1.003   **c.** .08   **d.** .075   **e.** .3

Less than 30 percent of 7100 students answered this question correctly.[4] Explain how to determine the correct answer by describing Decimal Squares for these decimals.

Approximation

8. a. Using a blank Decimal Square for tenths, determine how many complete parts should be shaded to best approximate $\frac{1}{3}$ of the whole square. Shade these parts. Beneath the square, record the decimal that represents the shaded part.

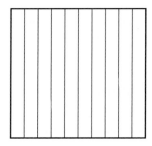

      ————

  b. Shade complete parts of each of these two blank Decimal Squares to best approximate $\frac{1}{3}$ of a whole square. Beneath each square, record the decimal that represents the shaded portion of the square.

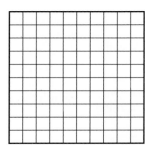   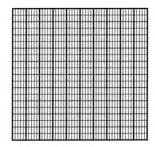

   ————   ————

[4]A. Grossman, "Decimal Notation: An Important Research Finding," *Arithmetic Teacher* 30 (May 1983): 32–33.

*c. Shade complete parts of each of these Decimal Squares to best approximate $\frac{1}{6}$ of a whole square. Write the decimal that represents the shaded part of each square.

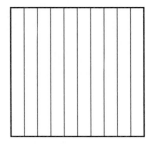

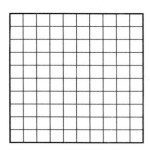

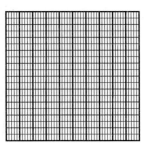

JUST FOR FUN

In Decimal Bingo you practice identifying equal decimals. The Decimal Place-Value Game provides more insight on place values.

DECIMAL BINGO (2 to 4 players)

Each player selects one of the following four bingo mats with decimals. The deck of Decimal Squares should be spread face down. Each player in turn takes a square and circles the decimal or decimals on the bingo mat that equal the decimal for the square. The winner is the first player to circle four decimals in any row, column, or diagonal.

.30	.400	.1	.70
.7	.55	.3	.8
.10	.40	.85	.95
.8	.300	.05	.550

Mat 1

.60	.50	.3	.10
.1	.75	.600	.5
.450	.30	.15	.525
.500	.45	.425	.750

Mat 2

.70	.2	.50	.40
.5	.4	.450	.65
.20	.700	.375	.675
.400	.45	.475	.650

Mat 3

.75	.300	.60	.4
.600	.9	.30	.350
.40	.750	.325	.25
.35	.6	.575	.90

Mat 4

DECIMAL PLACE-VALUE GAME (2 to 4 players)

Players each draw a place-value table like the one next to the dice. Each player in turn rolls two dice until he or she obtains a sum less than 10. The player then records this number in one of the three columns in his or her place-value table. Only one number is written in one column on each turn, and the number cannot be moved to another column after it has been written down. After each player has had three turns, the player with the greatest three-place decimal is the winner. The first player to win five rounds wins the game.[5]

Variation: Use a place-value table with four columns, and roll the dice to obtain the digits in a four-place decimal.

Place-Value Table

Tenths	Hundredths	Thousandths

---

[5]Another way to generate numbers for this game is to write each digit from 0 to 9 on a separate card and then draw one card at random from this deck. Replace the card before the next draw.

Follow-Up Questions and Activities **6.1**

1. *School Classroom:* The students in your class are discussing the relative values of several decimals. Richard claims that 0.15 is smaller than 0.125 since 15 parts is always less than 125 parts and Susan insists he has it backward but cannot explain why. How might you help these students use a Decimal Square model and correct decimal language to resolve this discussion?

2. *School Classroom:* Elementary students learn that one or more zeros can be placed at the end of a decimal without changing its value, but they usually do not understand why. Use Decimal Squares to illustrate 0.3 = 0.30 = 0.300 and write an explanation involving the use of additional zeros that would make sense to students. Copy Blank Decimal Squares from the companion website.

3. *School Classroom:* Illustrate and explain how you would use both the Decimal Squares model and the place value chart on the **Elementary School Text** page at the beginning of this section to help an elementary school student see that 2.3 > 2.29. Copy Blank Decimal Squares from the companion website.

4. *Math Concepts:* Use Decimal Squares to find a few decimal numbers between 0.5 and 0.6, a few decimal numbers between 0.49 and 0.5, and a few decimal numbers between 0.311 and 0.312. In each case, give the name of the decimal, illustrate the decimal with a Decimal Square sketch and explain your thinking. Copy Blank Decimal Squares from the companion website.

5. *Math Concepts:* Open the **Math Investigation 6.1: Read Me—Repeating Decimals Instructions** from the companion website and investigate the relationship between fractions and their decimal expansions as described in question 1 of the *Starting Points for Investigations 6.1.* Describe your investigation and explain your thinking.

6. *Math Concepts:* Sketch each of the following decimals on a blank Decimal Square and describe how you can use the Decimal Square representation to express each of these decimals as fraction. Copy Blank Decimal Squares from the companion website.

   a. 0.7

   b. 0.15

   c. 0.250

   d. 0.125

7. *NCTM Standards:* Read the **Grades 3–5 and 6–8 Number and Operations Standards** in the back pages of this book. Pick two *Expectations,* one from each level, which the activities in this section address. State the *Expectations* and the *Standards* they are under. Explain which activities from this section address these *Expectations* and how they do so.

BENNETT-BURTON-NELSON WEBSITE

www.mhhe.com/bbn

Virtual Manipulatives	Grid and Dot Paper	Links and Readings
Interactive Chapter Applets	Color Transparencies	Geometer Sketchpad Modules
Puzzlers	Extended Bibliography	

Activity Set **6.2**   # OPERATIONS WITH DECIMAL SQUARES

PURPOSE

To use Decimal Squares to illustrate decimal addition, subtraction, multiplication, and division.

Virtual Manipulatives

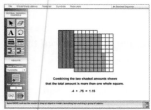

www.mhhe.com/bbn

MATERIALS

Decimal Squares from the Manipulative Kit or from the Virtual Manipulatives.

INTRODUCTION

It is common when computing on a calculator to get decimal numbers. Because of our technology and the frequent occurrence of decimals, it has been suggested that decimal concepts be taught earlier in the elementary school curriculum.

> Calculators create whole new opportunities for ordering the curriculum and for integrating mathematics into science. No longer need teachers be constrained by the artificial restriction to numbers that children know how to employ in the paper-and-pencil algorithms of arithmetic. Decimals can be introduced much earlier since they arise naturally on the calculator. Real measurements from science experiments can be used in mathematics lessons because the calculator will be able to add or multiply the data even if the children have not yet learned how. They may learn first what addition and multiplication mean and when to use them, and only later how to perform these operations manually in all possible cases.[6]

Early introduction of the decimal concepts of addition, subtraction, multiplication, and division in the elementary school curriculum makes it imperative that children have good physical and visual models that embody these concepts. The goal is to develop concepts and a decimal number sense rather than paper-and-pencil manipulative skills. For example, a child may not know the traditional moving-the-decimal-point algorithm of computing $.35 \div .05$ but may "see" that the answer is 7 by using the Decimal Squares model—and then verify this result by using a calculator. These figures show that the shaded part for .05 fits into the shaded part for .35 seven times.

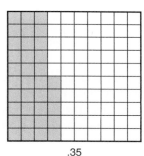

.35

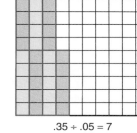

$.35 \div .05 = 7$

---

[6]National Research Council, *Everybody Counts: A Report to the Nation on the Future of Mathematics Education* (Washington, DC: The National Academy Press, 1989): 47–48.

Addition

1. Addition of decimals can be illustrated by determining the total shaded amount of two or more Decimal Squares. Fill in the missing number, and compute the sum by counting the total number of shaded parts.

a.

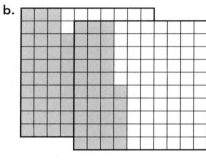

.3 + _____ = _____

b.

.38 + _____ = _____

c.

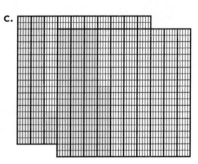

_____ + .355 = _____

d.

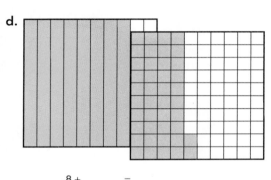

.8 + _____ = _____

e.

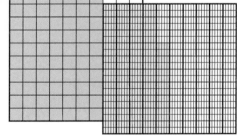

_____ + .470 = _____

f.

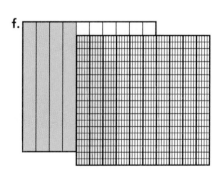

.4 + _____ = _____

I will learn to subtract decimals.

28.5 Subtract Decimals

Learn

Miguel's go-cart is 2.50 yards long. Sam's go-cart is 1.75 yards long. How much longer is Miguel's go-cart than Sam's go-cart?

Find: 2.50 − 1.75

Let's see how to connect models to paper and pencil.

Make Connections

	Models	Paper and Pencil
STEP 1 Shade to show 2.50.	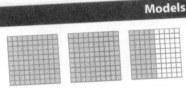	Line up the decimal points. $$\begin{array}{r} 2.50 \\ -\,1.75 \\ \hline \end{array}$$
STEP 2 Cut 1 whole and 75 small squares to show taking 1.75 away.		Start with the hundredths. Subtract each place. Regroup as needed. $$\begin{array}{r} \overset{\scriptstyle 14}{\underset{}{}}\\ 1\ \overset{}{4}\ 10 \\ \cancel{2}.\cancel{5}\cancel{0} \\ -\,1.75 \\ \hline 0\ 75 \end{array}$$
STEP 3 Count to find the difference.	You can also use a calculator.	Place the decimal point in the difference. 0.75

Miguel's go-cart is 0.75 yards longer than Sam's go-cart.

Try It   Subtract.

1. 3.4 − 1.7
2. 6.8 − 2.7
3. 0.76 − 0.37
4. 6.52 − 1.29

5. **Write About It**   **Explain** how you can check the answer when subtracting decimals.

2. Shade each Decimal Square to represent the decimal written beneath it. Add the decimals by determining the total shaded amount of the two squares. Explain how you arrived at your answer.

*a.

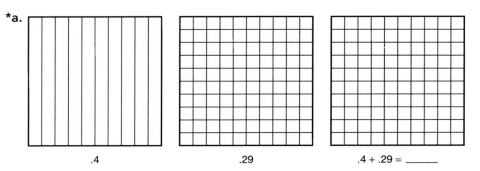

.4   .29   .4 + .29 = _____

Explanation:

b.

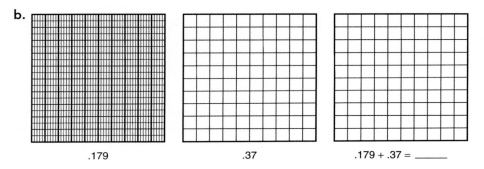

.179   .37   .179 + .37 = _____

Explanation:

*c.

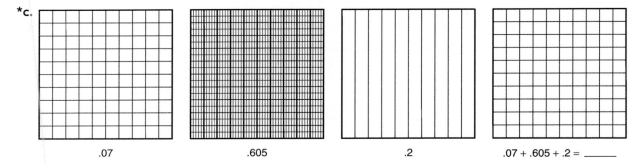

.07   .605   .2   .07 + .605 + .2 = _____

Explanation:

Subtraction

Take away

3. Subtraction of decimals can be illustrated with Decimal Squares by circling the amount to be taken away—*take-away concept for subtraction*—and counting the number of shaded parts that remain.

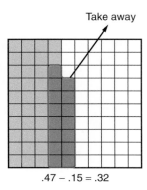

.47 − .15 = .32

For each of the following, outline the amount to be taken away and complete the equation.

a.

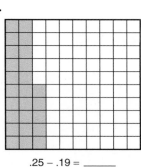

.25 − .19 = _____

b.

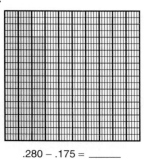

.280 − .175 = _____

c.

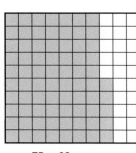

.75 − .08 = _____

4. Shade each Decimal Square to represent the decimal written beneath it. Determine the difference by *comparing* the shaded parts of the squares. In part a, for example, you may find the difference by determining what must be added to .07 to get .5. Briefly explain how you arrived at each answer.

*a.

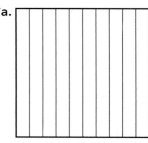

.5

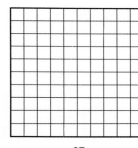

.07

.5 − .07 = _____

Explanation:

b.

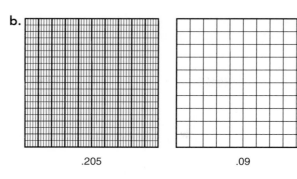

.205   .09   .205 − .09 = _____

Explanation:

*c.

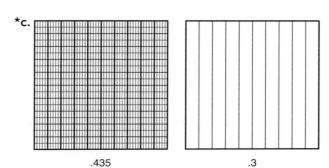

.435   .3   .435 − .3 = _____

Explanation:

Multiplication

5. Here is the Decimal Square for .45. If there were 3 of these Decimal Squares, there would be a total of 3 × 45 = 135 shaded parts. Since there are 100 parts in each whole square, the total shaded amount would be 1 whole square and 35 parts out of 100.

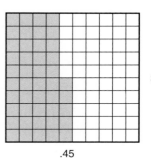

3 × .45 = 1.35

.45

In a similar manner, compute the following products and explain your answers in terms of the shaded parts of Decimal Squares.

a. 6 × .83 = _____

*b. 4 × .725 = _____

*c. Explain, using a Decimal Square for .35, why multiplication by 10 results in a decimal number with the same digits but with the decimal point in a different place.

6. The product .3 × .2 means "take 3 tenths of 2 tenths." To do this, we split the shaded amount of the .2 square into 10 equal parts and take 3 of them. The result is 6 hundredths. This blue region shows that .3 × .2 = .06.

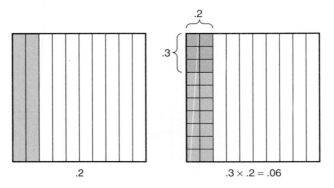

The shaded portion of the first figure below represents the decimal 1.2. When the shaded area representing 1.2 is split into 10 equal parts and 3 are taken, as shown by the blue region in the second figure, the result is 3 tenths and 6 hundredths, or 36 hundredths. Notice in the second figure that .3 and 1.2 are also the lengths of the edges of the blue rectangle. That is, we are using a rectangular model for decimal multiplication, similar to the rectangular model for multiplying two two-digit whole numbers.

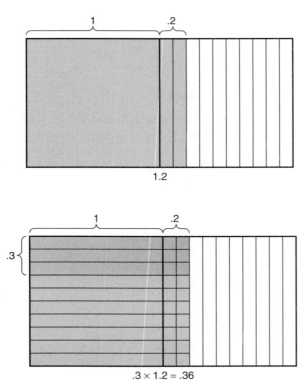

The product 1.3×1.2 can be found by forming a rectangle with dimensions 1.3×1.2, as shown below. The blue rectangular region represents 1 unit, 5 tenths, and 6 hundredths, so $1.3 \times 1.2 = 1.56$. Notice the top portion of the blue rectangle model shows 1×1.2 and the lower portion of the model shows $.3 \times 1.2$. The sum of these two partial products is 1.56. You can also think of this model as showing the four partial products (1×1, $1 \times .2$, $.3 \times 1$, $.3 \times .2$) whose sum is also 1.56.

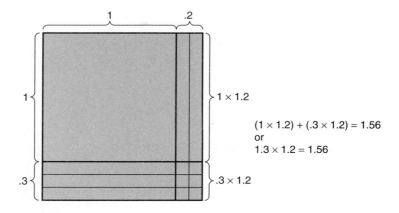

In a similar manner, sketch a Decimal Square diagram to illustrate each of the following. Label the dimensions of the rectangle, determine the product from the diagram, and explain your reasoning.

a. $.4 \times .3 =$ _____

b. $.4 \times 1.3 =$ _____

*c. $1.4 \times 1.3 =$ _____

d. $2.4 \times 1.3 =$ _____

Division

7. The *sharing method of division* can be used to illustrate the division of a decimal by a whole number. In the Decimal Square shown here, the shaded portion representing .60 has been divided into 3 equal parts to illustrate .60 ÷ 3. Since each of these parts has 20 shaded parts (out of 100), .60 divided by 3 is .20.

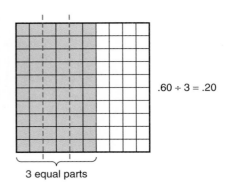

.60 ÷ 3 = .20

3 equal parts

Divide each Decimal Square into the given number of parts, and use the result to determine the quotient.

a.

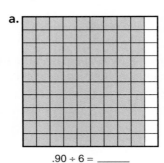

.90 ÷ 6 = _____

b.

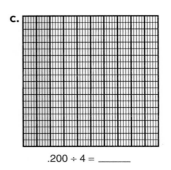

.75 ÷ 3 = _____

c.

.200 ÷ 4 = _____

8. Use the following Decimal Squares to determine the indicated quotients. Record each quotient beneath the square, and shade that amount for the quotient on the Decimal Square.

a.

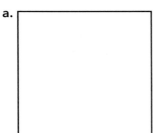

1 ÷ 10 = _____

b.

.1 ÷ 10 = _____

c.

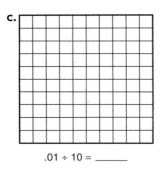

.01 ÷ 10 = _____

*9. In view of the results in activity 8, explain why dividing a decimal number, such as 2.87, by 10 results in a decimal with the same digits but the decimal point moved one place to the left.

10. The *measurement concept of division* involves repeatedly measuring off or subtracting one amount from another. It can be seen in the Decimal Square shown here that 15 of the shaded parts can be measured off from 75 parts 5 times.

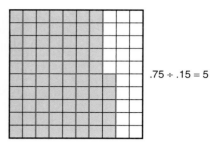

$.75 \div .15 = 5$

Draw lines on the following Decimal Squares to indicate how the measurement concept of division can be used to obtain each indicated quotient.

a.
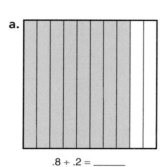

$.8 \div .2 =$ _____

*b.
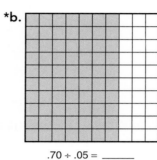

$.70 \div .05 =$ _____

c.
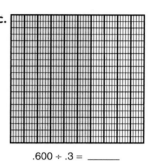

$.600 \div .3 =$ _____

*d. On the Second National Assessment of Educational Progress, students were asked to estimate $250 \div .5$. Only 39 percent of the 17-year-olds correctly estimated this quotient; 47 percent ignored the decimal point, giving an answer of 50.[7] Use the measurement concept of division to explain why $250 \div .5 = 500$.

All Four Operations

11. a. Complete the following equations by placing each of these 10 decimals in exactly one of the boxes.

.3   .75   .8   .650   .15   .2   .35   .45   .400   .350

☐ + ☐ = ☐

☐ − ☐ = ☐

4 × ☐ = ☐

☐ ÷ ☐ = 3

[7]National Assessment of Educational Progress, "Math Achievement Is Plus and Minus," *NAEP Newsletter* 12(5) (October 1979): 2.

b. Spread your Decimal Squares face down and select 10 of them. List your 10 decimals here. Using each of your decimals only once, complete as many of the following four equations as possible.

10 decimals selected: _____, _____, _____, _____, _____,

_____, _____, _____, _____, _____,

$$\boxed{} + \boxed{} = \boxed{}$$

$$\boxed{} - \boxed{} = \boxed{}$$

$$3 \times \boxed{} = \boxed{}$$

$$\boxed{} \div \boxed{} = 2$$

c. *Solitaire:* The activity in part b can be played like a solitaire game. See how many turns it takes you to complete the four equations by selecting only 10 Decimal Squares on each turn.

JUST FOR FUN

Build skills in performing operations on decimals with these games—addition in the first game, division in the second, and subtraction in the third.

DECIMAL SQUARES BLACKJACK
(2 to 4 players)

The dealer shuffles the deck of Decimal Squares and deals one square face down to each player. The dealer also gets one square. The object of the game is to use one or more squares to get a decimal or a sum of two or more decimals that is less than or equal to 1, without going over. To get an additional square from the dealer, a player says "Hit me." When a player wants no more additional squares, he or she says "I'm holding." After every player has said "I'm holding," the players show their squares. The player whose sum is closest to 1, but not greater than 1, wins 1 point. The winner is the first player to win 5 points.

GREATEST QUOTIENT (2 to 4 players)

Spread the Decimal Squares face down. Each player chooses two squares and computes the quotient of one decimal divided by the other. The object is to get the greatest quotient. The player with the greatest quotient wins all the squares used in that round, including any discarded squares. If there is a tie, the squares are placed aside and the winner of the next round gets them. Play continues until the deck has been played through and no more rounds are possible. The winner is the player who has won the most squares.

Chance Option: A player can attempt to increase a quotient by choosing a new square. However, before choosing a new square, the player must discard one of the previously chosen squares.

GREATEST DIFFERENCE (2 to 4 players)

This game is similar to the greatest quotient game except that the player with the greatest difference wins the round.

Follow-Up Questions and Activities 6.2

1. *School Classroom:* One of your students cannot understand how to add decimals by using the standard algorithm where decimal points are aligned before adding. Illustrate how you can use the Decimal Square model and correct decimal language to help the student resolve this issue using the sum of the decimals .5, .15, and .175 as an example.

2. *School Classroom:* Design a few questions that you believe are appropriate for helping an upper elementary school student understand how to subtract decimals using a Decimal Squares model and the comparison method of subtraction. Try this activity on an upper elementary school age child of your choice. Record your questions and the student's responses.

3. *School Classroom:* The Decimal Squares subtraction modeled on the **Elementary School Text** page at the beginning of this section used the Take Away Subtraction Method (see activity 7 in Activity Set 3.2). Draw a sketch and describe how this same subtraction would be modeled using Decimal Squares and the Missing Addend Subtraction Method.

4. *Math Concepts:* For each of the following, draw a sketch to show how a Decimal Squares model is used to compute the sum or difference and explain how the model matches the placement of decimal points in the standard paper-and-pencil algorithm. Copy Blank Decimal Squares from the companion website.

   a. $0.3 + 0.5$ **b.** $0.4 + 0.65$

   c. $0.85 - 0.2$ **d.** $0.7 - 0.15$

5. *Math Concepts:* For each of the following, draw a sketch to show how a Decimal Squares model is used to compute the product or quotient and explain how the model matches the standard paper-and-pencil algorithm. Copy Blank Decimal Squares from the companion website.

   a. $.2 \times .5$

   b. 1.2×1.5

   c. $.75 \div .15$

6. *Math Concepts:* In activity 10, the measurement concept of division is used as an approach to divide one decimal by another decimal. However, another way to compute the quotient is to multiply the dividend and the divisor by the same power of 10 and just do whole number division. For example, $.75 \div .15 = 75 \div 15$, $.8 \div .2 = 8 \div 2$, and $.70 \div .05 = 70 \div 5$. Use the Decimal Square model to explain why division of decimals like these can be replaced by division involving whole numbers.

7. *NCTM Standards:* Go to the **Grade 6–8 Number and Operations Standards** in the back pages of this book and find the *"Understand Meanings of Operations"* Standard. Explain how using a Decimal Square model can help a middle school student understand the meaning of decimal addition and subtraction.

BENNETT-BURTON-NELSON WEBSITE

www.mhhe.com/bbn

Virtual Manipulatives	Grid and Dot Paper	Links and Readings
Interactive Chapter Applets	Color Transparencies	Geometer Sketchpad Modules
Puzzlers	Extended Bibliography	

Activity Set **6.3**   A MODEL FOR INTRODUCING PERCENT

PURPOSE

To use base-ten pieces to introduce the concept of percent and to illustrate and solve various percent problems.

Virtual Manipulatives

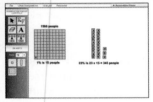

www.mhhe.com/bbn

MATERIALS

Base-Ten Pieces from the Manipulative Kit or from the Virtual Manipulatives.

INTRODUCTION

Percent is a common and widely used mathematical concept. From television to newspapers to shopping, the word percent enters our life almost daily, as noted in the following passage.

> Percentages are everywhere—in the food we eat ([a serving of] cornflakes contains 25% of our recommended daily allowance of vitamin A), in the clothes we wear (35% cotton), in our favorite television programs (watched by 55% of the television audience), and in the money we earn (27% tax bracket) and spend ($5\frac{1}{2}$% sales tax). In modern society, people who do not understand percentages will have difficulty reading articles and advertisements that appear in newspapers, determining if they are being cheated by financial institutions or retail establishments, or knowing if they are being misled by politicians.[8]

When something is divided into 100 equal parts, one part is called *one percent* and written 1%. The 10 by 10 grids from the base-ten pieces are divided into 100 equal parts so the smallest square is 1 percent and the whole grid is 100 percent. These number pieces will be used to explore the concept of percent and solve various percent problems.

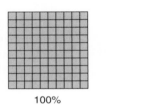
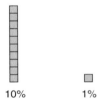

100%   10%   1%

The classical three cases of percent are visualized in this activity set using this model.

Percent and whole: 25% of 150 = ?
Part and whole: ?% of 150 = 90
Percent and part: 6% of ? = 24

At the end of this activity set, Fraction Bars are split into approximately 100 parts to provide percent and decimal estimations for fractions.

---

1. If the 10 by 10 grid represents 100%, determine what percent is represented by each of these collections of base-ten pieces.

*a.   b.   *c.   *d.   e.

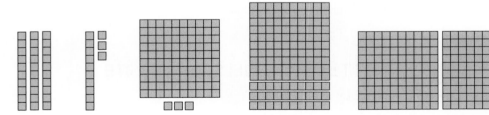

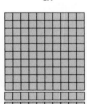

Percent: _____   _____   _____   _____   _____

[8]James H. Wiebe, "Manipulating Percentages," *The Mathematics Teacher* (January 1986): 23–26.

2. If the 10 by 10 grid represents 100%, use your base-ten pieces to form a collection to represent each of the percentages below. Draw sketches to record your answers.

   *a. 23%   **b.** 98%   ***c.** 105%

   d. 123%   **e.** 202%   ***f.** $\frac{1}{2}$%

Value 300

3. Suppose that a value of 300 is assigned to the 10 by 10 grid and that this value is spread evenly among all the small squares. Use this value for parts a–e.

   *a. Describe an easy method for performing a mental calculation to find the value of one small square.

   Using mental calculations determine the value of each of the following collections of base-ten pieces:

   b.

   Value: _____

   *c.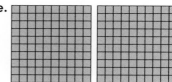

   Value: _____

   d.

   Value: _____

   e.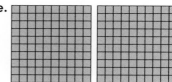

   Value: _____

Unit 14   Enrichment

Relating Fractions, Decimals, and Percents

VOCABULARY

percent

ratio

You have seen how fractions and decimals name parts of a whole. **Percent** is another way of naming part of a whole.

Percent means per hundred. The grid shows that 25 out of 100 squares are orange. You can write this as a percent: 25% of the grid is orange.

You can also write the amount as a fraction:
25 out of 100 $= \frac{25}{100} = \frac{1}{4}$

You can write the amount as a decimal:
25 out of 100 = 25 hundredths $= 0.25$

$25\% = \frac{25}{100} = 0.25$

25% of the squares are orange.

You can also write a ratio to compare the parts of the grid. A **ratio** compares two quantities. You can write a ratio as a fraction.

There are 25 orange parts out of 100 parts. You can also write this ratio in this form:
25 : 100, or 1 : 4

Write the percent for the shaded part. Then write the percent as a fraction in simplest form, as a decimal in simplest form and as a ratio.

1.

2.

3.

4.

5.

6.

Write the percent as both a fraction and a decimal.

7. 50%

8. 10%

9. 44%

10. 77%

11. What is 100% as a fraction? As a decimal?

Percent and Whole

Value 150

4. Suppose the 10 by 10 grid is assigned a value of 150 and this value is spread evenly among all the small squares. For each part a–e, select and sketch the collection of base-ten pieces that represents the given **percent** of a 10 by 10 grid. Determine the **value** of each collection without just doing paper-and-pencil computations.

*a. The value of 30% of 150 = ?

b. The value of 75% of 150 = ?

*c. The value of 7% of 150 = ?

d. The value of 111% of 150 = ?

e. The value of 210% of 150 = ?

f. Explain how you can use base-ten pieces to determine the value of a percent of a whole.

Part and Whole

Value 450

5. Assign a value of 450 to the 10 by 10 grid. For each part a–e, select and sketch the collection of base-ten pieces that represents the given **value**. Determine what **percent** of the 10 by 10 grid the value represents.

*a. ? % of 450 = 45

b. ? % of 450 = 108

c. ? % of 450 = 441

d. ? % of 450 = 585

e. ? % of 450 = 909

f. Explain how you can use base-ten pieces to determine what percent of the whole a given value (part) is.

Percent and part

6. For each part a–e, select and sketch the collection of base-ten pieces that represents the given **percent** of a 10 by 10 grid. In each part, if the collection has the given **value,** what is the value of the entire 10 by 10 grid?

*a. 6% of ? = 24

b. 40% of ? = 30

*c. 55% of ? = 132

d. 125% of ? = 180

e. Explain how you can use base-ten pieces to determine the value of a whole given the value of a percent of the whole.

Some Percent Statements

7. Many statements that deal with percent can be represented with the base-ten piece model. Consider the statement "Last year the charity benefit raised $6720, which was 120% of its goal." 120% can be represented with these base-ten pieces.

There are several observations that can be made by looking at the model:

(1) Because 120% has a value of $6720, one can see from the model that each long has a value of $560 ($6720 ÷ 12) or that each small square has a value of $56 ($6720 ÷ 120).

(2) Last year's goal (100%) must have been $5600 (10 × $560 or 100 × $56).

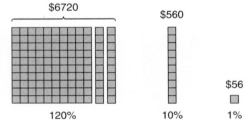

(3) The goal was exceeded by $1120 ($6720 − $5600).

Model each of the following statements with your base-ten pieces. Make a sketch of your model, record at least one *percent* observation, and explain how you arrived at it.

*a. 65% of the firm's 320 employees were women.

*b. 280 of the school's 800 students were absent.

c. I bought this sweater for $126 at the store's 30% off sale.

d. This year the charity benefit had a goal of $7000 and it raised 135% of its goal.

e. In a certain county, 57 of the schools have a student-to-teacher ratio that is greater than the recommendations for accreditation. The 57 schools are 38% of the number of schools in the county.

f. A new company entered the New York Stock Exchange in July and by December the price of each share of stock had risen (increased) 223% to $32.50 a share.

Fractions as Percents

8. Fractions with denominators that are factors of 100 can be readily expressed as percents. For example, if each part of a $\frac{3}{4}$ Fraction Bar is split into 25 equal parts, the bar will have 75 parts shaded out of 100 equal parts. So $\frac{3}{4}$ equals 75%, or the decimal .75.

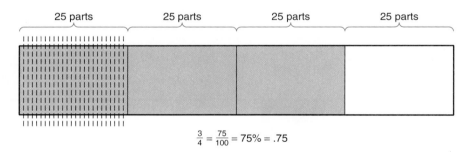

$$\frac{3}{4} = \frac{75}{100} = 75\% = .75$$

Imagine splitting each of the following Fraction Bars into 100 equal parts. Indicate above each part of a bar the number of new parts after splitting, and then determine the percent and decimal equivalents for each fraction.

a.

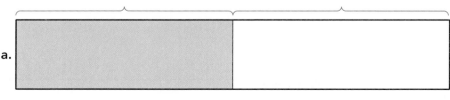

$$\frac{1}{2} = \frac{}{100} = \underline{\hspace{1cm}} \% = . \underline{\hspace{1cm}}$$

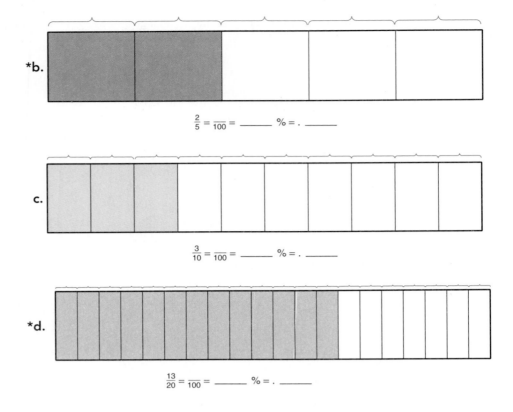

*b.

$$\frac{2}{5} = \frac{}{100} = \text{\_\_\_\_\_} \% = .\text{\_\_\_\_\_}$$

c.

$$\frac{3}{10} = \frac{}{100} = \text{\_\_\_\_\_} \% = .\text{\_\_\_\_\_}$$

*d.

$$\frac{13}{20} = \frac{}{100} = \text{\_\_\_\_\_} \% = .\text{\_\_\_\_\_}$$

Fractions as Approximate Percents

9. To obtain an approximate percent for the fraction $\frac{1}{7}$, visualize a $\frac{1}{7}$ Fraction Bar. This bar has 1 part shaded out of 7 parts. If each part of the bar is split into 14 equal parts, the result will be 14 shaded parts out of 98 parts.

14 parts

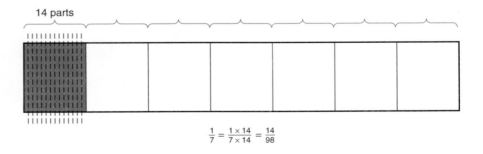

$$\frac{1}{7} = \frac{1 \times 14}{7 \times 14} = \frac{14}{98}$$

If each part of the $\frac{1}{7}$ bar is split in 15 equal parts, there will be 15 shaded parts out of 105 parts.

15 parts

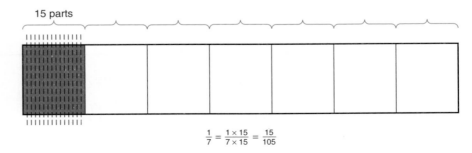

$$\frac{1}{7} = \frac{1 \times 15}{7 \times 15} = \frac{15}{105}$$

Because 105 is not as close to 100 as 98 is, we can say that $\frac{1}{7}$ is approximately 14%. Since 14% is $\frac{14}{100}$, the decimal .14 is also an approximation for $\frac{1}{7}$.

Determine a percent and decimal approximation for each of the following fractions by splitting the corresponding Fraction Bar into approximately 100 parts (or visualizing the splitting). Explain how you arrived at your percent for each fraction by indicating the number of parts due to splitting. (Remember, each part of the bar must be split into the same number of equal parts.)

a. $\frac{1}{3} \approx \overline{100} = $ _____ % = . _____

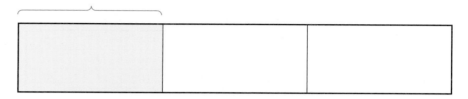

*b. $\frac{5}{6} \approx \overline{100} = $ _____ % = . _____

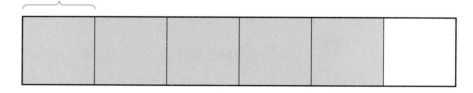

c. $\frac{2}{9} \approx \overline{100} = $ _____ % = . _____

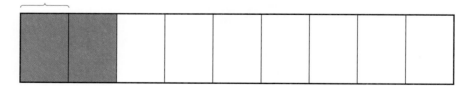

JUST FOR FUN

GAME OF INTEREST (2 to 4 players)

This game requires the Color Tiles (for markers), the 1-to-12 Spinner from the Manipulative Kit, and the game mat on Material Card 18.

Each player chooses markers of one color and players spin to see who will play first (high number). In turns, players spin to obtain a percent with the number 1–10 representing 1% to 10%. (If the spinner ends on the numbers 11 or 12 spin again.) The player spinning then mentally computes

that percent of one of the following amounts, $50, $100, $200, $300, $400, $500, or $600, and places a marker on the number in the table corresponding to the correct percent of that amount (the *interest*). The game continues until one player, the winner, gets 4 adjacent markers in a row either vertically, horizontally, or diagonally.

Example: Spin 7%; choose to take 7% of $400, which is $28; place a color marker on the number 28 on the gameboard.

Interest Gameboard

	$50	$100	$200	$300	$400	$500	$600	
.5	1	1.5	2	2.5	3	3.5	4	4.5	5
1	2	3	4	5	6	7	8	9	10
2	4	6	8	10	12	14	16	18	20
3	6	9	12	15	18	21	24	27	30
4	8	12	16	20	24	28	32	36	40
5	10	15	20	25	30	35	40	45	50
6	12	18	24	30	36	42	48	54	60

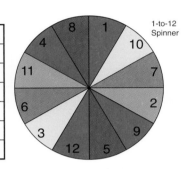

1-to-12 Spinner

COMPETING AT PLACE VALUE APPLET

This applet is a two-person game in which each player tries to form the largest possible four-place decimal by placing digits from the spinner into the place value table. In the following example, you are playing against the Robot. In which box of the place value table would you place the "5" from the spinner? As you play this game, try to determine the Robot's strategy in placing digits in the table. For example, since you have one more random number to place in the last box, in which box of the place value table would you place the "5" from the spinner?

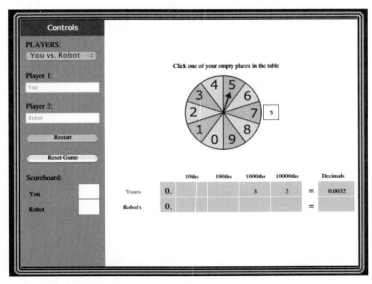

Competing at Place Value, Chapter 6
www.mhhe.com/bbn

Follow-Up Questions and Activities 6.3

1. *School Classroom:* Several of your students are unsure about how to determine the original price of an item, and their savings, when an item is advertised as "On sale for $10.99 at 30% of the original cost." How can you use the base-ten piece percent model to help your students? Include diagrams with your explanation.

2. *School Classroom:* Some of your students are in disagreement about the answer to the following question. Explain how you can use base-ten pieces or percent grids to help them with this problem.

   If an amount first increases in value by 50% and then decreases in value by 50%, will it return to its original value or to more or less than its original value?

3. *School Classroom:* Represent $\frac{1}{2}$ percent on a 10 by 10 grid. Then, as on the **Elementary School Text** page at the beginning of this section, explain how the diagram helps you express $\frac{1}{2}$ percent as a fraction, a decimal, and a ratio (of whole numbers).

4. *Math Concepts:* Model each of the following with your base-ten pieces; sketch the model, label the sketch clearly, and record at least one percent observation about each statement. In each case, explain your reasoning.

   a. 70 percent of the 120 students in the class are women.

   b. 10 of the 30 students in the class want to teach middle school.

   c. Jane spent $25 on teaching supplies at the education center's 35 percent off sale.

5. *Math Concepts:*

   a. If an amount doubles in value, by what percent has the amount increased? Include base-ten piece diagrams with your explanation of the solution.

   b. If an amount triples in value, by what percent has the amount increased? Include base-ten piece diagrams with your explanation of the solution.

6. *Math Concepts:* For each of the following, explain your thinking and include diagrams or sketches of base-ten pieces or percent grids to justify your solution.

   a. If 3% of an amount has a value of $45, what is the value of 100%?

   b. If 45% of an amount has a value of $3, what is the value of 100%?

   c. Are part a and part b the same question or different questions? Explain your thinking.

7. *NCTM Standards:* Go to http://illuminations.nctm.org/ and under "Lessons" select grade levels 6–8 and the **Number and Operations Standard.** Choose a lesson about percents.

   a. State the title of the lesson and briefly summarize the lesson.

   b. Referring to the **Standards Summary** in the back pages of this book as necessary, list the *Number and Operation Standard Expectations* that the lesson addresses and explain how the lesson addresses these *Expectations.*

 ## BENNETT-BURTON-NELSON WEBSITE

www.mhhe.com/bbn

Virtual Manipulatives	Grid and Dot Paper	Links and Readings
Interactive Chapter Applets	Color Transparencies	Geometer Sketchpad Modules
Puzzlers	Extended Bibliography	

Activity Set **6.4** IRRATIONAL NUMBERS ON THE GEOBOARD

PURPOSE

To use geoboards and/or dot paper to represent figures whose sides and perimeters have lengths that are irrational numbers.

Virtual Manipulatives

www.mhhe.com/bbn

MATERIALS

A geoboard and rubber bands (optional). There is a template for making a rectangular geoboard on Material Card 8 or you may wish to use the geoboard in the Virtual Manipulatives.

INTRODUCTION

When we used the rod model for greatest common factors (Activity Set 4.2), we saw that any two rods with whole number lengths could be cut evenly into pieces of equal common length. In some cases, the lengths of the rods may be relatively prime, like 3 and 8, but the rods can still be cut evenly into pieces with common length 1.

If two rods do not have whole number lengths but do have rational number lengths, can they still be cut evenly into rods of equal common length? Again the answer is yes. Suppose, for example, the rods have lengths $3\frac{1}{3}$ and $5\frac{1}{2}$. Because these numbers are equal to $3\frac{2}{6}$ and $5\frac{3}{6}$, the rods can both be cut evenly into pieces of length $\frac{1}{6}$.

Does it then follow that any two lengths can be evenly cut into pieces of equal common length? About 2300 years ago, mathematicians would have answered yes. They thought that any two lengths are *commensurable*—that is, have a common unit of measure. This unit might be very small, such as a millionth or a billionth of an inch, but surely there would always be such a length. When the Greek mathematician Hippasus (470 B.C.E.) discovered that the side and the diagonal of a square are *incommensurable*—that is, do not have a common unit of measure—he caused such a crisis in mathematics that, reportedly, he was taken to sea and never returned. His discovery ultimately led to new types of numbers, called *irrational numbers,* which are represented by infinite nonrepeating decimals.

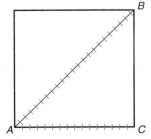

In a square, diagonal $\overline{AB}$ and side $\overline{AC}$ cannot be cut into pieces of equal common length.

1. Region *X* represents 1 unit of area on the geoboard. Region *Y* can be subdivided into 6 unit squares and 4 halves so that it has an area of 8 square units. If this figure is formed on the geoboard, it may be helpful to use rubber bands to subdivide it into unit squares and halves. Region *Z* is half of a rectangle of area 6 square units, so *Z* has an area of 3 square units.

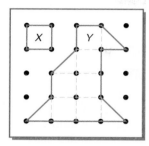 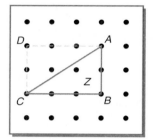

Assuming each small square represents 1 square unit, determine the area of each of the following geoboard regions. Record the areas inside the figures.

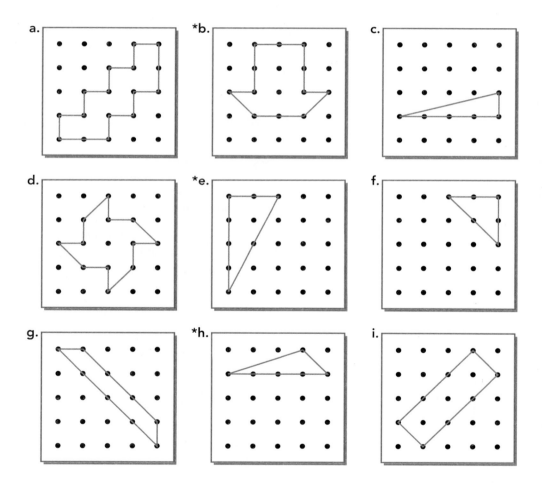

11-3a   HANDS-ON LAB   *A Preview of Lesson 11-3*

The Pythagorean Theorem

What You'll LEARN

Find the relationship among the sides of a right triangle.

Materials

• centimeter grid paper
• ruler
• scissors

INVESTIGATE *Work as a class.*

Four thousand years ago, the ancient Egyptians used mathematics to lay out their fields with square corners. They took a piece of rope and knotted it into 12 equal spaces. Taking three stakes, they stretched the rope around the stakes to form a right triangle. The sides of the triangle had lengths of 3, 4, and 5 units.

STEP 1   On grid paper, draw a segment that is 3 centimeters long. At one end of this segment, draw a perpendicular segment that is 4 centimeters long. Draw a third segment to form a triangle. Cut out the triangle.

STEP 2   Measure the length of the longest side in centimeters. In this case, it is 5 centimeters.

STEP 3   Cut out three squares: one with 3 centimeters on a side, one with 4 centimeters on a side, and one with 5 centimeters on a side.

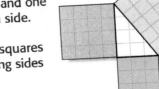

STEP 4   Place the edges of the squares against the corresponding sides of the right triangle.

STEP 5   Find the area of each square.

Writing Math

Work with a partner.

1. What relationship exists among the areas of the three squares?

Repeat the activity for each right triangle whose perpendicular sides have the following measures. Write an equation to show your findings.

2. 6 cm, 8 cm

3. 5 cm, 12 cm

4. **Write** a sentence or two summarizing your findings.

5. **MAKE A CONJECTURE** Determine the length of the third side of a right triangle if the perpendicular sides of the triangle are 9 inches and 12 inches long.

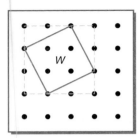

2. One way to determine the area of square W is to enclose it inside the larger square. If each small square represents 1 square unit, then the larger square has area 9 square units. Since each triangular region between the square W and the large square has an area of 1 square unit, the area of square W is (9 square units − 4 square units) = 5 square units.

Here are seven other squares that can be constructed on the geoboard. Determine the area of each square. Record the areas inside the squares.

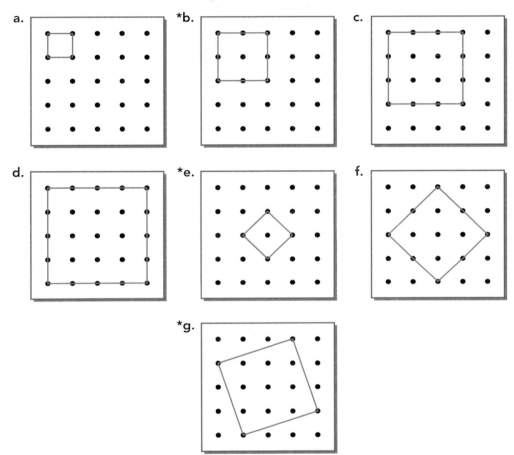

3. For any square, the length of a side times itself gives the area of the square.

$$\text{side length} \times \text{side length} = \text{area}$$

Square W in activity 2 has an area of 5 square units. The length of a side of square W is $\sqrt{5}$ units because by definition $\sqrt{5}$ is *the positive number that, when multiplied times itself, gives 5.* That is, $\sqrt{5} \times \sqrt{5} = 5$. One of the squares in activity 2 has an area of 9 square units, and the length of a side is $\sqrt{9} = 3$ units.

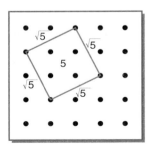
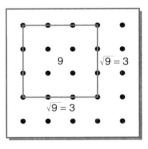

Finish recording the areas (from least to greatest) and the corresponding side lengths for the eight squares in activity 2.

Area of square (square units): _____ _____ _____ 5 _____ 9 _____ _____

Length of side (units):   _____ _____ _____ $\sqrt{5}$ _____ 3 _____ _____

*4. Determine the lengths of the three line segments in the next figure by first drawing a square on each segment and finding the area of the square. (The corners of a sheet of paper can be used to draw the sides and locate the corners of the square. The corners of each square will be on dots. The dotted lines form a square on segment a.) Record the side lengths by the line segments.

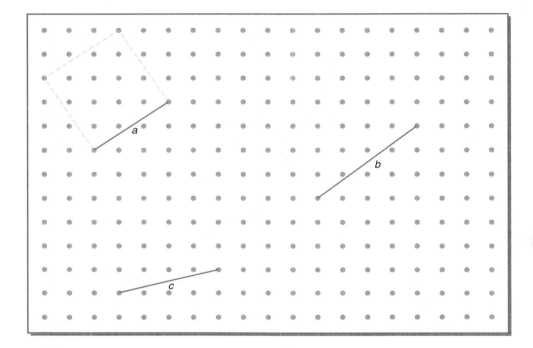

5. Calculator Activity: If n is a positive integer and not a perfect square (that is, n is not 1, 4, 9, 16, 25, 36, . . .), then $\sqrt{n}$ is an *irrational number.* For example, $\sqrt{5}$ is an irrational number. When written as decimals, irrational numbers have infinite and nonrepeating decimal expansions.

a. Use the $\sqrt{\ }$ key on your calculator to obtain an approximate value for $\sqrt{5}$. Record the decimal from your calculator display. (If you do not have a square root key you can raise 5 to the $\frac{1}{2}$ or .5 power.)

b. Multiply the calculator's decimal for $\sqrt{5}$ times itself and record the result. Did you get 5? Explain why a calculator might, or might not, produce a 5.

c. Explain the advantages of labeling the length of a segment with a symbol like √5 rather than writing out the digits for √5 that appear on a calculator display.

6. Each of the following figures has three squares surrounding a right triangle (a right triangle has one angle of 90°). For each figure, use the techniques from activity 2 to determine the area of each square and complete the table.

	Square A	Square B	Square C
a. Figure 1	_____	_____	_____
*b. Figure 2	_____	_____	_____
c. Figure 3	_____	_____	_____
*d. Figure 4	_____	_____	_____

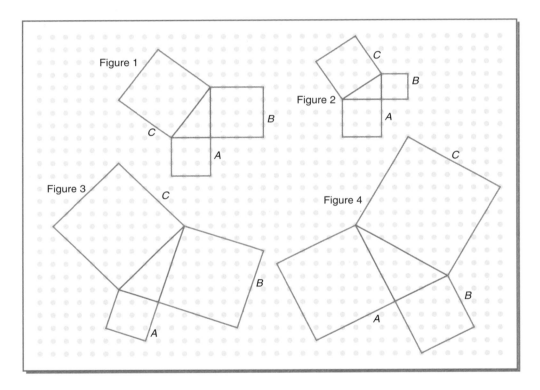

7. For every right triangle, the same relationship holds between the area of the square on the longest side (the hypotenuse) and the area of the squares on the other two sides (the legs).

a. Use the data from activity 6 to make a conjecture, in writing, about this relationship.

b. Use the relationship from part a to find the area of the square on the hypotenuse for each of the following figures by completing the first two columns of the table and using the results to determine the length of each hypotenuse.

	Total Area of Squares on Two Legs	Area of Square on Hypotenuse	Length of Hypotenuse
(1) Figure 1	————	————	————
*(2) Figure 2	————	————	————
(3) Figure 3	————	————	————
*(4) Figure 4	————	————	————

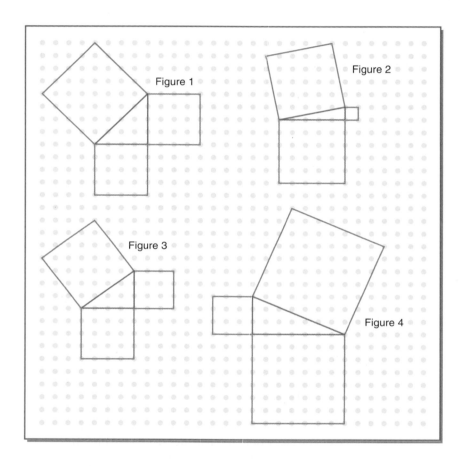

JUST FOR FUN

GOLDEN RECTANGLES

Some rectangles are more aesthetically pleasing than others. One in particular, the *golden rectangle,* has been the favorite of architects, sculptors, and artists for over 3000 years. The Greeks of the fifth century B.C.E. were fond of this rectangle. The front of the Parthenon in Athens fits into a golden rectangle.

Parthenon

In the nineteenth century, the German psychologist Gustav Fechner found that most people unconsciously favor the golden rectangle. Which one of the following rectangles do you feel has the most pleasing dimensions?

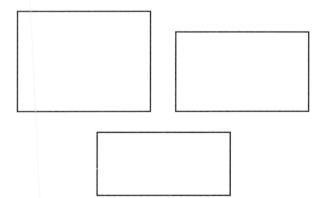

The length of a golden rectangle divided by its width is an irrational number that, when rounded to three decimal places, is 1.618. Measure the preceding rectangles to determine which is closest to a golden rectangle. Measure some other rectangles, such as greeting cards, credit cards, business cards, index cards, pictures, and mirrors, to see if you can find a golden rectangle. (A ratio of 1.6 is close enough.) Check the ratio of the length of the front of the Parthenon to its width in the diagram on this page.

A golden rectangle can be constructed from a square such as *ABCD* by placing a compass on the midpoint of side $\overline{AB}$ and swinging an arc *DF.* Then *FBCE* is a golden rectangle.

Make a golden rectangle, and check the ratio of its sides. If the sides of the square have length 2, then $BF = 1 + \sqrt{5}$. Use your calculator to determine $(1 + \sqrt{5}) \div 2$ (the ratio of the sides of the rectangle) to three decimal places. Cut out your rectangle and fold it in half along its longer side. Is the result another golden rectangle?

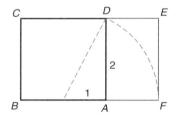

The ratio of the sides of a golden rectangle is called the *golden mean* or *golden ratio.*[9] It is surprising that this number (approximately 1.618) is also associated with the Fibonacci numbers: 1, 1, 2, 3, 5, 8, 13, ... The ratios of successive terms in this sequence ($\frac{1}{1}, \frac{2}{1}, \frac{3}{2}, \frac{5}{3}, \frac{5}{8}, \dots$) get closer and closer to the golden ratio. The ratio $\frac{8}{5}$, for example, is 1.6. Use your calculator to determine how far you must go in the Fibonacci sequence before the ratio of numbers is approximately 1.618.

[9]Several occurrences of the golden ratio are described in C. F. Linn, *The Golden Mean* (New York: Doubleday, 1974).

Follow-Up Questions and Activities 6.4

1. *School Classroom:* Marthona often mixes up the Pythagorean theorem and will use $a^2 + b^2 = c^2$ as well as $a^2 = b^2 + c^2$ or $b^2 = a^2 + c^2$ when a and b are the legs and c is the hypotenuse of a right triangle. How can you help her understand the theorem and resolve this issue?

2. *School Classroom:* Suppose that you are teaching an elementary school class that is studying decimal operations. Design an activity for the class that uses decimal operations and that involves the golden rectangle (described in the **Just for Fun** activity in this section), the golden ratio (1.618 rounded), and measuring. Describe your activity in detail.

3. *School Classroom:* Copy Rectangular Geoboards from the companion website and draw an obtuse triangle. Construct a square on each side of this triangle and then determine the area of each square. Compare the sum of the areas of the two squares on the short sides of the triangle to the area of the square on the long side of the triangle. Repeat for two different obtuse triangles. Form a conjecture about the relationship between the sums of the areas of squares on the short sides of an obtuse triangle and the area of the square on the long side. Include your drawings as you explain your conjecture.

4. *Math Concepts:* Copy Dot Paper from the companion website. For each of the following use the region X described in activity 1 as the unit square.
   a. Create a fun shape that would fit on a 5 by 5 geoboard by using only line segments with rational lengths.
   b. Determine the area of the shape you created in part a. Show your work clearly on the dot paper.
   c. Create a fun shape that would fit on a 5 by 5 geoboard using at least three line segments with irrational lengths and at least one line segment with rational length for the edges of your shape.
   d. Determine the area of the shape you created in part c. Show your work clearly on the dot paper.
   e. Create a fun shape that would fit on a 5 by 5 geoboard by using only line segments with irrational lengths.
   f. Determine the area of the shape you created in part e. Show your work clearly on the dot paper.

5. *Math Concepts:* How many line segments of different length can be constructed on a 5 by 5 geoboard? Sketch the segments and record the length of each segment. Explain your thinking. Copy Rectangular Geoboards or Dot Paper from the companion website.

6. *Math Concepts:* Golden rectangles, described in the **Just for Fun** activity in this section, have proportions that have been favored by people since antiquity. Two familiar rectangles are the 3" by 5" index card and the common business card (2" by 3.5"). Which of these two cards has proportions closest to a golden rectangle? Explain your answer and how you arrived at it.

7. *Math Concepts:* Open the **Math Laboratory Investigation 6.4: Read Me—Pythagorean Theorem Instructions** from the companion website and investigate the physical model of the Pythagorean theorem as described in questions 1 and 2 of the *Starting Points for Investigations 6.4.* Describe your investigation and explain your thinking.

8. *NCTM Standards:* The Pythagorean relationship is only specifically mentioned in the **Grade 6–8 Geometry Standards** in the back pages of this book, but understanding the theorem and being computationally fluent with the theorem addresses other *Expectations* in other *Content Standards.* List two such *Expectations* and describe how fluency with the Pythagorean theorem addresses these *Expectations.*

BENNETT-BURTON-NELSON WEBSITE
www.mhhe.com/bbn

Virtual Manipulatives	Grid and Dot Paper	Links and Readings
Interactive Chapter Applets	Color Transparencies	Geometer Sketchpad Modules
Puzzlers	Extended Bibliography	

Elementary School Activity

INTRODUCING DECIMALS WITH BASE-TEN PIECES

Purpose: To introduce elementary school students to decimals using base-ten pieces.

Connection: Ask each student to write an example of a decimal on a piece of paper. Record some of their examples on the overhead and ask them where they have seen decimals written. Pick one of their examples, or write the decimal .3 on the overhead and ask them to draw a picture or sketch to represent that decimal. Let them share their examples with the class and, if no one has a part-to-whole sketch showing 3 out of 10 parts, then provide an example. Tell them that today they are going to look at decimals using base-ten pieces.

Materials: Sets of base-ten pieces can be created by copying base-ten grid paper from the companion website onto cardstock and cutting out units, longs, and Base-ten pieces transparencies can also be made with the base-ten pieces image. Sets of base-ten pieces can be placed in plastic sealable bags. Each group of two to four students will need one set of base-ten pieces.

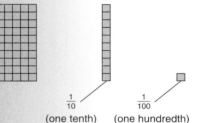

1

$\frac{1}{10}$
(one tenth)

$\frac{1}{100}$
(one hundredth)

1. Have the students select one piece of each size from their base-ten pieces. Ask each group to discuss how the pieces are related and to determine a value for each piece if the largest piece represents 1 unit. Ask for volunteers to describe their findings.

2. Put 11 hundredth pieces and 12 tenths pieces on the overhead and ask the students for suggestions about how the same collection could be represented by the fewest pieces. Then, if no one suggests it, model exchanging 10 hundredth pieces for 1 tenth piece and 10 tenths for 1 unit piece. When all agree that no more trades can reduce the number of pieces, record the minimum number of pieces in a table like the following.

1 pieces	$\frac{1}{10}$ pieces	$\frac{1}{100}$ pieces
1	3	1

3. Ask the students to form each of the following collections, find the minimum collection, and record their results in a table like the one above.

   a. 9 tenths and 12 hundredths   **b.** 1 unit, 4 tenths, and 11 hundredths

   c. 14 tenths   **d.** 16 hundredths

   e. 1 unit, 9 tenths, and 10 hundredths   **f.** 2 units, 13 tenths, and 15 hundredths

4. Ask the students what the number 102 means. Tell them that the collection in part (a) of the table they just made will be written as 1.02 so it is not confused with 102. The period or dot separates the units from the tenths and 1.02 means 1 unit, no tenths, and 2 hundredths. Ask them to write numbers with decimal points for the collections in parts (b) through (f) of their table.

5. Tell the students that decimal numbers like 1.32 can be read in several ways. Discuss the reason for each way.

   a. As "one point three two"

   b. As "one and thirty-two hundredths"

   c. As "one and three tenths and two hundredths"

6. Write the following numbers on the overhead and ask each group to form the collection of base-ten pieces represented by each of the numbers. Ask for volunteers to show or describe their collections.

   1.21   2.03   .23   .04   1.07

Using a 10 by 10 grid as the unit, this third grader is representing the decimal 2.563.

7

Statistics

In grades K–4, students begin to explore basic ideas of statistics by gathering data appropriate to their grade level, organizing them in charts or graphs, and reading information from displays of data. These concepts should be expanded in the middle grades. . . . Instruction in statistics should focus on the active involvement of students in the entire process: formulating key questions; collecting and organizing data; representing the data using graphs, tables, frequency distributions, and summary statistics; analyzing the data; making conjectures; and communicating information in a convincing way.[1]

Activity Set 7.1 COLLECTING AND GRAPHING DATA

PURPOSE

To collect and display data and to look for relationships or trends between two sets of data.

MATERIALS

A protractor and a tape measure from Material Card 19 or a ruler and string.

INTRODUCTION

Graphs provide a visual means of looking at sets of data and examining relationships and trends in the data. There are many ways to display data and a decision on which type of display to use often depends on the type of data you wish to display and on which display best illustrates the results.

Pie Graphs

Pie Graphs, like this one displaying percentage of fruit types in a fruit drink, show the relative sizes of certain quantities by dividing a circle into sectors with the same proportions.

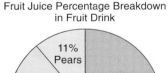

Fruit Juice Percentage Breakdown
in Fruit Drink

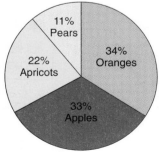

---

[1]*Curriculum and Evaluation Standards for School Mathematics* (Reston, VA: National Council of Teachers of Mathematics, 1989): 105.

I will learn how to choose the best graph.

6.7 Choose the Best Graph

Learn

VOCABULARY
circle graph

There are 100 fish and other animals at the local aquarium. Which type of graph would you use to show the information given in the table?

To choose the best graph, determine the type of data and how to analyze them.

Animals at the Aquarium				
Type of Animal	Tropical Fish	Sharks	Dolphins	Sea Horses
Number	30	15	20	35

Choosing a Graph

A **circle graph** or bar graph would be a good choice because both graphs can compare the number of animals at the aquarium.

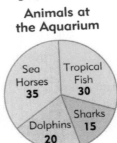

Animals at the Aquarium

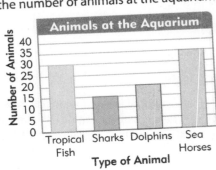

Other Ways to Display Data

Use a line graph to show changes over time.

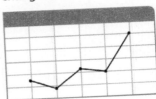

Use a pictograph to show multiples of numbers.

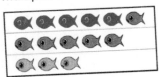

Key: Each fish represents 10 fish.

Use a stem-and-leaf plot to organize data by place value.

Stem	Leaf
7	1 3 6
8	4 7
9	5 5 6 7

Bar Graphs

Bar graphs such as the triple bar graph showing votes cast in presidential elections,[2] show data classified into distinct categories with equal width bars representing frequencies.

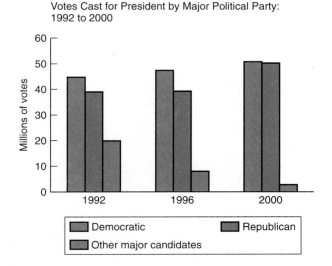

Line Plots

Line plots such as the plot shown here displaying the number of books read by a class of students, are often used to display numerical data that naturally falls into distinct numerical categories.

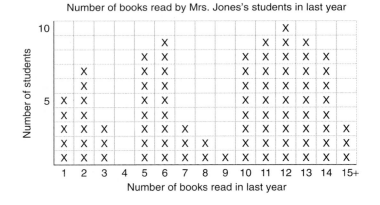

Stem-and-Leaf Plots and Histograms

The stem-and-leaf plot and the histogram on the next page both display a graphical representation of the same set of homework scores. The histogram shows the total number of scores within the noted interval (for example, there are 4 scores in the 20 to 29 range). The stem-and-leaf plot also shows scores in the same intervals but retains the actual data (for example, in the interval 20 to 29 the four scores are 22, 27, 28, and 28).

[2]*Statistical Abstract of the United States* (Washington, DC: Board of Census, 2004–2005): 238.

Homework Scores

Stem	Leaf
1	9
2	2788
3	022447779
4	01335567889
5	00

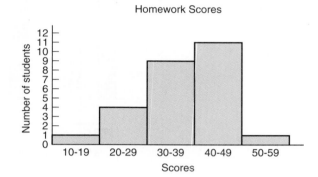

Homework Scores

Scatter Plots

Scatter plots provide a visual means of looking for relationships between two sets of data. In this scatter plot, a middle school student collected the heights of the mothers and fathers of her class-mates. By plotting a point that paired the heights of each set of parents she can look for a trend: Do taller mothers tend to be married to taller fathers?

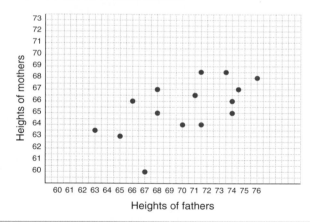

1. As a class, gather data on the eye color of the students in the class. Organize the data in the provided table.

Eye Color	Number of Students
Brown	
Blue	
Green	
Hazel	
Gray	

*a. Sketch a *single bar graph* corresponding to this data set by first marking a scale on the vertical axis, then marking the heights of the bars, and then sketching single bars of those heights centered over the eye colors. The bar edges in each data category should not touch, but each bar should be the same width.

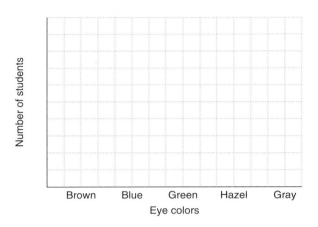

*b. Sketch a *pie graph* corresponding to the class data set of eye color by using a protractor to divide the circle into a set of pie slices of the appropriate size. To determine the appropriate size you must compute the central angle of each pie slice by multiplying the percentage of students with a particular eye color by 360°. Label each slice with the correct percentage and the correct eye color.

Eye Color	Number of Students	Percentage of Students	Central Angle
Brown			
Blue			
Green			
Hazel			
Gray			
Total			

Eye color comparison

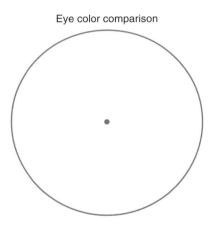

c. Which is the most common eye color? The least common?

d. In your opinion, does the bar graph or the pie graph display the eye color data the best? Explain your thinking.

e. List at least three observations each about these two data displays; what features does each display emphasize?

f. List several types of data sets that would be good to display with a bar graph. Explain your thinking.

g. List several types of data sets that would be good to display with a pie graph. Explain your thinking.

2. As a class, gather data on the number of individual writing tools (pencils, pens, highlighters, markers, etc.) that each student in the class has with them today. Organize the data in the provided table.

Number of Writing Tools	Number of Students	Number of Writing Tools	Number of Students
1		9	
2		10	
3		11	
4		12	
5		13	
6		14	
7		15+	
8			

*a. Complete the *line plot* corresponding to this data set by marking an X for each student with the indicated number of writing tools above the number.

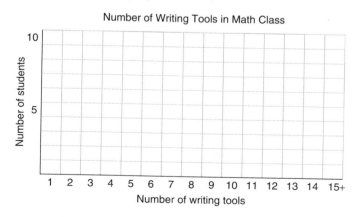

b. What is the most popular number of writing tools? The least popular?

c. List at least three observations about this data display; what feature does this display emphasize?

d. List several types of data sets that would be good to display with a line plot. Explain your thinking.

3. The following stem-and-leaf plot displays one randomly chosen temperature reading for each of the 50 U.S. states on February 14, 2006, at 12 noon PST (Pacific standard time).

Temperature	
Stem	**Leaf**
2	0678
3	025567777899
4	11246689
5	00555567789
6	0123344456
7	22344

a. How many states had temperatures 50° or less?

b. What is the highest temperature? The lowest?

*c. Another way to organize the temperature data would be to divide the data range into several intervals and note the frequency at which the temperatures in these intervals occurs. Organize your temperatures by frequency in the provided table.

Interval	15–24	25–34	35–44	45–54	55–64	65–74
Frequency						

d. Sketch a *histogram* displaying the temperature data by sketching bars of the correct height above the intervals on the horizontal axis. Consecutive bars should touch.

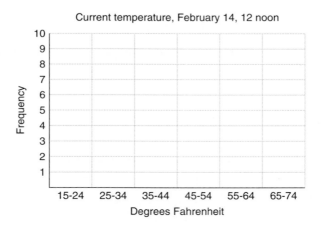

e. What is the most common range of temperatures?

f. In your opinion; which graph, stem-and-leaf plot or histogram, displays the temperature data the best? Explain your thinking.

g. List at least three observations each about these two data displays; what features does each display emphasize?

h. List several types of data sets that would be good to display with a stem-and-leaf plot. Explain your thinking.

i. List several types of data sets that would be good to display with a histogram. Explain your thinking.

4. a. As a class, gather data on the height of your mothers and fathers (in inches); give your best approximations if you don't know their exact heights. Organize the class data in the provided table.

Father's Height	Mother's Height	Father's Height	Mother's Height	Father's Height	Mother's Height	Father's Height	Mother's Height

b. Form a *scatter plot* of these data on the following grid:

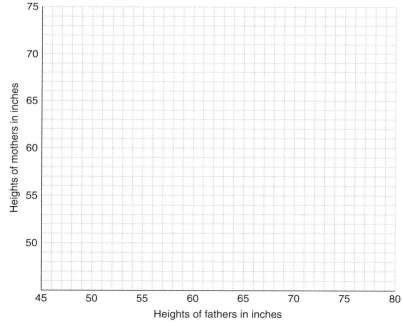

Use the scatter plot you formed in part b to answer the following questions.

c. What is the height of the shortest mother? The tallest mother?

d. What are the heights of the shortest and tallest fathers?

e. What is the difference in height between the shortest and tallest mother? The shortest and tallest father?

f. For how many couples was the woman taller than the man?

5. One method for determining a relationship or trend on a scatter plot is to draw a single straight line or curve that approximates the location of the points.

  a. On the scatter plot in activity 4, draw a single straight line through the set of points that you believe best represents the trend of the plotted points. This is called a *trend line*. (One strategy: Look for a directional pattern of the points from left to right and then draw a line in a similar direction so that approximately half the points are above the line and half of the points are below the line.)

  b. Do you think there is a trend or relationship between the two sets of data? That is, from the data collected, do taller people seem to marry taller people? Justify your conjecture in a sentence or two.

*6. a. Suppose that the middle school student's scatter plot in the introduction had looked as follows. Draw a trend line that you believe best represents this data set. Write a sentence or two summarizing the relationship between heights of fathers and mothers for this data.

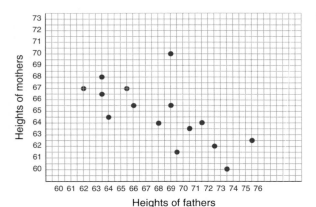

Summary:

*b. Now suppose that the student's data had looked like the scatter plot here. Draw a trend line for these points. Would you say there is a trend or relationship between the heights of the fathers and mothers for this data? Explain your reasoning.

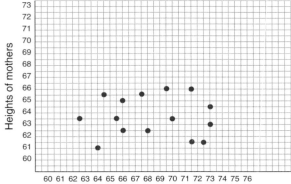

Summary:

c. The relationship between two sets of data can be described as positive, negative, or no relationship, depending on the slope of the trend line. Classify the relationships for the scatter plots in activities 4 and 6 on the preceding pages as positive, negative, or no relationship.

4b. _____   **6a.** _____   **6b.** _____

d. For a negative relationship, one set of data increases while the other corresponding set of data decreases; and for a positive relationship, as one set of data increases the corresponding data also increases. Describe two sets of data that will have a negative relationship and two that will have a positive relationship.

7. Form a scatter plot for each of the following sets of data and in each case sketch a trend line. Determine if there is a positive or negative relationship, or no relationship.

a. This table contains data on one aspect of child development—the time required to hop a given distance. The age of each child is rounded to the nearest half year. Use your trend line to predict the hopping time for an average 7.5-year-old and record it in the table.

Age (years)	5	5	5.5	5.5	6	6	6.5	7	7	7.5	8	8	8.5	8.5	9	9	9.5	10	11
Time (seconds) to hop 50 feet	10.8	10.8	10.5	9.0	8.4	7.5	9.0	7.1	6.7		7.5	6.3	7.5	6.8	6.7	6.3	6.3	4.8	4.4

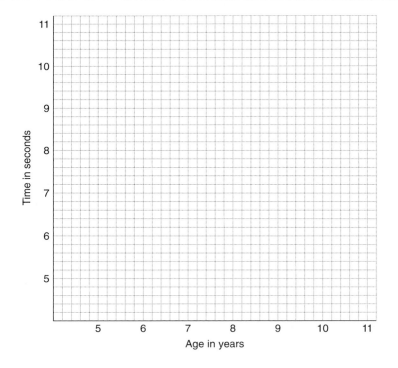

b. The following table was recorded by a forester who did a sample cutting of oak trees and recorded their diameters (in inches) and age (by counting rings). Use your trend line to predict the age of a tree that is 5.5 inches in diameter and the diameter of a tree that is 40 years old.

Age (years)	Diameter (inches)
10	2.0
8	1.0
22	5.8
30	6.0
18	4.6
13	3.5
38	7.0
38	5.0
25	6.5
8	3.0
16	4.5
28	6.0
34	6.5
29	4.5
20	5.5
4	0.8
33	8.0
23	4.7
14	2.5
35	7.0
30	7.0
12	4.9
8	2.0
5	0.8
10	3.5

Age of a tree that is 5.5

inches in diameter: _____

Diameter of a tree that

is 40 years old: _____

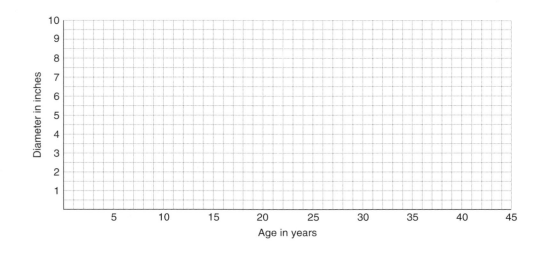

JUST FOR FUN

M&M'S®

Bag Number

	1	2	3	4	5	6	7	8	9	10	11	12	13	14	15	16	17	18	19	20	21	22	23	24
Red	9	12	5	10	9	11	11	11	11	14	10	14	12	8	11	11	12	5	10	18	14	13	11	9
Yellow	16	13	16	17	17	8	14	19	13	15	19	12	20	15	14	18	18	16	24	13	10	17	17	9
Blue	12	7	11	11	11	8	11	8	7	11	11	7	7	12	8	11	11	9	5	9	15	8	12	4
Orange	5	12	9	9	9	5	8	5	9	6	9	11	6	9	8	11	5	8	8	7	7	10	5	6
Green	6	5	5	6	9	10	6	7	8	2	2	4	10	7	9	2	8	5	4	5	6	4	9	16
Brown	8	6	9	5	1	12	5	5	8	8	3	10	5	5	7	5	2	12	10	5	5	3	3	11
Totals	56	55	55	58	56	54	55	55	56	56	54	58	60	56	57	58	56	55	61	57	57	55	57	55

The table here lists the color distributions in 24 bags of M&M's milk chocolate candies (net wt. 1.69 oz.).

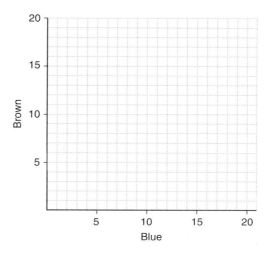

*1. The total number of pieces of candy varies little from bag to bag, but some color combinations vary greatly. As the number of one color changes in a bag, does if affect the number of any other color? For example, if the number of brown increases in a bag, does it affect the number of any other particular color? At the right is a grid for a scatter plot comparison for the two colors, blue and brown. Each bag determines a point on the grid. For example, on the grid point (12, 8) represents 12 blue and 8 brown from bag 1 and (7, 6) represents 7 blue and 6 brown from bag 2. Plot all blue/brown pairs on the grid. Draw a trend line to see if there is any relationship. (*Note:* If the number of brown increases as the number of blue increases, there is a positive relationship. If the number of brown decreases as the number of blue increases, there is a negative relationship. Or, there may be no relationship.)

*2. Assume that you purchase the same size bag of candy as those in the table. If your bag had 14 blue pieces, about how many brown pieces would you predict using your trend line? If there where 14 brown, how many blue would you predict?

*3. Try comparing yellow and green. Make a scatter plot and draw the trend line.

4. Pick other pairs of colors to compare.

Follow-Up Questions and Activities 7.1

1. *School Classroom:* A group of students studying a scatter plot comparing *Monthly Income* to *Frequency of Dining Out* are having trouble answering interpretive questions that don't correspond to plotted points on the scatter plot. For example, they don't know how to answer "How often do families with a monthly income of $4000 eat out?" The students say their trend line does not go through a point for $4000. How can you help these students?

2. *School Classroom:* The **Elementary School Text** page at the beginning of this section is from a grade 4 textbook. Explain how you would help students *construct* a circle graph (pie graph) to represent the aquarium data given in the table.

3. *School Classroom:* The students in a middle school class have built identical paper bridges and placed centimeter cubes on the bridges to determine bridge load strengths. In nine trials the students found the bridges broke under the following weights (in cm cubes):

	Trial 1	Trial 2	Trial 3	Trial 4	Trial 5	Trial 6	Trial 7	Trial 8	Trial 9
Number of cubes	688	851	787	832	1000	187	120	481	730

   a. Explain how you would help the students find effective graphical ways to display their data without just telling them which graphical displays to use.

   b. Which graphical display type do you think best displays the data? Why do you think it is best?

4. *Math Concepts:* Explore scatter plots and trend lines further by answering the questions about the distribution of M&M's in the **Just for Fun Activity** in this section.

5. *Math Concepts:* Review current periodicals (newspapers or magazines) and find at least two different types of data graphs explored in the activities in this section. For each graph, write three observations about the data that you can read from the graph. Include a reference for each periodical with a copy of the page on which you found the data display.

6. *Math Concepts:* List at least two similarities and at least two differences between each pair of graph types:
   a. Bar graph and stem-and-leaf graph
   b. Bar graph and histogram
   c. Stem-and-leaf graph and histogram

7. *NCTM Standards:* Read the **Data Analysis and Probability Standards** in the back pages of this book for each grade level: Pre-K–2, 3–5, and 6–8. For each grade level, list at least one *Expectation* that describes the types of graphs that should be studied at that level.

BENNETT-BURTON-NELSON WEBSITE

www.mhhe.com/bbn

Virtual Manipulatives	Grid and Dot Paper	Links and Readings
Interactive Chapter Applets	Color Transparencies	Geometer Sketchpad Modules
Puzzlers	Extended Bibliography	

Activity Set **7.2** ANALYZING DATA, SAMPLING, AND SIMULATION

PURPOSE

To analyze real data and apply the idea of randomness to sampling and simulations.

MATERIALS

Green and Red Tiles from the Manipulative Kit, the Table of Random Digits from Material Card 20, and containers such as boxes and bags for selecting tile samples.

INTRODUCTION

One of the main objectives of statistics is to make decisions or predictions about a population (students in schools, voters in a country, lightbulbs, fish, and so forth) based on information taken from a sample of the population. A poorly chosen sample will not truly reflect the nature of the population. An important requirement is that the sample be randomly chosen. *Randomly chosen* means that every member of the population is equally likely to be selected.

Once a sample has been chosen, it is useful to determine a single number that describes the data. An *average* is one type of value or measure that represents a whole set of data. There are three averages commonly used to describe a set of numbers: mean, median, and mode. Let's use these averages to describe the following set of numbers:

$$2, 3, 4, 6, 8, 11, 12, 12, 12, 18$$

The *mean,* which is commonly referred to as the average, is the sum of the values divided by the total number of values. The sum of the 10 numbers is 88, so the mean is 8.8 (88 ÷ 10). The *median* is the middle value when all the values are arranged in order. The median for these values is 9.5, which is halfway between the two middle values 8 and 11. The *mode* is the value (or values) that occurs most frequently—in this case, the mode is 12.

Simulations are processes that help answer questions about a real problem; they are experiments that closely resemble the real situation. These experiments usually involve random samples.

In this activity set, we will analyze time intervals between eruptions and duration of eruptions for Old Faithful geyser using stem-and-leaf plots, line plots, and scatter plots; experimentally select random samples; and use the idea of randomness to simulate a real situation.

---

1. The park rangers in Yellowstone National Park make predictions on the times of eruptions for Old Faithful geyser to inform visitors at the park. The data in the table shows the length of time in minutes between 16 consecutive eruptions.

57	87	73	94	52	88	72	88	62	87	57	94	51	98	59

   *a. Examine the data and list three observations about the length of time between eruptions.

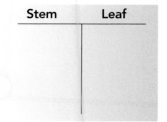

   b. Complete the stem-and-leaf plot at the left and a line plot on page 207 for this data.

I will explore choosing samples of a population.

6.3 Explore Sampling

Hands On Activity

A **population** is a group about which information is desired. Sometimes surveying everyone in an entire population is too difficult, time-consuming, or expensive.

When this is the case, a **sample** can be surveyed. A sample is a part of a population chosen to get information about the whole population.

Use a sample to estimate how many students in your classroom will see a movie this weekend.

VOCABULARY
population
sample

You Will Need
• paper bag

Use Models

STEP 1
Have each student answer the question "Will you see a movie this weekend?" by writing *Yes* or *No* on a slip of paper. Place the slips of paper in a paper bag and mix them up.

STEP 2
Select 10 slips of paper, one at a time, without looking. Record the number of students in your sample who wrote *Yes*.

STEP 3
Use the sample findings to predict the number of students in your class who will see a movie this weekend.

STEP 4
Replace the 10 slips of paper and repeat the sampling experiment two more times to get three predictions in all.

STEP 5
Once the three predictions are found, empty the bag onto a table and find the total number of students in the class who wrote *Yes*.

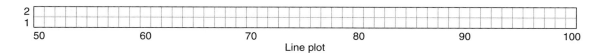

Line plot

c. What information is revealed by each of the plots in part b and what information about the data is not revealed?

d. Compute the mean, median, and mode(s) for the data.

e. Compute the mean, median, and mode(s) for eight shortest time intervals between eruptions and then for the seven longest time intervals. Explain why these averages are more important in analyzing the data than those in part d.

f. Assume that you know the time interval between two eruptions. Using the information above, describe a possible method for estimating the length of the next time interval between eruptions.

*2. The following data is for 15 consecutive eruptions of Old Faithful. For each duration of an eruption in minutes, there is an interval in minutes before the next eruption.[3]

Duration	4.4	2.0	4.7	1.9	4.2	1.6	1.6	2.1	4.5	1.7	4.5	1.9	4.6	1.7	4.6
Interval to next eruption	81	60	91	51	85	55	98	49	85	65	102	56	86	62	91

a. Form a scatter plot for the given data and sketch a trend line.

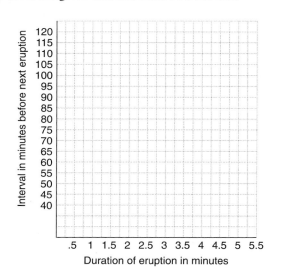

[3]For lesson plans about the eruptions of Old Faithful, see Linda C. Foreman and Albert B. Bennett, Jr., *Math Alive* (Salem, OR: The Math Learning Center, 1998): 399–417.

b. The following starting times and durations are for several randomly selected eruptions from a 2-day period. Use your scatter plot and trend line to make the following predictions.

Starting Time	Duration	Predicted Interval Before Next Eruption	Predicted Time of Next Eruption
11:22 a.m.	1 min 50 sec	_____	_____
8:30 a.m.	4 min 26 sec	_____	_____
12:40 p.m.	3 min 46 sec	_____	_____

3. **Sampling and Predictions:** The objective of sampling is to make predictions about a large population. Samples are usually relatively small. For example, some national television ratings are based on a sample of only 1100 people. The following activity is designed to show how a sample can represent the given population.

Have a classmate put any one of the following three populations of tiles in a container, without your knowing the numbers of red and green tiles. *Don't look at the contents of the container until you have completed all parts of this activity.*

Population 1	Population 2	Population 3
25 red tiles	20 red tiles	10 red tiles
5 green tiles	10 green tiles	20 green tiles

Draw a tile and check off its color in the following table. Return the tile to the container and repeat this activity. After every five draws, make a prediction as to which population you think is in the container. Continue the experiment until you have selected 25 times.

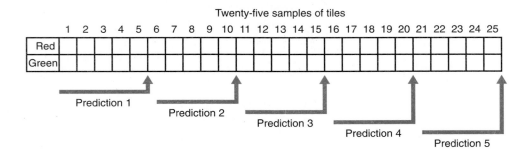

a. Compute the percentage of red tiles in each of the following groups.

First 5   First 10   First 15   First 20   All 25

b. As the size of the sample increases, the likelihood that it represents the population becomes greater. Based on your sample of 25 tiles, predict which of the three given populations you have sampled. Would you have selected the same population if your sample size had been only the first 5 tiles? The first 10? Now look at the contents of the container to check your prediction.

4. **Stratified Sampling:** The following are the annual incomes and the regional living areas for 18 households. Write the information for each household on a separate piece of paper, and place the pieces of paper in a container.

Lake Property	Lake Property	Lake Property	Suburban	Suburban	Suburban	Suburban	Suburban	Suburban
$400,000	$250,000	$185,000	$100,000	$120,000	$105,000	$175,000	$159,000	$135,000
City	City	City	City	City	City	City	City	City
$179,000	$226,000	$175,000	$193,000	$221,000	$300,000	$325,000	$105,000	$168,000

a. The average of all 18 incomes is $195,611.11. Select 6 pieces of paper at random from the container. Compute the average (mean) income of your sample and record it here. By how much does it differ from the average of all 18 incomes?

*b. There are many different samples of 6 incomes that you could have selected. Suppose, for example, your sample contained the 6 greatest incomes. What is the average of these 6 incomes? What is the average of the 6 smallest incomes?

c. The average of the 6 greatest incomes and the average of the 6 smallest incomes differ significantly from the average of all 18 incomes. By using a technique called *stratified sampling,* you can avoid getting an unrepresentative sample. Separate the total population of 18 incomes by living area into 3 different containers. Notice that the lake property, suburban, and city salaries represent $\frac{1}{6}$, $\frac{1}{3}$, and $\frac{1}{2}$ of the population, respectively. To obtain a proportional *stratified sample* of 6 incomes, select 1 lake property income ($\frac{1}{6}$ of 6), 2 suburban incomes ($\frac{1}{3}$ of 6), and 3 city incomes ($\frac{1}{2}$ of 6) from their individual containers. Compute the average of these 6 incomes. By how much does it differ from the average of all 18 incomes?

*d. If the stratified sampling procedure in part c is used, what is the greatest possible average that can be obtained for 6 incomes?

What is the smallest possible average that can be obtained?

Compare these averages to those in part b and discuss the advantages of stratified sampling.

5. **Simulation:** People with type O blood are called universal donors because their blood can be used in transfusions to people with different blood types. About 45 percent of the population has type O blood. If blood donors arrive at the blood bank with random blood types, how many donors, on the average, would it take to obtain five donors with type O blood? Make a conjecture.

   a. There are 100 pairs of digits from 00 to 99 and the pairs (00, 01, 02, . . . , 44) represent 45 percent of them. These 45 pairs of digits will represent the donors with type O blood. Without looking, put your pencil point on the table of random digits on Material Card 20. Beginning with the digit closest to the pencil point, start listing consecutive pairs of digits from the table of random digits until your list includes exactly five pairs from the list (00, 01, 02, . . . , 44). If each pair of digits represents a donor, then according to this trial how many donors would have to arrive at the blood bank to obtain five donors with type O blood?

   b. The procedure you followed in part a is a *simulation*—a way to answer a problem by running an experiment which resembles the problem.[4] Assuming that blood donors who go to the blood bank have random blood types and that 45 percent have type O, your experiment simulated the number of donors needed to obtain five donors with type O blood. Run the same experiment a total of 10 times and record your results here.

| | Tallies | | Number of Donors Needed |
Experiment	Digit Pairs from 00 to 44	Digit Pairs from 45 to 99	to Obtain 5 of Blood Type O
1			
2			
3			
4			
5			
6			
7			
8			
9			
10			
		Experimental Mean	

   c. The mean of the numbers of donors in the 10 experiments (third column) is the *average number* for these experiments. Based on your experimental results, what is the average number of donors the blood bank would have to receive to obtain five donors with type O blood?

[4]An excellent source for simulation activities is M. Gnanadesikan, R. Scheaffer, and J. Swift, *The Art and Techniques of Simulation* (Palo Alto, CA: Dale Seymour Publications, 1987).

JUST FOR FUN

SIMULATED RACING GAME (2 players)

In this race, one player flips a coin and the other rolls a die. At the start of play, each player rolls the die, and the high roller gets to use the die in the game. The race track is 12 steps long, and the racers move simultaneously. That is, the coin is flipped and the die is rolled at the same time. The coin tosser can move 1 step for heads and 2 steps for tails. The die roller can move the number of steps that comes up on the die. The race continues until one person lands on the last step. However, *the winner must land on the last step by exact count*. It is possible for this race to end in a tie. Find a person to race against and complete several races using a die and a coin.

1. Does this appear to be a fair race? That is, do the wins seem to be evenly distributed between the die roller and the coin tosser? You may wish to have a larger sample of completed races on which to base your conclusions. Use the table of random digits on Material Card 20 to simulate die rolling and coin flipping as follows:

- *Coin Flipping:* Select an arbitrary digit in the table of random digits. If the digit is even, call the outcome heads. If the digit is odd, call the outcome tails. For the next flip, move to the next digit in the table and do the same. Repeat this process until the game is complete.
- *Die Rolling:* Select an arbitrary digit in the table of random digits. If the closest digit is a 1, 2, 3, 4, 5, or 6, let it represent your first roll of the die. If that digit is a 0, 7, 8, or 9, move to the next digit in the table that is not a 0, 7, 8, or 9 and let that digit represent your die roll. For the succeeding roll, move to the next digit in the table and do the same. Repeat this process until the game is complete.

2. What happens when the length of the race (number of steps) is shortened? For example, will a two-step race be won more frequently by one player than the other? Try races of different lengths. List some conjectures or conclusions about the fairness of the race and its length.

	Race Track											
Start	**1**	**2**	**3**	**4**	**5**	**6**	**7**	**8**	**9**	**10**	**11**	**Finish**
Coin flipping												
Die rolling												

Follow-Up Questions and Activities 7.2

1. *School Classroom:* A group of 10 students was asked to count the change in their pockets (which was 25, 25, 43, 50, 50, 50, 50, 50, 75, and 100 cents) and to compute the mean, median, and mode. The students thought a mode and a median of 50 cents made sense but a mean of 51.8 cents did not seem reasonable because that was not an amount of money anyone could have. How would you explain the meaning of mean in this case to the students?

2. *School Classroom:* Design a color tile sampling activity (for example, see activity 3 in this activity set) that you believe is appropriate for an elementary school student and write a few questions that you can ask about your activity. Try this activity on an elementary school age child of your choice. Describe your activity, record your questions, and record the student's responses.

3. *School Classroom:* Read the sampling activity on the **Elementary School Text** page at the beginning of this section. If you were the teacher in this sixth-grade classroom, list three additional questions you could ask your students as "step 6" to promote discussion and understanding of the sampling process and their results from this activity. Briefly describe the usefulness of each of your three questions.

4. *Math Concepts:* With a classmate, play the *Racing Game* described in the **Just for Fun Activity** in this section. Answer the two questions after you and your partner have played the game.

5. *Math Concepts:* The following table displays housing prices for three types of houses in Monmouth, Oregon.

City Home	City Home	City Home	City Home	City Home	City Home
$180,000	$220,000	$150,000	$135,000	$147,000	$165,000
Luxury Home	Luxury Home	Country Home	Country Home	Country Home	Country Home
$375,000	$410,000	$200,000	$190,000	$220,000	$250,000

   a. Pick a stratified sample of six houses from the data set and explain your procedure.

   b. What is the difference between the median of the entire data set and the median of your stratified sample? Are either the median of the entire set or the median of a stratified sample a good indicator of housing prices in Monmouth?

   c. What is the largest possible difference between the median of the entire data set and the median of any stratified sample of six houses?

6. *Math Concepts:* For each of the following, design a data set with 10–15 entries satisfying the stated criteria. In each case, give a real-world example of where such a data set might occur.

   a. The mean is a better measure of central tendency than the median or the mode.

   b. The median is a better measure of central tendency than the mean or the mode.

   c. The mode is a better measure of central tendency than the mean or the median.

7. *NCTM Standards:* Read the *Expectations* in the **Grades 6–8 Data Analysis and Probability Standards** in the back pages of this book under the *Standard* "Develop and evaluate inference . . .". For each *Expectation,* give an example of an activity from this section that addresses the *Expectation.*

BENNETT-BURTON-NELSON WEBSITE
www.mhhe.com/bbn

Virtual Manipulatives	Grid and Dot Paper	Links and Readings
Interactive Chapter Appolets	Color Transparencies	Geometer Sketchpad Modules
Puzzlers	Extended Bibliography	

Activity Set **7.3**   STATISTICAL DISTRIBUTIONS: OBSERVATIONS AND APPLICATIONS

PURPOSE

To construct and apply frequency distributions.

MATERIALS

The Table of Random Digits on Material Card 20.

Alexander Hamilton

James Madison

INTRODUCTION

Once measurements from a population sample have been collected, they are arranged by grouping similar measurements together in a table, chart, or graph. A *frequency distribution* is a tabulation of values by categories or intervals. An interesting illustration of the use of frequency distributions was in the resolution of the controversy over authorship of the *Federalist Papers.*[5] This is a collection of 85 political papers written in the eighteenth century by Alexander Hamilton, John Jay, and James Madison. There is general agreement on the authorship of all but 12 of these papers. In order to determine who should be given credit for the 12 disputed papers, frequency distributions were compiled for certain filler words such as *by, to, of,* and *on.*

Forty-eight of Hamilton's papers and 50 of Madison's papers were analyzed to determine how many times each author used the word "by" in every 1000 words of text. You will notice from figure a on the next page, for example, that in approximately 16 papers Hamilton used the word "by" seven or eight times in every 1000 words whereas in roughly the same number of papers Madison used "by" 11 or 12 times in every 1000 words. In some papers Madison used "by" more than 13 times for every 1000 words while Hamilton never used "by" more than 12 times per 1000 words.

A comparison of the frequency distributions for usage of "by" indicates that Madison used that word more frequently than Hamilton did. Notice that Madison's distribution looks like the distribution of the word "by" in the distribution of the disputed papers in the bottom of figure a. An analysis for the use of the word "to" is shown in figure b. These and similar distributions for other filler words support the contention that Madison was the author of the disputed papers.

[5]F. Mosteller et al., *Statistics: A Guide to the Unknown* (New York: Holden-Day, 1972): 164–175.

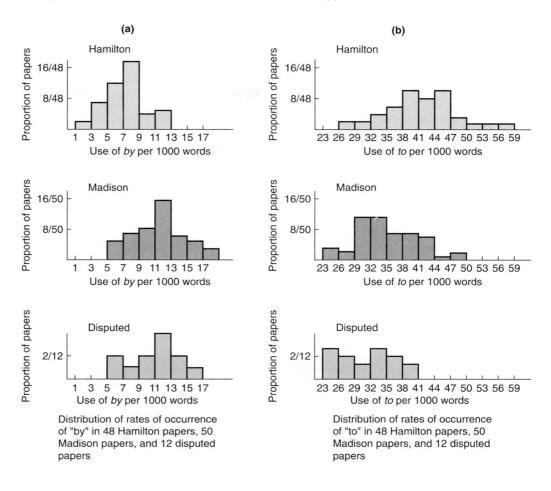

(a)

Hamilton — Proportion of papers (16/48, 8/48) vs. Use of *by* per 1000 words (1, 3, 5, 7, 9, 11, 13, 15, 17)

Madison — Proportion of papers (16/50, 8/50) vs. Use of *by* per 1000 words (1, 3, 5, 7, 9, 11, 13, 15, 17)

Disputed — Proportion of papers (2/12) vs. Use of *by* per 1000 words (1, 3, 5, 7, 9, 11, 13, 15, 17)

Distribution of rates of occurrence of "by" in 48 Hamilton papers, 50 Madison papers, and 12 disputed papers

(b)

Hamilton — Proportion of papers (16/48, 8/48) vs. Use of *to* per 1000 words (23, 26, 29, 32, 35, 38, 41, 44, 47, 50, 53, 56, 59)

Madison — Proportion of papers (16/50, 8/50) vs. Use of *to* per 1000 words (23, 26, 29, 32, 35, 38, 41, 44, 47, 50, 53, 56, 59)

Disputed — Proportion of papers (2/12) vs. Use of *to* per 1000 words (23, 26, 29, 32, 35, 38, 41, 44, 47, 50, 53, 56, 59)

Distribution of rates of occurrence of "to" in 48 Hamilton papers, 50 Madison papers, and 12 disputed papers

Several types of frequency distributions commonly occur. If each category or interval of the distribution has approximately the same number of values, the distribution is called a *uniform distribution*. For example, the following histogram shows the frequency distribution for the outcomes of rolling a die 3000 times. The frequency of each outcome varies between approximately 480 and 520.

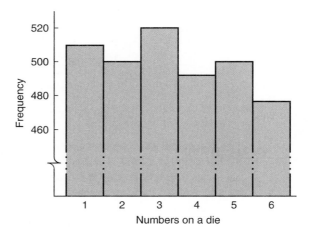

Frequency (460, 480, 500, 520) vs. Numbers on a die (1, 2, 3, 4, 5, 6)

One of the most useful distributions in statistics is the *normal distribution.* This distribution often occurs in the physical, social, and biological sciences. The graph of a normal distribution is the familiar bell-shaped curve. This curve is symmetric about the mean, with a gradual decrease at both ends. The heights of a large sample of adult men will be *normally distributed,* as shown in the following graph.

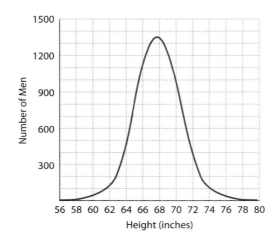

1. When four coins are tossed, there are six ways to get exactly two heads. Think of the coins as being a penny, nickel, dime, and quarter. The penny and dime may be heads and the nickel and quarter tails; the penny and nickel heads and the dime and quarter tails; and so forth. Fill in the remaining four ways of getting exactly two heads. Then fill in all other possible ways the coins can come up. There are 16 outcomes in all.

H	H	T	T				
H	T	H	T				

The graph at the top of the next page shows the number of different outcomes for tosses of four coins at a time. The frequency of 6 above 2 heads corresponds to the six different outcomes that have exactly two heads. There are frequencies of 1 above 0 heads and 4 heads, because each of these two events can occur in only one way, if the tosses result in all tails or in all heads respectively. This distribution looks like a normal curve. As the number of tosses of four coins increases, the distribution of outcomes theoretically gets closer to a normal curve.

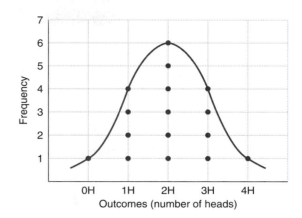

a. Use the table of random digits on Material Card 20 to simulate the tossing of six coins. Pick an arbitrary starting point in the table and look at the first six digits. Count each even digit as heads and each odd digit as tails and record the number of heads on line one of the table below. Then look at the next six random digits and record the number of heads on line two. Continue to use groups of six random digits to simulate 64 tosses of six coins, and record the number of heads for each toss in the table below.

1	2	3	4	5	6	7	8	9	10	11	12	13
14	15	16	17	18	19	20	21	22	23	24	25	26
27	28	29	30	31	32	33	34	35	36	37	38	39
40	41	42	43	44	45	46	47	48	49	50	51	52
53	54	55	56	57	58	59	60	61	62	63	64	

b. Plot the frequency of each outcome on the grid at the top of the next page. For example, the number of times you got exactly two heads should be plotted above 2H on the graph. Theoretically, about 78 percent of the outcomes should be 2, 3, or 4 heads. What percent of your outcomes are 2, 3, or 4 heads?

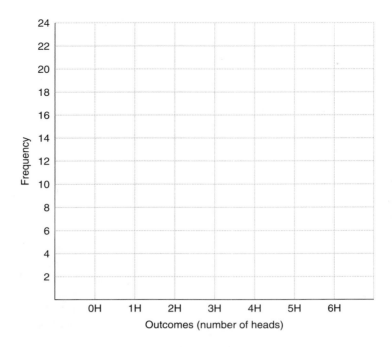

*c. Suppose that an outcome of heads represents the birth of a girl and an outcome of tails represents that of a boy. In addition, suppose that each of the coin tosses in part a represents a family that is planning to have six children. Explain how you would use the data to predict approximately what percent of those families will have *at least* three girls.

2. When measurements such as weight, range of eyesight, or IQ are compiled for a large number of people, they are usually normally distributed. The following list contains the pulse rates of 60 students. Use these data to complete the histogram here and then answer the questions on the following page.

Pulse rates (beats per minute)/Frequency

Pulse	53	56	57	58	61	62	63	64	65	66	67	68	69	70	71	72	73	74	75	76	77	78	79	80	81	82	84	86	89	91	92
Freq.	1	2	1	1	1	3	1	1	3	1	2	2	2	6	1	4	3	4	2	3	1	1	2	3	1	1	2	2	1	1	1

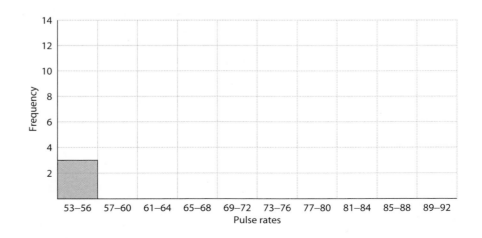

a. Do the pulse rates appear to you to be fairly close to a normal distribution?

*b. *Standard deviation* is a measure of the variation and spread of a distribution. One property of a normal distribution is that 68 percent of the measurements are within 1 standard deviation on either side of the mean, 95 percent are within 2 standard deviations on either side of the mean, and 99.7 percent of the measurements are within 3 standard deviations on either side of the mean, as illustrated here. The set of pulse rates has a mean of 72 and a standard deviation of 8.7. Determine the percentage of pulse rates within ±1 standard deviation, ±2 standard deviations and ±3 standard deviations of the mean, and record your results below. Does the distribution of pulse rates approximately satisfy this property?

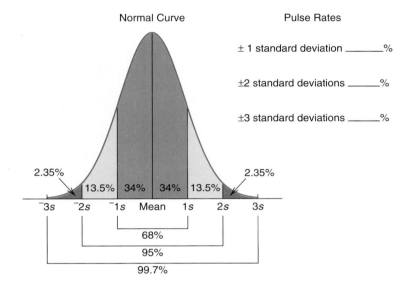

c. Even smaller collections of measurements may tend to be normally distributed. Draw a bar graph of your classmates' pulse rates taken over a 10-second interval. One property of approximately normal curves is that the mean, median, and mode are approximately equal. Determine the mean, median, and mode for the pulse rates of your class. Are they approximately equal?

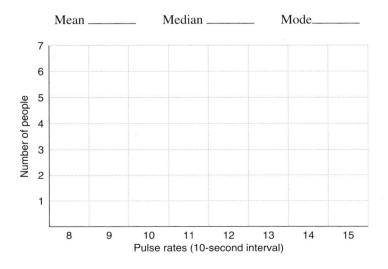

3. Some people are not aware of the uneven distribution of letters which occurs in words. One such person may have been Christofer Sholes, the inventor of the typewriter. He gave the left hand 56 percent of all the strokes, and he gave the two most agile fingers on the right hand two of the least often used letters of the alphabet, *j* and *k*. This table shows the frequencies, in terms of percentages of occurrence, of letters in large random samples.

E	12.3%	S	6.6%	U	3.1%	B	1.6%	J	0.1%
T	9.6%	R	6.0%	P	2.3%	G	1.6%	Z	0.1%
A	8.1%	H	5.1%	F	2.3%	V	0.9%		
O	7.9%	L	4.0%	M	2.2%	K	0.5%		
N	7.2%	D	3.7%	W	2.0%	Q	0.2%		
I	7.2%	C	3.2%	Y	1.9%	X	0.2%		

*a. There are 350 letters in the preceding paragraph. Count the number of times that *e, s, c, w,* and *k* occur and compute their percentages. Compare your answer with the percentages that have been computed for large random samples.

	Tally	Frequency	Percent
e			
s			
c			
w			
k			

b. The most frequently occurring letter in the English language is *e*. In 1939 a 267 page novel entitled *Gadsby* was released by the Wetzel Publishing Company. The novel was known not for its literary merit, but rather for one distinctive feature: Not 1 of its 50,000 words contained the letter *e*. Compose a sentence of at least ten words that does not use the letter *e*. (It is interesting for classmates to share their sentences.)

*c. In Morse code, letters are represented by dots and dashes so that they can be sent by electrical impulses. A dot consumes 1 time unit, a dash consumes 3 time units, and 1 time unit is needed for each space between symbols. In 1938 Samuel Morse assigned the symbols with the shortest time intervals to the letters that occurred most frequently, according to his sample of 12,000 words from a Philadelphia newspaper. Although Morse's code assignment is more efficient than it would have been if he had assigned letters haphazardly, it can still be improved. In the table at the top of the next page, devise a new and more efficient assignment by changing and reassigning the code symbols so that in moving down the column each letter does not use more time units than the next letter. How many fewer time units will this new assignment require for these nine letters than that used by Samuel Morse?

Code Symbol	Number of Time Units	Letters	Reassigned Code Symbol
•	1	e	_____
—	3	t	_____
• —	5	a	_____
— — —	11	o	_____
— •	5	n	_____
••	3	i	_____
•••	5	s	_____
• — •	7	r	_____
••••	7	h	_____

4. It is surprising to learn that the leading digits of any numerous set of large numbers *do not occur with the same frequency*—that is, are not evenly distributed.[6] Find a partner to help you tally the first digit in the list of metropolitan populations below and play the following game. For each number in the table beginning with a 1, 2, 3, or 4, you win; for each number beginning with a 5, 6, 7, 8, or 9, your partner wins. Record your tallies in the table at the end of the next page and determine the total for each digit to see who wins. Then answer the questions on page 223.

Populations of 166 Selected Metropolitan Areas

Philadelphia to Atlantic City

Cecil	82,522	Beaver	184,406	**Richmond-Petersburg**	
Chester	421,686	Allegheny	1,268,446	Powhatan	21,950
New Castle	482,807	**Portland-Salem**		Hanover	81,975
Bucks	587,942	Clark	326,943	Goochland	17,823
Gloucester	247,897	Washington	399,697	New Kent	13,052
Burlington	420,323	Yamhill	82,085	Chesterfield	245,915
Montgomery	719,718	Polk	61,560	Henrico	246,052
Atlantic	238,047	Clackamas	334,732	Charles City	7,092
Cape May	98,069	Columbia	44,416	Dinwiddie	24,657
Cumberland	140,341	Marion	268,541	Prince George	30,135
Camden	505,204	Multnomah	631,082	Colonial Heights	16,955
Salem	64,912	**Providence-Warwick-Pawtucket**		Hopewell	22,529
Delaware	542,593	Washington	120,649	Richmond	194,173
Philadelphia	1,436,287	Bristol	49,114	Petersburg	34,724
Phoenix-Mesa		Kent	161,811	**Rochester**	
Maricopa	2,784,075	Providence	574,038	Wayne	94,977
Pinal	146,929	**Raleigh-Durham-Chapel Hill**		Orleans	44,518
Pittsburgh		Wake	570,615	Livingston	66,000
Butler	170,785	Johnston	106,582	Ontario	99,662
Westmoreland	372,103	Franklin	44,743	Genesee	60,654
Washington	205,566	Orange	110,116	Monroe	716,072
Fayette	144,847	Chatham	45,406		
		Durham	202,411	*Continued*	

[6] An explanation of this phenomenon can be found in W. Weaver, *Lady Luck* (New York: Doubleday, 1963): 270–277.

Sacramento-Yolo

Placer	229,259
El Dorado	158,502
Sacramento	1,144,202
Yolo	153,849

St. Louis

St. Charles	272,353
Lincoln	36,556
Warren	24,600
Monroe	26,586
Jefferson	195,675
Franklin	91,763
Clinton	35,591
Jersey	21,373
Madison	259,351
St. Louis County	998,696
St. Clair	261,941
City of St. Louis	339,316

Salt Lake City-Ogden

Davis	233,013
Salt Lake	850,667
Weber	184,065

San Antonio

Comal	73,391
Wilson	31,423
Guadalupe	80,472
Bexar	1,353,052

San Diego

San Diego	2,780,592

San Francisco Bay Area

Contra Costa	918,200
Sonoma	433,304
Solano	377,415
Santa Clara	1,641,215
San Mateo	700,765
Napa	119,288
Alameda	1,400,322
Santa Cruz	242,994
San Francisco	745,774
Marin	236,770

Sarasota-Bradenton

Manatee	239,682
Sarasota	303,400

Scranton-Wilkes-Barre-Hazleton

Wyoming	29,149
Columbia	64,120
Luzerne	313,767
Lackawanna	208,455

Seattle Area

Snohomish	587,783
Thurston	202,255
Kitsap	232,623
Island	70,319
Pierce	676,505
King	1,654,876

Springfield, Mass.

Hampshire	149,384
Hampden	439,609
Stockton-Lodi	550,445
San Joaquin	550,445

Syracuse

Madison	71,069
Oswego	124,006
Cayuga	81,264
Onondaga	458,301

Tampa-St. Petersburg-Clearwater

Hernando	127,227
Pasco	325,824
Hillsborough	925,277
Pinellas	878,231

Toledo

Fulton	41,895
Wood	119,498
Lucas	448,542

Tucson

Pima	790,755

Tulsa

Rogers	68,128
Wagoner	55,259
Creek	67,142
Tulsa	543,539
Osage	42,838

Washington-Baltimore

Loudoun	143,940
Spotsylvania	83,692
Stafford	87,055
Calvert	71,877
Manassas Park	8,711
King George	17,236
Manassas	35,336
Howard	236,388
Frederick	186,777
Carroll	149,697
Prince William	259,827
Berkeley	70,970
Culpeper	33,083
Harford	214,668
Queen Anne's	39,672
Charles	117,963
Warren	30,126
Jefferson	41,368
Fredericksburg	21,686
Fairfax County	929,239
Anne Arundel	476,060
Fauquier	54,109
Montgomery	840,879
Prince George's	777,811
Alexandria	118,300
Clarke	12,779
Falls Church	10,042
Washington County	127,352
Baltimore County	721,874
City of Fairfax	20,697
Arlington	177,275
City of Baltimore	645,593
Washington	523,124

West Palm Beach-Boca Raton

Palm Beach	1,032,625

Wichita

Butler	61,932
Sedgwick	448,050
Harvey	34,361

Youngstown-Warren

Columbiana	111,521
Trumbull	225,066
Mahoning	255,165

First Digit of Number	1	2	3	4	5	6	7	8	9
Tallies									
Totals									

a. Would you have won the game if you had used the digits 1, 2, and 3 only? Justify your answer by showing the percentage of numbers with these leading digits.

b. Use the results from the table to make one or more conjectures regarding the occurrence of the leading digits of large numbers from sets of data.

c. The populations in the list of metropolitan areas are four-, five-, six-, and seven-digit numbers. The least number is 7,092 and the greatest number is 2,784,075. In the table below, all numbers from 7,092 to 2,784,075 have been separated into six intervals. There are 2,908 numbers (9,999 − 7,092 + 1) in the first interval and all have leading digits of 7, 8, and 9. The second interval has numbers with leading digits 1, 2, 3, 4. Determine the number of numbers in each of the remaining intervals and whether you win or lose the game with leading digits 1, 2, 3, and 4.

Interval	Number of Numbers	Win or Lose
7,092 to 9,999	2,908	LOSE
10,000 to 49,999	_____	_____
50,000 to 99,999	_____	_____
100,000 to 499,999	_____	_____
500,000 to 999,999	_____	_____
1,000,000 to 2,784,075	_____	_____

*d. Considering *all* numbers from 7,092 to 2,784,075, how do the number of numbers with leading digits 1, 2, 3, and 4 compare to those with leading digits of 5, 6, 7, 8, and 9? Describe how this result can explain why it is likely that the person choosing digits 1, 2, 3, and 4 will win using the list of populations of metropolitan areas or any numerous set of large numbers.

Follow-Up Questions and Activities 7.3

1. *School Classroom:* A middle school student is confused by the term "skewed to the right" when the data are "piled up" on the left and "skewed to the left" when the data are "piled up" on the right. Explain how you would help the student make sense out of these terms.

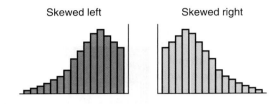

2. *School Classroom:* How would you help a middle school student who states you can never *really* have a normal distribution since all data sets will be finite and the frequency histogram will always be bumpy and never perfectly smooth like a normal distribution?

3. *Math Concepts:* The following table contains the results of using a table of random digits to simulate throwing three dice, 30 times. For example, in roll #1, the simulated throw of three dice resulted in the numbers 3, 3, and 2.

Roll #	1	2	3	4	5	6	7	8	9	10
Dice	332	356	642	332	234	225	353	311	365	411
Roll #	11	12	13	14	15	16	17	18	19	20
Dice	211	243	423	343	422	416	234	332	414	234
Roll #	21	22	23	24	25	26	27	28	29	30
Dice	324	221	352	212	426	551	214	153	415	141

a. Use the table to determine the sum of each roll of the dice. Tabulate the sum data and sketch a bar graph showing the sum data. Clearly label the graph. Does the sum data appear to be approximately normally distributed? Explain the reasons for your conclusion.

b. The set of dice sums has a mean of 8.8 and a standard deviation of 2.5. Determine the percentage of sums ± 1 standard deviation from the mean, ± 2 standard deviations from the mean, and ± 3 standard deviations from the mean.

c. Based on your calculations in part b, is the data set approximately normally distributed? Explain your reasons for your conclusion.

4. *Math Concepts:* Read the **Just for Fun Activity** in this section and:

a. Use the Caesar cipher to decipher the message on the pictured scroll.

b. Follow the instructions and use a frequency distribution to help decipher the secret message given on the top of page 224.

5. *Math Concepts*

a. Using an organized table, list all of the possible results for tossing five coins (there are 32 possibilities). What percentage of your outcomes are 0 heads, 1 head, 2 heads, 3 heads, 4 heads, and 5 heads?

b. Using the number of heads as the outcome of each possible toss, plot the frequency of each outcome on a grid similar to the grid used for activity 1b.

c. Given a mean of 2.5 heads and a standard deviation of 1.1 heads, does the distribution of number of heads seem approximately normally distributed? Explain your reasoning.

6. *NCTM Standards:* Read the first *Expectation* in the **Grade 3–5 Data Analysis and Probability Standard** under "Formulate Questions." Then propose a statistical investigation that you think would be of interest for elementary students to pursue in which they formulate questions and then collect, analyze, and interpret data to answer the questions. With regard to the *Expectation,* how could, "data-collection methods affect the nature of the data set" for the investigation you suggest?

7. *NCTM Standards*: Go to http://illuminations.nctm.org/ and under "Lessons" select grade levels 3–5 and the **Data Analysis and Probability Standard.** Choose a lesson that involves graphing data.

   a. State the title of the lesson and briefly summarize the lesson.

   b. Referring to the **Standards Summary** in the back pages of this book as necessary, list the **Data Analysis and Probability Standard Expectations** that the lesson addresses and explain how the lesson addresses these *Expectations.*

 **BENNETT-BURTON-NELSON WEBSITE**

www.mhhe.com/bbn

Virtual Manipulatives	Grid and Dot Paper	Links and Readings
Interactive Chapter Applets	Color Transparencies	Geometer Sketchpad Modules
Puzzlers	Extended Bibliography	

FINDING AVERAGES WITH COLOR TILES

Purpose: To provide elementary school students with a visual introduction and meaning to finding the average of whole numbers.

Connections: Ask the class what the word "average" means. They may suggest several meanings, such as an average person or an average score. Discuss a few meanings of this word and tell them that today we are going to discover the meaning of the word "average" in mathematics.

Materials: Sets of color tiles may be created by copying 2-centimeter grid paper on four different colors of cardstock or by copying the color tile images from the companion website. Color tile transparencies can also be made with the color tile images. Sets of 20 of each of four colors can be placed in plastic sealable bags for storage. Each group of two to four students will need one set of color tiles. Students will also need centimeter grid paper for recording averages with fractional parts.

7   3

1. Place two towers of tile on the overhead, one of height 7 and the other of height 3 and have the students form the same towers at their tables. Ask the students to level off the towers by shifting tiles so that towers both have the same height. Tell them that this leveling off process can be used to find the average of numbers. Ask them, "What is the average of 7 and 3?"

2. Ask the students to find the average of 1 and 5 by building two towers and leveling them off. Then, without building towers, ask them to imagine towers of heights 20 and 26 and mentally find the average of 20 and 26. Have student volunteers share the different ways they determined the average was 23.

8   5   6.5   6.5

3. Ask the students to find the average of 5 and 8 by building towers or doing it mentally. Discuss that it is permissible to use half tiles (or fractions of tiles). Allow students to use grid paper to record this new idea. See the two towers at the left.

4. Place the five towers shown at the left on the overhead and ask the students to find the average of the five numbers by leveling off the towers. Discuss the average and then pose questions like the following (keep the original towers of heights 4, 5, 2, 1, and 3 on your overhead so students can refer back to the original towers):

   a. Tell the students that each tower represents the feet of snow that fell in Nisswa, Minnesota, for each of the past 5 years. Ask each group to discuss and report what they believe is the average snowfall for Nisswa during this 5-year period.

   b. If it snowed 6 feet the next year, have them use their tile and grid paper to determine the 6-year average.

   c. If it did not snow at all during the sixth year ask them to discuss and determine what the 6-year average would be.

4   5   2   1   3

Students find the average of 7, 2, and 6 by leveling off towers of 7 cubes, 2 cubes, and 6 cubes to a height of 5 cubes.

8 Probability

In prekindergarten through grade 2, the treatment of probability ideas should be informal. Teachers should build on children's developing vocabulary. . . . We'll probably have recess this afternoon, or It's unlikely to rain today. . . . In grades 3–5 students can consider ideas of chance through experiments—using coins, dice, or spinners—with known theoretical outcomes or through designating familiar events as impossible, unlikely, likely, or uncertain. . . . Middle grade students should learn and use appropriate terminology and should be able to compute probabilities for simple compound events. . . .[1]

Activity Set 8.1 PROBABILITY EXPERIMENTS

PURPOSE

To determine probabilities experimentally and then analyze the experiments to determine the theoretical probabilities, when possible.

MATERIALS

A penny, 10 identical tacks, Two-Penny and Three-Penny Game Grids on Material Cards 21 and 22 respectively, and the Table of Random Digits on Material Card 20.

INTRODUCTION

The word *stochastic,* strange sounding but currently very popular in scientific circles, means random, chancy, chaotic. It is pronounced "stoh-kastic." The stochastization of the world (forgive this tongue-twister) means the adoption of a point of view wherein randomness or chance or probability is perceived as real, objective and fundamental aspect of the world. . . .

Of the digits that crowd our daily papers many have a stochastic basis. We read about the percentage of families in New York City that are childless, the average number of cars owned by four-person families in Orlando, Florida, the probability that a certin transplant operation will succeed. . . . It is implied that a certain attitude is to be engendered by these disclosures, that a course of action should be set in motion. If it is reported that the English scores of Nebraskan tenth-graders are such and such while that of Iowan tenth-graders are this and that, then presumably someone believes that something ought to be done about it.

The stochastization of the world so permeates our thinking and our behavior that it can be said to be one of the characteristic features of modern life. . . .[2]

[1]*Principles and Standards for School Mathematics* (Reston, VA: National Council of Teachers of Mathematics, 2000): 51.
[2]P. J. Davis and R. Hersh, *Descartes Dream* (New York: Harcourt Brace Jovanovich, 1986): 18–19.

I will explore organizing and displaying outcomes.

26.6 Explore Finding Outcomes

Hands On Activity

You can use a 2-color counter to explore the results of probability experiments.

You Will Need
- a 2-color counter

VOCABULARY
equally likely
possible outcomes

Find out what the results would be if you flipped a counter 20 times.

Use Models

It is **equally likely** to get red or yellow. You can show the probability as a fraction.

$\frac{1}{2}$ ← number of chances it will be red
← total number of possible outcomes

STEP 1

Copy the table. Predict the possible outcomes if you toss the counter 20 times. **Possible outcomes** are any of the results that could occur in an experiment. Record in the table.

There are 2 possible outcomes: landing on red or landing on yellow.

Outcomes		
Counters	Prediction	Tallies
⬤		
⬤		

STEP 2

Toss 1 counter 20 times. Record the outcome each time.

STEP 3

Write the total results for each outcome.

The importance of an understanding of probability and the related area of statistics to becoming an informed citizen is widely recognized. The *Principles and Standards for School Mathematics* recommends probability activities at all grade levels, K–12, and that a spirit of investigation, exploration, experimentation, and discussion permeate this study. Probability is rich in interesting problems and provides opportunities for using fractions, decimals, ratio, and percent.

In this activity set, we will consider both *experimental probabilities,* which are determined by observing the outcomes of experiments, and *theoretical probabilities,* which are determined by mathematical calculations. The theoretical probability of rolling a 4 on a die is $\frac{1}{6}$ because there are 6 faces on a die, each of which is equally likely to turn up, and only one of these faces has a 4. The experimental probability of obtaining a 4 is found by rolling a die many times and recording the results. Dividing the number of times a 4 comes up by the total number of rolls gives us the experimental probability.

1. Suppose someone wanted to bet that a tack would land with its point up when dropped on a hard surface. Would you accept the bet? Before you wager any money, try the following experiment. Take 10 identical tacks and drop them on a hard surface. Count the number of tacks that land point up. Do this experiment 10 times and record your results in the following table.

Trial Number	1	2	3	4	5	6	7	8	9	10
Number with points up	___	___	___	___	___	___	___	___	___	___

   a. Out of the 100 tacks you dropped, how many landed point up? On the basis of this experiment, explain why you would or would not accept the bet.

   b. Based on your results, what is the experimental probability that this type of tack will land point up?

   $$\frac{\text{Number with point up}}{\text{Total number dropped}} =$$

c. Based on your results, about how many tacks would you expect to land point up if you dropped 300 tacks?

d. Based on your results, what is the experimental probability that this type of tack will land point down? How is this probability related to the probability in part b?

2. Games of chance like the following are common at carnivals and fairs. A penny is spun on a square grid, and if it lands inside a square you win a prize. Compare the diameter of a penny to the width of the Two-Penny Grid (Material Card 21). Do you think there is a better chance that the penny will land inside a square or on a line? Make and record a conjecture before you begin the experiment in part a below.

Conjecture:

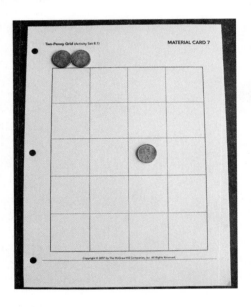

a. Spin a penny 24 times on the Two-Penny Grid and tally the results below.

	Tally	Total
Penny inside square		
Penny on line		

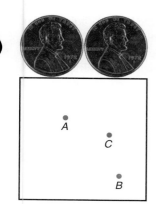

b. Based on your experiment, compute and record the experimental probability that a penny will land inside a square.

$$\frac{\text{Number inside squares}}{\text{Total number of spins}} =$$

c. The length of a side of a square is twice the diameter of a penny. Which of the points to the left labeled *A*, *B*, and *C* will be winning points if they represent the center of a penny?

d. Shade the region of the square in which the center of every *winning* penny must fall. What fractional part of the square is the shaded region? This is the theoretical probability that a penny will land inside the square.

*e. Is this a fair game, in the sense that there is a 50 percent chance of winning?

3. The sides of the squares on the Three-Penny Grid (Material Card 22) are three times the diameter of a penny. When a penny is spun on this grid, do you think the chances of its landing inside the lines are better than the chances of its landing on a line? Make and record a conjecture before you begin the experiment.

Conjecture:

a. Spin a penny 24 times, tally your results, and compute the experimental probability of not landing on a line.

	Tally	Total
Penny inside square		
Penny on line		

$$\frac{\text{Number inside squares}}{\text{Total number of spins}} =$$

b. Shade the region of the square in which the centers of winning pennies must fall. What is the theoretical probability that a penny will land inside the square?

c. Explain why this is or is not a fair game.

c. Using your data, what is the experimental probability the student will wear the same T-shirt more than once in a five-day week?

4. Cut out three cards of the same size. Label both sides of one with the letter A, both sides of the second with the letter B, one side of the third with A, and the other side of the third with B. Select a card at random and place it on the table. The card on the table will have either an A or a B facing up. What is the probability that the letter facing down will be different from the letter facing up? Make a conjecture and record it below. Then repeat this experiment 24 times and use the table to record the number of times that the letter facing down is different from the letter facing up. Compute and record the experimental probability.

Conjecture:

JUST FOR FUN

RACETRACK GAME (2 or 3 players)

Each player chooses three tracks on the race track game board and places a marker on its starting square. In turn, the players roll two dice. If the sum of the numbers on the dice matches the number of a track on which the player's marker is located, the player may move one square toward the finish line on this track. The first player to have a marker reach the last square on the track is the winner. Play the game a few times. What are the three tracks that are most likely to produce a winner, and which of the three gives the best chance of winning?

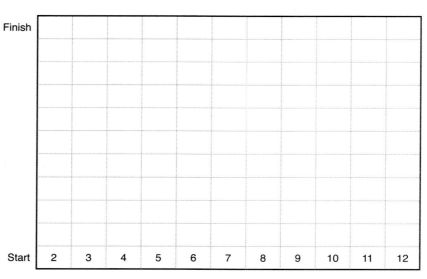

Variation: Use the sum of the numbers on three dice rather than on two dice and the following game board. Which tracks give you the best chance of winning?

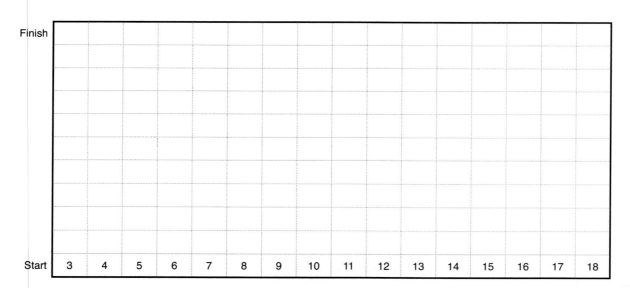

Follow-Up Questions and Activities 8.1

1. *School Classroom:* After a class of students played the penny spin games described in activities 2 and 3 of this activity set, some wanted to know the grid square width for which the game becomes a fair game. Determine this size and write a description of how you would help students discover and understand this result.

2. *School Classroom:* Suppose that you wanted your students to play the *Racetrack Game* described in the **Just for Fun Activity** in this section but had no dice in the classroom. Devise two ways that you could have the students simulate the random roll of a pair of dice to successfully play the game. Describe your methods in detail.

3. *Math Concepts:* For the card game described in activity 4 of this activity set, does the probability that the letter facing up will be different than the letter facing down increase or decrease as you increase the number of cards and letters? Explore this idea and find the theoretical probability that the letter facing up will be different than the letter facing down on a randomly selected card from the following set of cards. Explain your thinking.

Six Card Set	
Card 1: A on both sides	Card 4: One side A, one side B
Card 2: B on both sides	Card 5: One side A, one side C
Card 3: C on both sides	Card 6: One side B, one side C

4. *Math Concepts:* Design a game similar to the *Racetrack Game* in the **Just for Fun Activity** in this section. Instead of sums, use the product of the numbers when two dice are rolled.
   a. List the set of numbers that must be placed in the start boxes for the game (order the list from least to greatest).
   b. What is the theoretical probability of obtaining each of the different products? Explain your reasoning.

5. *Math Concepts*
   a. Suppose the Penny Spin game in activity 3 uses a Four-Penny diameters wide by Three-Penny diameters high Grid instead of a Three-Penny Grid. Is the game fair now? Explain your reasoning and support your answer with theoretical probability calculations.
   b. Suppose the Penny Spin game in activity 3 uses a Four-Penny Grid instead of a Three-Penny Grid. Is the game fair now? Explain your reasoning and support your answer with theoretical probability calculations.

6. *NCTM Standards:* Go to http://illuminations.nctm.org/ and under "Lessons" select grade levels 6–8 and the **Data Analysis and Probability Standard.** Choose a lesson that involves probability.
   a. State the title of the lesson and briefly summarize the lesson.
   b. Referring to the **Standards Summary** in the back pages of this book as necessary, list the **Number and Operation Standard** *Expectations* that the lesson addresses and explain how the lesson addresses these *Expectations*.

7. *NCTM Standards:* The probability activity on the **Elementary School Text** page at the beginning of this section is taken from a third grade textbook. In what ways does this activity meet the *Expectations* described in the **Grade 3–5 Data Analysis and Probability Standard**?

BENNETT-BURTON-NELSON WEBSITE

www.mhhe.com/bbn

Virtual Manipulatives
Interactive Chapter Applets
Puzzlers

Grid and Dot Paper
Color Transparencies
Extended Bibliography

Links and Readings
Geometer Sketchpad Modules

Activity Set **8.2**   MULTISTAGE PROBABILITY EXPERIMENTS

PURPOSE

To perform multistage probability experiments and then compare the resulting experimental probabilities with the corresponding theoretical probabilities.

MATERIALS

Green and Red Tiles from the Manipulative Kit, four coins, a pair of dice, the Spinners on Material Card 23 and containers such as boxes and bags for selecting tile samples.

INTRODUCTION

It once happened in Monte Carlo that red came up on 32 consecutive spins of a roulette wheel. The probability that such a run will occur is about one out of 4 billion.

   The probability of two or more events occurring is called *compound probability* or *multistage probability*. When one event does not influence or affect the outcome of another event, the two are called *independent events*. For example, because the second spin of a roulette wheel is not affected by the first spin, the two are considered independent events. When one event does influence the outcome of a second, the events are said to be *dependent events*.

   Consider, for example, the probability of randomly drawing 2 red tiles from a box containing 3 red tiles and 4 green tiles. On the first draw, the probability of obtaining a red tile is $\frac{3}{7}$. If the first tile is replaced before the second draw, the probability of drawing another red tile is $\frac{3}{7}$, because the numbers of each color of tiles in the box are the same as they were on the first draw. These two drawings are *independent* events because the result of the first draw does not affect the outcome of the second draw. The probability of drawing 2 red tiles in this case is $\frac{3}{7} \times \frac{3}{7} = \frac{9}{49}$, as illustrated by the probability tree on page 241.

Tree Diagrams

HANDS-ON Mini Lab

Materials
• 2 counters
• marker

What You'll LEARN

Use tree diagrams to count outcomes and find probabilities.

NEW Vocabulary

fair game
tree diagram
sample space

Work with a partner.

Here is a probability game that you can play with two counters.

• Mark one side of the first counter A. Mark the other side B. Mark both sides of the second counter A.

• Player 1 tosses the counters. If both sides shown are the same, Player 1 wins a point. If the sides are different, Player 2 wins a point. Record your results.

• Player 2 then tosses the counters and the results are recorded. Continue alternating the tosses until each player has tossed the counters ten times. The player with the most points wins.

1. Before you play, **make a conjecture**. Do you think that each player has an equal chance of winning? Explain.

2. Now, play the game. Who won? What was the final score?

3. Collect the data from the entire class. What is the combined score for Player 1 versus Player 2?

4. Do you want to change the conjecture you made in Exercise 1? Explain.

A game in which players of equal skill have an equal chance of winning is a **fair game**. One way you can analyze whether games are fair is by drawing a **tree diagram**. A tree diagram is used to show all of the possible outcomes, or **sample space**, in a probability experiment.

EXAMPLE Draw a Tree Diagram

1 GAMES Refer to the Mini Lab above. Draw a tree diagram to show the sample space. Then determine whether the game is fair.

There are four equally-likely outcomes with two favoring each player. So, the probability that each player can win is $\frac{1}{2}$. Thus, the game is fair.

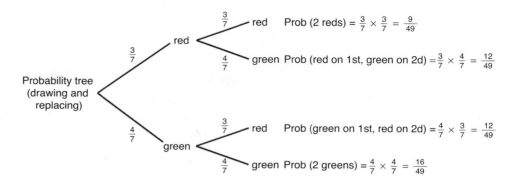

A completely different situation exists if the tile obtained on the first draw is not returned to the box before the second tile is drawn. In this case, the probability of drawing a red tile on the second draw depends on what happens on the first draw. That is, these events are *dependent*. For example, if a red tile is taken on the first draw, the probability of selecting a red tile on the second draw is $\frac{2}{6}$. In this case, the probability of drawing 2 red tiles is $\frac{3}{7} \times \frac{2}{6} = \frac{6}{42}$. The following probability tree illustrates this case.

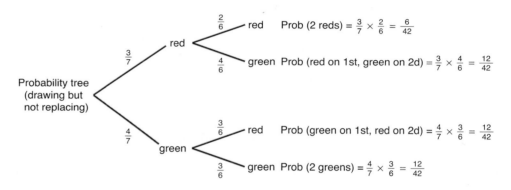

In both cases, the set of all possible outcomes shown in the probability tree is the *sample space* of the experiment. Both experiments have the same sample space {red-red, red-green, green-red, green-green}, but the probabilities of the various outcomes are different.

In the following activities, there are several experiments involving compound probabilities with both independent and dependent events. In each case, the experimental probability will be compared with the theoretical probability.

---

1. The following experiment has a result likely to be contrary to your intuition. Suppose that 3 red and 3 green tiles are placed in a container and that 2 are selected at random (both at once). What is the probability of getting 2 tiles of different colors? Write a conjecture below about the probability, and then perform the experiment 40 times and tally your results in the following table.

Conjecture:

	Tally	Total
Two tiles of different colors		
Two tiles of the same color		

a. Based on your results, what is the experimental probability of drawing the following?

2 tiles of different colors _____

2 tiles of the same color _____

*b. One way to determine the *theoretical* probability is to systematically list all 15 possible pairs that could be drawn from the container. Complete the sample space of all possible outcomes started below. (Notice that the tiles of each color have been numbered to preserve their identity.) Complete the list and use it to determine the theoretical probabilities by forming the following ratio. Compare the theoretical probabilities to the experimental probabilities from part a.

$$\frac{\text{Number of favorable outcomes}}{\text{Total number of outcomes}} =$$

Probability of 2 tiles of a different color _____

Probability of 2 tiles of the same color _____

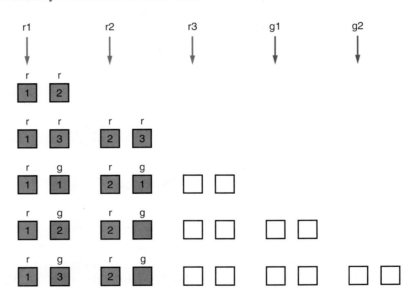

c. Drawing 2 tiles is the same as drawing 1 tile and then, without replacing it, drawing a second tile. The probability of drawing a red tile is $\frac{1}{2}$. The probability of then drawing a second red tile is $\frac{2}{5}$. The probability of drawing a red followed by a red is $\frac{1}{2} \times \frac{2}{5} = \frac{1}{5}$, as shown on the following probability tree. Determine the theoretical probabilities of the remaining three outcomes.

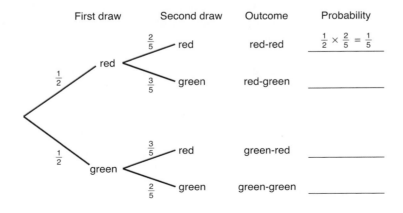

*d. The theoretical probability of drawing 2 tiles of different colors can be obtained from the preceding tree diagram. (Note in this case, the order of the tiles does not matter; green-red and red-green both count as drawing 2 tiles of different colors.) Record and explain how you determined the theoretical probability from the tree diagram. Compare this result to the theoretical probability determined in part b.

2. What is the probability that, on a toss of 4 coins, 2 will come up heads and 2 will come up tails? First make a conjecture about the probability and then perform the experiment by tossing 4 coins and recording the numbers of heads and tails in the table below. Do this experiment 32 times.

Conjecture:

	1	2	3	4	5	6	7	8	9	10	11	12	13	14	15	16	17	18	19	20	21	22	23	24	25	26	27	28	29	30	31	32
H																																
T																																

a. According to your table, what is the experimental probability of obtaining exactly 2 heads on a toss of 4 coins?

b. Tossing 4 coins at once is like tossing a single coin 4 times. Complete the tree diagram at the top of the next page to determine the sample space of all possible outcomes when a coin is tossed 4 times in succession. There will be 16 possible outcomes. How many of these will have 2 heads and 2 tails?

*a. What is the theoretical probability of rolling a double 6 in 1 roll of the dice?

b. What is the theoretical probability of not rolling a double 6 in 1 roll of the dice?

*c. What is the theoretical probability of not rolling a double 6 in 2 rolls of the dice?

d. Indicate how you would find the theoretical probability of not rolling a double 6 in 24 rolls of the dice. (Do not multiply your answer out.)

*e. The product $\frac{35}{36} \times \frac{35}{36} \times \ldots \times \frac{35}{36}$, in which $\frac{35}{36}$ occurs 24 times, is approximately .51. How can you use the result of part d to determine the theoretical probability of rolling at least one double 6 in 24 rolls of the dice?

6. Simulation: A TV game show offers its contestants the opportunity to win a prize by choosing 1 of 3 doors. Behind 1 door is a valuable prize, but behind the other 2 doors is junk. After the contestant has chosen a door, the host opens 1 of the remaining doors, which has junk behind it, and asks if the contestant would like to *stick* with the initial choice or *switch* to the remaining unopened door. If you were the contestant, would you stick, switch, or, possibly, choose the options at random? You may be surprised to discover that your chances of winning vary and depend on your strategy.

a. *Probability of Sticking:* Suppose you always stick with your first choice. To simulate the sticking strategy, imagine using the spinner from Material Card 23 and spinning the paper clip to simulate choosing a door at random. Since you are sticking with your first choice, you will win if you spin the door with a prize. What is the theoretical probability of winning the prize if you always stick with your first choice?

b. *Probability of Switching:* No matter what door the contestant chooses, the host will always open a door with junk behind it and ask if the contestant wants to switch. Imagine choosing the first door randomly, using the spinner as in part a. With the switch strategy, you win if the pointer stops on "junk," but you lose if the pointer stops on "prize." Explain why this happens. What is the theoretical probability of winning the prize with a switch strategy?

c. *Experimental Probability of Randomly Sticking or Switching:* Maybe the best strategy would be to choose a door and then decide on a stick or switch strategy by chance. Perform the following experiment to simulate this strategy. Choose your first door randomly, using the spinner as above in parts a and b. Then use the second spinner (from Material Card 23) to decide whether you should stick or switch. Perform the experiment 50 times and compute the experimental probability of winning the prize with this strategy. First fill in the following blanks so you can quickly complete the table of tallies from the spins.

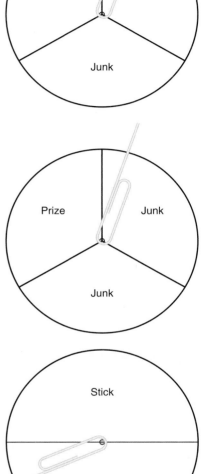

1st spinner	2nd spinner		1st spinner	2nd spinner	
junk	switch	_Prize_	prize	switch	_____
junk	stick	_____	prize	stick	_____

		Tally		Total
Prize		_____		_____
No prize		_____		_____

Experimental probability _____

d. *Theoretical Probability of Randomly Sticking or Switching:* This two-stage tree diagram represents picking a door at random and then deciding to stick or switch at random. The uppermost branch shows that if you randomly choose a junk door and then randomly spin "switch," you win the prize. Finish labeling the outcomes of the second stage and determine the theoretical probability of winning a prize with the random selection of stick or switch.

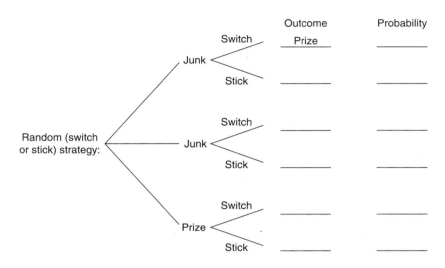

e. Suppose you were chosen to be a contestant for this game show. Write a short summary explaining what strategy you would choose and why you would choose it.

JUST FOR FUN

TRICK DICE

The four dice shown next have the following remarkable property: no matter which die your opponent selects, you can always select one of the remaining three dice so that the probability of winning when you each roll your die is in your favor. (Winning means having a greater number of dots facing up.) Make a set of these dice, either by altering regular dice or by using the dice on Material Card 24.

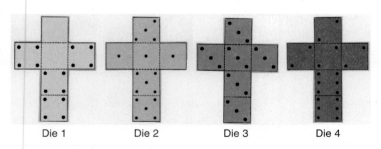

Die 1   Die 2   Die 3   Die 4

Try the following experiment with die 2 and die 4. Roll both dice 21 times and record the resulting numbers in the appropriate boxes of the following table. Then circle the numbers for which die 4 wins over die 2. Before beginning the experiment, try to predict which die has the better chance of winning.

Die 2																					
Die 4																					

1. For the winning die in the experiment above, what is the experimental probability of winning.

*2. Complete this table to show all 36 pairs of numbers that can result from the two dice. Circle the pairs in which die 4 has the greater number. What is the theoretical probability that die 4 will win over die 2? Compare this result to the experimental probability in question 1.

Die 2

Die 4	5	5	5	1	1	1
2	2, 5	2, 5	2, 5	(2,1)	(2,1)	(2,1)
2						
2						
2						
6						
6						

*3. If a 2 is rolled on die 4 and a 1 is rolled on die 2, then die 4 wins. What is the probability of these events happening? (*Hint*: Multiply the 2 probabilities.)

*4. If a 6 is rolled on die 4, it wins over every number on die 2. What is the chance of rolling a 6 on die 4?

*5. The theoretical probability that die 4 will win over die 2 is the sum of the probabilities in questions 3 and 4. What is this probability? Compare this result to your answer in problem 2.

Similar approaches can be used to show that die 2 wins over die 1, die 1 wins over die 3, and die 3 wins over die 4. Surprisingly, the first die of each of these pairs has a $\frac{2}{3}$ probability of winning over the second die. Try this experiment with some of your friends. Let them choose a die first, and you will always be able to select one with a greater chance of winning.

 DOOR PRIZES APPLET: STICK OR SWITCH?

You may have heard of the TV game show where the contestant picks one of three doors in hopes there is a prize behind it. The host then opens one of the remaining doors with junk behind it and asks if the contestant wishes to stick with the original choice or switch. Would you *Stick* or *Switch*? This applet will help you discover the winning strategy. The results may be surprising.

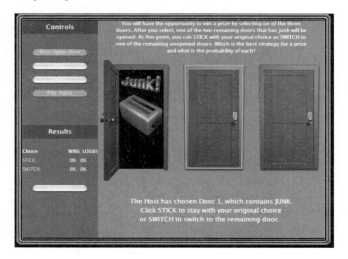

Door Prizes Applet, Chapter 8
www.mhhe.com/bbn

Follow-Up Questions and Activities 8.2

1. *School Classroom:* When asked to determine the probability of drawing two green tiles from a box containing three red tiles and three green tiles, one pair of students disagreed about an approach to the problem. One student said you must reach into the container and randomly pull out two tiles in one draw. The other said that you reach in and randomly draw one tile, then reach in again and randomly draw the second tile. Explain how you would help the students settle this difference without simply telling them what to do.

2. *School Classroom:* Several of your students insist that the probability of rolling two dice and obtaining a 2 on one die and a 3 on the other, is $\frac{1}{6} + \frac{1}{6}$. Explain how you can help them understand the error in their reasoning and how you can help them discover the correct probability.

3. *School Classroom:* Read the probability game on the **Elementary School Text** page at the beginning of this section. Describe what you would say or do as the teacher to help a student who does not understand how to construct a tree diagram to analyze this game.

4. *Math Concepts:* Suppose you are dealing cards from a 16-card set with 4 each of the cards numbered 1, 2, 3, and 4.
    a. What is the probability of being dealt a pair (two cards with the same number) if you are dealt two cards at a time? Set up a probability tree to explore this idea. Show your procedure and explain your thinking.
    b. What is the probability of being dealt two cards that sum to at most 5? Set up a probability tree to explore this idea. Show your procedure and explain your thinking.

5. *Math Concepts:*
    a. Does rolling two four-sided tetrahedral dice with sides numbered 1, 2, 3, and 4 instead of two standard cubical dice with sides numbered 1, 2, 3, 4, 5, and 6 increase or decrease your chances of rolling doubles? Set up a probability tree to explore this idea. Show your procedure and explain your thinking.
    b. Does rolling two eight-sided octahedral dice with sides numbered 1, 2, 3, 4, 5, 6, 7, and 8 instead of standard cubical dice with sides numbered 1, 2, 3, 4, 5, and 6 increase or decrease your chances of rolling doubles? Set up a probability tree to explore this idea. Show your procedure and explain your thinking.

6. *NCTM Standards:* Design a simple probability experiment that you believe is appropriate for an elementary school class. Describe your experiment and write a few questions for the students. For the probability experiment you designed, state the *Standard(s)* and *Expectation(s)* from the **Data Analysis and Probability Standard(s)** in the back pages of this book that your experiment addresses. Explain how your experiment addresses these *Expectations*.

 BENNETT-BURTON-NELSON WEBSITE

www.mhhe.com/bbn

Virtual Manipulatives	Grid and Dot Paper	Links and Readings
Interactive Chapter Applets	Color Transparencies	Geometer Sketchpad Modules
Puzzlers	Extended Bibliography	

Elementary
School Activity

PROBABILITY EXPERIMENTS WITH DICE

Purpose: To provide elementary school students with an example of an experimental approach to understanding simple probability.

Connections: Ask the class the meaning of the following phrase "There is a 50-50 chance it will rain." They may suggest several meanings such as, there is a good chance it will rain; or they don't know for sure; etc. Then discuss what it means to say, "There is a less than a 50-50 chance it will rain." Tell them that the chance something will happen is sometimes difficult to determine and that today they will perform an experiment to look at the chance of getting certain numbers when rolling two dice.

Materials: One pair of dice per pair of students, overheads or poster paper for creating class probability charts, and one or two probability charts per pair of students like the probability chart below.

1. Post a probability chart like the one here in front of the class and then follow the steps below the chart.

This third grade student conjectured that the 6-column would fill up first.

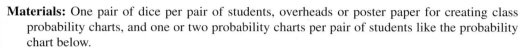

Sum of Two Dice Probability Chart

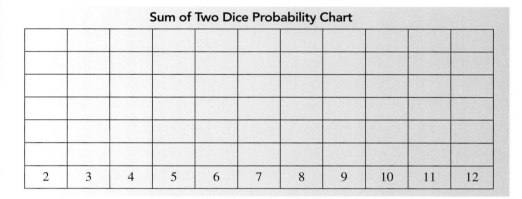

2	3	4	5	6	7	8	9	10	11	12

(i)   Have each pair of students roll their dice and write down the sum.

(ii) Ask each pair of students what sum they rolled and record an X in the table above that number.

(iii) Repeat these steps until one column on the chart is filled.

2. Pass out the blank probability charts and pairs of dice to each pair of students and have them repeat the experiment until one of their columns is filled.

3. Now repeat the experiment described in #1 with the whole class and with a new chart, but first ask each student to pick the number of the column they think will fill up first. Record the student names (or initials) under the column they choose. When the experiment is completed, start a discussion by asking the students why they chose the columns they did.

4. Repeat the experiment, if desired, always asking the students to choose the column they think will fill up first and asking the students why they are choosing this number. Discuss the results of each experiment. The experiments should lead the students to the conclusion that some sums have a greater chance of occurring than others. Ask them to list the numbers of the columns that appear to fill up fastest and the numbers that have the least chance of filling a column.

9 Geometric Figures

The study of geometry in grades 3–5 requires thinking and doing. As students sort, build, draw, model, trace, measure, and construct, their capacity to visualize geometric relationships will develop. At the same time they are learning to reason and to make, test, and justify conjectures about these relationships.[1]

Activity Set 9.1   FIGURES ON RECTANGULAR AND CIRCULAR GEOBOARDS

PURPOSE

To use rectangular geoboards to illustrate geometric figures and circular geoboards to study inscribed and central angles.

Virtual Manipulatives

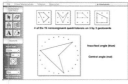

www.mhhe.com/bbn

MATERIALS

Rectangular and circular geoboards and rubber bands (optional). Templates for making rectangular and circular geoboards are on Material Cards 8 and 26 respectively and are also available in the Virtual Manipulatives. Recording paper for activity 1 is on Material Card 25 and the three-circle Venn diagram is on Material Card 6. A protractor is on Material Card 19. Scissors are needed for activity 1.

INTRODUCTION

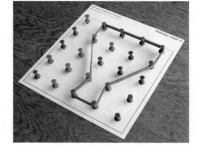

The geoboard is a popular physical model for illustrating geometric concepts and solving geometric investigations. The most familiar type of geoboard has a square shape, with 25 pins arranged in a 5 by 5 array. Rubber bands can be placed around the pins to form models for segments, angles, and polygons. For example, here is a 8-sided polygon.

The circular geoboard is very helpful for developing angle concepts. The one shown at the top of page 255 has a pin at the center and an outer circle of 24 pins. Many of the angles and polygons that can be formed on this circular geoboard cannot be made on the rectangular geoboard. The circular geoboard will be used to form central and inscribed angles and to establish an important relationship between them.

---

[1]*Principles and Standards for School Mathematics* (Reston, VA: National Council of Teachers of Mathematics, 2000): 165.

Draw a line or lines to make the new shapes.

1 Make 2 triangles.

2 Make 2 squares.

3 Make 4 squares.

4 Make 2 triangles.

5 Make 2 rectangles.

6 Make 6 triangles.

7 Make 3 triangles.

8 Make 1 triangle and 1 square.

9 Make 1 triangle and 1 rectangle.

LOG ON   www.mmhmath.com
For more Practice

Since most geoboard activities can be carried out on dot paper by drawing figures, the use of geoboards is optional in the following activities. However, geoboards provide insights because of the ease with which figures can be shaped and reshaped during an investigation. They also encourage experimentation and creativity. If geoboards are not available, you may wish to make them from boards and thumb tacks or finishing nails using the templates on Material Cards 8 and 26.

Rectangular Geoboards

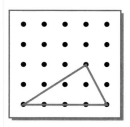

1. This figure shows a geoboard triangle with its base along the bottom row of pins. Determine all possible geoboard triangles that have the same base and the third vertex on a pin. Record your results by drawing each triangle on geoboard recording paper (Material Card 25).

    a. Assuming each small square = 1 square unit, determine the area of each of the triangles you drew using methods developed in Activity Set 6.4. Record the area inside the triangle.

    *b. Cut out each geoboard that has a triangle drawn on it. (Cut around the entire geoboard, not just the triangles.) Group the triangles that have the same area. Describe the characteristics that triangles of equal area have in common.

    *c. The two triangles shown here are *congruent* because one can be cut out and placed on the other so that they coincide. Sort all of the triangles into sets of congruent triangles. Select one triangle from each set of congruent triangles to form a new collection of noncongruent triangles. How many noncongruent triangles do you have?

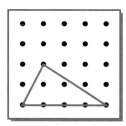 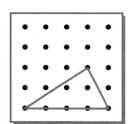

    d. Label the three-circle Venn diagram, Material Card 6, as shown here. Sort the collection of noncongruent triangles from part c by placing them in the appropriate regions of the Venn diagram. Record the number of triangles in each region on the diagram at the right. (*Note:* A *scalene triangle* has all sides of different length; an *isosceles triangle* has at least two sides of equal length; and a *right triangle* has one right angle.)

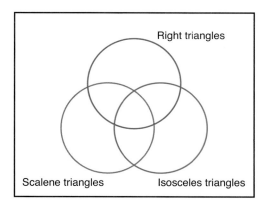

e. For the regions of the Venn diagram in part d which have no entries, can triangles that cannot be constructed on a 5 pin by 5 pin geoboard be drawn that belong to those regions? Explain how you arrived at your answer.

2. The first geoboard here shows three segments of different lengths. A geoboard segment has its endpoints on geoboard pins. Use your geoboard to determine how many geoboard segments of *different* lengths can be constructed. Record your solutions on these geoboards.

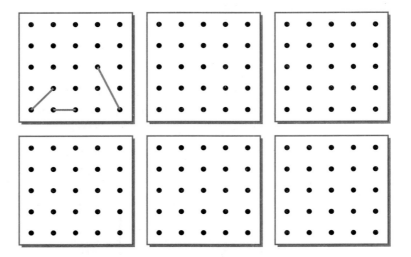

3. The following geoboards have a rubber band around the outer pins to form as large a square as possible. Additional rubber bands have been used to divide the squares into two *congruent* halves. (Congruent figures have the same size and shape.)

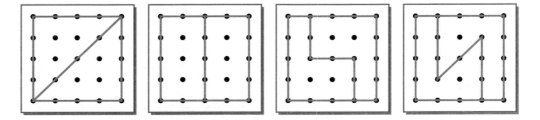

Find at least seven other ways to divide the square into congruent halves, and draw them below.

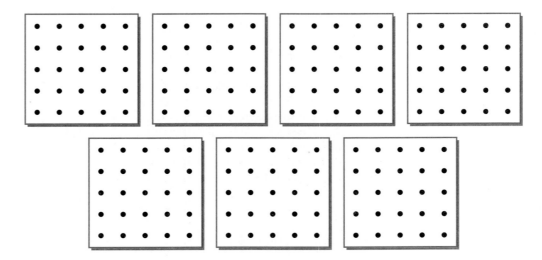

*4. There are 16 noncongruent quadrilaterals that can be formed on a 3 pin by 3 pin geoboard. Each of the quadrilaterals has its vertices at geoboard pins. Sketch them here.

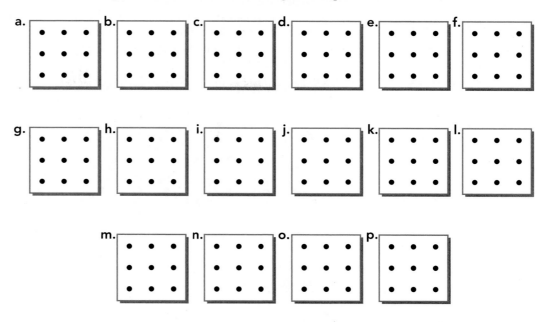

Classify each of the preceding quadrilaterals by recording the letter of its geoboard after each description that applies to it. (A *parallelogram* has two pairs of opposite parallel sides, a *trapezoid* has exactly one pair of parallel sides, a *convex polygon* is not "caved in," i.e., the line segment connecting any pair of points on the polygon lies within the polygon and a *concave polygon* is nonconvex.)

Square   _____

Rectangle, but not square   _____

Parallelogram, but not rectangle   _____

Trapezoid   _____

Convex   _____

Concave   _____

5. On each geoboard sketch a polygon whose vertices are points of the geoboard and which satisfies the given conditions. (An octagon is an 8-sided polygon, a nonagon is 9-sided, a decagon is 10-sided, and a dodecagon is 12-sided.)

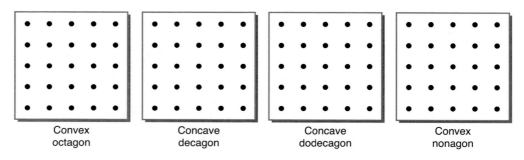

Convex   Concave   Concave   Convex
octagon   decagon   dodecagon   nonagon

Circular Geoboards

6. **Central Angles:** An angle whose vertex is located at the center of the circle and whose sides intersect the circle is called a *central angle*. The portion of the circle that is cut off by the sides of the angle is called the *intercepted arc* (see the diagram by activity 7). The central angle on this geoboard has a measure of 15 degrees (15°) because its intercepted arc is $\frac{1}{24}$ of a whole circle (360° ÷ 24 = 15°).

   *a. Under each geoboard, write the number of degrees in the indicated central angle.

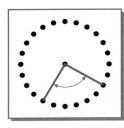  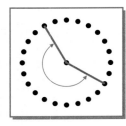 

   _____   _____   _____   _____

   *b. On your geoboard form central angles that have the following angle measures. Then draw the angles here.

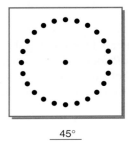 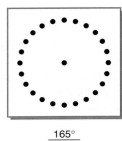 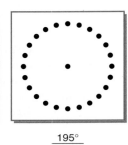 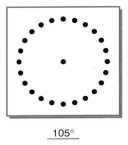

   <u>45°</u>   <u>165°</u>   <u>195°</u>   <u>105°</u>

7. **Inscribed Angles:** An angle is *inscribed* in an arc of a circle when the vertex of the angle is on the arc and its sides contain endpoints of the arc. In the figure at the left angle *ABC* is inscribed in the dark blue arc *ABC* and angle *ABC intercepts* the green arc *AC*.

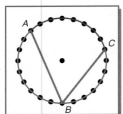

   *a. Construct the following inscribed angles on your circular geoboard and measure them with your protractor. (There is a protractor on Material Card 19. If you do not have a circular geoboard, draw the angles lightly, in pencil, on the geoboard template on Material Card 26.)

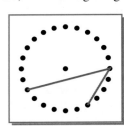 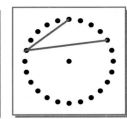 

   _____   _____   _____

 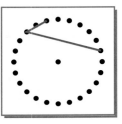

   _____   _____

*b. Look at the inscribed angles in part a that have the same angle measure. Make and record a conjecture about the *equality* of inscribed angles and the size of their corresponding intercepted arcs. Test your conjecture by drawing and measuring more inscribed angles. Record your conclusions.

Conjecture:

*c. Angle *PQR* is inscribed in a semicircle (half a circle). Using your circular geoboard and protractor, form and measure angle *PQR* as well as several other inscribed angles whose sides intersect the ends of a diameter. Record the angles and their measures below. Make and record a conjecture about the measure of these angles.

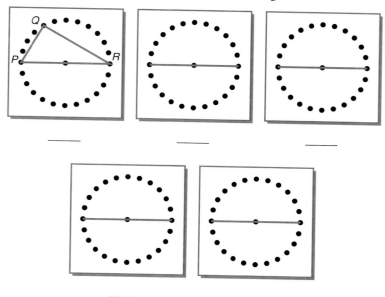

_____   _____   _____

_____   _____

Conjecture:

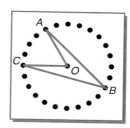

Angle *AOC* _____

Angle *ABC* _____

8. Form central angle *AOC* and inscribed angle *ABC* on your circular geoboard (or draw them on your circular geoboard template). Determine the measure of central angle *AOC*. Measure angle *ABC* with your protractor. Record both measures beneath the figure.

*a. Form each of the following inscribed angles on your geoboard, measure the angle with your protractor, and record the inscribed angle measure below the figure. Then, on each geoboard, form and determine the measure of the central angle that intercepts the same arc as the inscribed angle and record it.

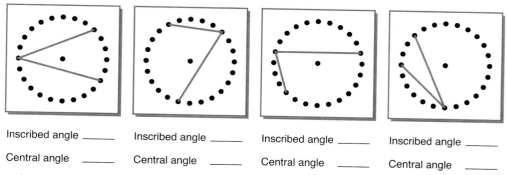

Inscribed angle _____   Inscribed angle _____   Inscribed angle _____   Inscribed angle _____

Central angle _____   Central angle _____   Central angle _____   Central angle _____

*b. There is a relationship between the measure of an inscribed angle and that of its corresponding central angle. Write a conjecture about that relationship.

Conjecture:

Cross Sections of a Cube Applet, Chapter 9
www.mhhe.com/bbn

JUST FOR FUN

Follow-Up Questions and Activities **9.1**

1. *School Classroom:* While working on an activity to divide geoboard squares into two congruent halves, several students could see that halves as in figures A and B were congruent but could not see that the parts of figures C and D were also congruent halves. Explain how you can help students determine when two plane figures are congruent so they can apply this knowledge to geoboard figures as well as other plane figures.

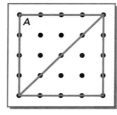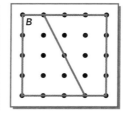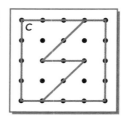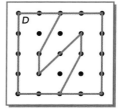

2. *School Classroom:* Several of your students insist that the following is a nonsquare rhombus because the sides are at a diagonal. How can you help your students resolve this issue?

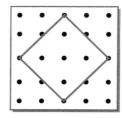

3. *School Classroom:* The second grade **Elementary School Text** page at the beginning of this section asks students to draw geometric shapes. Suppose you had students in your class who could recognize triangular, square, and rectangular shapes but were not able to dissect the **Elementary School Text** page figures into different shapes as requested. Describe at least two different ways you could help these students.

4. *Math Concepts:* Each triangle in the following family of triangles formed on a circular geoboard has base $T_1 T_{23}$. Downloadable Circular Geoboards and printable Virtual Geoboards are available at the companion website.

Determine which triangles are congruent and which triangles are acute, obtuse, scalene, isosceles, equilateral, or right; identify each triangle by its vertex angle (T_2 through T_{22}) and list the triangles in each category. Sketch or print the triangles you have formed and explain why each triangle belongs in the category you have put it in.

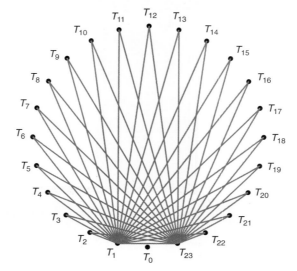

5. *Math Concepts:* Which regular polygons (all sides congruent and all angles congruent) can you form on a 24-pin circular geoboard? Illustrate each regular polygon on a circular geoboard and explain how you know it is a regular polygon. Circular Geoboards are available for download at the companion website.

6. *Math Concepts:* Downloadable Rectangular Geoboards and printable Virtual Geoboards are available at the companion website.

   a. Form polygons with 13, 14, 15, and 16 sides whose vertices are pins of a 5 pin by 5 pin geoboard. Sketch or print your work.

   b. Classify the polygons in part a as convex or concave.

   c. What is the polygon with the most number of sides you can form with vertices on the pins of a 5 pin by 5 pin geoboard? Is the polygon convex or concave? Sketch or print your work.

7. *NCTM Standards:* Go to http://illuminations.nctm.org/ and under "Lessons" select grade levels 3–5 and the **Geometry Standard.** Choose a lesson that involves polygons.

   a. State the title of the lesson and briefly summarize the lesson.

   b. Referring to the **Standards Summary** in the back pages of this book as necessary, list the *Geometry Standard Expectations* that the lesson addresses and explain how the lesson addresses these *Expectations*.

BENNETT-BURTON-NELSON WEBSITE

www.mhhe.com/bbn

Virtual Manipulatives	Grid and Dot Paper	Links and Readings
Interactive Chapter Applets	Color Transparencies	Geometer Sketchpad Modules
Puzzlers	Extended Bibliography	

Activity Set **9.2** REGULAR AND SEMIREGULAR TESSELLATIONS

PURPOSE

To study regular and semiregular tessellations of the plane.

MATERIALS

Pattern Blocks and Polygons for Tessellations from the Manipulative Kit or from the Virtual Manipulatives. You may wish to use scissors for activity 4.

Giant's Causeway, County Antrim, Ireland.

INTRODUCTION

The hexagonal-shaped basalt columns in the photographs above occur off the coast of Northern Ireland. The partitioning of surfaces by hexagons or nearly hexagonal figures is common in nature.[3] A figure, such as a regular hexagon, that can be used repeatedly to cover a surface without gaps or overlaps is said to *tile* or *tessellate* the surface. The resulting pattern is called a *tessellation*. An infinite variety of shapes can be used as the basic figure for a tessellation. The famous Dutch artist Maurits C. Escher (1898–1972) is noted for his tessellations with drawings of birds, fish, and other living creatures. Techniques for creating Escher-type tessellations are developed in Activity Set 11.2.

Pattern Block Tessellations

1. Figure 1, on the next page, shows the beginnings of a tessellation with the yellow hexagon pattern block and figures 2 and 3 show the beginnings of two different tessellations with the red trapezoid.

---

[3]For some examples of hexagonal patterns and a discussion of why they occur in nature, see H. Weyl, *Symmetry* (Princeton: Princeton University Press, 1952): 83–89.

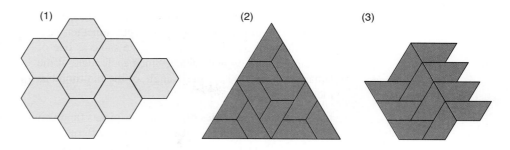

(1)   (2)   (3)

a. Find at least one other way to tessellate with the red trapezoid. Record your pattern.

b. All of the pattern block pieces other than the hexagon have more than one tessellation pattern like the trapezoid. For the square and for the blue parallelogram, sketch enough of at least two patterns so that a reader will be able to extend your patterns.

*2. When 3 acute angles (an angle measuring between 0° and 90°) of tan rhombuses are put together at a point, the sum of their measures is the same as one of the angles of an orange square. Since each angle of the square measures 90°, a small angle of the tan rhombus measures 30°.

 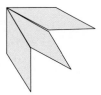

By comparing the angles of the various pieces (and using no angle-measuring instruments), determine the measures of the other seven different angles of the pieces in the pattern block collection. Draw pattern block sketches below and describe or show briefly how you reached your conclusions. Then record the angle measures on the pattern blocks below.

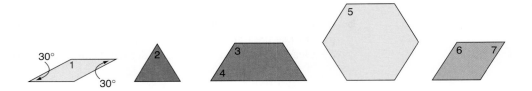

3. Both of the figures at the right have been formed by taping two pattern blocks together to form new shapes. The first figure, which uses a trapezoid and a blue parallelogram, is a hexagon (6 sides and 6 interior angles) and the second, which uses a triangle and a tan parallelogram, is a pentagon (5 sides and 5 interior angles). On the diagrams, record the measure of each interior angle in the new shapes.

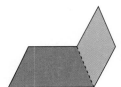 

a. Use tape and pattern blocks to form the hexagon and pentagon shown on the previous page and test each of them to see if they will tessellate. If so, sketch enough of the beginnings of a pattern so the reader has sufficient information to extend it. If not, explain why it will not work.

b. Tape two other pattern block pieces together to create a new shape that will not tessellate. Sketch your figure and explain why it will not tessellate.

a. There are six semiregular tessellations that can be formed using combinations of two different regular polygons about each vertex. Find and sketch at least one of these tessellations. (*Hint:* Look for combinations of angles whose measures add up to 360°.)

b. There are two semiregular tessellations that use combinations of three different regular polygons about each vertex. Find and sketch one of these tessellations. (*Hint:* Look for combinations of angles whose measures add up to 360°.)

*c. *Pattern Block Tessellations:* It is possible to tile a plane with combinations of polygons that do not form a semiregular tessellation. These tilings may have a regular pattern, but not every vertex point is surrounded by the same arrangement of polygons and not every polygon need be regular. Use your pattern blocks to create such a tiling and sketch it here.

JUST FOR FUN

THE GAME OF HEX (2 players)

Hex, a game of deductive reasoning, is played on a game board of hexagons similar to the 11 by 11 grid shown here (see Material Card 27). Player 1 and player 2 take turns placing their markers or symbols on any unoccupied hexagon. Player 1 attempts to form an unbroken chain or string of symbols from the left side of the grid to the right, and player 2 tries to form a chain of symbols from the top of the grid to the bottom. The first player to complete a chain is the winner. In this sample game, player 2 (using O's) won against player 1 (using X's).

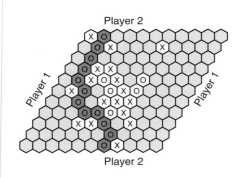

Winning Strategy: There will always be a winner in the game of Hex, since the only way a player can prevent the other from winning is to form an unbroken chain of markers from one side of the grid to the other. On a 3 by 3 game board, the person who plays first can easily win in 3 moves. What should be the first move? Find a first move on the 4 by 4 and 5 by 5 game boards that will ensure a win regardless of the opponent's moves.

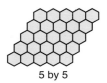

3 by 3   4 by 4   5 by 5

It is tempting to conclude that a winning strategy on an 11 by 11 game board begins with a first move on the center hexagon. However, there are so many possibilities for plays on a grid of this size that no winning strategy has yet been found. There is a type of proof in mathematics, called an *existence proof*, which shows that something exists even though no one is able to find it. It has been proved that a winning strategy does exist for the first player in a game of Hex on an 11 by 11 grid, but just what that strategy is, no one knows.[4]

---

[4]For an elementary version of this proof, see M. Gardner, "Mathematical Games," *Scientific American* 197 (1) (1957): 145.

Follow-Up Questions and Activities **9.2**

1. *School Classroom:* Bees form tessellations when they create their honeycombs. How might you use this idea to design an activity for your classroom? Explain your activity ideas and your thinking.

(a)   (b)

2. *School Classroom:* One of your students claims that she has formed regular polygons of 3, 4, and 6 sides on her rectangular geoboard and shows you the following figures. Explain how you would help her determine which of these figures are regular and which are not.

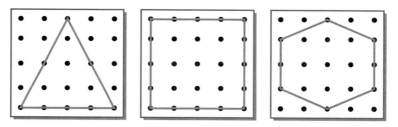

3. *School Classroom:* Do an Internet search and find a website that features a game or math applet focused on tessellations for kids. Print a one-page view of the game or applet, describe the game or applet, and discuss how you would use such an activity in your own class. Give the URL of the game or math applet you found.

4. *Math Concepts:* On Dot Paper or Grid Paper draw a seven-sided polygon that tessellates and show the tessellation. Dot Paper and Grid Paper are available for download at the companion website.

5. *Math Concepts:* Copy this concave quadrilateral in the center of a page of dot paper. Dot Paper is available for download at the companion website.

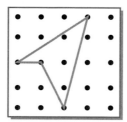

   a. Form a tessellation with this figure. Draw enough of the tessellation so it is obvious that the tessellation can be continued in all directions. Dot Paper is available for download at the companion website.

   b. What observations can you make about the angles around the points where the vertices of the quadrilaterals meet?

6. *Math Concepts:* Use Polygons for Tessellations and create a semiregular tessellation different from the tessellation you produced for activity 5a. Sketch or print your work. Printable Virtual Polygons for Tessellations are available at the companion website.

7. *NCTM Standards:* Read over the **Standards Summary** in the back pages of this book. Tessellations are not mentioned. What *Content Standards* and *Expectations* does the study of these topics address? List the *Standards* and *Expectations* and explain your thinking.

BENNETT-BURTON-NELSON WEBSITE

www.mhhe.com/bbn

Virtual Manipulatives	Grid and Dot Paper	Links and Readings
Interactive Chapter Applets	Color Transparencies	Geometer Sketchpad Modules
Puzzlers	Extended Bibliography	

Activity Set **9.3** MODELS FOR REGULAR AND SEMIREGULAR POLYHEDRA

PURPOSE

To construct and use models in order to observe and examine the properties of regular and semi-regular polyhedra.

MATERIALS

Scissors and patterns for constructing regular polyhedra on Material Cards 28 and 29. Two-Centimeter Grid Paper from Material Card 30.

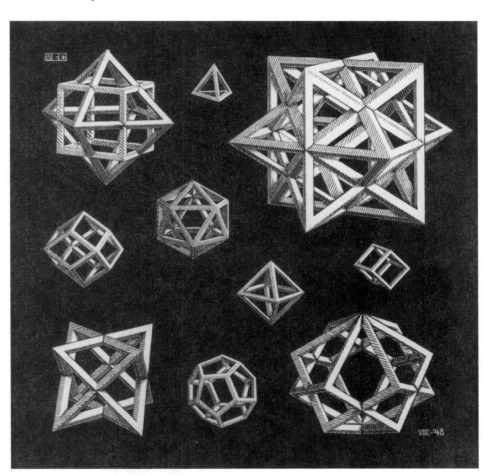

INTRODUCTION

The term polyhedron comes from Greek and means "many faces." A *regular polyhedron* is a convex polyhedron whose faces are regular polygons and whose vertices are each surrounded by the same number of these polygons. The regular polyhedra are also called *Platonic solids* because the Greek philosopher Plato (427–347 B.C.E.) immortalized them in his writings. Euclid (340 B.C.E.) proved that there were exactly five regular polyhedra. Can you identify the Platonic solids in M. C. Escher's wood engraving *Stars?*

*c. The following polyhedra are not Platonic solids. Count their vertices, faces, and edges and record your results. Test your conjecture from part b on these polyhedra.

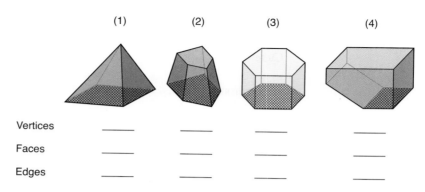

	(1)	(2)	(3)	(4)
Vertices	_____	_____	_____	_____
Faces	_____	_____	_____	_____
Edges	_____	_____	_____	_____

4. Net Patterns for Cubes: The shaded areas in parts a–f below were formed by joining 6 squares along their edges. A two-dimensional pattern that can be folded into a three-dimensional shape without overlap is called a *net* for the three-dimensional shape. Three of the following patterns are nets for a cube and three are not. Identify the patterns in parts a–f that are nets for a cube. Use Two-Centimeter Grid Paper (Material Card 30) to create at least five more nets for a cube (there are 11 nets in total that have 6 squares adjoined along their edges.). You may wish to cut your patterns out to test them. Sketch the nets in the provided grids.

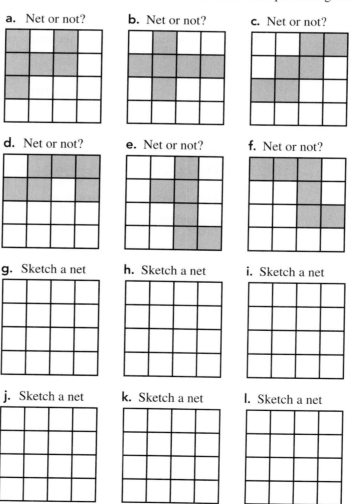

a. Net or not?

b. Net or not?

c. Net or not?

d. Net or not?

e. Net or not?

f. Net or not?

g. Sketch a net

h. Sketch a net

i. Sketch a net

j. Sketch a net

k. Sketch a net

l. Sketch a net

5. Archimedean Solids: A *semiregular polyhedron* is a polyhedron that has as faces two or more regular polygons and the same arrangement of polygons about each vertex. There are a total of 13 semiregular polyhedra shown below, and they are called *Archimedean solids.* These were known to Archimedes (287–212 B.C.E.) who wrote a book on these solids, but the book has been lost.

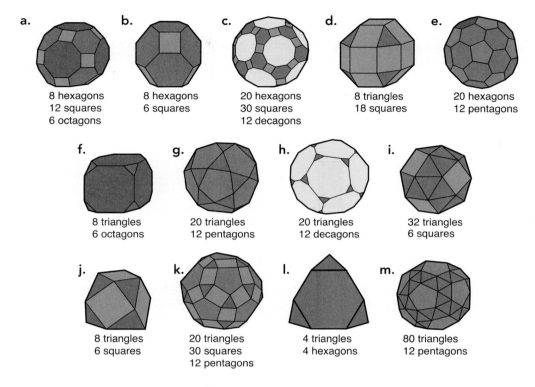

a.
8 hexagons
12 squares
6 octagons

b.
8 hexagons
6 squares

c.
20 hexagons
30 squares
12 decagons

d.
8 triangles
18 squares

e.
20 hexagons
12 pentagons

f.
8 triangles
6 octagons

g.
20 triangles
12 pentagons

h.
20 triangles
12 decagons

i.
32 triangles
6 squares

j.
8 triangles
6 squares

k.
20 triangles
30 squares
12 pentagons

l.
4 triangles
4 hexagons

m.
80 triangles
12 pentagons

The seven Archimedean solids shown in b, e, f, g, h, j, and l can be obtained by truncating Platonic solids. For example, if each vertex of a tetrahedron is cut off, as shown in the figure at the right, we obtain a truncated tetrahedron whose faces are regular hexagons and triangles, as shown in figure l above.

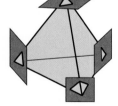

Tetrahedron

- Identify which Platonic solid is truncated to obtain each of the semiregular solids in b, e, f, g, h, and j.
- Note: Vertices may also be cut off all of the way to the midpoints of the edges.
- It may be helpful to look at the Platonic solids you constructed in activity 1.

6. Archimedean solids such as the one shown here (made by a student using this book) can be created by cutting out the polygonal faces and taping them together.

a. How many pentagons and hexagons were needed to make this model?

b. What well-known sports ball has the same number of pentagon and hexagon faces?

An Archimedean solid created by a student at the University of New Hampshire.

JUST FOR FUN

INSTANT INSANITY

Instant Insanity is a popular puzzle that consists of four cubes with their faces colored either red, yellow, blue, or green. The object of the puzzle is to stack the cubes so that each side of the stack (or column) has one of each of the four colors.

Material Card 31 contains patterns for a set of four cubes. Cut out and assemble the cubes and try to solve the puzzle. Note; the arrangement of the cubes in the photo to the right is not a solution to this puzzle.

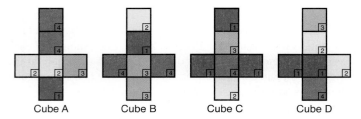

Cube A　　　Cube B　　　Cube C　　　Cube D

Robert E. Levin described the following method for solving this puzzle.[5] He numbered the faces of the cubes, using 1 for red, 2 for yellow, 3 for blue, and 4 for green, as shown below. To solve the puzzle you must get the numbers 1, 2, 3, and 4 along each side of the stack. The sum of these numbers is 10, and the sum of the numbers on opposite sides of the stack must be 20.

Levin made the following table showing opposite pairs of numbers on each cube and their sums. For example, 4 and 2 are on opposite faces of cube A and their sum is 6. The

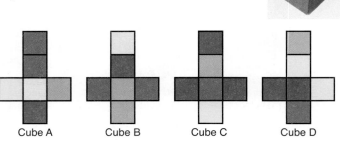

Cube A　　　Cube B　　　Cube C　　　Cube D

bottom row of the table contains the sums of opposite faces for each cube. For one combination of numbers whose sum is 20, the sums have been circled. Notice that above these circled numbers, the numbers 1, 2, 3, and 4 each occur only twice. This tells you how to stack the cubes so that two opposite sides of the stack will have a total sum of 20. (Both of these sides will have all four colors.) The two remaining sides of the stack must also have a sum of 20. Find four more numbers from the bottom row (one for each cube) such that their sum is 20 and each of the numbers 1, 2, 3, and 4 occurs exactly twice among the faces. The remaining two faces of each cube will be its top and bottom faces when it is placed in the stack.

	Cube A	Cube B	Cube C	Cube D
Pairs of opposite faces	4 4 3	4 1 2	1 1 3	1 1 4
	2 1 2	4 3 3	1 4 2	3 2 2
Sums of pairs	⑥5 5	8 4⑤	2⑤5	④3 6

[5]R. Levin, "Solving Instant Insanity," *Journal of Recreational Mathematics* 2 (July 1969): 189–192.

Follow-Up Questions and Activities 9.3

1. *School Classroom:* Suppose that your students are using sticks and gumdrops to create models of the five Platonic solids. How will you help them decide how many sticks and how many gumdrops they need and how to assemble their solids?

2. *School Classroom:* When asked to make a net for a cube, a drawing like net A is the usual response. Design an activity for middle school students that will lead them to draw nets like net B that are formed without using all squares. Describe your activity in such a way that another person could follow your directions. Submit a few designs for a net by sketching them on 2-Centimeter Grid Paper. 2-Centimeter Grid Paper is available for download at the companion website.

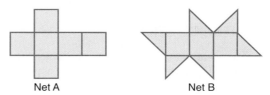

Net A   Net B

3. *Math Concepts:* Design a two-dimensional net for the following figure that is composed of four cubes. Describe your procedure for constructing this net and submit a copy of the net with your response.

4. *Math Concepts:* Open the **Math Laboratory Investigation 9.3: Read Me—Pyramid Patterns Instructions** from the companion website and investigate the pyramid patterns described in question 1 of the *Starting Points for Investigations 9.3.* Show your procedures and explain your thinking.

5. *Math Concepts:* Check your conjecture for Euler's formula (activity 3a) on the two-polygon Archimedean solids in activity 5 (parts b, d, e, f, g, h, i, j, and l) by listing and comparing the number of edges, vertices, and faces. You may wish to do an Internet search on a site such as Math World (mathworld.wolfram.com) to find movable three-dimensional views of the solids pictured here.

6. *NCTM Standards:* Read over the **Geometry Standards** in the back pages of this book. Pick one *Expectation,* from each grade level that the activities in this section address. State the *Expectations* and the *Standards* they are under. Explain which activities address these *Expectations* and how they do so.

BENNETT-BURTON-NELSON WEBSITE

www.mhhe.com/bbn

Virtual Manipulatives	Grid and Dot Paper	Links and Readings
Interactive Chapter Applets	Color Transparencies	Geometer Sketchpad Modules
Puzzlers	Extended Bibliography	

Activity Set **9.4**   CREATING SYMMETRIC FIGURES: PATTERN BLOCKS AND PAPER FOLDING

PURPOSE

To introduce investigations of symmetry.

MATERIALS

Pattern Blocks from the Manipulative Kit or the Virtual Manipulatives, Material Card 32, scissors and pieces of blank or scratch paper.

INTRODUCTION

The *wind rose,* shown below on the left, is a mariner's device for charting the direction of the wind. The earliest known wind rose appeared on the ancient sailing charts of the Mediterranean pilots, who charted eight principal winds. These are marked Nord, NE, EST, SE, Sud, SO, Ovest, and NO on the wind rose. Later, half-winds led to a wind rose with 16 points, and quarter-winds brought the total number of points to 32.[6]

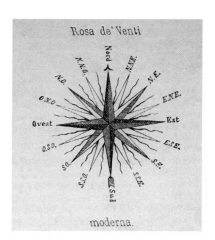

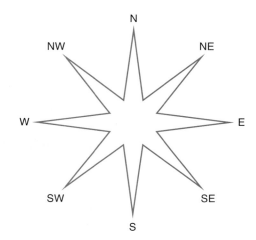

The eight-pointed wind rose shown above at the right is highly symmetric. It has eight lines of symmetry and eight rotational symmetries. For example, a line through any two opposite vertices of the wind rose is a *line of symmetry* because when the wind rose is folded on this line, the two sides will coincide. When a figure has a line of symmetry, the figure is also said to have *reflection symmetry.* The wind rose has *rotational symmetries* of 45°, 90°, 135°, 180°, 225°, 270°, 315°, and 360° because, when rotated about its center through any one of these angles, the figure will coincide with the original position of the wind rose.

Activities 3 to 6 have several basic patterns for cutting out symmetric figures. The variety of figures that can be obtained from slight changes in the angles of the cuts is surprising. The eight-pointed wind rose can be cut from one of these patterns. As you cut out these figures try to predict which one will produce the eight-pointed wind rose.

---

[6]M. C. Krause, "Wind Rose, the Beautiful Circle," *Arithmetic Teacher* 20 (May 1973): 375.

Pattern Block Symmetries

1. Use the square and the tan rhombus from your pattern block pieces to form figure 1. Notice that when another rhombus is attached as in figures 2 and 3, the new figures each have one line of symmetry. When the rhombus is attached as in figure 4, there are no lines of symmetry but there is rotational symmetry of 180°. Finally, when the rhombus is attached as in figure 5, there are no lines of symmetry or rotational symmetries (other than 360°).

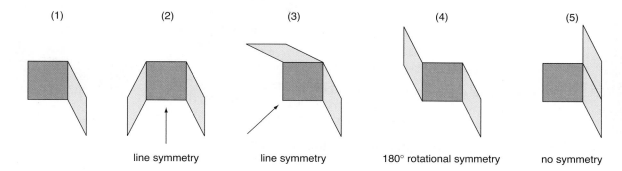

(1)   (2)   (3)   (4)   (5)

line symmetry   line symmetry   180° rotational symmetry   no symmetry

*a. Form this figure with your pattern block pieces. Determine the different ways you can attach exactly one more trapezoid to this figure to create figures with reflection symmetry. Use your pattern blocks to form at least four of these figures and sketch your results. Mark the lines of symmetry on your sketches.

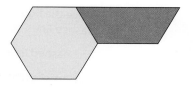

b. Do the same as in part a but find two ways to create figures with rotational symmetry (other than 360°) by attaching exactly one more trapezoid to the figure above. List the rotational symmetries for each figure.

I will learn to identify line symmetry and rotational symmetry.

20.3   Symmetry

Learn

VOCABULARY
line of symmetry
line symmetry
rotational symmetry
point of rotation

Artists use symmetry in their work. The artist's drawing to the right has two different types of symmetry.

A **line of symmetry** is a line that divides the figure into two halves that match exactly when the figure is folded on that line. A figure has **line symmetry** if it has at least one line of symmetry.

Does the artist's drawing have line symmetry?

Line Symmetry

Trace the figure on the right. If you fold it along either of the dashed lines, the two halves match exactly.

The dashed lines are the lines of symmetry in the artist's drawing.

The artist's drawing has line symmetry.

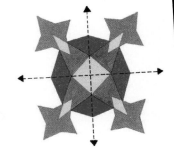

A figure has **rotational symmetry** if it can be rotated less than one full turn (360°) about a **point of rotation** and look exactly the same as it did before.

Does the artist's drawing have rotational symmetry?

Rotational Symmetry

Turn the tracing that you made of the artist's drawing around the point where its lines of symmetry meet until the tracing fits exactly over the original figure. This happens after you turn the tracing $\frac{1}{2}$ turn (180°).

The artist's drawing above has rotational symmetry.

Try It   Trace the figure. Does it have line symmetry? Write *yes* or *no*. If *yes*, draw the lines of symmetry.

1.   2.   3.   4.

5. **Write About It**   **Explain** the difference between line symmetry and rotational symmetry.

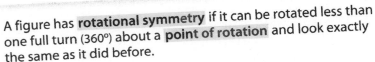

*c. By attaching 6 trapezoids to one hexagon, create the following four figures that have the given properties. Sketch your results.

Figure 1: One line of symmetry and no rotational symmetries (other than 360°)

Figure 2: Six rotational symmetries but no lines of symmetry

Figure 3: Three rotational symmetries and three lines of symmetry

Figure 4: No rotational symmetries (other than 360°) and no lines of symmetry.

2. a. Use your pattern blocks and Material Card 32 to build this design. Complete the design by adding additional pattern blocks so that the design has reflection symmetry about both perpendicular lines. Sketch the completed design on the given axes. Does the completed design have any rotational symmetries? If so, what are they?

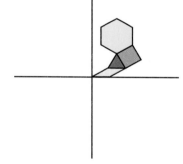

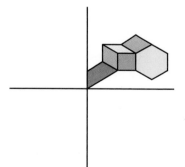

b. Build the design shown here and use additional pattern blocks to complete a design which has rotational symmetries of 90°, 180°, and 270° about the intersection of the perpendicular lines. Sketch the completed design on the given axes. Does the completed design have reflection symmetries? If so, how many? Mark any lines of symmetry on your sketch.

c. Arrange the pattern blocks as shown in this figure. Add additional pattern blocks so that the completed design has rotational symmetry of 90°, 180°, and 270°. Sketch the completed design on the given axes.

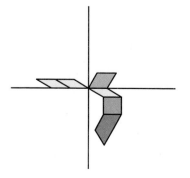

Paper-Folding Symmetries

3. Fold a rectangular piece of paper in half twice, making the second fold perpendicular to the first. Let *C* be the corner of all folded edges. Hold the folded paper at corner *C* and make one cut across as shown by segment *AB* on the diagram. Before opening the folded corner, predict what the shape (shaded part in unfolded) will be and how many lines of symmetry it will have.

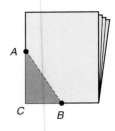

	Predicted Figure	Actual Result
Type of polygon	_____	_____
Number of lines of symmetry	_____	_____

a. Is it possible to draw a segment *AB* and make one cut across the folds so that the piece will unfold to a square? If so, describe how you made your cut. If not, explain why it cannot be done.

b. Experiment with other single cuts that start at point *A* but which exit from any of the other three sides of the twice-folded paper. Continue to predict before you unfold. Make a list of the different types of figures you obtain.

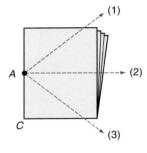

	Predicted Figure	Actual Result
(1)	_____	_____
(2)	_____	_____
(3)	_____	_____

4. Fold a rectangular piece of paper in half twice, making the second fold perpendicular to the first as in activity 3. Let *C* be the corner of all the folded edges. You will make two cuts from the edges to an inside point, as shown here. Before cutting the paper, predict what kind of polygon you will get, how many lines of symmetry the figure will have, and whether the figure will be convex or nonconvex. Cut and check your predictions.

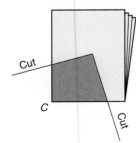

	Predicted Figure	Actual Result
Type of polygon	_____	_____
Number of lines of symmetry	_____	_____
Convex or not	_____	_____

*a. Find a way to make two cuts into an inside point so that you get a regular octagon; a regular hexagon. Sketch the location of your cuts on these folded-paper diagrams.

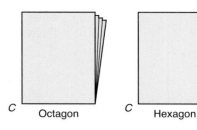

C   Octagon   C   Hexagon

b. Make a sketch of the figure you think will result when you cut a piece of double-folded paper as shown below. Then cut the paper and sketch the result.

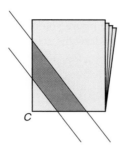

C

Predicted Figure	Actual Result

c. Vary the angle of the cuts in part b so that the two cuts are not parallel to each other. Experiment with cuts that will result in a rhombus inside a square; a square inside a rhombus. Sketch these lines on the folded-paper diagrams below.

Cuts for rhombus   Sketch of rhombus   Cuts for square   Sketch of square
inside square   inside square   inside rhombus   inside rhombus

5. The following pattern leads to a variety of symmetrical shapes. Begin with a standard sheet of paper as in figure a, and fold the upper right corner down to produce figure b. Then fold the upper vertex R down to point S to obtain figure c. To get figure d, fold the two halves inward so that points S and T are on line ℓ.

   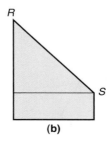   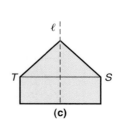   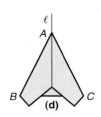

(a)   (b)   (c)   (d)

Make a horizontal cut, as indicated on this diagram, and draw a sketch of the resulting figure.

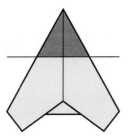

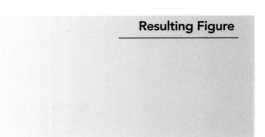

Resulting Figure

For each part a–d, draw a sketch of the figure you predict will result from the indicated cut. Then fold the paper, make the cut, and draw the actual result. Determine the number of lines of symmetry for each.

a. Slanted cut

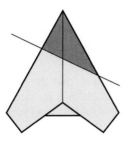

Predicted Figure   **Actual Result**

Number of lines of symmetry _____

b. Slanted cut (reversed)

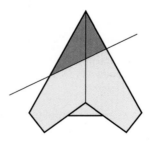

Predicted Figure   **Actual Result**

Number of lines of symmetry _____

c. Combination of two slanted cuts

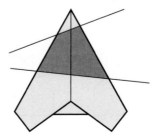

Predicted Figure   **Actual Result**

Number of lines of symmetry _____

*d. Two cuts to an inside point on the center line

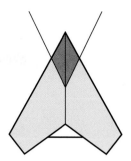

Predicted Figure	Actual Result

Number of lines of symmetry _____

*e. Find two cuts from the slanted sides of the following figure into a point on the center line that will produce a regular 16-sided polygon. Sketch the cuts on this diagram.

6. The five-pointed star has been used for badges and national symbols for centuries. It appears on the flags of over 40 countries and was once used on the back of a United States $4 piece.

  The four steps pictured in figures a through d illustrate a paper-folding approach to making a five-pointed star. To obtain figure a, fold a standard sheet of *paper* perpendicular to its longer side. Next, fold point *C* over to midpoint *M* of side $\overline{AD}$, as shown in figure b. To get figure c, fold up the corner containing point *D* and crease along $\overline{MZ}$. The final fold line is shown in figure d. Fold the right side of figure d over to the left side so that edge *NZ* lies along edge *MZ* resulting in figure e.

  a. Using your folded paper, as in figure e, make a cut from *Y* to *M* (not *N*) and sketch the

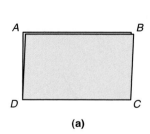

(a)

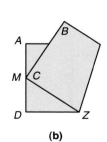

(b)

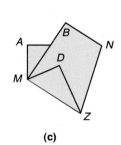

(c)

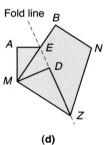

(d)

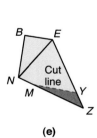

(e)

resulting figure here. Changing the position of *Y* will alter the thickness of the points on your star. *Hint:* Hold the paper tightly when cutting so it doesn't slip.

b. Begin with a new piece of paper and use the preceding four steps to obtain the pattern in figure d. Find a way to make a single cut so that the resulting figure is a regular pentagon; a regular decagon. Sketch the cut lines on the figures below.

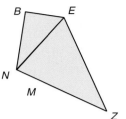
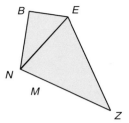

JUST FOR FUN

SNOWFLAKES

Snow is the only substance that crystallizes in many different figures. Yet in spite of the variations in the figures, all snow crystals have a common characteristic—their hexagonal shape.

A New England farmer, W. A. Bentley, began looking at snowflakes when he was given a microscope at the age of 15. A few years later he was given a camera, which he adapted to his microscope to take photographs of snowflakes. Shortly before his death in 1931, Bentley published a book containing 2500 pictures of snow crystals. His work has been used by artists, photographers, illustrators, jewelers, meteorologists, and crystallographers.[7]

To create your own snowflake, fold a standard-size sheet of paper according to the following directions.

1. Fold the paper in half twice, making the second fold perpendicular to the first as in activity 3. In figure a the corner C is also the center of the original piece of paper.

2. Fold to find the center line parallel to the longer edges, as indicated in figure b.

3. Bring corner X up to the center line and crease the paper along CY, as shown in figure c.

4. Fold corner B back until side $\overline{CB}$ lies along side $\overline{CY}$, and crease along $\overline{CX}$, as in figure d.

5. Cut off the portion of paper above $\overline{XY}$, as shown in figure e.

Now cut out designs along sides $\overline{CY}$, $\overline{CX}$, and $\overline{XY}$. Unfold the finished product carefully to examine your snowflake design. What is its shape? What lines of symmetry and what rotational symmetries does it have? Experiment with other designs to obtain a variety of snowflakes.

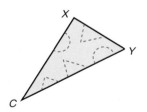

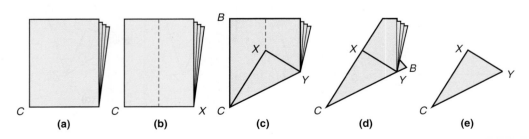

(a)	(b)	(c)	(d)	(e)

[7]F. Hapgood, "When Ice Crystals Fall from the Sky Art Meets Science," *Smithsonian* (January 1976): 67–72.

Follow-Up Questions and Activities **9.4**

1. *School Classroom:* One of your students claims that any line drawn through the center of a square is a line of symmetry for the square. Describe what you believe this student was thinking and how you would help her determine the lines of symmetry of a square without actually showing her these lines.

2. *School Classroom:* Rydell has found a wonderful pattern. Squares have four lines of symmetry and four rotational symmetries, nonsquare rectangles have two lines of symmetry and two rotational symmetries. He is sure this pattern (the number of lines of symmetry equals the number of rotational symmetries) holds for all quadrilaterals. Is he correct and if not, how can you help him resolve this issue?

3. *School Classroom:* Determine and describe the rotational and line symmetries for each of the four figures in *Try It* at the bottom of the **Elementary School Text** page at the beginning of this section.

4. *Math Concepts:* For each of the following use any combination of Pattern Blocks (cardstock or virtual) to form the figure with the stated properties; but do not duplicate any figures formed in this activity set. Sketch or print your work. Printable Virtual Pattern Blocks are available at the companion website.
   a. Figure a: One line of symmetry and no rotational symmetries (other than 360°).
   b. Figure b: Six rotational symmetries but no lines of symmetry
   c. Figure c: Three rotational symmetries and three lines of symmetry
   d. Figure d: No rotational symmetries (other than 360°) and no lines of symmetry.

5. *Math Concepts:* How many symmetrical shapes can be made by joining one more square to the ten square shape here? Use color tiles from the Manipulative Kit to find the shapes and record your answers on centimeter grid paper. Describe the type of symmetry. Centimeter Grid Paper is available for download at the companion website.

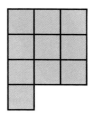

6. *Math Concepts:* Open the **Math Laboratory Investigation 9.4: Read Me—Mirror Cards Instructions** from the companion website and investigate the mirror patterns described in 1, 2, and 3 of the *Starting Points for Investigations 9.4.* Show your procedures and explain your thinking. A small handheld mirror will be helpful.

10 Measurement

Since the customary English system of measurement is still prevalent in the United States, students should learn both customary and metric systems and should know some rough equivalences between the metric and customary systems. . . .

Students should begin to develop formulas for perimeter and area in the elementary grades. Middle-grade students should formalize these techniques, as well as develop formulas for the volume and surface area of objects like prisms and cylinders.[1]

Activity Set **10.1**   MEASURING WITH METRIC UNITS

PURPOSE

To use estimation and measurement activities to introduce the basic metric units.

MATERIALS

The Metric Ruler from Material Card 19, the Metric Measuring Tape from Material Card 32, and pieces of paper.

© 1974 United Feature Syndicate, Inc.

INTRODUCTION

The metric system of measurement is used by most nations of the world. The basic metric units for length, mass, and volume are the *meter* (a little longer than a yard), the *gram* (about the weight of a paper clip), and the *liter* (a little more than a quart). If larger and smaller measures

---

[1]*Principles and Standards for School Mathematics* (Reston, VA: National Council of Teachers of Mathematics, 2000): 45–46.

I will learn to estimate and measure length in metric units;
and to choose an appropriate metric unit for measuring length.

Explore Metric Length

Hands On Activity

You can use a centimeter ruler or
a meterstick to measure.

You need to know how long a two-
way radio is. How can you measure
its length?

You Will Need

- centimeter ruler or
  meterstick

**Use a centimeter ruler to measure
the two-way radio.**

Use a Ruler

STEP 1

The two-way radio is:

▶ 107 millimeters long.
▶ 11 centimeters to the
nearest centimeter.

Note:
The millimeter (mm),
centimeter (cm), meter (m),
and kilometer (km) are
common metric units
of length.

STEP 2

Find 5 items in your classroom to measure.
Estimate and then measure with a centimeter ruler
or a meterstick. Copy and extend the chart and
record your measurements.

Remember: You
will never have an
exact measurement.
All measurements are
approximations.

Object	Length		Width		Height	
	Estimated	Measured	Estimated	Measured	Estimated	Measured

are needed in the metric system, they are obtained by using the following prefixes. The four prefixes marked with an asterisk are most commonly used. There are additional prefixes that extend this system to even larger and smaller measures for scientific purposes.

kilo*	1000 times
hecto	100 times
deka	10 times
deci*	$\frac{1}{10}$
centi*	$\frac{1}{100}$
milli*	$\frac{1}{1000}$

The prefixes differ by powers of 10. For example,

$$10 \text{ millimeters (mm)} = 1 \text{ centimeter (cm)}$$

$$10 \text{ centimeters} = 1 \text{ decimeter (dm)}$$

$$10 \text{ decimeters} = 1 \text{ meter (m)}$$

$$1000 \text{ meters} = 1 \text{ kilometer (km)}$$

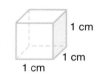

One cubic centimeter (1 cm³) equals 1 milliliter (ml) and, if water, has a mass of about 1 gram (g).

Here is one simple relationship among the metric units for length, mass, and volume: One cubic centimeter of water equals one milliliter of water and has a mass of about one gram.

The following activities involve the metric units for length and volume. If you are not familiar with the metric system and are unaccustomed to thinking of length in terms of centimeters and meters, the estimation and measuring game in activity 1 will give you expertise quickly. Another measuring game is in Just for Fun, at the end of this activity set.

1. **Centimeter and Meter Guessing Games (2 players):** One player marks two points on a sheet of paper. The opponent guesses the distance in centimeters between these two points. The distance is then measured with a ruler. If the guess is within 1 centimeter of being correct, the guessing player scores 1 point. If not, there is no score. The players alternate picking points and guessing distances until someone has scored 11 points. Use the score chart on page 298 and play the game with a partner.

   Challenging: If a player thinks an opponent's guess is not within 1 centimeter, that player may challenge the guess by giving his or her own estimate of the distance. If the challenger's estimate is within 1 centimeter and the opponent's is not, then the challenger receives 1 point and the opponent receives no score. However, if the opponent is within 1 centimeter, he or she receives 2 points for the insult, regardless of the challenger's estimate, and the challenger receives no score.

   Variation 1: Players estimate the lengths of objects around them. Since they will be estimating in centimeters, these objects should be reasonably small, such as pencils, books, width and length of desks, etc.

   Variation 2: This game is called the Meter Guessing Game. On a player's turn, he or she selects an object in the room, and the opponent guesses its length in meters. If the guess is within $\frac{1}{2}$ meter, the guessing player scores 1 point. If not, there is no score. The players alternate picking objects and guessing lengths. As before, a player's guess may be challenged.

Guess in cm	Actual Distance in cm	Score	
		Player 1	Player 2
————	————	————	————
————	————	————	————
————	————	————	————
————	————	————	————
————	————	————	————
————	————	————	————
————	————	————	————
————	————	————	————
————	————	————	————
————	————	————	————
————	————	————	————
————	————	————	————

2. Your handspan is a convenient ruler for measuring lengths. Stretch out your fingers and use your metric ruler (Material Card 19) to measure the maximum distance from your little finger to your thumb in centimeters.

a. Use your handspan to approximate the width and length of this page in centimeters. Record your results below and then check your approximations by measuring.

	Width	Length
Approximation	————	————
Measurement	————	————

b. Select some objects around you and estimate their lengths in centimeters. Check your estimates by measuring. Repeat this activity 10 times, and see how many lengths you can predict to within 1 centimeter. Record the objects, your estimates of lengths, and your measurements. In the last column record the difference between your estimation and measurement as a positive number, and then compute the average difference.

Object	Estimation	Measurement (nearest cm)	Difference
————	————	————	————
————	————	————	————
————	————	————	————
————	————	————	————
————	————	————	————
————	————	————	————
————	————	————	————
————	————	————	————
————	————	————	————
————	————	————	————

Average of differences ————

3. A millimeter is the smallest unit on your metric ruler. Obtain the measurements of the objects in parts a through c to the nearest millimeter.

  *a. The length of a dollar bill

  *b. The diameter of a penny

  c. The width of one of your fingernails. Do you have one with a width of 1 centimeter?

  d. What fraction of a millimeter is the thickness of one page of this book? (*Hint:* Measure several pages at once.)

4. This table contains some body measurements that are useful for buying and making clothes. Estimate or use your handspan to approximate these measurements. Then use your metric measuring tape and your metric ruler to obtain these measurements to the nearest centimeter.

	Estimate	Measurement
Waist	_____	_____
Height	_____	_____
Arm length	_____	_____
Foot length	_____	_____
Width of palm	_____	_____
Circumference of head	_____	_____

5. Use your metric measuring tape (Material Card 33) for the following.

  a. Measure the distance from the middle of your chest to your fingertips with your arm outstretched. Is this distance greater than or less than 1 meter? This body distance was once used by merchants to measure cloth. It is the origin of the English measure called the yard.

  b. Measure the distance from the floor up to your waist. How does this distance compare with a meter?

c. Select some objects around you whose lengths are greater than 1 meter, and try to estimate their length to within $\frac{1}{2}$ meter (50 cm). For example, estimate the height, width, and length of a room and then measure these distances with your metric measuring tape. Repeat this activity for 10 different objects. Record the objects, your estimates of lengths, and the measurements in the following table. In the last column of the table, record the difference between your estimation and measurement, as a positive number, and then compute the average of the differences.

Object	Estimation	Measurement (nearest $\frac{1}{2}$ m)	Difference
_____	_____	_____	_____
_____	_____	_____	_____
_____	_____	_____	_____
_____	_____	_____	_____
_____	_____	_____	_____
_____	_____	_____	_____
_____	_____	_____	_____
_____	_____	_____	_____
_____	_____	_____	_____
_____	_____	_____	_____

Average of differences _____

6. Your *pace* is the distance you cover in one normal pace. The single pace shown here is approximately 51 centimeters. To gather information about your pace, measure off a distance of 10 meters. Record the time in seconds and the number of paces it takes you to walk this distance.

Number of paces needed to walk 10 meters: _____

Time, in seconds, needed to walk 10 meters: _____

Using this information, explain how to determine each of the following.

a. The length of a single pace, in centimeters

b. The number of paces it will take you to walk 1 kilometer

c. The time in minutes that it will take you to walk 1 kilometer

7. A liter is very close to the English measure the quart. A liter is equal to 1000 cubic centimeters, the volume of a 10 cm by 10 cm by 10 cm cube.

*a. Use the dimensions on this drawing of a quart container to approximate the number of cubic centimeters in a quart. Which is greater, a liter or a quart?

One quart container

19.3 cm

7 cm

7 cm

*b. Suppose you wanted to cut off the top of a two-quart milk container to use for measuring 1 liter. What height should be marked on this container to measure 1 liter?

Two-quart container

Milk
Half Gallon (1.89 L)

Milk

Half Gallon (1.89 L)

20.5 cm

9.6 cm

9.6 cm

JUST FOR FUN

CENTIMETER RACING GAME (2 or more players)

This game is played on a racing mat (Material Card 34). The object of the game is to go from the center of the circle to a point inside the triangle, square, pentagon, and hexagon, in that order. Each player in turn rolls two dice. The two numbers may be added, subtracted, multiplied, or divided. The resulting computation is the number of centimeters the player moves. A metric ruler (Material Card 19) should be used to draw the line segment whose length is the player's number.

On each subsequent turn, players draw another line segment, beginning at the end of their last line segment. Before players can pass through a polygon or proceed from one polygon to the next, they must land inside the polygon with the end of a line segment. The first player to draw a line segment that ends inside the hexagon is the winner.

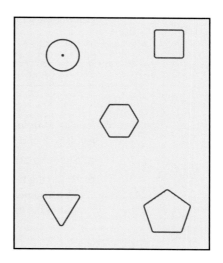

Follow-Up Questions and Activities 10.1

1. *School Classroom:* In a half page or more, make a case for one of the following approaches to teaching the metric system.

   a. The metric system should be taught from the point of view that it is secondary to the standard English system and learning how to convert between the two systems is the primary goal.

   b. The metric system should be taught so students can operate in the metric system with the facility we expect them to have with the standard English system.

2. *School Classroom:* While doing a measurement activity, one of your students asks you what it means to record a measurement to the nearest centimeter. Explain how you would help him understand what it means to measure "to the nearest centimeter."

3. *School Classroom:* Many measuring activities using millimeters and centimeters can be done *inside* a school classroom. What common objects can students estimate or measure *outside* a school classroom to develop a facility with measuring with meters? Read the **Elementary School Text** page at the beginning of this section and then describe two estimation and measuring activities using meters that students can do outside of their school classroom.

4. *Math Concepts:* In the metric system of measures, "meters" are used instead of "yards" from the English system. What used to be the 100-yard dash in track has now become the 100-meter dash (even though the distances are different).

   a. What lengths in the metric system do you think are used instead of these common units of length in the English system: quarter of an inch, inch, foot, and mile?

   b. Give examples to explain the advantage of the metric system over the English system with respect to the numerical relationship between the common units of length within each system.

5. *Math Concepts:* The Celsius scale is used for temperature in the metric system. Freezing is 0C and boiling is 100C on the Celsius scale. The corresponding temperatures on the Fahrenheit scale are 32° and 212° respectively. Viewing the two temperature scales side-by-side as below, and using arithmetic but no formulas, explain how you can determine the equivalent Fahrenheit temperature for 20C.

0C	20C		100C
32°			212°

6. *NCTM Standards:* Go to http://illuminations.nctm.org/ and under "Lessons" select grade levels 6–8 and the **Measurement Standard.** Choose a lesson involving measurement.

   a. State the title of the lesson and briefly summarize the lesson.

   b. Referring to the **Standards Summary** in the back pages of this book as necessary, list the *Measurement Standard Expectations* that the lesson addresses and explain how the lesson addresses these *Expectations*.

7. *NCTM Standards:* Using the **Standards Summary** at the back of this book, describe what metric measuring experiences are being suggested at each level: Pre-K–2, Grades 3–5, and Grades 6–8.

BENNETT-BURTON-NELSON WEBSITE

www.mhhe.com/bbn

Virtual Manipulatives   Grid and Dot Paper   Links and Readings
Interactive Chapter Applets   Color Transparencies   Geometer Sketchpad Modules
Puzzlers   Extended Bibliography

Activity Set **10.2**   AREAS ON GEOBOARDS

PURPOSE

To use rectangular geoboards to develop area concepts.

MATERIALS

A Rectangular Geoboard and rubber bands (optional). There is a template for making a rectangular geoboard on Material Card 8 or you may wish to use the Rectangular Geoboard in the Virtual Manipulatives.

Virtual Manipulatives

www.mhhe.com/bbn

INTRODUCTION

The virtual geoboard shown to the left has a rectangular array of 25 pins around which rubber bands have been placed. Notice the red polygon on the geoboard, is divided into 6 squares and 7 half squares by blue bands. If one small square serves as a unit of area, then the total area of the polygon is $9\frac{1}{2}$ unit squares or $9\frac{1}{2}$ square units.

In the following activities you will examine different methods for determining areas of polygons and discover how the formulas for the areas of rectangles, parallelograms, and triangles are related. The unit square for the areas in these activities is the smallest square with pins at its corners (1 unit by 1 unit) and the area of a polygon is the number of unit squares needed to cover the polygon.

1. In the figure for part a, the upper shaded triangle has an area of 1 square unit because it is half of a 2-unit by 1-unit rectangle. Similarly, the lower shaded triangle has an area of $1\frac{1}{2}$ square units because it is half of a 3-unit by 1-unit rectangle. Determine the areas of these figures by subdividing them into squares, halves of squares, and triangles that are halves of rectangles.

   *a. 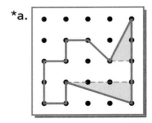   *b. 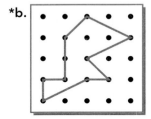   c.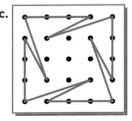

   _____   _____   _____

2. Sometimes it is easier to find the area outside a figure than the area inside. The hexagon in part a has been enclosed inside a square. What is the area of the shaded region? Subtract this area from the area of the 3-unit by 3-unit square to find the area of the hexagon. Use this technique to find the areas of the other figures.

   *a. 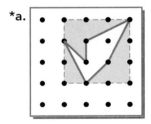   *b. 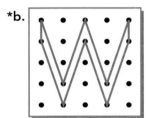   c.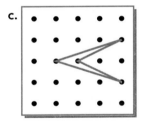

   _____   _____   _____

3. The *height, or altitude, of a triangle* is the perpendicular distance from a vertex to the line containing the opposite side. The *height of a parallelogram* is the perpendicular distance from a line containing one side to the line containing the opposite side. Using the length between two consecutive vertical or horizontal pins as the unit length, determine the heights, base length, and area of each triangle and each parallelogram.

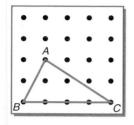 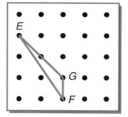 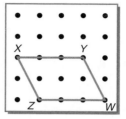 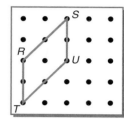

Height from vertex *A:* _____   Height from vertex *E:* _____   Height from side $\overline{ZW}$: _____   Height from side $\overline{RS}$: _____

Base $\overline{BC}$ length: _____   Base $\overline{FG}$ length: _____   Base $\overline{ZW}$ length: _____   Base $\overline{RS}$ length: _____

Area: _____   Area: _____   Area: _____   Area: _____

4. Use your geoboard techniques to determine the area and the perimeter of each of these parallelograms.

a.   **b.**   **c.**   **d.**

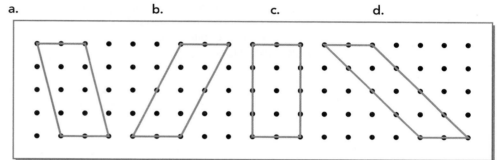

Area: _____   Area: _____   Area: _____   Area: _____

Perimeter: _____   Perimeter: _____   Perimeter: _____   Perimeter: _____

e. Each of the preceding parallelograms has one pair of sides of length 2 units and the same height. Make a conjecture about how to determine the area of a parallelogram if you know the length of a side and the height from that side. Sketch three additional parallelograms here with different areas to test your conjecture. If your conjecture appears to be valid, record it in the provided space.

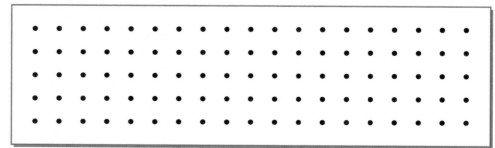

Conjecture:

f. It is a common thought that the area of some polygons is directly connected to the perimeter of the polygon. That is, when the perimeter of a polygon increases or decreases, so does the area. Is this true for parallelograms? Explain your thinking.

5. Use geoboard techniques to determine the areas of these triangles.

a.   b.   c.   d.

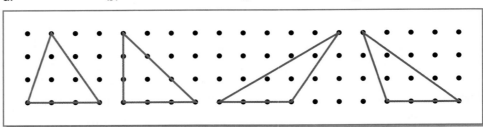

Area: _____   Area: _____   Area: _____   Area: _____

Make a conjecture about the area of triangles with bases of equal length and common heights. Sketch three additional noncongruent triangles with bases of length 5 units and altitudes of length 4 units to test your conjecture. If your conjecture appears to be valid, record it in the provided space below.

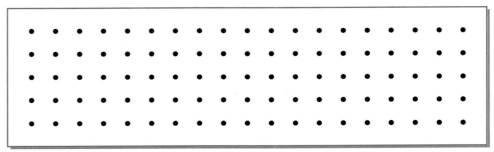

Conjecture:

6. One approach to discovering the formula for the area of a triangle is to use the formula for the area of a parallelogram. The triangle in part a below is enclosed in a parallelogram that shares two sides with the triangle. Enclose each triangle (parts b, c, and d) in a parallelogram that shares two sides with it. Then record the area of the triangle and the area of the parallelogram.

*a.   b.   *c.   d.

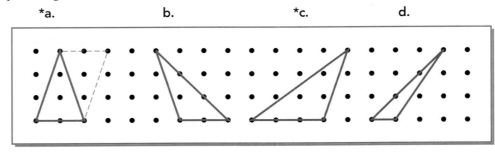

Parallelogram area: _____   Parallelogram area: _____   Parallelogram area: _____   Parallelogram area: _____

Triangle area: _____   Triangle area: _____   Triangle area: _____   Triangle area: _____

*7. The formula for the area of a triangle is one-half of the base length times the height to that base [$A = (\frac{1}{2})bh$]. Based on the observations you have made in activities 3, 4, 5, and 6, write a statement that explains why this formula works.

JUST FOR FUN

PENTOMINOES

Pentominoes are shapes that can be formed by joining five squares along their edges. Surprisingly, there are 12 such shapes. Pentominoes are used in puzzles, games, tessellations, and other problem-solving activities.

A complete set of pentomino pieces is on Material Card 35. Material Card 36 has a grid that can be used for questions 2, 3, and 4. (*Note:* Pieces can be turned over for the activities.)

1. Selecting the appropriate pieces from your pentomino set, form the 4 by 5 rectangular puzzle shown here. Outline this rectangle with pencil, and see how many other combinations of pieces you can find that will exactly fill the outline. There are at least five others.

2. The best-known challenge is to use all 12 pieces to form a 6 by 10 rectangle. Supposedly there are over 2000 different solutions. Find one solution and record it on this grid.

3. It is possible to form several puzzles by constructing an 8 by 8 grid of squares and then removing 4 unit squares. In one of these, the unit squares are missing from the corners, as shown here. Use all 12 pieces to cover a grid with this shape. Record your solution here.

*4. Pentomino Game (2 players): This game is played on an 8 by 8 grid. The players take turns placing a pentomino on uncovered squares of the grid. Play continues until someone is unable to play or all the pieces have been used. The player who makes the last move wins the game. The first seven plays of a game are shown on this board. Player A has made four moves, and player B has made three moves. Find a way player B can make the eighth move (with one of the remaining pentominoes) so that no more moves can be made. Play a few games and look for strategies.

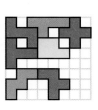

*5. It is possible to place 5 different pentomino pieces on an 8 by 8 grid so that no other piece from the same set can be placed on the grid. Find 5 such pieces.

Follow-Up Questions and Activities **10.2**

Downloadable Dot Paper, Rectangular Geoboards and printable Virtual Rectangular Geoboards are available at the companion website.

1. *School Classroom:* One of your students says that she can find the area of any geoboard figure that has no pins inside of it by counting the number of pins on the boundary of the figure, subtracting 2, and then dividing that number by 2. Form and record several figures that satisfy her conditions and determine their areas to test her conjecture. What would you say to this student?

2. *School Classroom:* Design a geoboard activity connecting the exploration of perimeter and area in parallelograms that you believe is appropriate for an elementary school student and write a few questions that you can ask about your activity. Try this activity on an elementary school age child of your choice. Describe your activity and record your questions and the student's responses.

3. *Math Concepts:* Determine the areas of the following figures using any technique or combination of techniques from the activities in this section. Notice that the hexagon in part a has a vertical line of symmetry, so you can determine the area of half the hexagonal region and then double the result to obtain the area of the entire hexagonal region.

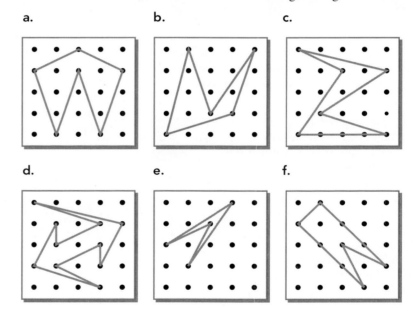

4. *Math Concepts:*

    a. Use geoboard techniques to determine the areas of these six trapezoids without using any known formulas (see Activity Set 9.1 for the definition of trapezoid).

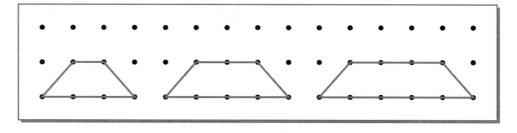

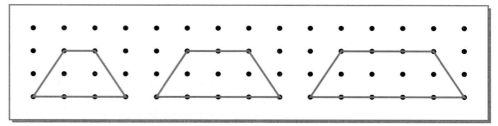

    b. Make a conjecture about the area of trapezoids with upper bases of equal length and lower bases of equal length but with different heights.

    c. Sketch three additional noncongruent trapezoids and determine their areas to test your conjecture.

5. *Math Concepts:* On a 5 by 5 geoboard:

    a. Determine a triangle of *least* area that can be formed with vertices on pins. Repeat for the triangle of greatest area. Record your triangles and justify your answers.

    b. Is it possible to form a triangle with area 1 square unit and a triangle with area 8 square units on a geoboard? Is it possible to form triangles with area 2, 3, 4, 5, 6, or 7 square units on a geoboard? Record your triangles and justify your answers.

6. *NCTM Standards:* Using the **Standards Summary** at the back of this book, list the *Expectations* that suggest using activities with non-standard units of measurements (such as the width of your hand span) for Pre-K–2. Determine if these ideas extend to Grades 3–5 and Grades 6–8 and describe your results.

 BENNETT-BURTON-NELSON WEBSITE

www.mhhe.com/bbn

Virtual Manipulatives	Grid and Dot Paper	Links and Readings
Interactive Chapter Applets	Color Transparencies	Geometer Sketchpad Modules
Puzzlers	Extended Bibliography	

Activity Set **10.3**   MODELS FOR VOLUME AND SURFACE AREA

PURPOSE

To construct three-dimensional figures and measure their volume.

MATERIALS

Patterns for a Prism, Pyramid, and Cylinder from Material Card 37; a Centimeter Ruler, a Compass, and a Protractor from Material Card 19; sand or rice for activity 6; and pieces of standard paper. For activity 7 an unopened cylindrical can, a baseball, and a container that can be used to submerge the baseball and the can in water.

INTRODUCTION

One of the greatest mathematicians of all time was Archimedes (287–212 B.C.E.), a native of Syracuse on the Island of Sicily. You may have heard the story of how Archimedes was able to solve a problem King Hieron had with his crown. The king had weighed out the exact amount of pure gold he wanted used for a crown, but upon receiving the crown he became suspicious that it was a mixture of gold and silver. The crown weighed as much as the original amount of gold, so there seemed to be no way of exposing the fraud. Archimedes was informed of the problem, and a solution occurred to him while he was taking a bath. He noticed that the amount of water that overflowed the tub depended on the extent to which his body was immersed. In his excitement to try his solution with gold and silver, Archimedes leaped from the tub and ran naked to his home, shouting, "Eureka! Eureka!"

As Archimedes discovered, the volume of a submerged object is equal to the volume of the displaced water. Finding the volumes of objects by submerging them in water is especially convenient with metric units, because the number of milliliters of water that is displaced is equal to the volume of the object in cubic centimeters. This relationship will be used in the following activities. You will also need the formulas for volumes of prisms and cylinders (area of base $\times$ height), pyramids and cones ($\frac{1}{3} \times$ area of base $\times$ height), and spheres [$(\frac{4}{3})\pi r^3$].

*1. To understand Archimedes' solution, consider two cubes both weighing the same amount, one of pure gold and one of pure silver. Since gold is about twice as heavy as silver, the cube of gold will be smaller than the cube of silver. Therefore, when each is submerged in water, there will be more water displaced for the cube of silver. To apply his theory, Archimedes used the crown and an amount of pure gold weighing the same as the crown. He submerged them separately in water and measured the amount of overflow. There was more water displaced for the crown than for the pure gold. What does this show about the volume of the crown as compared to the volume of the gold? Was King Hieron cheated?

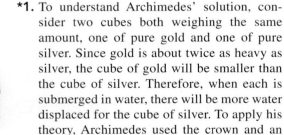

Gold

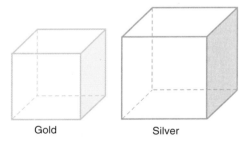

Silver

*2. Patterns for prisms, pyramids, and cylinders are easy to make. Three such patterns are contained on Material Card 37. Cut them out and tape their edges. Complete the first two lines of the following table below and then determine the volumes and surface areas of these figures. You may wish to fill them with sand or salt to check your volume answers. (The area of the base of a cylinder is πr^2. Use 3.14 for π.)

	Hexagonal Prism	Hexagonal Pyramid	Cylinder
Area of base	_____	_____	_____
Height (altitude)	_____	_____	_____
Volume	_____	_____	_____
Surface area	_____	_____	_____

*3. A standard 21.5 cm × 28 cm sheet of paper can be made into a cylinder in the two ways shown in the following figures. Make a cylinder (without bases) so that its circumference is 21.5 centimeters and its height is 28 centimeters. Then use another sheet of paper to form a cylinder with a circumference of 28 centimeters and a height of 21.5 centimeters. Predict which cylinder has the greater volume. As you compute the volume of each cylinder, record your methods and answers below the figures.

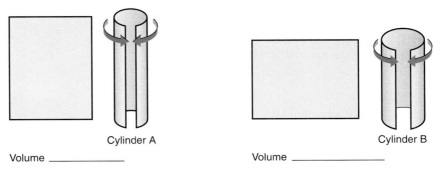

Cylinder A   Cylinder B

Volume _____   Volume _____

4. Cut a standard sheet of paper in half lengthwise and tape the two halves end to end, as shown below. Make a cylinder without bases and compute its volume. Compare the volume of this cylinder with that of cylinder B in activity 3. What happens to the volume of a cylinder as the height is halved and the circumference (thus, radius and diameter) is doubled?

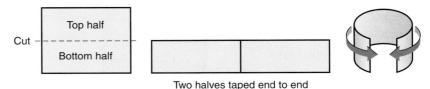

Cut ┄┄┄┄┄┄┄ Top half / Bottom half

Two halves taped end to end

I will learn to find the surface area of cylinders.

22.5   Explore Surface Area of Cylinders

Hands On Activity

You can use cans and paper to explore the relationship between the surface area of a cylinder, its height, and the area of its base.

You Will Need

- cylindrical cans, unopened
- paper
- pencils
- rulers
- scissors

Use Models

STEP 1

Trace the top and bottom of a can. Measure the diameter. Then find the circumference in inches.

STEP 2

Measure the height of the can in inches.
Draw a rectangle with width equal to the height of the can and length equal to the circumference of the top.

circumference

STEP 3

Cut out the two circles and the rectangle. Demonstrate that these pieces represent the surface area of the can.

STEP 4

Find the area of each piece. Add to find the total surface area. Use the table to record your findings.

Repeat for other cans.

Can	Area of Top (in.²)	Area of Bottom (in.²)	Area of Rectangle (in.²)	Surface Area (in.²)

5. Make a set of six different cones by cutting out three disks, each of radius 10 centimeters. (There is a compass and protractor on Material Card 19.) Each disk can be used for making two cones, as shown here. Cut from these disks sectors with central angles of 45°, 90°, 135°, 225°, 270°, and 315°, and *number the sectors from 1 to 6 according to the size of the central angle*. After cutting each disk into two parts, bend and tape the edges to form the cones.

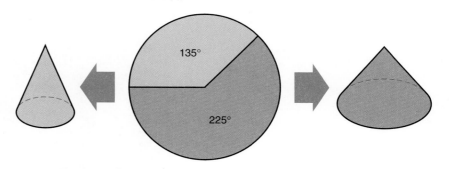

a. Without computing, line the cones up from left to right in what you estimate to be increasing volumes. Record your estimated order by recording the numbers of the cones.

_____   _____   _____   _____   _____   _____

Least volume   Greatest volume

*b. Compute the base areas and volumes (to the nearest two decimal places) of the cones, and enter them in the following table. Compare the results with the estimated order of the cones in part a. (The area of the base of a cone is πr^2. Use 3.14 for π.)

Computations:

	1	2	3	4	5	6
Central angle of disk	45°	90°	135°	225°	270°	315°
Radius (cm) of base	1.25	2.50	3.75	6.25	7.50	8.75
Base area (cm²)	_____	_____	_____	_____	_____	_____
Height (cm) of cone	9.92	9.68	9.27	7.81	6.61	4.84
Volume (cm³) of cone	_____	_____	_____	_____	_____	_____

*c. What will happen to the volume of the cone as sectors with central angles of less than 45° are used? As sectors with central angles of greater than 315° are used?

Central angles less than 45°:   Central angles greater than 315°:

6. Choose one of your cones from activity 5, and place a mark on the surface halfway from the vertex to the base (moving along the height from the vertex to the center of the cone).

   a. If the cone were filled to this mark, estimate what fractional part of the total volume of the cone would be filled. Circle the fraction that best represents your estimate.

$$\frac{1}{8} \quad \frac{1}{7} \quad \frac{1}{6} \quad \frac{1}{5} \quad \frac{1}{4} \quad \frac{1}{3} \quad \frac{1}{2}$$

   b. To experimentally test your estimate, fill the cone up to the mark with water (or sand or rice) and then pour its contents into an identical cone, repeating the process until the second cone is full. How many "fillings" are required?

   *c. Determine the radius and height of your "half-cone" and compute its volume. Compare this volume to the volume of the whole cone. Assume the cone has radius r and height h and that the half-cone has radius $\frac{r}{2}$ and height $\frac{h}{2}$. What fraction in part a represents the relationship between the volume of the half-cone compared to the volume of the whole cone? Show all of your work here.

7. The basketball and hand together displace 7715 milliliters of water and the hand alone displaces 480 milliliters. The marked line shows the original height of the water.

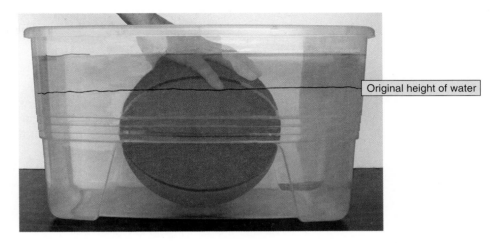

Original height of water

*a. What is the volume of the basketball in cubic centimeters?

b. What is the diameter of this ball to the nearest centimeter? [Sphere volume $= (\frac{4}{3})\pi r^3$, where r is the radius. Use 3.14 for π.] Explain how you arrived at your conclusions.

c. Submerge a baseball in water and measure the displaced water in milliliters. According to this experiment, what is the volume of a baseball in cubic centimeters? A baseball has a diameter of approximately 7.3 centimeters. Compute its volume in cubic centimeters, and compare this answer with the results of your experiment. Record your results.

d. Submerge an unopened cylindrical can in water and measure the overflow. Then measure the diameter and height of the can and compute its volume. Compare the computed volume with the results of your experiment. Record your results.

8. Spherical objects such as Christmas tree ornaments and basketballs are packed in cube-shaped compartments and boxes.

  a. If a sphere just fits into a box, estimate what fraction of the box is "wasted space." Circle the fraction that best represents your estimate.

$$\frac{1}{6} \qquad \frac{1}{5} \qquad \frac{1}{4} \qquad \frac{1}{3} \qquad \frac{1}{2}$$

Compute the amount of wasted space when a sphere of diameter 25 centimeters is placed in a 25 cm × 25 cm × 25 cm box. What fraction of the total volume of this box is wasted space?

  b. Spheres are also packed in cylinders. A cylinder provides a better fit than a box, but there is still extra space. If 3 balls are packed in a cylindrical can whose diameter equals that of a ball and whose height is 3 times the diameter of a ball, estimate what fraction of the space is unused.

$$\frac{1}{6} \qquad \frac{1}{5} \qquad \frac{1}{4} \qquad \frac{1}{3} \qquad \frac{1}{2}$$

Compute the amount of unused space. Assume that each ball and the cylinder have radius r and then express the height of the can in terms of r.

  *c. Tennis ball cans hold 3 balls. Determine the amount of wasted space in these cans if the balls have a diameter of 6.3 centimeters and the can has a diameter of 7 centimeters and a height of 20 centimeters. What fraction from part b is closest to representing the amount of wasted space? Check the reasonableness of your answer by experimenting with a can of balls and water.

JUST FOR FUN

SOMA CUBES

Soma cubes are a seven-piece puzzle invented by the Danish author Piet Hein. Piece 1 has 3 cubes, and the other pieces each have 4 cubes. Soma cubes can be purchased, or they can be constructed by gluing together cubes, such as sugar cubes, wooden cubes, or dice.

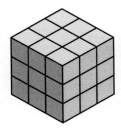

Surprisingly, these 7 pieces can be assembled to form a 3 by 3 by 3 cube. You may wish to try this challenging puzzle.

A common activity with soma cubes is constructing certain well-known figures. Each of the shapes in figure 1 requires all 7 pieces. Try to build them.

There are several elementary techniques for determining when a figure cannot be constructed with soma cubes. The simplest of these is counting the number of cubes. For example, a figure with 18 cubes cannot be formed because there is no combination of 4s and one 3 that adds up to 18.[2]

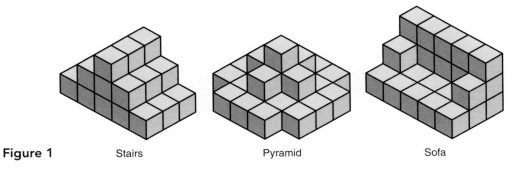

Figure 1   Stairs   Pyramid   Sofa

[2]Additional techniques can be found in G. Carson, *"Soma Cubes," The Mathematics Teacher* 66 (November 1973): 583–592.

FILLING 3-D SHAPES APPLET

How does the volume of a cube compare with the volume of a square pyramid that just fits into the cube? (Their bases have the same area and their altitudes are equal.) This applet enables you to experiment by pumping water from one figure to another to discover relationships. In a similar manner, you can compare the volumes of other solids.

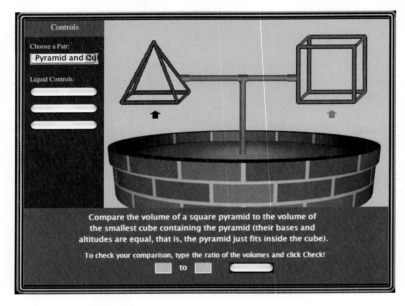

Filling 3-D Shapes Applet, Chapter 10
www.mhhe.com/bbn

Follow-Up Questions and Activities 10.3

1. *School Classroom:* Katrina is convinced that the two cylinders made by rolling a standard piece of paper left-to-right or top-to-bottom, must have the same volume. Describe how you can help Katrina explore this concept without using any formulas.

2. *School Classroom:* Make paper models to illustrate the following relationships and explain how you would illustrate the relationships in classroom experiences with maximum student involvement.

    a. The volume of a square pyramid is one-third the volume of a box with the same base and the same height as the pyramid.

    b. The volume of a right circular cone is one-third the volume of a cylinder with the same base and the same height as the cone.

    c. The volume of an inverted right circular cone has eight times the volume as an identical inverted cone that is filled to one-half its height.

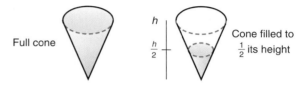

3. *School Classroom:* The surface area activity described on the **Elementary School Text** page at the beginning of this section assumes the students know certain formulas for area. Describe how you can restructure this activity so that students can obtain an approximation of the surface area without knowing any area formulas.

4. *Math Concepts:* If you have a cubical box that measures 3 inches on each edge and want to make a box with three times the volume, how long must each edge of the larger box be (to the nearest tenth of an inch)? Explain your thinking.

5. *Math Concepts:* Imagine that you have a cube of modeling clay that measures 4 inches on each edge.

    a. What is the surface area of that cube of clay?

    b. If you formed the same piece of clay (same volume) into a sphere, predict which clay object would have more surface area, the cube or the sphere. Then compute the surface area of the sphere to test your prediction (surface area of a sphere is $4\pi r^2$). Explain in detail how you determined the surface area of the clay sphere.

6. *Math Concepts:* Go to the companion website and open the Chapter 10 Applet: Filling 3D Shapes. Compare the volumes of the various shapes and record your observations.

7. The **Standards Summary** at the back of this book mentions *Volume* at every grade level. Give three simple examples of grade level appropriate activities exploring volume, one each for Pre-K–2, grades 3–5, and grades 6–8. Explain how these activities address *Expectations* in the **Geometry Standards.** State the *Expectations* with your explanation.

BENNETT-BURTON-NELSON WEBSITE

www.mhhe.com/bbn

Virtual Manipulatives	Grid and Dot Paper	Links and Readings
Interactive Chapter Applets	Color Transparencies	Geometer Sketchpad Modules
Puzzlers	Extended Bibliography	

Elementary School Activity

FINDING AREAS ON GEOBOARDS

Purpose: To introduce elementary school students to finding areas of figures by dividing regions into square units.

Connections: Ask the class if they know the meaning of the word "area" or if they can use the word in a sentence. Maybe they have heard the expression "work area" or "play area" or maybe they have seen signs such as: "This area is for construction workers" or "This area is closed." Tell them that today they will use the word "area" in a different way.

Materials: Per student or pair of students: One geoboard, one large rubber band, and 10 to 12 small rubber bands.

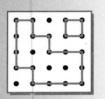

1. Show the students a geoboard with the two figures at the left marked with rubber bands and ask them to form both figures on their geoboards using their rubber bands. Tell the students to use more bands to divide the large figure into small squares the size of the small square on their geoboard. When this has been done, select a student to show her geoboard to the class. Ask the students to count the number of small squares contained in the large figure. Tell them that this shows that the area of the large figure is 10 square units.

2. Show the students the following figures, ask them to form the figures on their geoboards and determine the area of each figure. Ask volunteers to state the areas they found and to explain their methods. Some students may find it helpful to subdivide the figures into small squares, while others may have different methods.

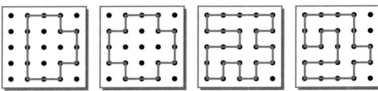

3. The areas of the following figures can be found by dividing the figures into squares and half-squares. Show the students the figures and ask them to form the figures and determine their areas. Discuss each by asking volunteers to explain their methods.

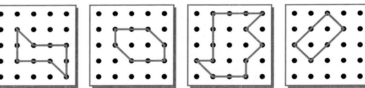

Student is determining area of geoboard figure by placing squares and half-squares in the figure.

4. (Optional) The areas of each of the triangles on these geoboards can be found by enclosing the triangle in a rectangle and taking half the area of the rectangle. Have the students form the first geoboard figure and ask for suggestions as to how its area can be found. Some students may say that the lower part of the triangle is almost one square unit and the top half of the triangle can be used to make a whole square. If no one suggests the method of using rectangles, have the students enclose the triangle in the smallest possible rectangle and find the area of the rectangle. Ask how this can be used to find the area of the triangle. (Area is 1 square unit.)

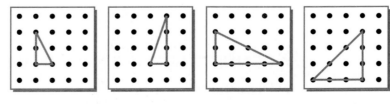

11 Motions in Geometry

Students need to learn to physically and mentally change the position, orientation, and size of objects in systematic ways as they develop their understandings about congruence, similarity, and transformations.[1]

Activity Set 11.1   LOCATING SETS OF POINTS IN THE PLANE

PURPOSE

To locate and sketch sets of points in a plane that satisfy given conditions.

MATERIALS

A ruler, compass, and protractor from Material Card 19, pieces of paper, two index cards, and scissors.

INTRODUCTION

Look at the two identical coins here. If the left coin is carefully rolled halfway around the other, what will be the position of the point *A*? Make a conjecture and test it by experimenting with two identical coins.

In this activity set, we will be locating the positions of points in the plane. Many geometric figures are described or defined as sets of points with certain conditions placed on them. Suppose, for example, that we are asked to locate and sketch *the set of points in the plane that are 2 cm from a given point P.* We can begin to identify points by using a ruler to locate points 2 cm from

[1]*Principles and Standards for School Mathematics* (Reston, VA: National Council of Teachers of Mathematics, 2000): 43.

I will learn to describe and draw circles and parts of circles.

20.1   Circles

Learn

Kenneth Noland's painting *Turnstole* has many circles on the canvas. How are a circle and its parts defined?

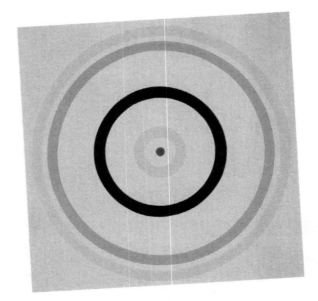

VOCABULARY

circle	diameter
center	radius
chord	central angle

Parts of a Circle

A **circle** is a closed figure in a plane with all of its points the same distance from the center. It has no beginning point and no ending point.

A circle can be named by its **center**.

A **chord** is a line segment that connects any two points on the circle.

A **diameter** is a chord that passes through the center of the circle.

A **radius** is a line segment that connects the center to a point on the circle. The plural of radius is *radii*.

A **central angle** is an angle formed between two radii. ∠CFA, ∠AFD, ∠DFB, and ∠BFC are central angles in circle F. The sum of the measures of the central angles of a circle is always 360 degrees.

You can confirm this fact by looking at the four right angles formed by two perpendicular diameters.

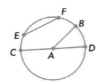

This circle is called circle A. Center: A

$\overline{EF}$ is a chord of circle A. Chord: $\overline{EF}$

$\overline{CD}$ is a diameter of circle A. Diameter: $\overline{CD}$

$\overline{AB}$ is a radius of circle A. Radius: $\overline{AB}$

 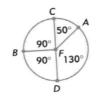

The sum of the measure of those angles is 4 × 90° = 360°.

point P, as shown in figure a. As more and more points are added to the collection of points, we can see that a smooth curve drawn through the points, as in figure b, visually describes the set of all points 2 cm from P as a circle with center P and radius 2 cm.

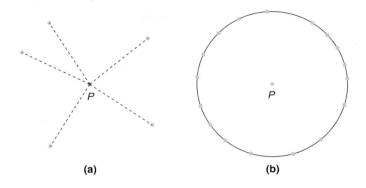

(a)   (b)

1. For parts a and b, place 10 to 20 points on each figure that satisfy the stated condition. Then draw a smooth curve through all points satisfying the condition and describe the outcome in your own words.

   a. The set of all points in the plane that are the same distance from point K as from point L.

   $K \bullet$

   $L \bullet$

   *b. The set of all points in the plane that are the same distance from line m as from line n. (The distance from a point to a line is along the perpendicular from the point to the line.)

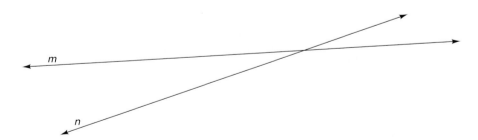

2. A *chord* is a line segment joining two points on a circle. Parts a through c involve chords of circles. Locate as many points as you need to feel confident about sketching the curve that satisfies the conditions. Describe each result in words, as specifically as possible.

*a. The set of all points that are midpoints of chords of length 4 cm on this circle.

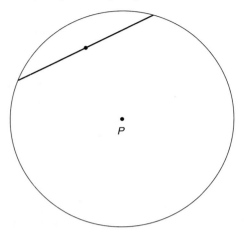

b. The midpoints of all chords of this circle that have point *R* as one endpoint.

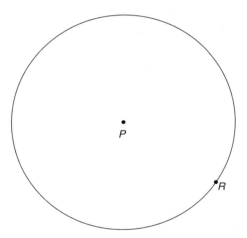

*c. The midpoints of all chords of this circle that pass through point *S*.

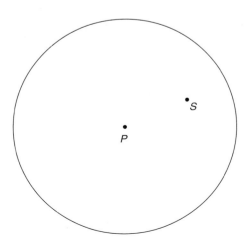

3. Draw and cut out a circle with radius 1.5 cm.

    a. Suppose the circle rolls around the inside of the square shown below always tangent to at least 1 edge. Sketch the path traced by the center of the circle and then describe it in words.

    b. Sketch and describe the path of the circle's center if the circle rolls around the outside of the square.

*4. Point *B* is the center of a circle with radius 1 cm, and point *A* is the center of a circle with radius 2 cm. Both *X* and *Y*, which are the intersections of these two circles, are twice as far from point *A* as from point *B*. Find more points that are twice as far from *A* as from *B*. Sketch and describe the set of all points in the plane that satisfy the conditions. (*Hint:* You may find it helpful to locate these points by drawing circles about *A* and *B*, with the radius about *A* twice the radius about *B*.)

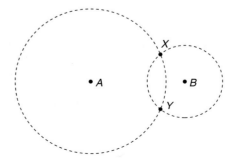

5. Cut out a narrow strip of cardstock or paper having a length of 5 cm and punch a small hole at its midpoint. Place this strip on the two perpendicular lines so that each end touches one of the lines as illustrated in figure 1. Place a pencil at the midpoint, *M*, and with the help of a classmate, move the strip so that its endpoints always touch the two perpendicular lines in figure 2. What curve is traced by point *M*?

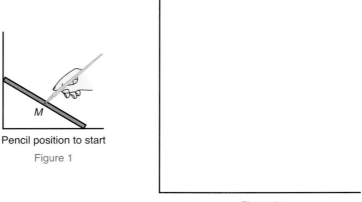

Pencil position to start

Figure 1

Figure 2

6. On a piece of paper draw a line segment $\overline{PQ}$ of length 7 cm. Place an index card (any piece of paper with a 90° corner will work) on top of segment $\overline{PQ}$ so that its adjacent sides pass through points *P* and *Q*. It is possible to shift the index card to new positions so that *P* and *Q* are still on adjacent edges of the index card but the corner of the card is at different points, such as point *X* and point *Y* in the following figure. Locate and mark several other different corner points by repositioning the index card in this manner.

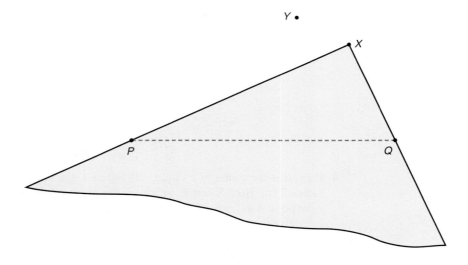

*a. Describe the curve made up of all possible corner points.

b. Bisect one corner of the index card, and cut along the angle bisector to obtain a 45° angle. The point W is the vertex point of the 45° angle. This card is placed on top of segment $\overline{RS}$ so that its sides pass through points R and S. Shift the card to locate other vertex points with R and S on the adjacent sides of the 45° angle. Describe the set of all such vertex points.

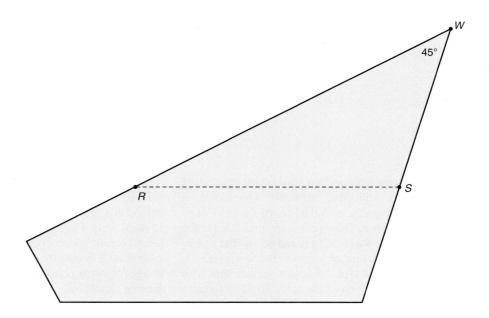

c. Suppose the vertex angle W of the card in part b were greater than 90°, for example, 110°. Draw a sketch of what you think the set of vertex points would look like. Test your conjecture by cutting an angle greater than 90° and locating points on segment $\overline{AB}$.

A ——————————————————————— B

JUST FOR FUN

LINE DESIGNS

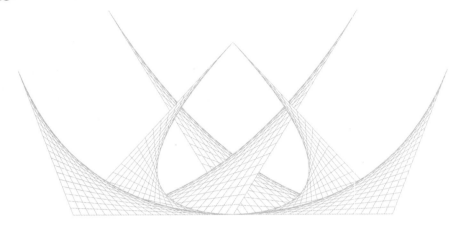

Line designs are geometric designs formed by connecting sequences of points with line segments. One common method is to connect equally spaced points on the sides of an angle, as shown in figure a. These points are connected in the following order: *A* to *a*, *B* to *b*, *C* to *c*, and so on. The resulting design gives the illusion of a curve that is a parabola. Experiment with different types of angles. Experiment with different types of angles such as the acute angle in figure a and the obtuse angle in figure b to see if the resulting designs give similar illusions of parabolas. Combining several angles, as in the figure above, and varying the colors can lead to interesting and beautiful designs.

Another way to create line designs is to draw chords in a circle according to certain rules. The design in figure d is being formed in a circle whose circumference has been divided into 36 equal parts. The first chord connects point 1 to point 2; the second chord connects point 2 to point 4; the third chord connects point 3 to point 6; and so on. This figure shows the first 18 chords, with point 18 connected to point 36. Continue drawing chords by connecting point 19 to point 2, point 20 to point 4, etc., until you reach point 36. The resulting figure has the shape of a heart. A curve with this shape is called a *cardioid*. The front ends of the chords for this cardioid traveled twice as fast around the circle as the back ends of the chords.

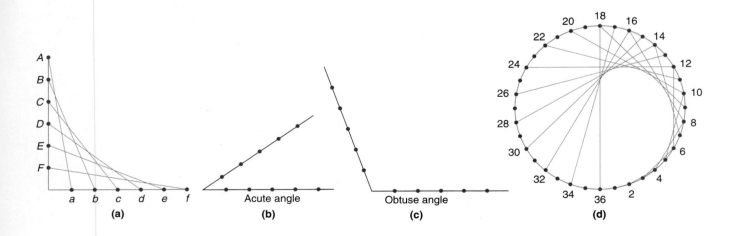

In the next figure let the front ends of the chords travel 3 times as fast. That is, connect point 1 to point 3, 2 to 6, 3 to 9, and so forth. Continue drawing these chords until the back ends of the chords have made one revolution and the front ends have made three revolutions. The cardioid on the preceding page has 1 *cusp* (inward point). How many cusps will this curve have?

Experiment with some more patterns. For example, let the front ends of the chords move 4 times faster $(1 \rightarrow 4, 2 \rightarrow 8, 3 \rightarrow 12, \ldots)$ or 5 times faster $(1 \rightarrow 5, 2 \rightarrow 10, \ldots)$. Can you predict the number of cusps in each case? (The 36 spaces around a circle will work for 2, 3, 4, or 6 cusps. For 5 cusps, use 40 spaces or some other multiple of 5 that conveniently divides into 360.) Many of these designs can be stitched with colored thread or yarn on cloth or poster-board or formed with nails and string or rubber bands. Below is an example of a variety of line art designs stitched on poster board with multicolored thread. The student who made this piece used a compass and protractor to sketch geometric shapes and mark points on the back of the poster before stitching the final art piece.

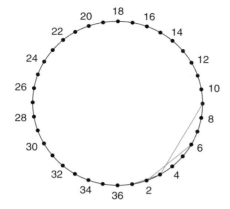

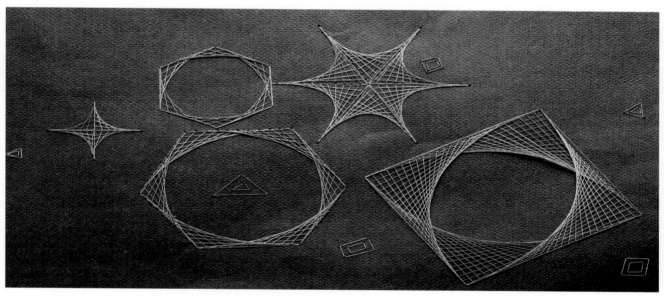

A line art poster created by a student at Western Oregon University.

Follow-Up Questions and Activities **11.1**

1. *School Classroom:* Cresedeo is having trouble sorting out the following four geometric terms: circle, diameter, chord, and arc. Describe several hands-on ways you might use to help Cresedeo and other students make sense of these terms.

2. *School Classroom:* One way to introduce students to definitions involving sets of points in the plane is to ask them to place or locate small objects (beans, rice, counters, etc.) that satisfy certain conditions. For example, placing a bean on a table and having your students place many pieces of rice all an equal distance from the bean leads to the definition of a circle. Create two activities concerning the location of sets of points that are appropriate for the elementary school classroom. Describe your activities in detail and accompany them with diagrams.

3. *Math Concepts:* Analyze the line design at the beginning of the **Just for Fun Activity** in this section. Write a set of directions that will enable your reader to construct this figure. Using your directions, construct the figure. If you refine your directions while drawing, explain the refinement.

4. *Math Concepts:* Suppose a point *P* is placed above a line and many line segments are drawn from *P* to the line. Describe the shape the set of midpoints of all of the line segments would form. Draw a sketch to accompany your conclusion.

5. *Math Concepts:* Open the **Math Laboratory Investigation 11.1: Read Me—Paper Folding Instructions** from the companion website and investigate the triangle constructions as described in 1, 2, 3, and 4 of the *Starting Points for Investigations 11.1*. Describe your investigation and explain your thinking.

6. *NCTM Standards:* Read over the **Geometry Standards** for all grade levels in the back pages of this book; list any *Expectations* that you believe are satisfied by activities that ask students to describe sets of points whose location is determined by given conditions. State the *Expectations,* the *Standards,* and the grade levels they are under.

BENNETT-BURTON-NELSON WEBSITE

www.mhhe.com/bbn

Virtual Manipulatives
Interactive Chapter Applets
Puzzlers

Grid and Dot Paper
Color Transparencies
Extended Bibliography

Links and Readings
Geometer Sketchpad Modules

Activity Set **11.2**   DRAWING ESCHER-TYPE TESSELLATIONS

PURPOSE

To create nonstandard tessellations and Escher-type drawings that illustrate motions in geometry.

MATERIALS

Tracing paper and a ruler and compass from Material Card 19.

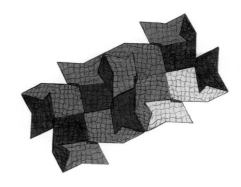

Tessellations created by students at Portland State University.

INTRODUCTION

The Dutch artist M. C. Escher was fascinated by the tile patterns he observed on the walls, floors, and ceilings of the Alhambra—a thirteenth-century Moorish palace in Granada, Spain. He considered pure geometric tessellations his "richest source of inspiration." Many of his own works are filled with images of living things as is the following Escher-type student drawing.

A tessellation involving life forms created by a student at Portland State University.

Escher-type drawings can be constructed by altering polygons that tessellate (triangles, quadrilaterals, and regular hexagons) by using congruence mappings (translations, rotations, reflections, and glide reflections). In this activity set, you will devise drawings and have the opportunity to create your own artistic work.

6-9b   HANDS-ON LAB

A Follow-Up of Lesson 6-9

Tessellations

Maurits Cornelis Escher (1898–1972) was a Dutch artist whose work used tessellations. A **tessellation** is a tiling made up of copies of the same shape or shapes that fit together without gaps and without overlapping. The sum of the angle measures where vertices meet in a tessellation must equal 360°. For this reason, equilateral triangles and squares will tessellate a plane.

Symmetry drawing E70 by M.C. Escher. © 2002 Cordon Art-Baarn-Holland. All rights reserved.

What You'll LEARN

Create Escher-like drawings using translations and rotations.

Materials

- index cards
- scissors
- tape
- paper

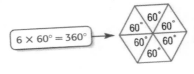

$6 \times 60° = 360°$

$4 \times 90° = 360°$

ACTIVITY

1   Create a tessellation using a translation.

STEP 1   Draw a square on the back of an index card. Then draw a triangle inside the top of the square as shown below.

STEP 2   Cut out the square. Then cut out the triangle and translate it from the top to the bottom of the square.

STEP 3   Tape the triangle and square together to form a pattern.

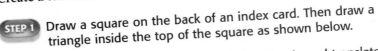

Step 1   Step 2   Step 3

STEP 4   Trace this pattern onto a sheet of paper as shown to create a tessellation.

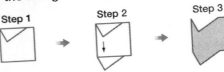

Your Turn   Make an Escher-like drawing using each pattern.

a.   b.   c.

1. **Translation Tessellations:** The rectangle in figure a tessellates. In figure b, one side of the rectangle is modified by a jagged line design. The design is then *translated* to the opposite side of the rectangle as a modification in figure c.

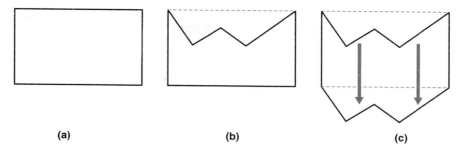

(a)   (b)   (c)

 *a. Explain why the new shape in figure c will also tessellate the plane.

In figure d, one of the remaining parallel sides of the rectangle is altered by a different design. This design is then translated to the opposite side in figure e, producing the final shape in figure f.

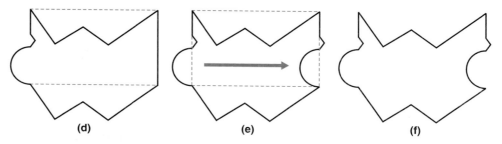

(d)   (e)   (f)

The tessellation formed by the modified rectangle is shown in figure A. This tessellation becomes an Escher-type drawing when details and/or color are added to the basic design. In figure B, the tessellation has been rotated 90° and a few details have been added to make a simple Escher-type drawing.

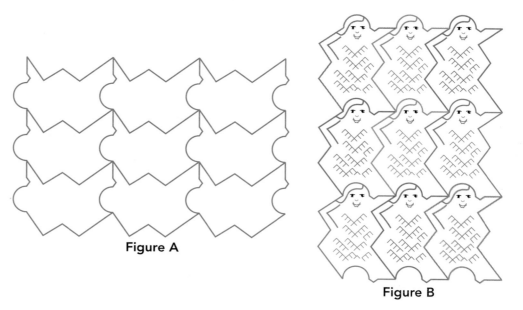

Figure A

Figure B

b. Create your own translation tessellation pattern by modifying and translating the sides of this parallelogram according to steps 1 to 3 given below.

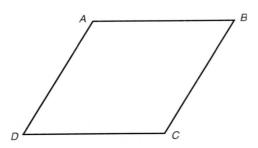

(1) Modify side $\overline{AB}$ by creating a design.

(2) Translate the design to $\overline{DC}$ by carrying out the following steps: Place a piece of tracing paper over the parallelogram. Mark points A and B and trace your modification for side $\overline{AB}$. Slide the tracing paper so that point A coincides with D and point B coincides with C. Use a pointed object (ballpoint pen, compass point) to make enough imprints through the tracing paper so that when you remove the paper you can draw the translated design on $\overline{DC}$.

(3) Repeat steps 1 and 2 to translate a modification of side $\overline{AD}$ to side $\overline{BC}$.

c. Use the pattern you have just created to form a tessellation. An easy way to do this is to place a clean piece of tracing paper over the pattern you created and carefully trace the pattern. Then move the tracing paper up, down, right, or left, and trace additional patterns adjacent to your first copy on the tracing paper. Make an Escher-type drawing by sketching in details.

2. Rotation Tessellations: The following figures illustrate the modification and rotation of the sides of an equilateral triangle. First, side $\overline{AB}$ is modified as in figure a. Then the design is rotated about vertex A to adjacent side $\overline{AC}$, as shown in figure b, so that vertex B is mapped onto vertex C.

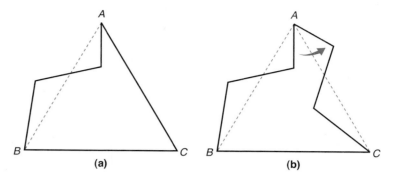

(a)   (b)

Side $\overline{BC}$ can be modified by rotating a design about its midpoint. In figure c, a design is created between the midpoint M and vertex C. The pattern is completed by rotating this design $180°$ about midpoint M so that vertex C is mapped onto vertex B, as shown in figure d.

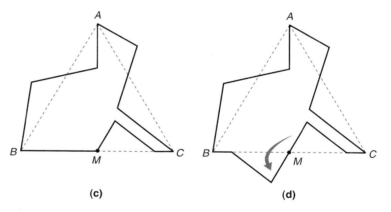

(c)   (d)

This pattern was used to create the following tessellation. Notice that this tessellation can be mapped onto itself by rotations about certain vertex points.

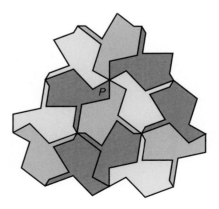

List all the rotations about point P that will map this tessellation onto itself.

a. Create a rotation tessellation pattern from square *ABCD* by first modifying side $\overline{AB}$ and rotating the design about vertex *B* to adjacent side $\overline{BC}$ and then modifying side $\overline{AD}$ and rotating the design about vertex *D* to adjacent side $\overline{DC}$. Use your pattern to form a tessellation and list all the rotations of the tessellation onto itself about one of the vertex points of the tessellation.

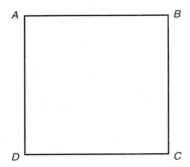

b. Use the following scalene triangle to design a rotation tessellation pattern. Because no two sides have equal length, you cannot rotate one side to another about a vertex, as in figure b at the beginning of activity 2. However, half a side can be rotated about the midpoint of that side, as was done in figures c and d of activity 2. The midpoint of each side has been marked. For each side, create a design between a vertex and the midpoint, and then rotate the design 180° about the midpoint. Show that this pattern tessellates by forming a tessellation. For a vertex point of the tessellation, what is the number of rotations of the tessellation into itself?

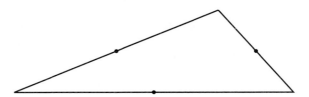

c. Convert one or both of your tessellation patterns from part a and part b to an Escher-type drawing.

3. Glide-Reflection Tessellations: A *glide reflection* can be used to create a tessellating figure from parallelogram *ABCD*. Side $\overline{AD}$ is modified in figure a, and the design is translated to side $\overline{BC}$ in figure b. Next, side $\overline{DC}$ is modified as shown in figure c.

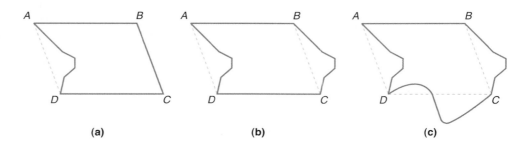

(a)   (b)   (c)

The design on $\overline{DC}$ is then translated to side $\overline{AB}$, as shown in figure d. Finally, the design along side $\overline{AB}$ is reflected about a line ℓ perpendicular to the midpoint of *AB*, as illustrated in figure e. The two motions (translation followed by reflection) shown in figures d and e produce a *glide reflection*.

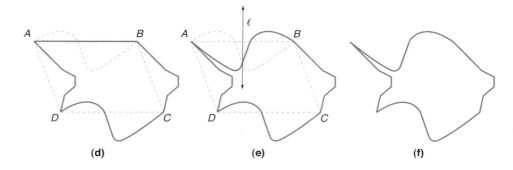

(d)   (e)   (f)

a. The pattern created above in figures a–f was used to form the following tessellation. What single mapping will map each row of this tessellation onto the row below it?

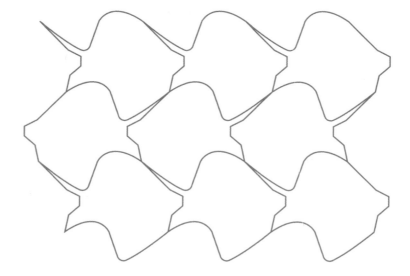

Mapping:

b. Modify the square *ABCD*, using two glide reflections to produce a figure that tessellates. To do this create a design along side $\overline{AD}$, translate the design to side $\overline{BC}$, and then reflect it about a line perpendicular to the midpoint of $\overline{BC}$. Similarly, modify side $\overline{AB}$ and translate that design to side $\overline{DC}$ through a glide reflection. (*Suggestion:* Use tracing paper to perform the glide reflection.)

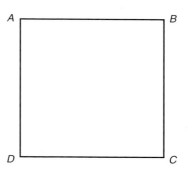

JUST FOR FUN

PAPER PUZZLE 1: PAPER-STRIP CUBE

Draw a strip of eight squares that each measure 3 cm on a side. Cut out the strip of squares, and fold it to make a cube that measures 3 cm on each edge.

PAPER PUZZLE 2: FOLDING NUMBERS IN ORDER

The following rectangle with the eight numbered squares can be folded so that the numbers are in order from 1 through 8 by carrying out the three folds shown in figures a, b, and c. (*Note:* The numbers will be in order, but not all will be facing up.)

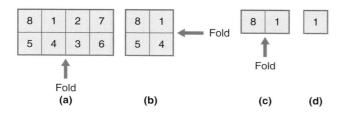

Each of these four numbered rectangles can be folded so that the numbers from 1 to 8 are in order. Make copies of the rectangles, and fold them to get the numbers in order. Devise a way, perhaps similar to that shown above, to record your solutions so that another person can understand your procedures.

2	1	3	4
7	8	6	5

6	7	5	8
3	2	4	1

8	7	2	5
1	6	3	4

1	8	7	4
2	3	6	5

Design a similar puzzle. One method is to *work backwards* by creatively folding a rectangle with blank squares, numbering the squares in order, and then unfolding it to write the numbers right side up on the rectangle.

PAPER PUZZLE 3: STEPPING THROUGH A PIECE OF PAPER

It is possible to cut a piece of $8\frac{1}{2}$-by-11-inch paper in such a way that you create a hole large enough to step through. A paper and scissors are all you need. No taping, gluing, or refastening the paper is needed or permitted. Try it.

Hint: Fold a sheet of paper and mark three points, *A, B,* and *C,* on the fold line. Make three cuts, as indicated by the dotted lines. Note that the cuts pass through points *A* and *C*

on the fold and the cut in line with *B* passes through the edge of the paper but not through the fold. Then cut along the fold from *A* to *C*. Carefully unfold the piece of paper to see the size of the hole you have created. To create a larger hole with a new sheet of paper, extend this procedure by making more cuts, alternating cutting from the fold and cutting from the edge.

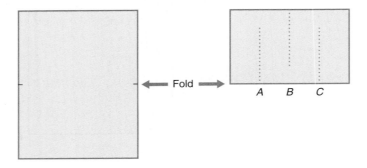

TESSELLATIONS APPLET

If you have ever formed a tessellation by tracing figures on paper or at a window, you will be amazed at the power of this applet. By creating one of several different polygons, you will be able to quickly modify its sides and then to click and see the resulting tessellation. You will be pleasantly surprised.

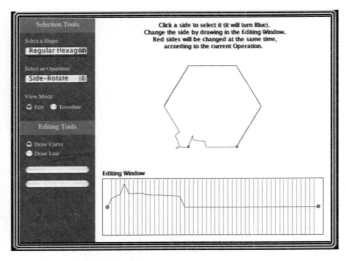

Tessellations Applet, Chapter 11
www.mhhe.com/bbn

Follow-Up Questions and Activities 11.2

1. *School Classroom:* Make a list of the geometric knowledge and skills that you believe elementary school students will learn by successfully creating a translation tessellation. What can you add to your list if students also successfully create rotation tessellations and glide reflection tessellations? Explain in detail.

2. *School Classroom:* Find and copy at least two Escher-type drawings that you believe would be appropriate to discuss with elementary students. Accompany the drawings with a list of questions you could pose to an elementary class to begin a discussion of the mathematical aspects of the drawings. Explain what you would like the students to notice.

3. *Math Concepts:* Every quadrilateral tessellates the plane. However, can an arbitrary quadrilateral such as the one shown here have all its sides altered and still tessellate the plane? Decide which methods described in this section you can use to alter the sides of this quadrilateral and tessellate the plane. In the pictured quadrilateral, no sides are of equal length and no sides are parallel. For each method you use, make a template for your figure and determine whether or not it will tessellate the plane. Describe your results and include any clarifying diagrams.

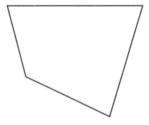

4. *Math Concepts:* Go to the companion website and launch the Tessellation Applet in Chapter 11. Choose one of the tessellations discussed in this section and create it online. Print your results.

5. *Math Concepts:* One way to create a shape for tessellation is to use tracing paper to trace and reproduce the transformed edges as demonstrated in activity 1. Another way is to use an index card or cardstock paper, design how you will alter an edge, cut off the design, and then tape that piece appropriately on another edge as shown in figure 1.

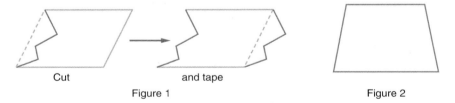

Cut   and tape

Figure 1   Figure 2

   a. Which tessellation-shaping techniques described in this activity set can be accomplished with this cut and tape process? Explain your thinking.

   b. Alter an isosceles trapezoid like the trapezoid shown in figure 2 and use the cut-and-tape method to form a template. Use this to form an Escher-type tessellation; sketch enough of the beginnings of a pattern so the reader has sufficient information to extend your pattern.

6. *NCTM Standards:* In the **Standards Summary** in the back pages of this book there are five **Process Standards.** The **Process Standards** discuss ways of acquiring and using content knowledge. Describe in detail how an activity in this section addresses an *Expectation* in one of the **Process Standards.** State the *Expectation* and the *Standard*.

BENNETT-BURTON-NELSON WEBSITE

www.mhhe.com/bbn

Virtual Manipulatives
Interactive Chapter Applets
Puzzlers

Grid and Dot Paper
Color Transparencies
Extended Bibliography

Links and Readings
Geometer Sketchpad Modules

Activity Set **11.3** DEVICES FOR INDIRECT MEASUREMENT

PURPOSE

To devise methods and simple instruments for measuring distances based on knowledge of similar triangles.

MATERIALS

Tape, drinking straws, string, paper-towel tube, small weights, yardstick, push-pins, hypsometer-clinometer from Material Card 38 and ruler and protractor from Material Card 19 (depending on which instruments you make). Cardstock or heavy weight paper for activity 4.

INTRODUCTION

It was in the second century B.C.E. that the Greek astronomer Hipparchus applied a simple theorem from geometry to measure distances indirectly. He computed the distance to the moon and many other astronomical distances. The theorem that Hipparchus applied states that if two triangles are *similar* (have the same shape), their sides are proportional. This important theorem is used in surveying, map-making, and navigation.

All that is needed to establish that two triangles are similar is that two angles of one are congruent to two angles of the other. The two triangles shown here are similar because $\angle A$ is congruent to $\angle D$ and $\angle C$ is congruent to $\angle F$. (When two angles of one triangle are congruent to two angles of another, the remaining angles also must be congruent. Why?)

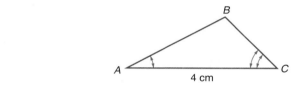

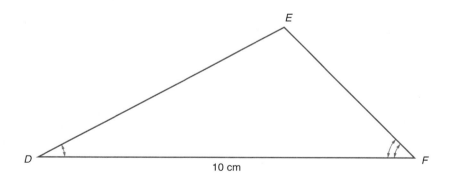

Hipparchus knew that for two similar triangles their side lengths are proportional. For example, side $\overline{DF}$ corresponds to side $\overline{AC}$ and is 2.5 times as long. You can check by measuring that this same relationship holds for all three pairs of corresponding sides. That is,

$$DF = 2.5 \times AC \qquad FE = 2.5 \times CB \qquad ED = 2.5 \times BA$$

Notice also that the ratios of the lengths of sides in one triangle are equal to the corresponding ratios in a similar triangle. For example,

$$\frac{AB}{AC} = \frac{DE}{DF} \quad \text{since} \quad \frac{AB}{AC} = \frac{3}{4} \quad \text{and} \quad \frac{DE}{DF} = \frac{2.5 \times 3}{2.5 \times 4}$$

Similarly, the following ratios are also equal.

$$\frac{AB}{BC} = \frac{DE}{EF} \quad \text{and} \quad \frac{BC}{AC} = \frac{EF}{DF}$$

All of the estimating methods and instruments in this activity set use the fact that the length of corresponding sides of similar triangles are proportional.

1. **Sighting Method:** Distances can be estimated when the size of an object at that distance is roughly known. For example, stretch your arm out in front of you, holding a ruler in a vertical position. Select some distant object such as a person and estimate his or her height. Hold the ruler so that the top is in line with your eye and the top of the person's head. Position your thumb on the ruler so that it is in line with the person's feet.

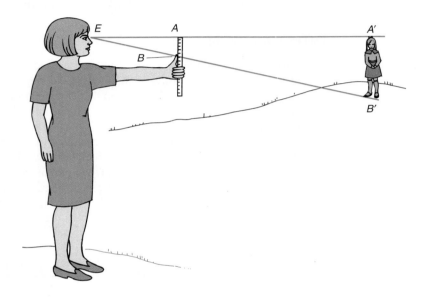

*a. The lines of sight from your eye (point E) to the top of your ruler and your thumb form triangle EAB. The lines of sight from E to the head and feet of the observed person form triangle $EA'B'$. *Why are these triangles similar?*

b. Obtain the length of $\overline{EA}$ by measuring the distance from your eye to a ruler, as shown in the figure. Obtain the length of $\overline{AB}$ from the ruler. Record these two lengths and your estimate of the height of the person ($\overline{A'B'}$) you are measuring the distance to.

c. Use the fact that triangle EAB is similar to triangle $E'A'B'$ to estimate the distance to the person, $\overline{EA'}$.

2. Scout Sighting Method: Here is an old scout trick for getting a rough estimate of the distance to an object. This variation of the sighting method does not require a ruler. The scout stretches out his or her arm and, with the left eye closed, sights with the right eye along the tip of one finger to a distant object, T, they wish to know the distance to. Next the scout closes the right eye and sights with the left eye along the unmoved finger to a second object, R. The scout then estimates the distance between the two objects and multiplies by 10 to estimate the distance to these objects.[2]

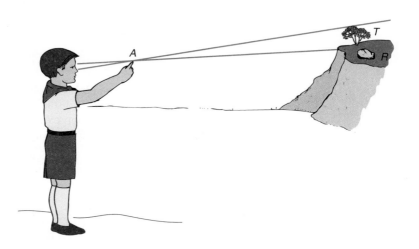

a. In the following diagram, E_1 and E_2 represent the eyes, A the finger, T the tree, and R the rock. Why is triangle E_1E_2A similar to triangle TRA?

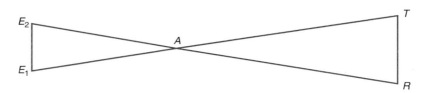

b. Assume the distance between the scout's eyes is 7.5 cm, and the distance from the scout's eye to fingertip is 75 cm. If the scout estimates the distance between the tree and the rock to be about 90 meters (the length of a football field), how far is it from the scout's finger to the tree? That is, what is length AT? Explain your thinking.

[2]For several more elementary sighting methods, see C. N. Shuster and F. L. Bedford, *Field Work in Mathematics* (East Palistine, OH: Yoder Instruments, 1935): 56–57.

c. The scout sighting method is based on the assumption that E_1A (the distance from eye to fingertip) is 10 times E_1E_2 (the distance between the eyes). Stretch your arm out in front of you and measure the distance from your eye to your raised index finger. Then measure the distance between your eyes. Record your distances on the following diagram. Should you be using the number 10 for the scout sighting method? If not, what number should you be using?

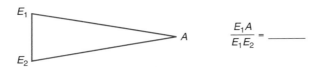

$$\frac{E_1A}{E_1E_2} = \underline{\qquad}$$

*d. When you measure your distance from an object you are fairly close to, such as something in a room, you should add the distance from eye to finger to the result obtained from the scout sighting method. In approximating greater distances, you can ignore the distance from eye to finger, E_1A. Explain why.

3. Stadiascope: The stadiascope works on the same principle as the sighting method with the ruler (see activity 1). This instrument has a peep sight at one end and cross threads at the other. The stadiascope shown here was made from a paper-towel tube having a length of 27 cm. At one end of the tube, six threads have been taped in horizontal rows. These threads are 1 cm apart. A piece of paper has been taped over the other end, and a peep sight has been punched on the same level as the lowest thread.

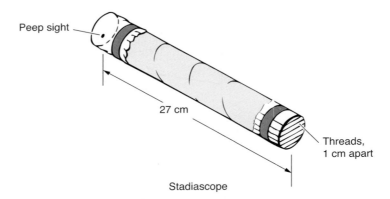

Peep sight

27 cm

Threads,
1 cm apart

Stadiascope

The following diagram shows a stadiascope being used to measure the distance to a truck. The truck fills 4 spaces at the end of the stadiascope. Let's assume that the truck has a height of 3 m.

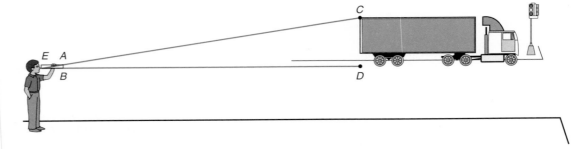

a. Point E is the peep sight, and points A and B mark the upper thread and lower thread of the 4 spaces of the stadiascope between which the truck is seen. Triangle EBA and triangle EDC are right triangles. Explain why they are similar.

*b. Since triangle EBA is similar to triangle EDC, the ratios of their corresponding sides are equal. Use the ratios given here to compute the length of ED in meters. (*Note: EB* and *AB* can be left in centimeters and *CD* in meters.)

$$\frac{ED}{EB} = \frac{CD}{AB}$$

*c. Suppose you sight a person who fills 2 spaces of the stadiascope and you estimate this person's height to be 180 cm. How many meters is this person from you?

d. Make a stadiascope and use it to measure some heights or distances indirectly. Check your results with direct measurements.

4. Clinometer: The clinometer, used to measure heights of objects, is an easy device to construct (see Material Card 38). It is a simplified version of the quadrant, an important instrument in the Middle Ages, and the sextant, an instrument used for locating the positions of ships. Each of these devices has arcs that are graduated in degrees for measuring angles of elevation. The arc of the clinometer is marked from 0 to 90°. When an object is sighted through the straw, the number of degrees in angle BVW can be read from the arc. Angle BAC is the angle of elevation of the clinometer.

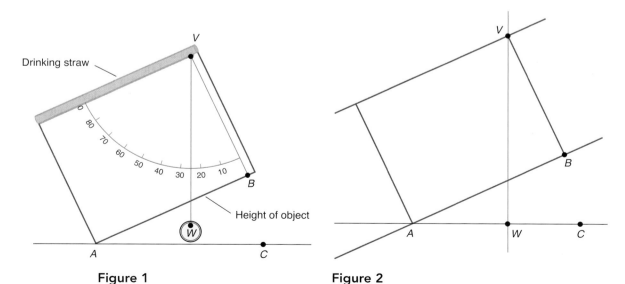

Figure 1   Figure 2

6. Transit: The transit (or theodolite) is one of the most important instruments for measuring horizontal and vertical angles in civil engineering. In its earliest form, this instrument was capable of measuring only horizontal angles, much like the simplified version shown below. To make a transit, tape a protractor (Material Card 19) to one end of a meterstick (or long thin board) and pin a drinking straw at the center point of the protractor.

The next diagram shows how the transit can be used to find the distance between two points. Line segment $\overline{AB}$ has been marked by posts on the left bank of the river. By standing at point B and holding the stick of the transit parallel to $\overline{AB}$, you can measure angle FBA. Similarly, by standing at point A and holding the stick parallel to $\overline{AB}$, you can measure angle FAB. The distance between the posts can be found by using a tape measure or by pacing off. This distance is 500 m. On paper, a similar triangle can be drawn to represent the real triangle formed by the fort and the posts. This small triangle will be similar to the real triangle if angle A and angle B have been drawn to be congruent to the angles measured with the transit.

a. Use a ruler to set up a scale on $\overline{AB}$ in the diagram below to represent 500 m. The actual distance from A to the fort, point F, can be found by using your scale. What is this distance to the nearest meter?

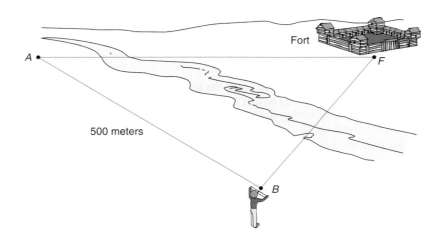

*b. Explain how you would use the transit to make a map of the objects in this field. What is the least number of angles and distances you would have to measure?

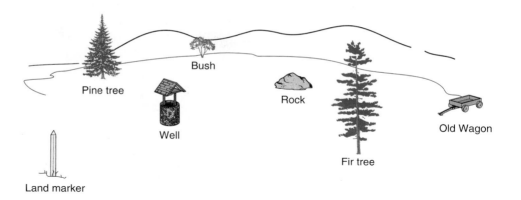

Pine tree

Bush

Well

Rock

Fir tree

Old Wagon

Land marker

JUST FOR FUN

ENLARGING DRAWINGS

Figure a shows a drawing of a rabbit. Suppose you wish to copy and double the size of the drawing. Here is one method that works when you do not have immediate access to a copy machine that automatically enlarges. Draw or place a transparent grid over the bunny as shown in figure b.

A grid whose edges are 2 times the length of those in figure b, is drawn on the next page. The sketch of the rabbit is then copied square by square from the small grid to the

(a)

(b)

larger grid. On the grid below, five squares have been copied from figure b on the previous page. Complete the enlargement by copying the remaining squares.

Choose a picture, cartoon, or drawing and enlarge it using the grid method. You can make it as large as you wish by choosing an appropriate grid.

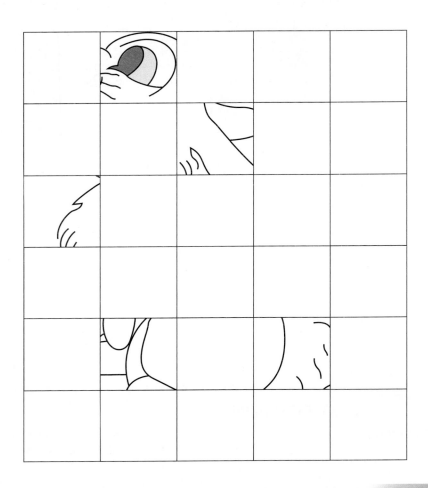

Follow-Up Questions and Activities 11.3

1. *School Classroom:* One of your students asks you if all squares are similar. Explain how you would explore this idea with your student.

2. *School Classroom:* A student says that a way to test whether or not two rectangles are similar is to put the smaller rectangle on the corner of the larger rectangle (as shown in the figure). Then, if the corner X on the smaller rectangle is on the diagonal AC of the larger rectangle, the two rectangles are similar. Explain whether or not this student is correct and why.

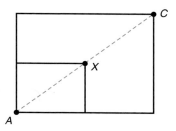

3. *Math Concepts:* Use your pattern blocks to form figure 1 below. Then use pattern blocks to form a new figure similar to figure 1 whose sides are in a ratio of 2 to 1 to figure 1. Sketch your resulting figure.

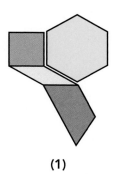

(1)

4. *Math Concepts:* On Centimeter Grid paper draw a new figure, similar to figure 2 below, so that the ratio from the sides of figure 2 to the sides of the new figure is 2 to 3. Compare the area of the new figure to the area of figure 2; how many times larger is the area of the new figure than figure 2? Centimeter Grid paper is available for download at the companion website.

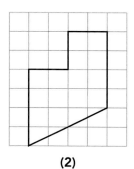

(2)

5. *NCTM Standards:* Give an example of an activity for exploring similarity for Grades 3–5. What *Expectations* and *Standards* does your activity address? State the *Expectations* and *Standards* and explain why your activity addresses these recommendations.

 BENNETT-BURTON-NELSON WEBSITE

www.mhhe.com/bbn

Virtual Manipulatives	Grid and Dot Paper	Links and Readings
Interactive Chapter Applets	Color Transparencies	Geometer Sketchpad Modules
Puzzlers	Extended Bibliography	

Elementary
School Activity

CREATING ESCHER-TYPE TESSELLATIONS

Purpose: To introduce elementary school students to methods for creating an Escher-type tessellation.

Connections: Books, posters or calendars of Escher's tessellation artwork are available in libraries and bookstores. Bring examples of his artwork to class for students to examine. Many students may have seen some of his work already. Ask students to look at the shapes of the interlocking pieces. Tell them that today they will be creating their own Escher-type drawings.

Materials: Scotch tape, scissors, and rulers for each group of students. A cardstock rectangle and large sheet of drawing paper for each student. (Cut a cardstock rectangle (2" by 4") ahead of time for each student—old file folders work well.)

This Escher-type tessel-
lation was created by a
fourth grader, who is
putting in some finish-
ing touches.

1. Distribute the rectangles and other materials to the students. Have the students put two points (like *P* and *Q*) on their rectangle and draw line segments from the points to the vertices and edge of the rectangle as shown. You may wish to illustrate the process for your students using an overhead.

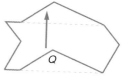

2. Ask the students to cut out the triangle from the end of their rectangle and carefully tape the triangle on the other end of the rectangle without turning it.

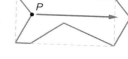

3. Similarly, have the students cut out their bottom triangle, slide it to the upper edge, and tape it to the top of the rectangle. (It must be placed along the top edge directly above the place where it was cut from the lower edge).

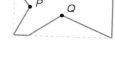

4. The students now have a template. Ask them to place the template in the center of their piece of drawing paper and trace around it with a pencil. Then fit the template to the edges of the traced figure and continue tracing to create a tessellation by expanding the drawing in all directions around their original figure.

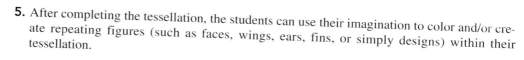

Proudly displaying
her tessellation.

5. After completing the tessellation, the students can use their imagination to color and/or create repeating figures (such as faces, wings, ears, fins, or simply designs) within their tessellation.

6. (Optional) Some students may wish to start over or create other tessellations. The beginning shape can be a square, parallelogram, or rectangle. The shapes cut from the end and bottom edges can be shapes other than triangular, but they must be taped directly across, as described above.

Activity Set 1.3

2. a.

b. The perimeter of the triangle can be represented with 5 variable pieces and 6 units. The perimeter is 66, so the 5 variable pieces represent 60 units. Therefore, each single variable piece represents 12 units. The sides of the triangle are 12 units, 24 units, and 30 units.

4.

Short piece of rope ▭

Long piece of rope ▭

End to end ▭

End to end, the length is 75 m. Then 2 variable pieces represent 68 m (75 − 7) and one variable piece is 34 m. So the short piece is 34 m and the long piece is 41 m.

6.

Number of dimes Greg has ▭

Number of nickels Andrea has ▭

Suppose Greg exchanges his dimes for nickels.

Number of nickels Greg will have ▭

Number of nickels Andrea will have ▭

Andrea has 80 cents more than Greg, so 2 variable pieces represent 80 cents, which is the amount of money that Greg has.

8.

Number of men ▭

Number of women ▭

Double number of men ▭

Increase women by 9 ▭

Suppose each variable piece represents one-fifth of the students. Then 2 variable pieces represent the total number of men and 3 pieces the number of women. The equality given by doubling the number of men and increasing the women by 9, shows that each variable piece represents 9 people. The original class has 45 people, 18 men and 27 women.

Activity Set 2.1

2. a. By asking yes or no questions that refer to a single attribute, a player can identify any piece in at most 6 guesses. For example: Is it large? Is it red? Is it blue? Is it triangular? Is it square? Is it circular?

4. b. LRC, SRT, SBT, LRS, LRH, SRC, SRS, SRH, LRT, SYT, LYT, LBT

5. a. LRC, LYC, SRC, SYC

6. b. LARGE RED pieces, or LARGE AND RED pieces

c. LYT, SYT, LBT, LBS, LBC, LBH, SBT, SBS, SBC, SBH, LRT, LRH, LRS, LRC, SRT, SRH, SRS, SRC

7. b. (2) The large blue hexagon and the large red hexagon.

(5) All of the hexagons except for the small yellow hexagon. Or: The large yellow hexagon, the small red hexagon, the large red hexagon, the small blue hexagon, and the large blue hexagon.

Activity Set 2.2

2. c. Both of these line segments have slope $-\frac{4}{3}$

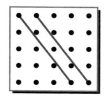

4. a. The slope of line segment A is $-\frac{2}{3}$, the slope of line segment C is $\frac{3}{2}$.

5. d. The slope of the line using points P and Q is $\frac{4-3}{2-5} = \frac{1}{-3} = -\frac{1}{3}$.

The slope of the line using point Q and any point R should also be $-\frac{1}{3}$.

6. a. $y = \frac{5}{2}x$

7. a. The equation of line K is $y = x$. The equation of line L is $y = x + 2$.

Activity Set 2.3

3. Math—*Robinson*, English—*Smith*, French—*Brown*, Logic—*Jones*

4. Pilot—*Jones*, Copilot—*Smith*, Engineer—*Robinson*

Activity Set 3.1

1. c. 0 long-flats, 0 flats, 4 longs, 4 units

2. c. 1 long-flat, 0 flats, 0 longs, 1 unit

f. 453 unit squares

3. c. 1001_{five}

f. 3303_{five}

4. b. 142 unit squares

5. a. base three

6. b. 425_{seven}. Total number of unit squares: 215

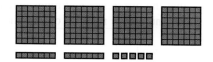

7. b.

123_{nine}

Just for Fun 3.1

Mind-Reading Cards

2. $27 = 1 + 2 + 8 + 16$, cards 1, 2, 8, and 16

4. A number k is on a card if and only if the number of the card is a term in the sum of the binary numbers that equals k. So the sum of the numbers of the cards on which a person's age appears is the person's age.

5. Since $44 = 32 + 8 + 4$, the number 44 must be written on cards 4, 8, and 32.

Game of Nim

3. Crossing out 1 stick in the second row leaves an even number of binary groups.

4. It is not possible in 1 turn to change an even situation into another even situation. Therefore, if you leave your opponent with an even situation, there will be an odd situation on your turn.

Activity Set 3.2

2. b. Since the maximum amount you can win in a roll is 2 longs and 2 units, it will take you at least 11 turns to win the game. (If you win the maximum amount on each turn, then in 2 turns you will be 1 unit short of a flat. So in 10 turns you will be 5 units short of a long-flat, and it will take at least 1 more turn to win.)

6. b. GCF(280, 168) = GCF(112, 168) = GCF(112, 56) = GCF(56, 56) = 56

   d. GCF(306, 187) = GCF(119, 187) = GCF(119, 68) = GCF(51, 68) = GCF(51, 17) = GCF(34, 17) = GCF(17, 17) = 17

7. b. LCM(14, 21) = 42

   d. LCM(8, 10) = 40

8. a.

A	B	GCF(A, B)	LCM(A, B)	A × B
(3) 14	21	7	42	294
(5) 8	10	2	40	80

9. a. GCF(9, 15) = 3 and 9 × 15 = 135, 135 ÷ 3 = 45. So LCM(9, 15) = 45.

   c. GCF(140, 350) = 70 and (140 × 350) ÷ 70 = 70. So LCM(140, 350) = 700.

Just for Fun 4.2

1. Yes

Star (8, 3)   Star (9, 4)   Star (7, 2)   Star (7, 4)

2. Star (n, s) is congruent to (has the same size and shape as) star (n, r).

Star (12, 5)   Star (12, 7)   Star (10, 3)   Star (10, 7)

3. Star (5, 1) has 1 path; star (10, 4) has 2 paths; star (12, 4) has 4 paths; and star (6, 3) has 3 paths.

Star (5, 1)   Star (10, 4)   Star (12, 4)   Star (6, 3)

4. n and s must be relatively prime; that is, GCF(n, s) = 1. These stars have 1 continuous path: (1) star (15, 2) = star (15, 13); (2) star (15, 4) = star (15, 11); and (3) star (15, 7) = star (15, 8).

Star (15, 2)   Star (15, 4)   Star (15, 7)

5. Star (9, 2) has 1 path and requires 2 orbits. Star (8, 6) has 2 paths and each path requires 3 orbits. Star (14, 4) has 2 paths and each path requires 2 orbits.

Star (9, 2)   Star (8, 6)   Star (14, 4)

6. b. The number of orbits for star (n, s) is LCM(n, s) divided by n.

7. b. 11

Activity Set 5.1

2. a. 37   8   29   21

   c. 20   6   14   8

   f. 24   13   11   ⁻2

3. c. 13; ⁻59; ⁻62

4. b. If there are more red tiles than black tiles, subtract the number of black tiles from the number of red tiles and make the answer negative. If the number of black tiles is greater than or equal to the number of red tiles, subtract the number of red tiles from the number of black tiles.

5. b.

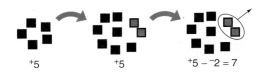

  ⁺5   ⁺5   ⁺5 − ⁻2 = 7

6. Notice that in each of the preceding examples, taking out a given number of tiles of one color is equivalent to putting in the same number of tiles of the opposite color. For example, in 5b, 2 red tiles and 2 black tiles were put in the set and then 2 red tiles were withdrawn from the set. The same result could be accomplished by simply adding 2 black tiles to the set.

7. b.

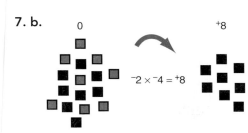

$$^-2 \times ^-4 = ^+8$$

9. c. In the sharing approach, $^-3$ represents the number of groups, which is not possible. In the measurement approach, groups of 3 red tiles cannot be formed from 12 black tiles.

10. c. i. $15 \div 3 = 5$; divide 15 black tiles into 3 equal piles, each pile contains 5 black tiles *or* measure off 3 black tiles at a time from 15 black tiles. Five sets of 3 black tiles can be measured off.

iii. $^-15 \div 3 = ^-5$; divide 15 red tiles into 3 equal piles, each pile contains 5 red tiles.

Activity Set 5.2

1. a.

Fraction	No. of Bars with Equal Fractions
$\frac{0}{4}$	5
$\frac{1}{2}$	4
$\frac{2}{3}$	3
$\frac{6}{6}$	5
$\frac{1}{4}$	2

2. a. $\frac{1}{12} < \frac{1}{6} < \frac{1}{4} < \frac{1}{3} < \frac{5}{12} < \frac{1}{2} < \frac{7}{12} < \frac{2}{3} < \frac{3}{4} < \frac{5}{6} < \frac{11}{12}$

3. b. Here are 10 inequalities; there are others.

$\frac{1}{2} < \frac{2}{3}, \frac{1}{2} < \frac{3}{4}, \frac{1}{2} < \frac{4}{6}, \frac{1}{2} < \frac{5}{6}, \frac{1}{3} < \frac{2}{4}, \frac{1}{3} < \frac{3}{4},$

$\frac{1}{4} < \frac{1}{2}, \frac{1}{4} < \frac{1}{3}, \frac{1}{4} < \frac{2}{6}, \frac{1}{4} < \frac{3}{6}$

4. b. $\frac{2}{3} < \frac{3}{4}$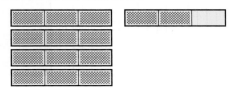

d. $\frac{7}{7} = \frac{5}{5}$ since they are both whole bars.

5. a. Nearest whole number is 5

c. Nearest whole number is 1

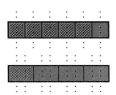

6. b.

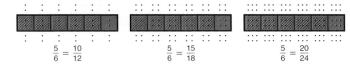

$\frac{6}{7} = \frac{18}{21}$ $\frac{5}{8} = \frac{15}{24}$ $\frac{1}{6} = \frac{3}{18}$

7. b. $\frac{2}{3} = \frac{2 \times 17}{3 \times 17} = \frac{34}{51}$

d.

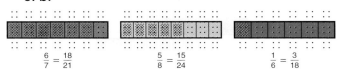

$\frac{5}{6} = \frac{10}{12}$ $\frac{5}{6} = \frac{15}{18}$ $\frac{5}{6} = \frac{20}{24}$

8. a.

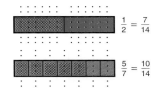

$\frac{1}{2} = \frac{7}{14}$

$\frac{5}{7} = \frac{10}{14}$

9. d. $\frac{7}{9} = \frac{70}{90}$ and $\frac{8}{10} = \frac{72}{92}$ so $\frac{8}{10} > \frac{7}{9}$

f. $\frac{11}{15} = \frac{121}{165}$ and $\frac{8}{11} = \frac{120}{165}$ so $\frac{11}{15} > \frac{8}{11}$

10. b. $2 \div 3 = \frac{2}{3}$

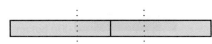

Activity Set 5.3

1. a.   **c.**

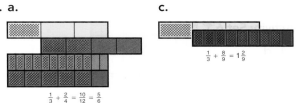

$\frac{1}{3} + \frac{2}{4} = \frac{10}{12} = \frac{5}{6}$ $\frac{1}{3} + \frac{8}{9} = 1\frac{2}{9}$

e.

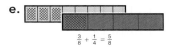

$\frac{3}{8} + \frac{1}{4} = \frac{5}{8}$

3. a.

$\frac{13}{12} = 1\frac{1}{12}$ **g.** $\frac{7}{12}$

d.

6. a. Value of grid is 400: Since 6% has value 24, 1% has value 4, and the value of the 10 by 10 grid is 400.

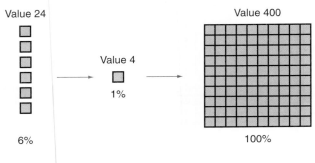

Value 24

Value 4

1%

Value 400

6%

100%

c. Value of the grid is 240: Since 55% has value 132, 1% has value 2.4 (132 ÷ 55), and 100% has value 240.

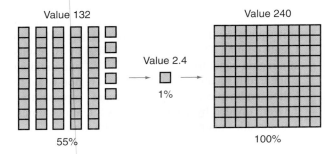

Value 132

Value 2.4

1%

Value 240

55%

100%

7. a. Some possible observations: There are 208 women employees; 35% of the employees are men; there are 112 men employees.

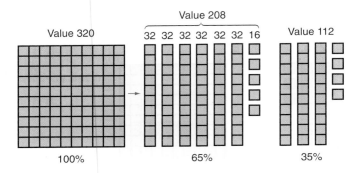

Value 320

Value 208

32 32 32 32 32 32 16

Value 112

100%

65%

35%

b. Some observations: 35% of the students were absent; 65% of the students were present.

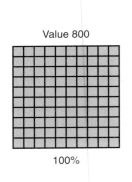

Value 800

Value 280

80 80 80 40

100%

8. b. $\frac{2}{5} = 40\% = .4$

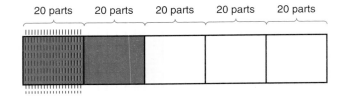

20 parts   20 parts   20 parts   20 parts   20 parts

d. $\frac{13}{20} = \frac{65}{100} = .65\% = .65$

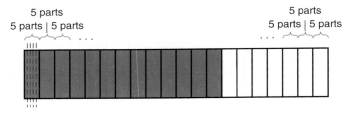

5 parts

5 parts | 5 parts   5 parts | 5 parts

. . .   . . .

9. b. $\frac{5}{6} \approx 85\% = .85$

17 parts

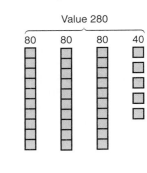

Activity Set 6.4

1. b. 7 square units   **e.** 4 square units
    h. 2 square units
2. b. 4 square units   **e.** 2 square units
    g. 10 square units
4. a. $\sqrt{13}$ **b.** 5   **c.** $\sqrt{17}$
6.

	Square A	Square B	Square C
b. Fig. 2	9	4	13
d. Fig. 4	45	20	65

7. b.

	Total Area of Squares on Two Legs	Area of Square on Hypotenuse	Length of Hypotenuse
(2) Fig. 2	1 + 25 = 26	26	$\sqrt{26}$
(4) Fig. 4	9 + 49 = 58	58	$\sqrt{58}$

Activity Set 7.1

1. a. A typical bar graph display of eye color might look like

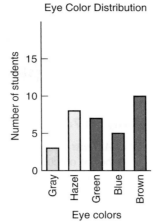

Eye Color Distribution

b. A typical distribution and Pie Graph might look like

Eye Color	Number	Percentage	Central Angle (degrees)
Brown	10	30.3	109.1
Blue	5	15.2	54.5
Green	7	21.2	76.4
Hazel	8	24.2	87.3
Gray	3	9.1	32.7
Total	33	100.0	360

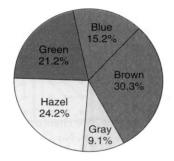

2. a. A typical line plot might look like

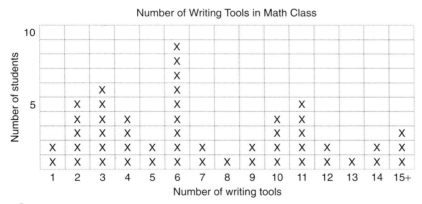

3. c.

Interval	15–24	25–34	35–44	45–54	55–64	65–74
Frequency	1	5	14	6	17	7

6. a. The trend line for this data has a negative slope. It indicates that the taller the father the shorter the mother.

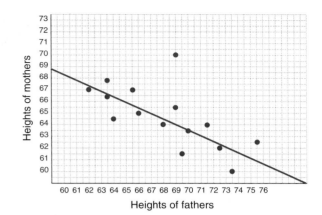

b. The horizontal trend line for this data has zero slope. Short fathers are paired with short and tall mothers and the same is true for taller fathers. There seems to be no apparent trend.

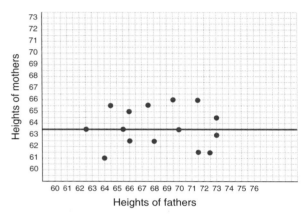

4. c. Each interior angle of a regular polygon with more than 6 sides is greater than 120° and less than 180°. The measures of such angles are not factors of 360.

Just for Fun 7.1

1. There is a negative relationship. As the number of blue increases the number of brown decreases. (A correlation of about −.5.)

2. Based on the scatter plot trend line, if you had 14 blue

4. **b.** $287,000 is the average for the 6 greatest incomes; $120,667 is the average for the 6 smallest incomes.

   d. $264,167 is the greatest average and $139,667 is the least average. Both are closer to the mean of $195,611 than the greatest average and least average from part b.

5. **c.** Here are two examples of pattern block tessellations that are neither regular nor semi-regular.

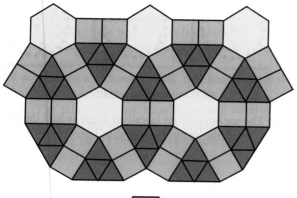

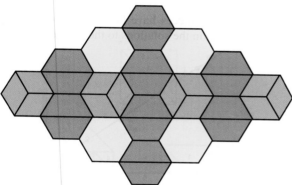

Just for Fun 9.2

The winning strategy on a 3 by 3 or 5 by 5 grid is to occupy the center hexagon on the first move. On a 4 by 4 grid, the winning first move is any of those marked here.

4 by 4

Activity Set 9.3

3. **a.**

	Vertices (V)	Faces (F)	Edges (E)
Tetrahedron	4	4	6
Cube	8	6	12
Octahedron	6	8	12
Dodecahedron	20	12	30
Icosahedron	12	20	30

c.

	(1)	(2)	(3)	(4)
Vertices	5	10	12	10
Faces	5	7	8	7
Edges	8	15	18	15

5. **b.** Octahedron   **e.** Icosahedron   **f.** Cube
   g. Icosahedron or dodecahedron
   h. Dodecahedron   **j.** Cube or octahedron

Activity Set 9.4

1. **a.**

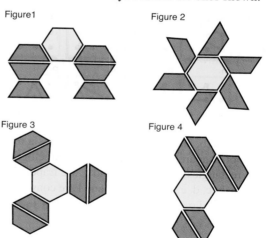

c. There are other ways besides the ones shown.

Figure 1   Figure 2

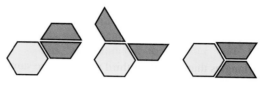

Figure 3   Figure 4

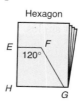

4. **a.** Angle *ABC* has a measure of 135°; $AD = DC$ and $AB = BC$.

Octagon

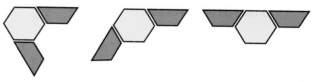

Angle *EFG* has a measure of 120°; $FG = HG = HF$ and $EF = \frac{1}{2}$ of *FG*.

Hexagon

5. d. The eight-pointed wind rose.

  e. A regular 16-sided polygon can be obtained by cutting a 157.5° angle as shown here, with $AB = AC = AD$. *Note:* Some of the lines of symmetry are not crease lines.

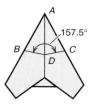

Activity Set 10.1

3. a. 156 mm   **b.** 19 mm

7. a. A quart contains approximately 946 cm³. A liter contains slightly more than a quart.

  b. Approximately 10.9 cm

Activity Set 10.2

1. a. 9 sq. units   **b.** 6 sq. units

2. a. 3 sq. units   **b.** 4 sq. units

6. a. Parallelogram, 6 square units; triangle, 3 square units.

  c. Parallelogram, 9 square units; triangle, $4\frac{1}{4}$ square units.

7. The area of a parallelogram is equal to the length of a side multiplied by the height from that side. A triangle with base of length b units and height of length h units has half the area of a parallelogram with base length b and height of length h from that side.

Just for Fun 10.2

4. The squares with an X in the following figure show one possible final move in the pentomino game.

5. Here are 5 pieces that work.

Activity Set 10.3

1. The volume of the crown was greater than the volume of the gold. King Hieron was cheated.

2.

	Hexagonal Prism	Hexagonal Pyramid	Cylinder
Area of base	9.1 cm²	9.1 cm²	12.6 cm²
Height (altitude)	5.0 cm	5.0 cm	3.0 cm
Volume	45.5 cm³	15.2 cm³	37.7 cm³
Surface area	75.2 cm²	38.7 cm²	62.8 cm²

3. Cylinder A: 1030 cm³; cylinder B: 1342 cm³

5. b.

	1	2	3	4	5	6
Central angle of disk	45°	90°	135°	225°	270°	315°
Radius (cm) of base	1.25	2.50	3.75	6.25	7.50	8.75
Base area (cm²)	4.91	19.63	44.16	122.66	176.63	240.41
Height (cm) of cone	9.92	9.68	9.27	7.81	6.61	4.84
Volume (cm³) of cone	16.24	63.34	136.45	319.32	389.17	387.86

  c. For central angles of less than 45°, the smaller the angle is, the smaller the volume is. For central angles of more than 315°, the larger the angle is, the smaller the volume is. The maximum volume of approximately 403 cm³ occurs with a central angle of 294°.

6. c. A cone with a base of radius r and a height of h has a volume of $\frac{1}{3} \times \pi r^2 h$. The "half cone" has a base of radius $\frac{r}{2}$ and a height of $\frac{h}{2}$. Its volume is $\frac{1}{3} \times \pi(\frac{r}{2})^2(\frac{h}{2})$, which is equal to $\frac{1}{3} \times \pi r^2 h \times \frac{1}{8}$.

  Therefore, the volume of the "half cone" is $\frac{1}{8}$ of the volume of the original cone.

7. a. 7235 cm³

8. c. The volume of the 3 balls is $3 \times \frac{4}{3} \times \pi(3.15)^3 \approx$ 394 cm³. The volume of the can is $20 \times \pi(3.5)^2 \approx$ 769 cm³. Therefore, approximately $\frac{1}{2}$ of the space is wasted.

Activity Set 11.1

1. b. The points form 2 perpendicular lines that pass through the intersection of lines m and n and bisect the angles formed by the intersection of m and n.

2. a. The points form a circle with P as center and radius equal to the distance from P to the midpoint of the chords.

  c. The points form a circle whose center is the midpoint of segment $\overline{PS}$ and whose diameter is $\overline{PS}$.

4. A circle

6. a. A semicircle on diameter $\overline{PQ}$ (a circle if you reverse the card and repeat the process on the other side of segment $\overline{PQ}$)

Activity Set 11.2

1. a. The new figure will tessellate because the exact shape that has been adjoined to one edge of the rectangle was deleted from the opposite side of the rectangle.

Activity Set 11.3

1. a. Both triangles contain the angle at E, and the angles at A and $A´$ are right angles. When two angles of one triangle are congruent to two angles of another, the triangles are similar.

2. d. When you are estimating large distances, the distance from eye to finger is relatively small and ignoring it will not significantly affect the estimate. However, when you are estimating small distances, which may be only a few times greater than the distance from eye to finger, ignoring the distance from the eye to the finger will give a larger error. In the latter case, the distance should be added to the estimated distance.

3. b. 20.25 m   **c.** 24.3 m

4. c. $\overline{ET}$ in the figure measures 80 mm. So 80 mm represents 60 m, or 1 mm represents .75 m. The height of the tree from T to R in the diagram is 24 mm, so the height of the actual tree between those two points is $24 \times .75 = 18$ m.

5. c. Approximately 33 m plus 1.5 m, the height of the hypsometer above the ground, for a total of 34.5 m.

6. b. Use a line from the land marker to the pine tree as a base line and measure the distance between these two points. From the pine tree, measure the 5 angles between the base line and the remaining 5 objects. From the landmark, measure the 5 angles between the base line and the remaining 5 objects. With the 10 angles, a map can be made of the locations of each object. Using the distance from pine tree to the landmark, a scale can be set up to determine all distances between any pairs of objects in the field.

Credits

Photo Credits

Chapter 1
Page 11: © The Granger Collection; p. 15 (top): © H. Stanley Johnson/SuperStock RF; p. 15 (center): © Dr. Parvind Sethi; p. 15 (bottom right): © PhotoAlto/PunchStock; p. 15 (bottom left): *Patterns in Nature* by Peter S. Stevens, Atlantic Monthly/Little Brown, 1974. Reprinted by courtesy of Peter S. Stevens; p. 24: Photo by Albert B. Bennett, Jr.

Chapter 2
Page 32, 54: Photo by Albert B. Bennett, Jr.

Chapter 3
Page 55 (all), 74, 91, 93: Photo by Albert B. Bennett, Jr.

Chapter 4
Page 111 (both), 114: Photo by Albert B. Bennett, Jr.; p. 116: Courtesy Hamid Buhmard, Western Oregon University; p. 118: Photo by Albert B. Bennett, Jr.

Chapter 5
Page 126, 146: Photo by Albert B. Bennett, Jr.

Chapter 6
Pages 156: Photo by Albert B. Bennett, Jr.; p. 187: © Getty/RF; p. 190: Photo by Albert B. Bennett, Jr.

Chapter 7
Page 214 (all): Library of Congress; p. 216 (all): © Image Club RF; p. 228 (all): Photo by L. Ted Nelson.

Chapter 8
Page 231, 232: Photo by Albert B. Bennett, Jr.; p. 233 (all): © Image Club RF; p. 235, 236: Photo by Albert B. Bennett, Jr.; p. 239(top): © Comstock/Alamy RF; p. 239 (center): © Vol. 25 PhotoDisc/Getty RF; p. 239 (bottom): Photo by Albert B. Bennett, Jr.; p. 243 (all): © Image Club RF; p. 245, 248 (all), 249, 251: Photo by Albert B. Bennett, Jr.

Chapter 9
Page 253, 255, 260 (all): Photo by Albert B. Bennett, Jr.; p. 264 (left): © Stockbyte/Getty RF; p. 264 (right): © Stockbyte/Getty RF; p. 273a: © Comstock/PunchStock RF; p. 273b: © Digital Vision, Ltd. RF; p. 275: M.C. Escher's "Stars" © 2008 The M.C. Escher Company – Baarn – Holland. All rights reserved. www.mcescher.com; p. 276, (all), 279, 280: Photo by Albert B. Bennett, Jr.; p. 282: © Getty/RF; p. 293: Photo by Albert B. Bennett, Jr.

Chapter 10
Page 298, 300: Photo by Albert B. Bennett, Jr.; p. 301 (top): © The McGraw-Hill Companies, Inc./Dot Box, Inc.; p. 301 (bottom): © The McGraw-Hill Companies, Inc./Jacques Cornell, photographer; p. 307: Photo by Albert B. Bennett, Jr.; p. 310: © Comstock/Alamy; p. 314, 315, 316 (top): Photo by Albert B. Bennett, Jr.; p. 316 (bottom): © The McGraw-Hill Companies, Inc./Ken Karp, photographer; p. 317, 320: Photo by Albert B. Bennett, Jr.

Chapter 11
Page 321: © Image Club RF; p. 329: Photo courtesy Hamid Behmard, Western Oregon University; p. 331 (all): Photo by L. Ted Nelson; p. 350, 355 (all): Photo by Albert B. Bennett, Jr.

Activity Cards
Problem 1, Activity Set 2.3 (all): © Vol. 116 PhotoDisc/Getty RF and © Children's Portraits Punchstock/Stockbyte RF; Problem 2, Activity Set 2.3 (all): © Vol. 116 PhotoDisc/Getty RF; © Children's Portraits Punchstock/Stockbyte RF; and © IS490/Image Source Black RF; Activity Set 8.1 (all): © Image Club RF; Activity Set 10.2: Photo by Albert Bennett, Jr.

Illustrations and Text

Chapter 5
Page 106: Fraction Bar model from the Fraction Bars® materials by Albert B. Bennett, Jr., and Patricia Davidson © 2003. Permission of Scott Resources, Inc. Fort Collins, Colorado.

Chapter 6
Page 123: Decimal Squares model from the Decimal Squares® materials by Albert B. Bennett, Jr., © 2003. Permission of Scott Resources, Inc. Fort Collins, Colorado.

Chapter 7
Page 185: Graphs from *A Guide to the Unknown,* by Frederick Mosteller et al., copyright 1972. Reprinted by courtesy of Holden-Day, Inc.

Chapter 11
Page 287: Line designs from *Line Designs* by Dale Seymour, Linda Libey, and Joyce Snider. Reprinted by permission of Creative Publications, Palo Alto.

Index

Note: Page numbers preceded by A refer to the Appendix; those preceded by M refer to the Material Cards section.

A

Abacus-type models, 55
Acute angle, 328
Acute triangle, 262
Addition
 algorithm for, 66
 of decimals, 159–161, 167–168
 of fractions, 137–140, 142–143
 games, 66–67, 126–127, 143, 168
 of integers, 122–123
 models of, 66–69, 74
 of whole numbers, 66–69, 74
Algebra
 geometric model of, 19–22
 NCTM standards on, A4–A5
 story problems, solving, 19–22
Algebraic expressions cards, M–5
Algebraic Expressions Game, 22
Algebra pieces, M–3
 definition of, 19
 solving story problems with, 19–22
Altitude (height)
 of parallelogram, 304
 of triangle, 304
Angle(s)
 acute, 328
 central, 257–258, 259–260, 313–314
 on geoboard, 257–260
 inscribed, 258–260
 measurement of, 257–260, 266, 347–348
 obtuse, 328
 of pattern blocks, 266
 right, 255
 vertex, of regular polygons, 269
Approximation
 of decimals, 155–156
 of measurements, 302
Arabian Nights Mystery, 91, 92
Arc, intercepted, 258–259
Archimedean solids, 279
Archimedes, 279, 310
Area
 plane, 181–185, 255, 304–307, 319–320
 surface, 310–311
Area model. *See* Rectangular (area) model
Art and Techniques of Simulation, The (Gnanadesikan *et al.*), 210
Attribute-game grid, M–9
Attribute Grid Game, 28
Attribute Guessing Game, 27–28

Attribute Identity Game, 32, 52
Attribute label cards, M–7
Attribute pieces
 reasoning with, 54
 sorting and classifying with, 25–34
Average. *See* Mean

B

Bar graph, 193, 195–196
Base
 of cone, area of, 313
 of cylinder, area of, 310
Base-five numeral, 58
Base-five pieces, 55–58, 66–67, 69–72, 82
Base (numeration systems)
 five, 55–58, 66–67, 69–72, 82
 nine, 59–60
 seven, 52, 59
 ten, 59–60, 83–93
 three, 59, 69
 two, 52
Base ten pieces
 decimals and, 170–175, 190
 whole numbers and, 59–60, 83–93
Bedford, F. L., 345
Bell-shaped curve, 215–219
 standard deviation and, 219, 226
Bennett, Albert B., Jr., 111, 207
Bentley, W. A., 290
Binary numbers, 60–61
Black and red tile model, for integers, 119–128
Body measurement, 299
Bradford, C. L., 103

C

Caesar, Julius, 224
Caesar cipher, 224
Calculator(s)
 Cross-Number Puzzle, 81
 decimals on, 158, 184
 irrational numbers on, 184
 Keyboard Game, 91
 number tricks, 91
 square root on, 184
 whole numbers on, 81, 91

Cardioids, 328
Carpenter, T. P., 137, 147
Carson, G., 317
Celsius scale, 302
Center, 322
Centimeter, 297
 cubic, 297, 301, 310
Centimeter Guessing Game, 297–298
Centimeter Racing Game, 301
Centimeter racing mat, M–69
Centi (prefix), 297
Central angle, 257–258, 259–260, 313–314, 322
Chinese culture
 Game of Nim, 61
 model for integers, 119
 tangram puzzle, 260–261
Chip trading models, 55
Chord, 322
Chords, 323–324, 328–329
Circle, 322
 center, 322
 central angle, 322
 chord of, 322, 323–324, 328–329
 diameter, 322
 intercepted arc of, 258–259
 radius, 322
Circle graph, 192
Circular geoboard, 253–254, 257–260, 262–263
Circular geoboard template, M–53
Classroom connections. *See* Connections
Clinometer, 347–348
Codes, 220–221, 224
Color tiles
 averages with, 228
 seeing and extending patterns with, 9, 11–17, 24
Commensurable lengths, 180
Common denominator, 140
Common factor, 106
Common multiples, 106
Communication, NCTM standards on, A1
Comparison concept of subtraction, 71–72
Competing at Place Value Game, 161
Complementary probabilities, 245–246
Composite numbers, 96, 101–102, 118
Compound probability. *See* Multistage probability

Material Cards

1. Algebra Pieces (1.3)
2. Algebraic Expression Cards (1.3)
3. Attribute Label Cards (2.1)
4. Attribute-Game Grid (2.1)
5. Two-Circle Venn Diagram (2.1)
6. Three-Circle Venn Diagram (2.1, 9.1)
7. Follow Up Activities and Questions 2.1 No. 3
8. Rectangular Geoboard Template (2.2, 6.4, 9.1, 10.2)
9. Coordinate Guessing and Hide-a-Region Grids (2.2)
10. Logic Problem Clue Cards and People Pieces (Problem 1) (2.3)
11. Logic Problem Clue Cards and People Pieces (Problem 2) (2.3)
12. Logic Problem Clue Cards, Prize and People Pieces (Problem 3) (2.3)
13. Logic Problem Clue Cards, Career, Singer, People, and Location Pieces (Problem 4) (2.3)
14. Logic Problem Clue Cards (Problem 5) (2.3)
15. Logic Problem Object Pieces (Problem 5) (2.3)
16. Pica-Centro Recording Sheet (2.3)
17. Mind-Reading Cards (3.1)
18. Interest Gameboard (6.3)
19. Metric Ruler, Protractor, and Compass (7.1, 9.1, 10.1, 10.3, 11.1, 11.2, 11.3)
20. Table of Random Digits (7.2, 7.3, 8.1)
21. Two-Penny Grid (8.1)
22. Three-Penny Grid (8.1)
23. Simulation Spinners (8.2)
24. Trick Dice (8.2)
25. Geoboard Recording Paper (9.1)
26. Circular Geoboard Template (9.1)
27. Grid for Game of Hex (9.2)
28. Regular Polyhedra (9.3)
29. Regular Polyhedra (9.3)
30. Two-Centimeter Grid Paper (9.3)
31. Cube Patterns for Instant Insanity (9.3)
32. Perpendicular Lines for Symmetry (9.4)
33. Metric Measuring Tape (10.1)
34. Centimeter Racing Mat (10.1)
35. Pentominoes (10.2)
36. Pentomino Game Grid (10.2)
37. Prism, Pyramid, and Cylinder (10.3)
38. Hypsometer-Clinometer (11.3)

Algebra Pieces (Activity Set 1.3)

MATERIAL CARD 1

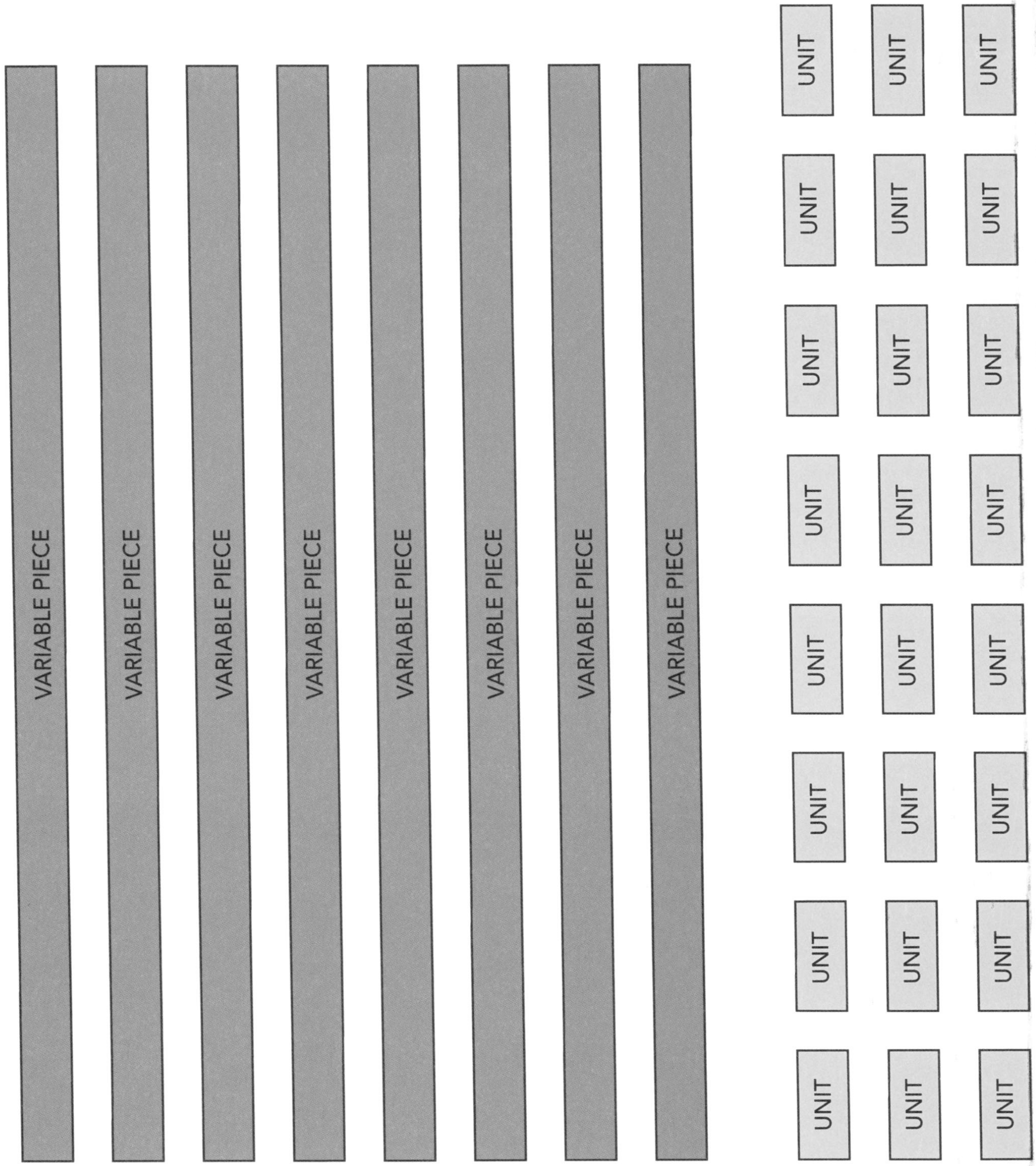

VARIABLE PIECE

VARIABLE PIECE

VARIABLE PIECE

VARIABLE PIECE

VARIABLE PIECE

VARIABLE PIECE

VARIABLE PIECE

VARIABLE PIECE

UNIT UNIT UNIT

UNIT UNIT UNIT

UNIT UNIT UNIT

UNIT UNIT UNIT

UNIT UNIT UNIT

UNIT UNIT UNIT

UNIT UNIT UNIT

UNIT UNIT UNIT

Team A   Team B

I have $n + 1$ **Who has** two less than a number	**I have** $4n + 5$ **Who has** two more than the square root of a number	**I have** $n + 2$ **Who has** five less than a number	**I have** $5n + 3$ **Who has** one more than three times the square of a number
I have $n - 2$ **Who has** one more than two times a number	**I have** $\sqrt{n} + 2$ **Who has** five less than eight times a number	**I have** $n - 5$ **Who has** two more than three times a number	**I have** $3n^2 + 1$ **Who has** two more than one-third of a number
I have $2n + 1$ **Who has** five less than seven times a number	**I have** $8n - 5$ **Who has** one more than four times the square of a number	**I have** $3n + 2$ **Who has** five less than six times a number	**I have** $\frac{n}{3} + 2$ **Who has** six less than the cube of a number
I have $7n - 5$ **Who has** seven more than the square of a number	**I have** $4n^2 + 1$ **Who has** four more than one-third of a number	**I have** $6n - 5$ **Who has** eight more than the square of a number	**I have** $n^3 - 6$ **Who has** nine more than four times a number
I have $n^2 + 7$ **Who has** three more than half of a number	**I have** $\frac{n}{3} + 4$ **Who has** seven less than the cube of a number	**I have** $n^2 + 8$ **Who has** five less than half of a number	**I have** $4n + 9$ **Who has** seven less than half of a number
I have $\frac{n}{2} + 3$ **Who has** five more than four times a number	**I have** $n^3 - 7$ **Who has** one more than a number	**I have** $\frac{n}{2} - 5$ **Who has** three more than five times a number	**I have** $\frac{n}{2} - 7$ **Who has** two more than a number

	TRIANGULAR
	HEXAGONAL
	CIRCULAR
	SQUARE
AND	RED
AND	BLUE

LARGE	SMALL	NOT	YELLOW
SMALL	NOT	OR	LARGE
SMALL	NOT	OR	LARGE

Rows, 1 difference (1 point)   Columns, 2 differences (2 points)   Diagonals, 3 differences (3 points)

		Place attribute piece here to start game		

Two-Circle Venn Diagram (Activity Set 2.1) MATERIAL CARD 5

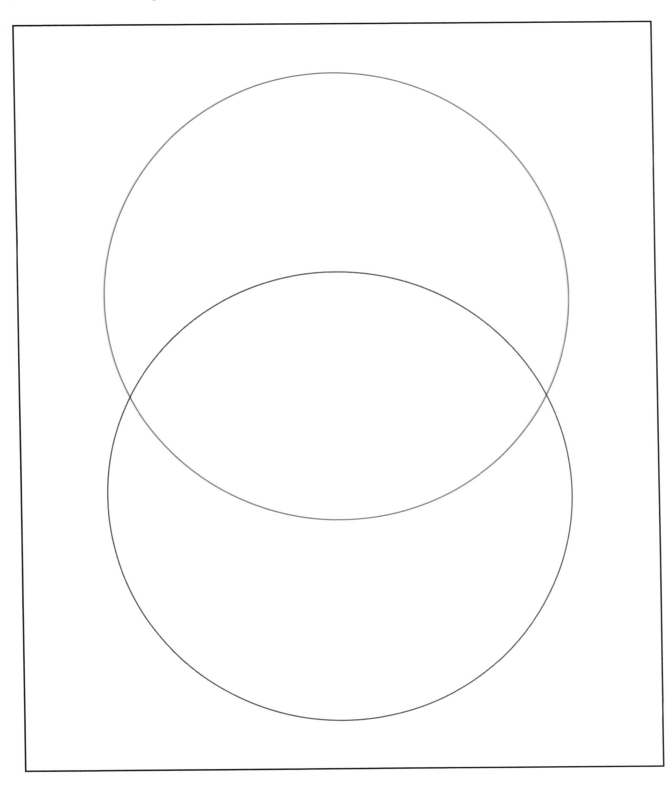

Three-Circle Venn Diagram (Activity Sets 2.1 and 9.1) **MATERIAL CARD 6**

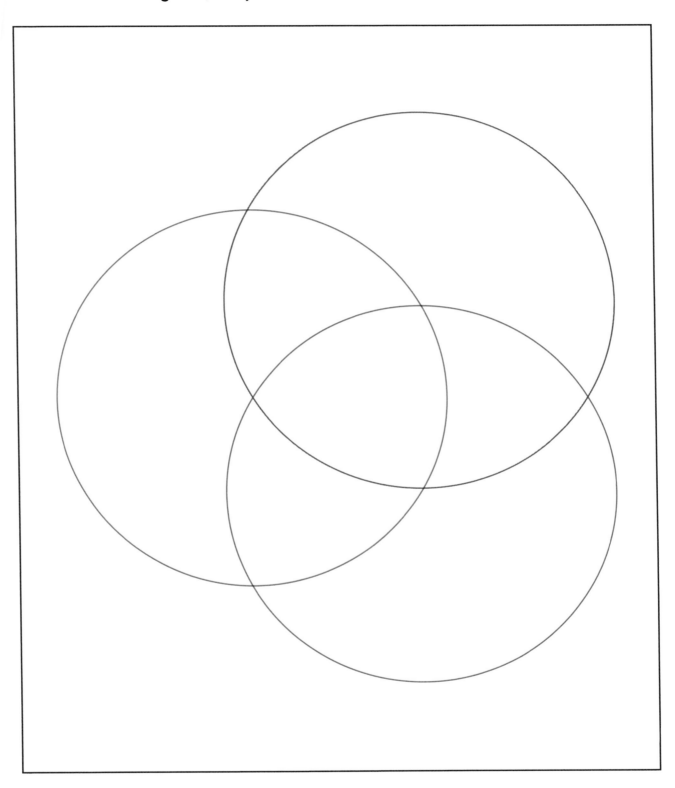

a.

SMALL   TRIANGULAR

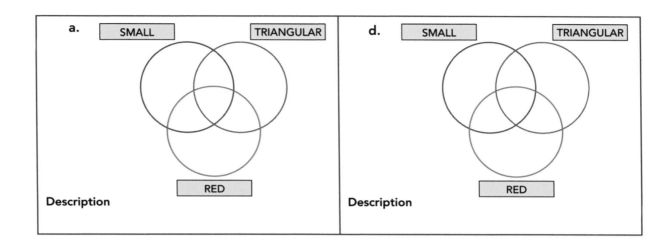

RED

Description

d.

SMALL   TRIANGULAR

RED

Description

b.

SMALL   TRIANGULAR

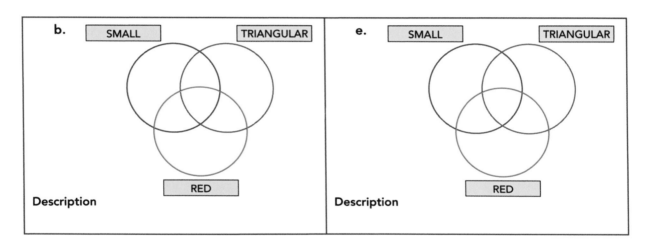

RED

Description

e.

SMALL   TRIANGULAR

RED

Description

c.

SMALL   TRIANGULAR

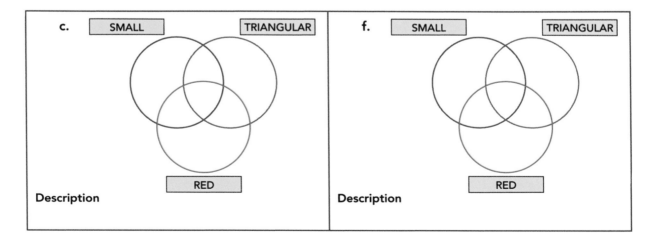

RED

Description

f.

SMALL   TRIANGULAR

RED

Description

Rectangular Geoboard Template

(Activity Sets 2.2, 6.4, 9.1, and 10.2)

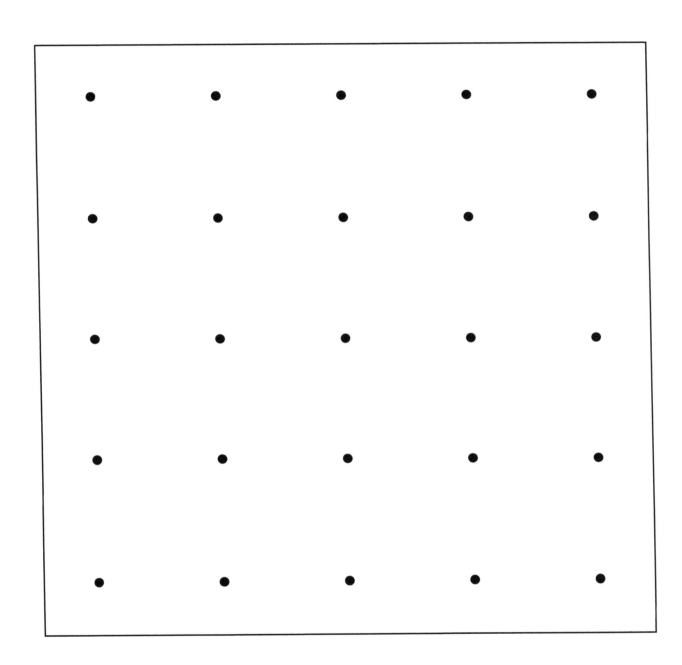

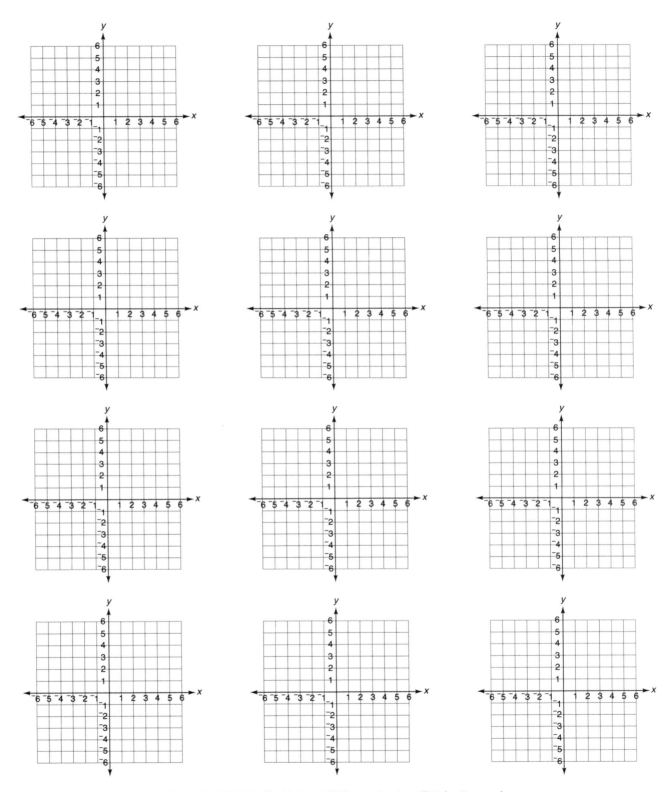

Paul, Nicky, Sally, Uri, Jane, Veneta, Monty, Marc, and Edith are standing in a row according to height, but not necessarily in the order given.

Edith is closer to Sally than she is to Nicky.

LOGIC PROBLEM 1   CARD A

Veneta, Edith, Marc, Sally, Monty, and Jane are shorter than Paul, Nicky, and Uri.

There is just one person between Uri and Paul.

Name the 9 people in order from shortest to tallest.

LOGIC PROBLEM 1   CARD B

Edith, Marc, Monty, Jane, and Veneta are shorter than the other four.

Uri is between Sally and Nicky.

Monty and Paul have 7 people between them.

LOGIC PROBLEM 1   CARD C

Uri, Nicky, Jane, Paul, and Sally are taller than the others.

Veneta and Monty are the only two people shorter than Edith.

LOGIC PROBLEM 1   CARD D

Nicky

Paul

Sally

Marc

Uri

Edith

Jane

Monty

Veneta

Mr. Racquet is coach of the tennis team.

McKenna said, "I won't play if Tyrone is on the team."

LOGIC PROBLEM 2   CARD A

Juan, McKenna, Tyrone, Derek, Ida and Anna play mixed doubles.

Tyrone said, "I won't play if either Derek or Ida is choosen."

LOGIC PROBLEM 2   CARD B

How can Mr. Racquet select four compatible players (two men and two women) for a road trip?

Derek said, "I'll only play if Anna plays."

LOGIC PROBLEM 2   CARD C

Juan said. "I'll only play if McKenna plays."

Anna had no likes or dislikes.

LOGIC PROBLEM 2   CARD D

Juan

Anna

Tyrone

Derek

McKenna

Ida

Smith, Brown, Jones, and Robinson are told that they have each won one of four academic prizes, but none of them knows which, so they are speculating.

Smith thinks that Robinson has won the logic prize.

LOGIC PROBLEM 3   CARD A

The four academic prizes are for outstanding work in mathematics, English, French, and logic.

Jones feels confident that Smith has not won the mathematics prize.

Who won each prize?

LOGIC PROBLEM 3   CARD B

Robinson is of the opinion that Brown has won the French prize.

The winners of the mathematics and logic prizes were correct in their speculations.

LOGIC PROBLEM 3   CARD C

The English and French prize winners were not correct in their predictions of the prize winners.

Brown thinks that Jones has won the English prize.

The math prize was awarded to Robinson.

LOGIC PROBLEM 3   CARD D

Math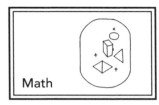

English

French

Logic

Jones

Smith

Robinson

Brown

On a plane, Smith, Jones, and
Robinson are pilot, copilot and
engineer, but not necessarily in that
order.

The copilot has the same name as
the singer living in the same town.

LOGIC PROBLEM 4   CARD A

On the plane there is a singing group,
The 3-Ms, whose names are M. Smith,
M. Robinson, and M. Jones.

The copilot lives in the city between
that of M. Jones and that of the
engineer.

LOGIC PROBLEM 4   CARD B

M. Robinson lives in New York City.

Jones consistently beats the engineer
in racquetball.

LOGIC PROBLEM 4   CARD C

The singers each reside in a different
city, New York, San Francisco and
Chicago, as do the members of the
plane crew.

What is the pilot's name?

LOGIC PROBLEM 4   CARD D

Pilot	Chicago
Copilot	New York
Engineer	San Francisco
M. Jones	Jones
M. Smith	Smith
M. Robinson	Robinson

The Chevrolet owner lives in the house next door to the house where the horses are kept.

The person in the red house is English.

The Japanese drives a Ford.

Each house is occupied by a person of different nationality.

The person in the ivory house does not drink milk.

LOGIC PROBLEM 5   CARD A

The Plymouth driver lives next door to the person with the fox.

The Honda owner drinks orange juice.

The Norwegian lives next to the blue house.

Coffee is drunk in the green house.

Who owns the skunk?

LOGIC PROBLEM 5   CARD B

The Chevrolet owner lives in the yellow house.

Milk is drunk in the middle house.

The Norwegian lives in the first house.

The Spaniard owns a dog.

If each person has one home, one pet, one car, a different nationality and a different drink, who drinks the water?

LOGIC PROBLEM 5   CARD C

The Ukrainian drinks tea.

The green house is immediately to the right of the ivory house.

The Mercedes driver owns snails.

The fox lives with the owner of the house farthest from the green house.

The five houses are in a row.

LOGIC PROBLEM 5   CARD D

Logic Problem Object Pieces
PROBLEM 5 (Activity Set 2.3)

English

Dog

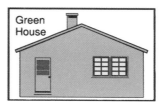
Green House

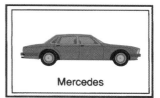
Mercedes

Norwegian

Horse

Red House

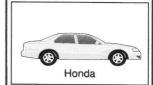
Honda

Japanese

Skunk

Ivory House

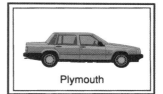
Plymouth

Ukrainian

Snails

Blue House

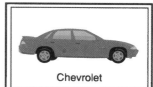
Chevrolet

Spaniard

Fox

Yellow House

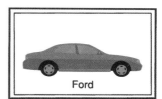
Ford

Water

Coffee

Orange Juice

Tea

Milk

Pica-Centro Recording Sheet
(Activity Set 2.3 JUST FOR FUN)

THREE-DIGIT RECORDING SHEETS

GUESSES		RESPONSES		GUESSES		RESPONSES		GUESSES		RESPONSES	
Digits		Pica	Centro	Digits		Pica	Centro	Digits		Pica	Centro

FOUR-DIGIT RECORDING SHEETS

GUESSES		RESPONSES		GUESSES		RESPONSES		GUESSES		RESPONSES	
Digits		Pica	Centro	Digits		Pica	Centro	Digits		Pica	Centro

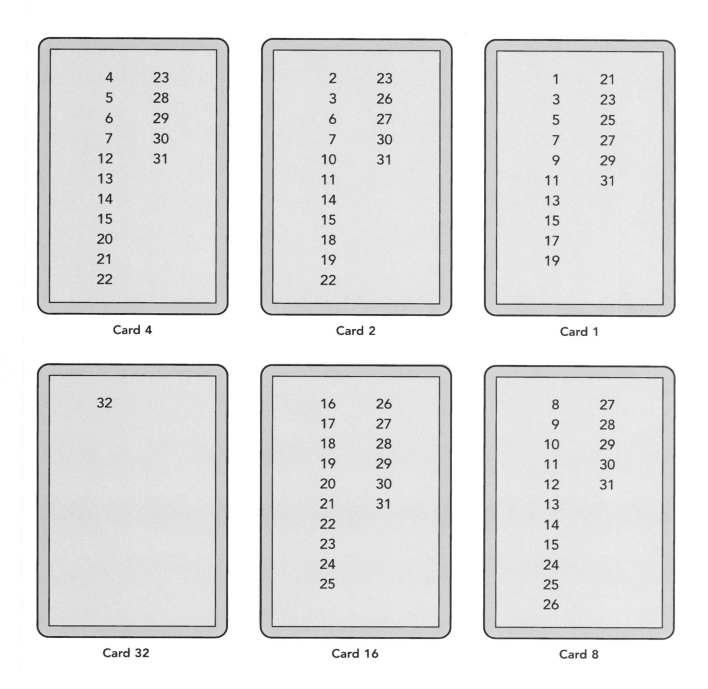

4	23
5	28
6	29
7	30
12	31
13	
14	
15	
20	
21	
22	

Card 4

2	23
3	26
6	27
7	30
10	31
11	
14	
15	
18	
19	
22	

Card 2

1	21
3	23
5	25
7	27
9	29
11	31
13	
15	
17	
19	

Card 1

32

Card 32

16	26
17	27
18	28
19	29
20	30
21	31
22	
23	
24	
25	

Card 16

8	27
9	28
10	29
11	30
12	31
13	
14	
15	
24	
25	
26	

Card 8

INTEREST GAMEBOARD

$600	5	10	20	30	40	50	60
	4.5	9	18	27	36	45	54
$500	4	8	16	24	32	40	48
$400	3.5	7	14	21	28	35	42
$300	3	6	12	18	24	30	36
	2.5	5	10	15	20	25	30
$200	2	4	8	12	16	20	24
$100	1.5	3	6	9	12	15	18
	1	2	4	6	8	10	12
$50	.5	1	2	3	4	5	6

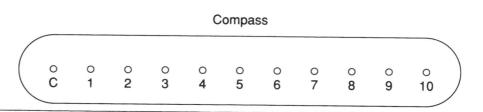

Compass

Punch out holes C, 1, 2, 3, ..., 10. Hold point C fixed for the center of a circle and place a pencil at hole 8 to draw a circle of radius 8 centimeters.

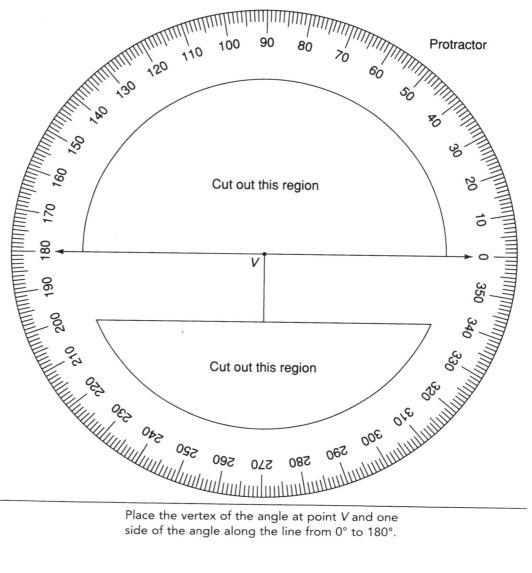

Protractor

Cut out this region

V

Cut out this region

Place the vertex of the angle at point V and one side of the angle along the line from 0° to 180°.

Table of Random Digits (Activity Sets 7.2, 7.3, and 8.1)

69588	18885	24831	28185	84019	91168	62187	69079	86492	24195
19797	27708	70288	72541	10576	79693	28704	97678	95777	46759
50212	65574	17333	21694	47617	71881	88513	62695	76222	42544
16380	57486	86835	82724	23964	77540	93652	75555	77283	29473
29826	51673	28082	85640	43062	21997	77247	14653	13471	03865
51427	10863	96787	43214	68955	13735	72107	63399	15951	53968
36037	55838	30244	28819	19794	72893	43642	89344	72686	17378
52421	74281	44363	37701	25103	06701	33100	00483	38208	57711
64936	77559	27432	27412	89263	50899	68524	54274	35905	40343
05013	22060	17792	96536	74156	88924	19652	84311	92236	18008
69970	37423	22837	28337	06347	84836	68812	06121	23216	64020
96601	64066	87785	41608	32193	67850	46509	70020	18435	75427
30984	17658	07126	96234	66401	05691	55657	29217	61037	83086
93775	97887	39692	84605	98008	43174	07226	17637	63106	11806
10975	47371	37928	71999	19339	87802	88208	23697	57359	64825
34487	51270	55303	80666	63115	97793	01883	46650	10668	04238
77876	02108	02420	23983	49776	29281	01665	04908	78948	09727
38781	58184	25008	00962	80002	22962	92127	49898	24259	61862
83788	62480	44711	21815	84629	06939	67646	06948	04529	45214
89704	30361	15988	83311	78147	00323	49940	68820	24291	44077
24113	92774	25852	01814	44175	64734	25392	58525	88314	97199
23041	81334	43410	28285	59247	22853	24395	17770	61573	38097
43123	25825	91840	79914	41137	99165	33796	95374	25960	35135
20585	11696	84826	43878	74239	98734	35854	82082	97416	20039
45699	87633	29489	57614	52384	88793	24228	60107	83502	28129
42060	77709	09509	58712	21415	38415	10841	93372	53568	70864
23038	92956	27304	20825	70350	33151	93654	81710	34692	58456
72936	52909	92458	61567	72380	00931	49994	38711	12237	49788
24631	18803	35690	70000	10040	38204	67146	85913	48332	86757
62397	54028	77523	24891	27989	02289	74513	26279	85382	82180
75724	78027	60675	01294	37607	84053	41144	94743	85633	50356
44997	49702	68073	99166	05851	22239	76340	79458	25968	75875
20733	42897	05445	46195	97046	16120	41546	04463	34074	05515
90448	49154	27693	90607	98476	50924	25067	01233	64588	31287
50151	76497	10878	87213	84640	35943	46320	03267	15324	95455
33944	22308	60879	07308	10759	75179	05130	66184	69554	65891
42837	55847	75893	54245	38752	68095	33158	81860	56469	84190
39357	40544	25447	96260	87283	22483	78031	91393	38040	82382
45673	87347	44240	61458	87338	62039	71825	52571	27146	86404
97714	52538	91976	52406	19711	99248	23073	43926	81889	47540

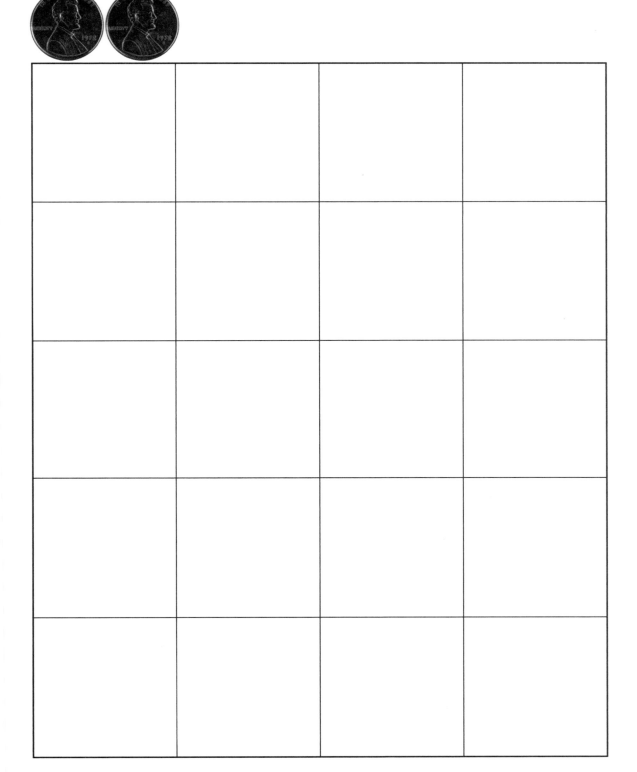

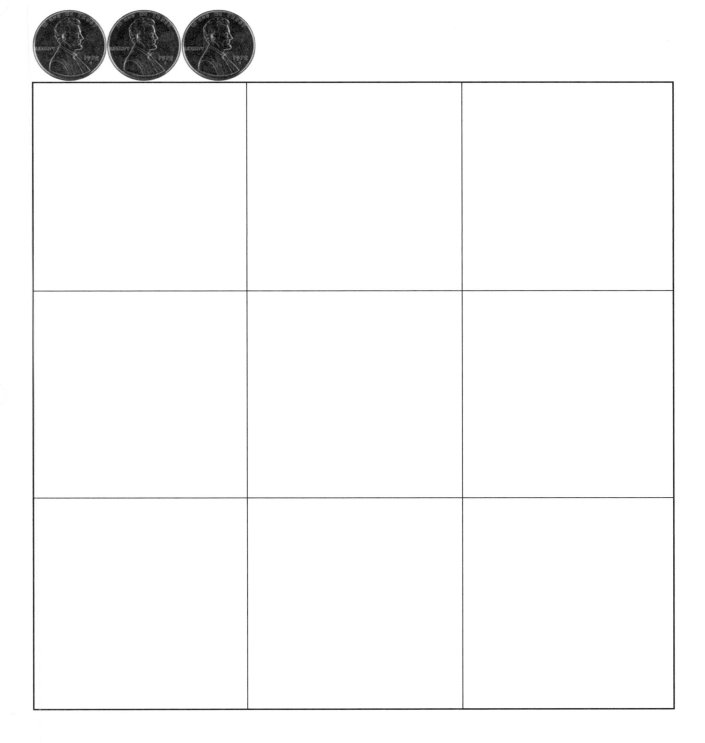

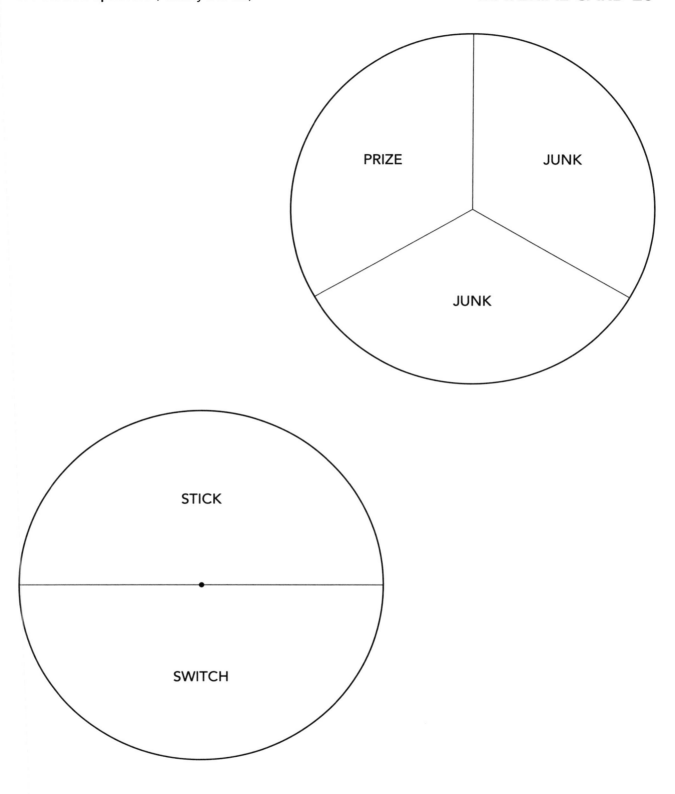

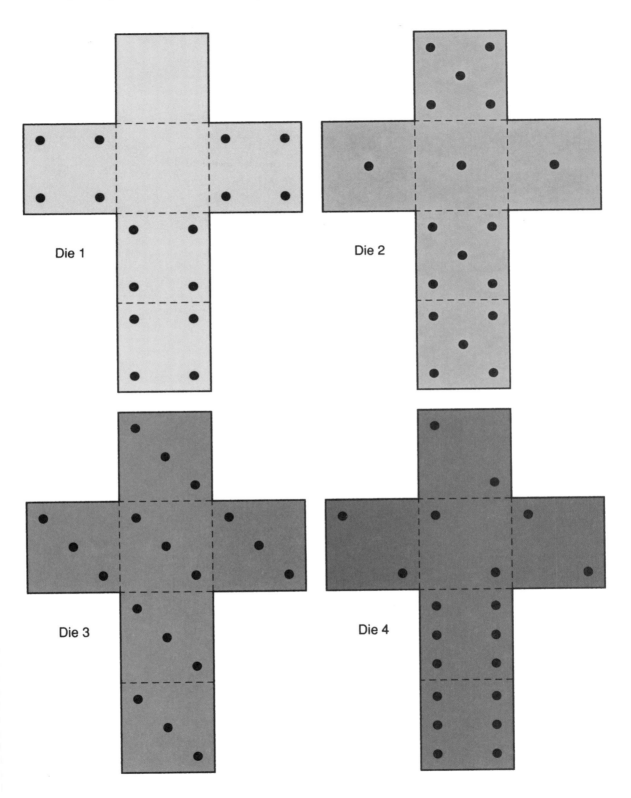

Die 1

Die 2

Die 3

Die 4

Geoboard Recording Paper (Activity Set 9.1)

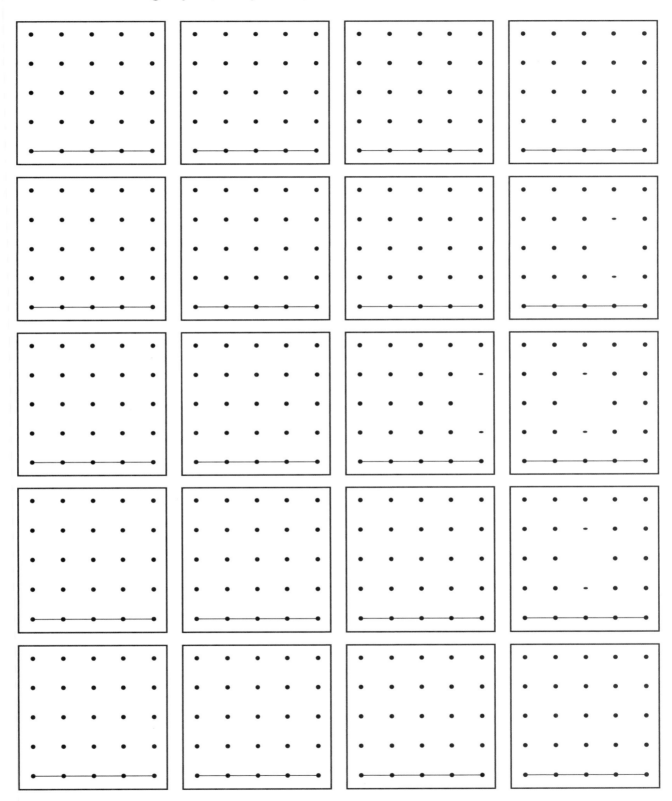

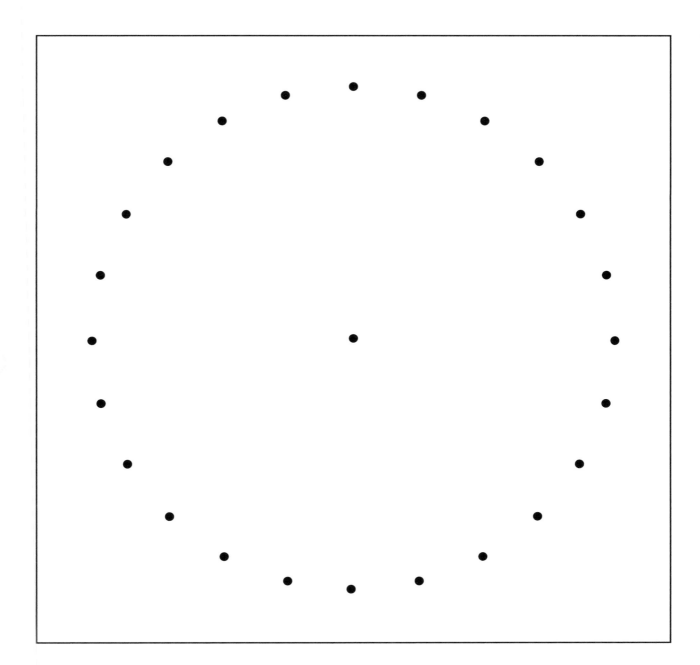

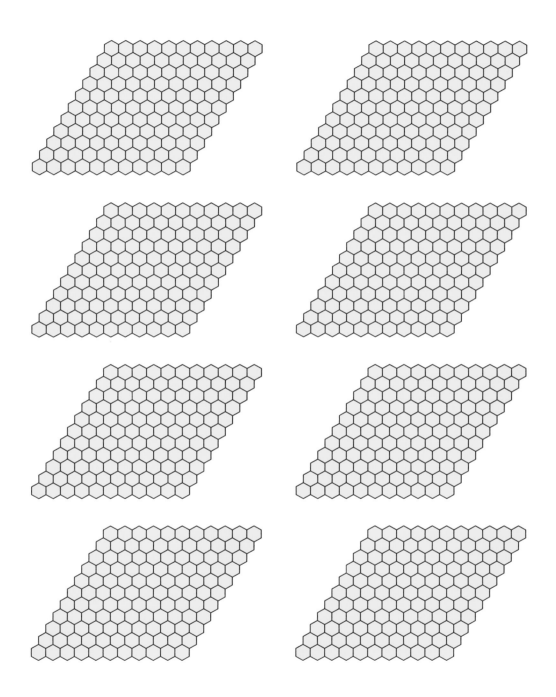

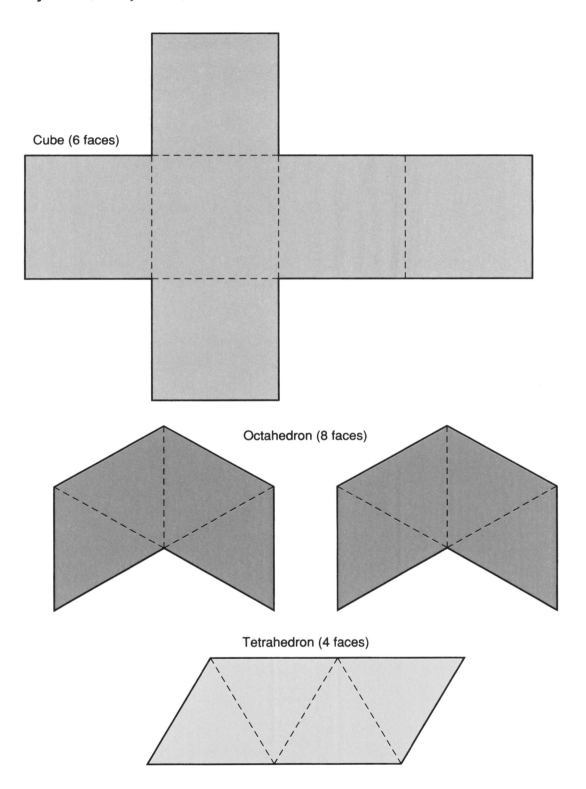

Cube (6 faces)

Octahedron (8 faces)

Tetrahedron (4 faces)

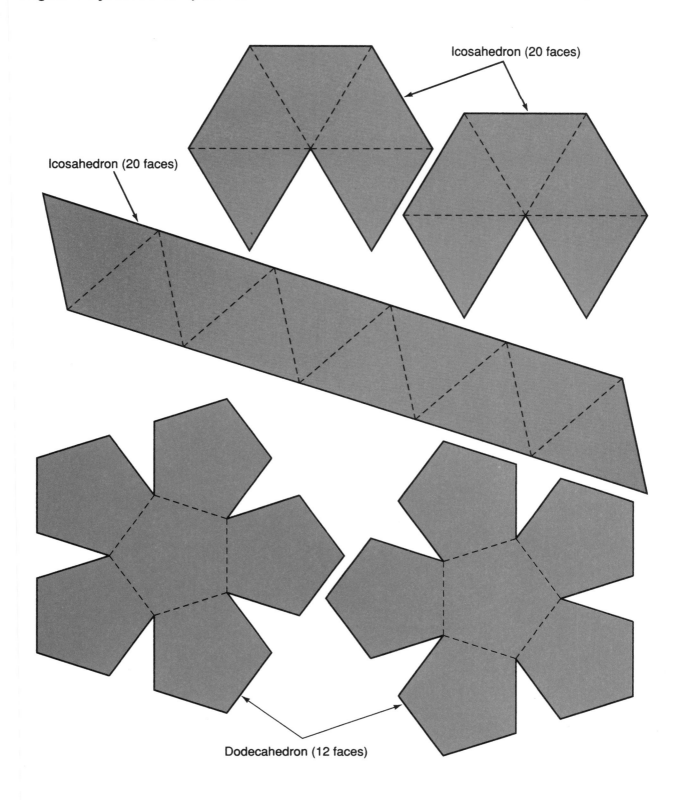

Icosahedron (20 faces)

Icosahedron (20 faces)

Icosahedron (20 faces)

Dodecahedron (12 faces)

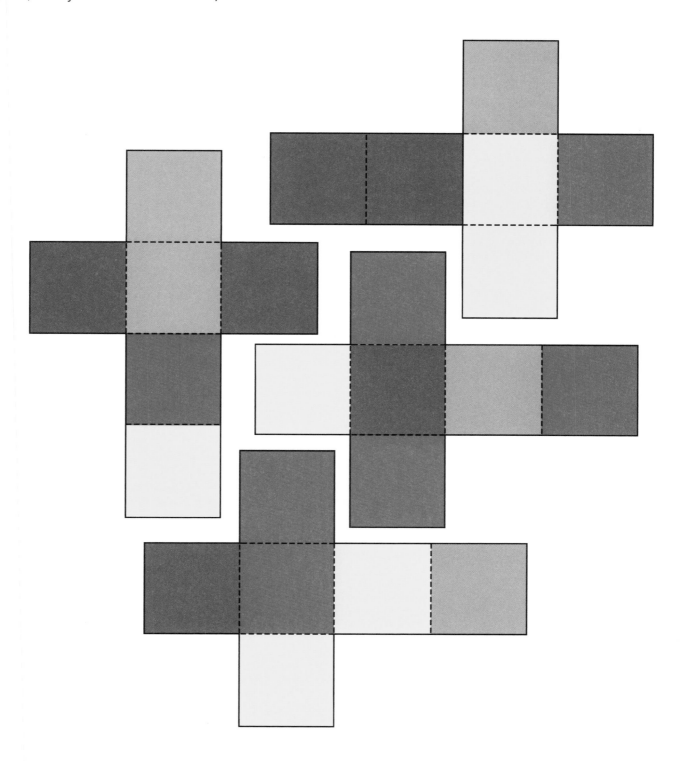

Metric Measuring Tape (Activity Set 10.1)

Cut out the five vertical strips and then tape or glue tab 2 under the edge labeled 2, tab 4 under the edge labeled 4, tab 6 under the edge labeled 6, and tab 8 under the edge labeled 8, to form a metric tape that is 100 centimeters long.

2	4	6	8	100 cm
15 cm	35 cm	55 cm	75 cm	95 cm
10 cm	30 cm	50 cm	70 cm	90 cm
5 cm	25 cm	45 cm	65 cm	85 cm
20	40	60	80	

Tabs →

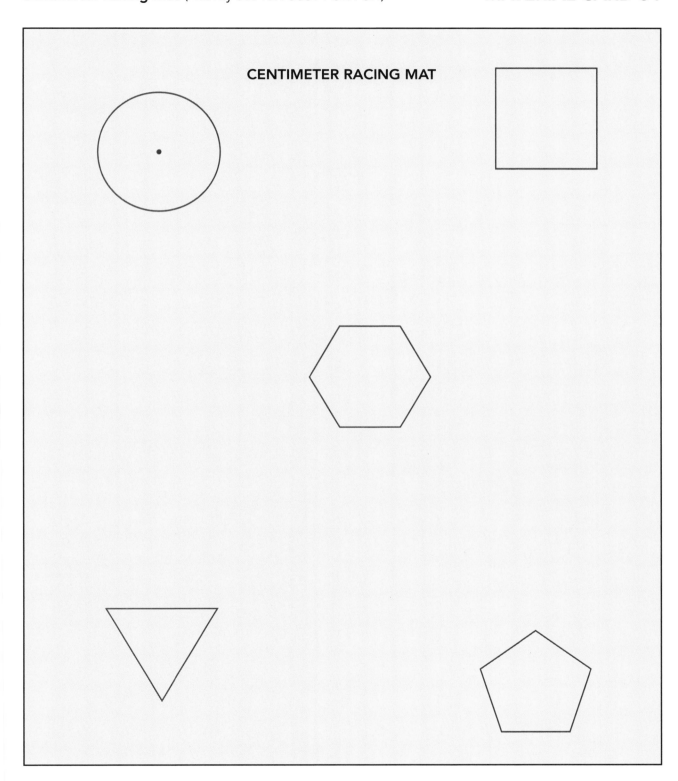

CENTIMETER RACING MAT

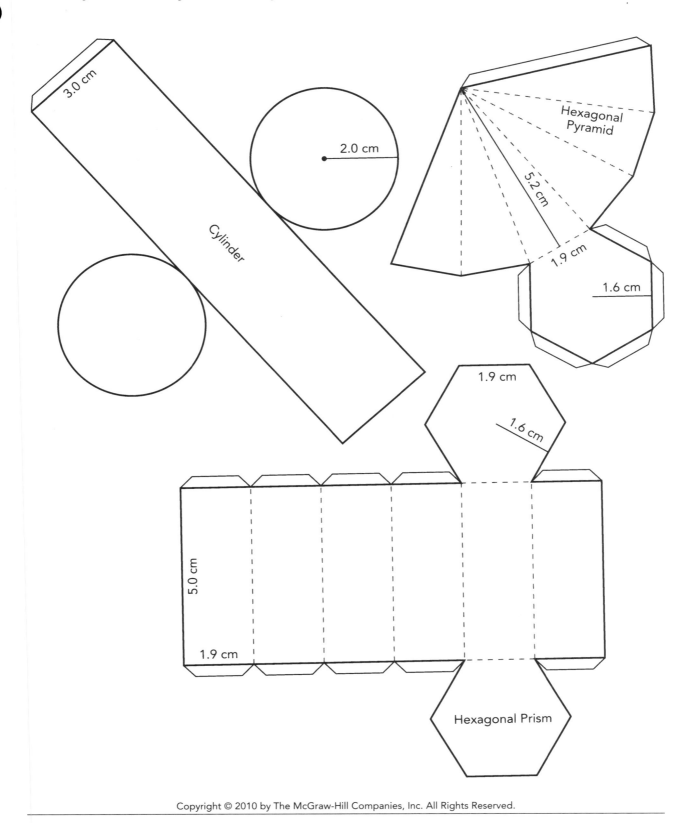

3.0 cm

Cylinder

2.0 cm

Hexagonal
Pyramid

5.2 cm

1.9 cm

1.6 cm

1.9 cm

1.6 cm

5.0 cm

1.9 cm

Hexagonal Prism

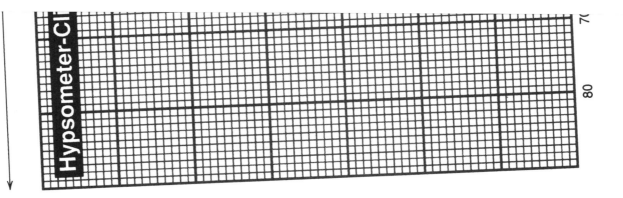

Hypsometer-Cl

70

80

Appendix

Table of NCTM
Standards and
Expectations

Content Standards

Number and Operations

STANDARD

Instructional programs from prekindergarten through grade 12 should enable all students to—

	Pre-K–2	Grades 3–5
	Expectations	**Expectations**
	In prekindergarten through grade 2 all students should—	In grades 3–5 all students should—
Understand numbers, ways of representing numbers, relationships among numbers, and number systems	• count with understanding and recognize "how many" in sets of objects; • use multiple models to develop initial understandings of place value and the base-ten number system; • develop understanding of the relative position and magnitude of whole numbers and of ordinal and cardinal numbers and their connections; • develop a sense of whole numbers and represent and use them in flexible ways, including relating, composing, and decomposing numbers; • connect number words and numerals to the quantities they represent, using various physical models and representations; • understand and represent commonly used fractions, such as 1/4, 1/3, and 1/2.	• understand the place-value structure of the base-ten number system and be able to represent and compare whole numbers and decimals; • recognize equivalent representations for the same number and generate them by decomposing and composing numbers; • develop understanding of fractions as parts of unit wholes, as parts of a collection, as locations on number lines, and as divisions of whole numbers; • use models, benchmarks, and equivalent forms to judge the size of fractions; • recognize and generate equivalent forms of commonly used fractions, decimals, and percents; • explore numbers less than 0 by extending the number line and through familiar applications; • describe classes of numbers according to characteristics such as the nature of their factors.
Understand meanings of operations and how they relate to one another	• understand various meanings of addition and subtraction of whole numbers and the relationship between the two operations; • understand the effects of adding and subtracting whole numbers; • understand situations that entail multiplication and division, such as equal groupings of objects and sharing equally.	• understand various meanings of multiplication and division; • understand the effects of multiplying and dividing whole numbers; • identify and use relationships between operations, such as division as the inverse of multiplication, to solve problems; • understand and use properties of operations, such as the distributivity of multiplication over addition.
Compute fluently and make reasonable estimates	• develop and use strategies for whole-number computations, with a focus on addition and subtraction; • develop fluency with basic number combinations for addition and subtraction; • use a variety of methods and tools to compute, including objects, mental computation, estimation, paper and pencil, and calculators.	• develop fluency with basic number combinations for multiplication and division and use these combinations to mentally compute related problems, such as 30 × 50; • develop fluency in adding, subtracting, multiplying, and dividing whole numbers; • develop and use strategies to estimate the results of whole number computations and to judge the reasonableness of such results; • develop and use strategies to estimate computations involving fractions and decimals in situations relevant to students' experience; • use visual models, benchmarks, and equivalent forms to add and subtract commonly used fractions and decimals; • select appropriate methods and tools for computing with whole numbers from among mental computation, estimation, calculators, and paper and pencil according to the context and nature of the computation and use the selected method or tool.

Number and Operations

STANDARD

Instructional programs from prekindergarten through grade 12 should enable all students to—	Grades 6–8	Grades 9–12
	Expectations	**Expectations**
	In grades 6–8 all students should—	In grades 9–12 all students should—
Understand numbers, ways of representing numbers, relationships among numbers, and number systems	• work flexibly with fractions, decimals, and percents to solve problems; • compare and order fractions, decimals, and percents efficiently and find their approximate locations on a number line; • develop meaning for percents greater than 100 and less than 1; • understand and use ratios and proportions to represent quantitative relationships; • develop an understanding of large numbers and recognize and appropriately use exponential, scientific, and calculator notation; • use factors, multiples, prime factorization, and relatively prime numbers to solve problems; • develop meaning for integers and represent and compare quantities with them.	• develop a deeper understanding of very large and very small numbers and of various representations of them; • compare and contrast the properties of numbers and number systems, including the rational and real numbers, and understand complex numbers as solutions to quadratic equations that do not have real solutions; • understand vectors and matrices as systems that have some of the properties of the real-number system; • use number-theory arguments to justify relationships involving whole numbers.
Understand meanings of operations and how they relate to one another	• understand the meaning and effects of arithmetic operations with fractions, decimals, and integers; • use the associative and commutative properties of addition and multiplication and the distributive property of multiplication over addition to simplify computations with integers, fractions, and decimals; • understand and use the inverse relationships of addition and subtraction, multiplication and division, and squaring and finding square roots to simplify computations and solve problems.	• judge the effects of such operations as multiplication, division, and computing powers and roots on the magnitudes of quantities; • develop an understanding of properties of, and representations for, the addition and multiplication of vectors and matrices; • develop an understanding of permutations and combinations as counting techniques.
Compute fluently and make reasonable estimates	• select appropriate methods and tools for computing with fractions and decimals from among mental computation, estimation, calculators or computers, and paper and pencil, depending on the situation, and apply the selected methods; • develop and analyze algorithms for computing with fractions, decimals, and integers and develop fluency in their use; • develop and use strategies to estimate the results of rational-number computations and judge the reasonableness of the results; • develop, analyze, and explain methods for solving problems involving proportions, such as scaling and finding equivalent ratios.	• develop fluency in operations with real numbers, vectors, and matrices, using mental computation or paper-and-pencil calculations for simple cases and technology for more-complicated cases. • judge the reasonableness of numerical computations and their results.

Algebra

STANDARD

Instructional programs from prekindergarten through grade 12 should enable all students to—	Pre-K–2 **Expectations** In prekindergarten through grade 2 all students should—	Grades 3–5 **Expectations** In grades 3–5 all students should—
Understand patterns, relations, and functions	• sort, classify, and order objects by size, number, and other properties; • recognize, describe, and extend patterns such as sequences of sounds and shapes or simple numeric patterns and translate from one representation to another; • analyze how both repeating and growing patterns are generated.	• describe, extend, and make generalizations about geometric and numeric patterns; • represent and analyze patterns and functions, using words, tables, and graphs.
Represent and analyze mathematical situations and structures using algebraic symbols	• illustrate general principles and properties of operations, such as commutativity, using specific numbers; • use concrete, pictorial, and verbal representations to develop an understanding of invented and conventional symbolic notations.	• identify such properties as commutativity, associativity, and distributivity and use them to compute with whole numbers; • represent the idea of a variable as an unknown quantity using a letter or a symbol; • express mathematical relationships using equations.
Use mathematical models to represent and understand quantitative relationships	• model situations that involve the addition and subtraction of whole numbers, using objects, pictures, and symbols.	• model problem situations with objects and use representations such as graphs, tables, and equations to draw conclusions.
Analyze change in various contexts	• describe qualitative change, such as a student's growing taller; • describe quantitative change, such as a student's growing two inches in one year.	• investigate how a change in one variable relates to a change in a second variable; • identify and describe situations with constant or varying rates of change and compare them.

Algebra

STANDARD

Instructional programs from prekindergarten through grade 12 should enable all students to—	Grades 6–8	Grades 9–12
	Expectations In grades 6–8 all students should—	**Expectations** In grades 9–12 all students should—
Understand patterns, relations, and functions	• represent, analyze, and generalize a variety of patterns with tables, graphs, words, and, when possible, symbolic rules; • relate and compare different forms of representation for a relationship; • identify functions as linear or nonlinear and contrast their properties from tables, graphs, or equations.	• generalize patterns using explicitly defined and recursively defined functions; • understand relations and functions and select, convert flexibly among, and use various representations for them; • analyze functions of one variable by investigating rates of change, intercepts, zeros, asymptotes, and local and global behavior; • understand and perform transformations such as arithmetically combining, composing, and inverting commonly used functions, using technology to perform such operations on more-complicated symbolic expressions; • understand and compare the properties of classes of functions, including exponential, polynomial, rational, logarithmic, and periodic functions; • interpret representations of functions of two variables.
Represent and analyze mathematical situations and structures using algebraic symbols	• develop an initial conceptual understanding of different uses of variables; • explore relationships between symbolic expressions and graphs of lines, paying particular attention to the meaning of intercept and slope; • use symbolic algebra to represent situations and to solve problems, especially those that involve linear relationships; • recognize and generate equivalent forms for simple algebraic expressions and solve linear equations.	• understand the meaning of equivalent forms of expressions, equations, inequalities, and relations; • write equivalent forms of equations, inequalities, and systems of equations and solve them with fluency—mentally or with paper and pencil in simple cases and using technology in all cases; • use symbolic algebra to represent and explain mathematical relationships; • use a variety of symbolic representations, including recursive and parametric equations, for functions and relations; • judge the meaning, utility, and reasonableness of the results of symbol manipulations, including those carried out by technology.
Use mathematical models to represent and understand quantitative relationships	• model and solve contextualized problems using various representations, such as graphs, tables, and equations.	• identify essential quantitative relationships in a situation and determine the class or classes of functions that might model the relationships; • use symbolic expressions, including iterative and recursive forms, to represent relationships arising from various contexts; • draw reasonable conclusions about a situation being modeled.
Analyze change in various contexts	• use graphs to analyze the nature of changes in quantities in linear relationships.	• approximate and interpret rates of change from graphical and numerical data.

Geometry

STANDARD

Instructional programs from prekindergarten through grade 12 should enable all students to—	Pre-K–2 **Expectations** In prekindergarten through grade 2 all students should—	Grades 3–5 **Expectations** In grades 3–5 all students should—
Analyze characteristics and properties of two- and three-dimensional geometric shapes and develop mathematical arguments about geometric relationships	• recognize, name, build, draw, compare, and sort two- and three-dimensional shapes; • describe attributes and parts of two- and three-dimensional shapes; • investigate and predict the results of putting together and taking apart two- and three-dimensional shapes.	• identify, compare, and analyze attributes of two- and three-dimensional shapes and develop vocabulary to describe the attributes; • classify two- and three-dimensional shapes according to their properties and develop definitions of classes of shapes such as triangles and pyramids; • investigate, describe, and reason about the results of subdividing, combining, and transforming shapes; • explore congruence and similarity; • make and test conjectures about geometric properties and relationships and develop logical arguments to justify conclusions.
Specify locations and describe spatial relationships using coordinate geometry and other representational systems	• describe, name, and interpret relative positions in space and apply ideas about relative position; • describe, name, and interpret direction and distance in navigating space and apply ideas about direction and distance; • find and name locations with simple relationships such as "near to" and in coordinate systems such as maps.	• describe location and movement using common language and geometric vocabulary; • make and use coordinate systems to specify locations and to describe paths; • find the distance between points along horizontal and vertical lines of a coordinate system.
Apply transformations and use symmetry to analyze mathematical situations	• recognize and apply slides, flips, and turns; • recognize and create shapes that have symmetry.	• predict and describe the results of sliding, flipping, and turning two-dimensional shapes; • describe a motion or a series of motions that will show that two shapes are congruent; • identify and describe line and rotational symmetry in two- and three-dimensional shapes and designs.
Use visualization, spatial reasoning, and geometric modeling to solve problems	• create mental images of geometric shapes using spatial memory and spatial visualization; • recognize and represent shapes from different perspectives; • relate ideas in geometry to ideas in number and measurement; • recognize geometric shapes and structures in the environment and specify their location.	• build and draw geometric objects; • create and describe mental images of objects, patterns, and paths; • identify and build a three-dimensional object from two-dimensional representations of that object; • identify and draw a two-dimensional representation of a three-dimensional object; • use geometric models to solve problems in other areas of mathematics, such as number and measurement; • recognize geometric ideas and relationships and apply them to other disciplines and to problems that arise in the classroom or in everyday life.

Geometry

STANDARD

Instructional programs from prekindergarten through grade 12 should enable all students to—	Grades 6–8	Grades 9–12
	Expectations In grades 6–8 all students should—	**Expectations** In grades 9–12 all students should—
Analyze characteristics and properties of two- and three-dimensional geometric shapes and develop mathematical arguments about geometric relationships	• precisely describe, classify, and understand relationships among types of two- and three-dimensional objects using their defining properties; • understand relationships among the angles, side lengths, perimeters, areas, and volumes of similar objects; • create and critique inductive and deductive arguments concerning geometric ideas and relationships, such as congruence, similarity, and the Pythagorean relationship.	• analyze properties and determine attributes of two- and three-dimensional objects; • explore relationships (including congruence and similarity) among classes of two- and three-dimensional geometric objects, make and test conjectures about them, and solve problems involving them; • establish the validity of geometric conjectures using deduction, prove theorems, and critique arguments made by others; • use trigonometric relationships to determine lengths and angle measures.
Specify locations and describe spatial relationships using coordinate geometry and other representational systems	• use coordinate geometry to represent and examine the properties of geometric shapes; • use coordinate geometry to examine special geometric shapes, such as regular polygons or those with pairs of parallel or perpendicular sides.	• use Cartesian coordinates and other coordinate systems, such as navigational, polar, or spherical systems, to analyze geometric situations; • investigate conjectures and solve problems involving two- and three-dimensional objects represented with Cartesian coordinates.
Apply transformations and use symmetry to analyze mathematical situations	• describe sizes, positions, and orientations of shapes under informal transformations such as flips, turns, slides, and scaling; • examine the congruence, similarity, and line or rotational symmetry of objects using transformations.	• understand and represent translations, reflections, rotations, and dilations of objects in the plane by using sketches, coordinates, vectors, function notation, and matrices; • use various representations to help understand the effects of simple transformations and their compositions.
Use visualization, spatial reasoning, and geometric modeling to solve problems	• draw geometric objects with specified properties, such as side lengths or angle measures; • use two-dimensional representations of three-dimensional objects to visualize and solve problems such as those involving surface area and volume; • use visual tools such as networks to represent and solve problems; • use geometric models to represent and explain numerical and algebraic relationships; • recognize and apply geometric ideas and relationships in areas outside the mathematics classroom, such as art, science, and everyday life.	• draw and construct representations of two- and three-dimensional geometric objects using a variety of tools; • visualize three-dimensional objects from different perspectives and analyze their cross sections; • use vertex-edge graphs to model and solve problems; • use geometric models to gain insights into, and answer questions in, other areas of mathematics; • use geometric ideas to solve problems in, and gain insights into, other disciplines and other areas of interest such as art and architecture.

Measurement

STANDARD

Instructional programs from prekindergarten through grade 12 should enable all students to—	Pre-K–2 **Expectations** In prekindergarten through grade 2 all students should—	Grades 3–5 **Expectations** In grades 3–5 all students should—
Understand measurable attributes of objects and the units, systems, and processes of measurement	• recognize the attributes of length, volume, weight, area, and time; • compare and order objects according to these attributes; • understand how to measure using nonstandard and standard units; • select an appropriate unit and tool for the attribute being measured.	• understand such attributes as length, area, weight, volume, and size of angle and select the appropriate type of unit for measuring each attribute; • understand the need for measuring with standard units and become familiar with standard units in the customary and metric systems; • carry out simple unit conversions, such as from centimeters to meters, within a system of measurement; • understand that measurements are approximations and understand how differences in units affect precision; • explore what happens to measurements of a two-dimensional shape such as its perimeter and area when the shape is changed in some way.
Apply appropriate techniques, tools, and formulas to determine measurements	• measure with multiple copies of units of the same size, such as paper clips laid end to end; • use repetition of a single unit to measure something larger than the unit, for instance, measuring the length of a room with a single meterstick; • use tools to measure; • develop common referents for measures to make comparisons and estimates.	• develop strategies for estimating the perimeters, areas, and volumes of irregular shapes; • select and apply appropriate standard units and tools to measure length, area, volume, weight, time, temperature, and the size of angles; • select and use benchmarks to estimate measurements; • develop, understand, and use formulas to find the area of rectangles and related triangles and parallelograms; • develop strategies to determine the surface areas and volumes of rectangular solids.

Measurement

STANDARD

Instructional programs from prekindergarten through grade 12 should enable all students to—	Grades 6–8	Grades 9–12
	Expectations In grades 6–8 all students should—	**Expectations** In grades 9–12 all students should—
Understand measurable attributes of objects and the units, systems, and processes of measurement	• understand both metric and customary systems of measurement; • understand relationships among units and convert from one unit to another within the same system; • understand, select, and use units of appropriate size and type to measure angles, perimeter, area, surface area, and volume.	• make decisions about units and scales that are appropriate for problem situations involving measurement.
Apply appropriate techniques, tools, and formulas to determine measurements	• use common benchmarks to select appropriate methods for estimating measurements; • select and apply techniques and tools to accurately find length, area, volume, and angle measures to appropriate levels of precision; • develop and use formulas to determine the circumference of circles and the area of triangles, parallelograms, trapezoids, and circles and develop strategies to find the area of more-complex shapes; • develop strategies to determine the surface area and volume of selected prisms, pyramids, and cylinders; • solve problems involving scale factors, using ratio and proportion; • solve simple problems involving rates and derived measurements for such attributes as velocity and density.	• analyze precision, accuracy, and approximate error in measurement situations; • understand and use formulas for the area, surface area, and volume of geometric figures, including cones, spheres, and cylinders; • apply informal concepts of successive approximation, upper and lower bounds, and limit in measurement situations; • use unit analysis to check measurement computations.

Data Analysis and Probability

STANDARD

Instructional programs from prekindergarten through grade 12 should enable all students to—	Pre-K–2	Grades 3–5
	Expectations	**Expectations**
	In prekindergarten through grade 2 all students should—	In grades 3–5 all students should—
Formulate questions that can be addressed with data and collect, organize, and display relevant data to answer them	• pose questions and gather data about themselves and their surroundings; • sort and classify objects according to their attributes and organize data about the objects; • represent data using concrete objects, pictures, and graphs.	• design investigations to address a question and consider how data-collection methods affect the nature of the data set; • collect data using observations, surveys, and experiments; • represent data using tables and graphs such as line plots, bar graphs, and line graphs; • recognize the differences in representing categorical and numerical data.
Select and use appropriate statistical methods to analyze data	• describe parts of the data and the set of data as a whole to determine what the data show.	• describe the shape and important features of a set of data and compare related data sets, with an emphasis on how the data are distributed; • use measures of center, focusing on the median, and understand what each does and does not indicate about the data set; • compare different representations of the same data and evaluate how well each representation shows important aspects of the data.
Develop and evaluate inferences and predictions that are based on data	• discuss events related to students' experiences as likely or unlikely.	• propose and justify conclusions and predictions that are based on data and design studies to further investigate the conclusions or predictions.
Understand and apply basic concepts of probability		• describe events as likely or unlikely and discuss the degree of likelihood using such words as *certain, equally likely,* and *impossible;* • predict the probability of outcomes of simple experiments and test the predictions; • understand that the measure of the likelihood of an event can be represented by a number from 0 to 1.

Data Analysis and Probability

STANDARD

Instructional programs from prekindergarten through grade 12 should enable all students to—	Grades 6–8 **Expectations** In grades 6–8 all students should—	Grades 9–12 **Expectations** In grades 9–12 all students should—
Formulate questions that can be addressed with data and collect, organize, and display relevant data to answer them	• formulate questions, design studies, and collect data about a characteristic shared by two populations or different characteristics within one population; • select, create, and use appropriate graphical representations of data, including histograms, box plots, and scatterplots.	• understand the differences among various kinds of studies and which types of inferences can legitimately be drawn from each; • know the characteristics of well-designed studies, including the role of randomization in surveys and experiments; • understand the meaning of measurement data and categorical data, of univariate and bivariate data, and of the term variable; • understand histograms, parallel box plots, and scatterplots and use them to display data; • compute basic statistics and understand the distinction between a statistic and a parameter.
Select and use appropriate statistical methods to analyze data	• find, use, and interpret measures of center and spread, including mean and interquartile range; • discuss and understand the correspondence between data sets and their graphical representations, especially histograms, stem-and-leaf plots, box plots, and scatterplots.	• for univariate measurement data, be able to display the distribution, describe its shape, and select and calculate summary statistics; • for bivariate measurement data, be able to display a scatterplot, describe its shape, and determine regression coefficients, regression equations, and correlation coefficients using technological tools; • display and discuss bivariate data where at least one variable is categorical; • recognize how linear transformations of univariate data affect shape, center, and spread; • identify trends in bivariate data and find functions that model the data or transform the data so that they can be modeled.
Develop and evaluate inferences and predictions that are based on data	• use observations about differences between two or more samples to make conjectures about the populations from which the samples were taken; • make conjectures about possible relationships between two characteristics of a sample on the basis of scatterplots of the data and approximate lines of fit; • use conjectures to formulate new questions and plan new studies to answer them.	• use simulations to explore the variability of sample statistics from a known population and to construct sampling distributions; • understand how sample statistics reflect the values of population parameters and use sampling distributions as the basis for informal inference; • evaluate published reports that are based on data by examining the design of the study, the appropriateness of the data analysis, and the validity of conclusions; • understand how basic statistical techniques are used to monitor process characteristics in the workplace.
Understand and apply basic concepts of probability	• understand and use appropriate terminology to describe complementary and mutually exclusive events; • use proportionality and a basic understanding of probability to make and test conjectures about the results of experiments and simulations; • compute probabilities for simple compound events, using such methods as organized lists, tree diagrams, and area models.	• understand the concepts of sample space and probability distribution and construct sample spaces and distributions in simple cases; • use simulations to construct empirical probability distributions; • compute and interpret the expected value of random variables in simple cases; • understand the concepts of conditional probability and independent events; • understand how to compute the probability of a compound event.

Process Standards

Problem Solving

STANDARD

Instructional programs from prekindergarten through grade 12 should enable all students to—

- Build new mathematical knowledge through problem solving
- Solve problems that arise in mathematics and in other contexts
- Apply and adapt a variety of appropriate strategies to solve problems
- Monitor and reflect on the process of mathematical problem solving

Reasoning and Proof

STANDARD

Instructional programs from prekindergarten through grade 12 should enable all students to—

- Recognize reasoning and proof as fundamental aspects of mathematics
- Make and investigate mathematical conjectures
- Develop and evaluate mathematical arguments and proofs
- Select and use various types of reasoning and methods of proof

Communication

STANDARD

Instructional programs from prekindergarten through grade 12 should enable all students to—

- Organize and consolidate their mathematical thinking through communication
- Communicate their mathematical thinking coherently and clearly to peers, teachers, and others
- Analyze and evaluate the mathematical thinking and strategies of others
- Use the language of mathematics to express mathematical ideas precisely

Connections

STANDARD

Instructional programs from prekindergarten through grade 12 should enable all students to—

- Recognize and use connections among mathematical ideas
- Understand how mathematical ideas interconnect and build on one another to produce a coherent whole
- Recognize and apply mathematics in contexts outside of mathematics

Representation

STANDARD

Instructional programs from prekindergarten through grade 12 should enable all students to—

- Create